Brilliant Microsoft® Windows Vista 2007

Steve Johnson

Perspection, Inc.

PEARSON
Prentice
Hall

Harlow, England • London • New York • Boston • San Francisco • Toronto
Sydney • Tokyo • Singapore • Hong Kong • Seoul • Taipei • New Delhi
Cape Town • Madrid • Mexico City • Amsterdam • Munich • Paris • Milan

Pearson Education Limited
Edinburgh Gate
Harlow
Essex CM20 2JE
England

and Associated Companies throughout the world

Visit us on the World Wide Web at:
www.pearsoned.co.uk

Original edition, entitled MICROSOFT WINDOWS VISTA ON DEMAND, 1st edition, 0789736454 by
JOHNSON, STEVE; PERSPECTION, INC., published by Pearson Education, Inc, publishing as
Que/Sams, Copyright © 2007 Perspection, Inc.

This UK edition published by PEARSON EDUCATION LTD, Copyright © 2007

This edition is manufactured in the USA and available for sale only in the United Kingdom, Europe,
the Middle East and Africa

The right of Steve Johnson to be identified as author of this work has been asserted
by him in accordance with the Copyright, Designs and Patents Act 1988.

ISBN: 978-0-136-13677-4

British Library Cataloguing-in-Publication Data
A catalogue record for this book is available from the British Library

10 9 8 7 6 5 4 3 2 1
10 09 08 07 06

Printed and bound in the United States of America

The publisher's policy is to use paper manufactured f   m sustainable forests

Brilliant Guides

What you need to know and how to do it

When you're working on your PC and come up against a problem that you're unsure how to solve, or want to accomplish something in an application that you aren't sure how to do, where do you look?? Manuals and traditional training guides are usually too big and unwieldy and are intended to be used as an end-to-end training resource, making it hard to get to the info you need right away without having to wade through pages of background information that you just don't need at that moment – and helplines are rarely that helpful!

Brilliant guides have been developed to allow you to find the info you need easily and without fuss and guide you through the task using a highly visual, step-by-step approach – providing exactly what you need to know when you need it!!

Brilliant guides provide the quick easy-to-access information that you need, using a detailed index and troubleshooting guide to help you find exactly what you need to know, and then presenting each task on one or two pages. Numbered steps then guide you through each task or problem, using numerous screenshots to illustrate each step. Added features include "See Also ..." boxes that point you to related tasks and information in the book, whilst "Did you know?..." sections alert you to relevant expert tips, tricks and advice to further expand your skills and knowledge.

In addition to covering all major office PC applications, and related computing subjects, the *Brilliant* series also contains titles that will help you in every aspect of your working life, such as writing the perfect CV, answering the toughest interview questions and moving on in your career.

Brilliant guides are the light at the end of the tunnel when you are faced with any minor or major task!

a

Acknowledgements

Perspection, Inc.

Brilliant Microsoft Windows Vista 2007 has been created by the professional trainers and writers at Perspection, Inc.

Perspection, Inc. is a software training company committed to providing information and training to help people use software more effectively in order to communicate, make decisions, and solve problems. Perspection writes and produces software training books, and develops multimedia and Web-based training. Since 1991, we have written more than 80 computer books, with several bestsellers to our credit, and sold over 5 million books.

This book incorporates Perspection's training expertise to ensure that you'll receive the maximum return on your time. You'll focus on the tasks and skills that increase productivity while working at your own pace and convenience.

We invite you to visit the Perspection Web site at:

www.perspection.com

Acknowledgements

The task of creating any book requires the talents of many hard-working people pulling together to meet impossible deadlines and untold stresses. We'd like to thank the outstanding team responsible for making this book possible: the writer, Steve Johnson; the technical editor, Alex Williams; the production team, Emily Atwood, Alex Williams, and Dori Hernandez; the editors and proofreaders, Emily Atwood and Holly Johnson; and the indexer, Katherine Stimson.

At Que publishing, we'd like to thank Greg Wiegand and Stephanie McComb for the opportunity to undertake this project, Michelle Newcomb for administrative support, and Sandra Schroeder for your production expertise and support.

Perspection

About The Author

Steve Johnson has written more than thirty-five books on a variety of computer software, including Microsoft Office 2003 and XP, Microsoft Windows XP, Apple Mac OS X Panther, Macromedia Flash MX 2004 and 8, Macromedia Director MX 2004, Macromedia Fireworks, and Adobe Photoshop CS and CS2. In 1991, after working for Apple Computer and Microsoft, Steve founded Perspection, Inc., which writes and produces software training. When he is not staying up late writing, he enjoys playing golf, gardening, and spending time with his wife, Holly, and three children, JP, Brett, and Hannah. When time permits, he likes to travel to such places as New Hampshire in October, and Hawaii. Steve and his family live in Pleasanton, California, but can also be found visiting family all over the western United States.

Contents

6 Exchanging Messages and Information   **165**

Introduction

Welcome to *Brilliant Microsoft Windows Vista 2007*, a visual quick reference book that shows you how to work efficiently with Microsoft Windows Vista. This book provides complete coverage of basic to advanced Windows Vista skills.

How This Book Works

You don't have to read this book in any particular order. We've designed the book so that you can jump in, get the information you need, and jump out. However, the book does follow a logical progression from simple tasks to more complex ones. Each task is presented on no more than two facing pages, which lets you focus on a single task without having to turn the page. To find the information that you need, just look up the task in the table of contents or index, and turn to the page listed. Read the task introduction, follow the step-by-step instructions in the left column along with screen illustrations in the right column, and you're done.

What's New

If you're searching for what's new in Windows Vista, just look for the icon: **New!**. The new icon appears in the table of contents and through out this book so you can quickly and easily identify a new or improved feature in Windows Vista. A complete description of each new feature appears in the New Features guide in the back of this book.

Keyboard Shortcuts

Most menu commands have a keyboard equivalent, such as Ctrl+P, as a quicker alternative to using the mouse. A complete list of keyboard shortcuts is available on the Web at *www.perspection.com*.

How You'll Learn

How This Book Works

What's New

Keyboard Shortcuts

Step-by-Step Instructions

Real World Examples

Workshop

Microsoft Office Specialist

Get More on the Web

Step-by-Step Instructions

This book provides concise step-by-step instructions that show you "how" to accomplish a task. Each set of instructions include illustrations that directly correspond to the easy-to-read steps. Also included in the text are time-savers, tables, and sidebars to help you work more efficiently or to teach you more in-depth information. A "Did You Know?" provides tips and techniques to help you work smarter, while a "See Also" leads you to other parts of the book containing related information about the task.

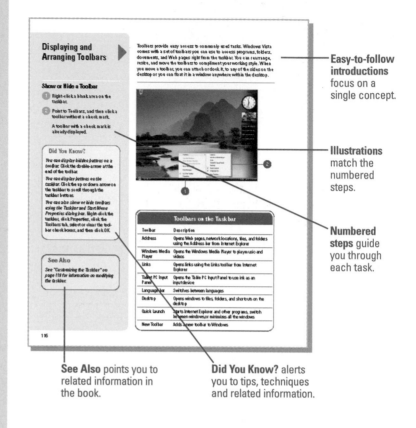

Easy-to-follow introductions focus on a single concept.

Illustrations match the numbered steps.

Numbered steps guide you through each task.

See Also points you to related information in the book.

Did You Know? alerts you to tips, techniques and related information.

Real World Examples

This book uses real world examples files to give you a context in which to use the task. By using the example files, you won't waste time looking for or creating sample files. You get a start file and a result file, so you can compare your work. Not every topic needs an example file, such as changing options, so we provide a complete list of the example files used through out the book. The example files that you need for project tasks along with a complete file list are available on the Web at *www.perspection.com*.

Real world examples help you apply what you've learned to other tasks.

Workshop

This book shows you how to put together the individual step-by-step tasks into indepth projects with the Workshop. You start each project with a sample file, work through the steps, and then compare your results with project results file at the end. The Workshop projects and associated files are available on the Web at www.perspection.com.

Microsoft Certified Applications Specialist

This book prepares you for the Microsoft Certified Applications Specialist (MCAS) exam for Microsoft Windows Vista. Each MCAS certification exam has a set of objectives, which are organized into broader skill sets. To prepare for the certification exam, you should review and perform each task identified with a MCAS objective to confirm that you can meet the requirements for the exam. Throughout this book, content that pertains to an objective is identified with the following MCAS logo and objective number next to it.

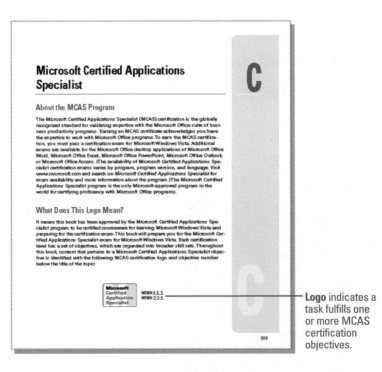

The **Workshop** walks you through indepth projects to help you put Access to work.

Logo indicates a task fulfills one or more MCAS certification objectives.

Get More on the Web

In addition to the information in this book, you can also get more information on the Web to help you get up to speed faster with Windows Vista. Some of the information includes:

Transition Helpers

◆ **Only New Features.** Download and print the new feature tasks as a quick and easy guide.

Productivity Tools

◆ **Keyboard Shortcuts.** Download a list of keyboard shortcuts to learn faster ways to get the job done.

More Content

◆ **Photographs.** Download photographs and other graphics to use in your Office documents.

◆ **More Content.** Download new content developed after publication. For example, you can download a complete chapter on Office SharePoint Server 2007.

You can access these additional resources on the Web at *www.perspection.com*.

Additional content is available on the Web. You can download a chapter on SharePoint.

Getting Started with Windows Vista

Introduction

Microsoft Windows Vista introduces a breakthrough user experience that is designed to help you intuitively view, find, and organize information on your computer. Windows Vista delivers better personal productivity and digital entertainment on your computer. Before you get started with Windows Vista, check out the new features, which includes the Windows Areo user experience, Instant Searches, Explorers, Sidebars and gadgets, improved Internet Explorer, Windows Media Center, and advanced security and protection. A complete description of each new feature appears in the New Features guide in the back of this book.

Microsoft Windows Vista is an **operating system**, a computer program that controls the basic operation of your computer and the programs you run. A **program**, also known as an **application**, is task-oriented software you use to accomplish a specific task, such as word processing, managing files on your computer, or performing calculations. Windows Vista displays programs in frames on your screen, called windows (thus the name of the operating system). A **window** can contain the contents of a file and the application in which it was created, **icons** (picture representations of a program or a file), or other usable data. A **file** is a collection of information (such as a letter or list of addresses) that has a unique name, distinguishing it from other files. This use of windows and icons is called a **graphical user interface** (**GUI**, pronounced "gooey"), meaning that you ("user") interact ("interface") with the computer through the use of graphics: icons and other meaningful words, symbols, and windows.

Introducing Windows Vista

Windows Vista Editions

Windows Vista comes in four main editions: the Home Basic Edition for consumers; the Home Premium Edition for consumer power users; the Business Edition for business and power users; and the Ultimate Edition for the complete package. Two other editions are available for specific needs: the Starter Edition and Enterprise Edition. The Starter Edition is for the beginning PC user and provides the most basic entry to Windows Vista, which is targeted to emerging markets. The Enterprise Edition is for large corporations with advanced data protection, compatibility, and international support needs.

The **Home Basic** Edition provides a basic secure entry point for using Windows Vista. The **Home Premium** Edition adds to the basic experience by providing the Windows Areo experience, the Mobility Center and Tablet PC support for laptops, Windows Meeting Space for sharing documents, and Windows Media Center for media entertainment.

The **Business** Edition modifies the Home Premium Edition by adding advanced hardware protection, business networking and remote desktop access, and by removing the Windows Media Center. The **Ultimate** Edition combines every thing from all the editions into one complete package.

Windows Vista User Experience

Windows Vista provides two distinct user interface experiences: a basic experience for entry-level systems, and a more visually dynamic experience called **Windows Aero** (**New!**). Both offer a new and intuitive navigation experience that help you more easily find and organize your applications and files, but Aero goes further by delivering a truly next-generation desktop experience.

The basic experience has been updated and streamlined so you can find and work with your programs and files more easily than in previous versions of Windows. Some of the important new features include Explorer windows, Live icons, Search Folders, and Instant Search.

Windows Vista uses Explorer windows (**New!**) to give you more information and control while simplifying how you work with your files. Each Explorer window includes a Command Bar, Live icons, column headers, and a Navigation pane. Command Bars display only the tasks that are most appropriate for the files being displayed. Live icons are scalable thumbnails that display the first page of documents, the actual image of a photo, or the album art for individual songs in your music collection, making it easier to find exactly what you are looking for. The Navigation pane contains Search Folders and traditional folders that you have created on your computer. A Search Folder (**New!**) is simply a search that you save. Opening a Search Folder instantly runs that saved search, displaying up-to-date results immediately.

With Windows Vista, you no longer have to remember where you store every file. Instead, to find a file, you need only to remember something about it. The updated Start menu integrates the Instant Search (**New!**) box to help you quickly find and start any program or file on your computer. After you add or edit file properties or data associated with a file, such as a keyword on a document, you can use the Instant Search box to quickly find a file by the file property.

Start Menu　　　Search folders　　　Windows Sidebar and gadgets

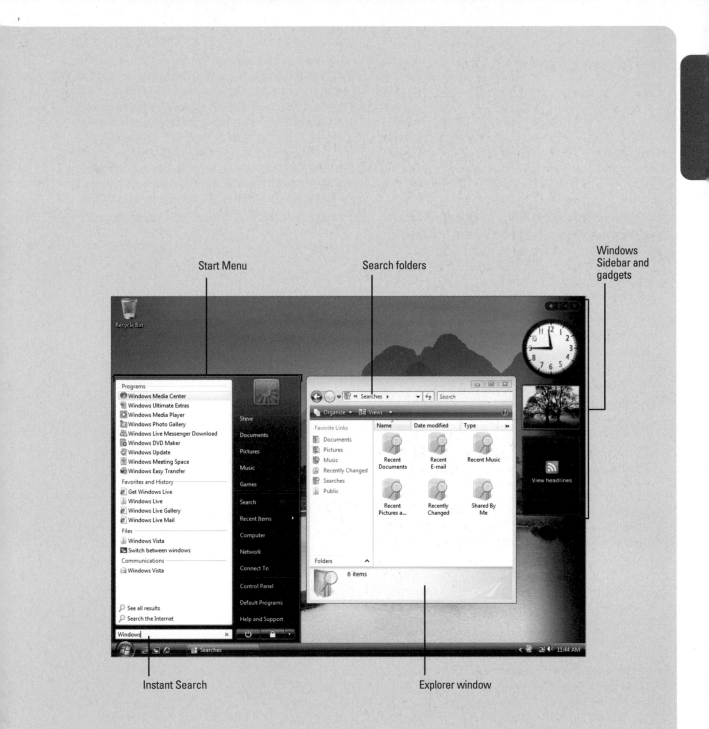

Instant Search　　　Explorer window

Starting Windows Vista

Windows Vista automatically starts when you turn on your computer. When you first start Windows Vista, you see a Welcome screen that you use to log on to Windows. The Welcome screen displays all the user accounts on the computer. Unlike Windows XP, the Welcome screen can't be turned off. After you click a user name, and enter a password, you see the Windows Vista desktop and the Welcome Center window (**New!**), which displays options to view basic computer details, transfer files and setting, add new users, connect to the Internet, install Windows Ultimate Extras, view new feature in Windows Vista, and view Microsoft offers available on the Web.

Start Windows Vista Using the Welcome Screen

1. Turn on your computer, and wait while Windows Vista loads and displays the Welcome screen.

2. If prompted for added security, press and then release the Ctrl, Alt, and Delete keys at the same time.

3. Click your user name.

4. Type your password. Be sure to use the correct capitalization.

5. Click the arrow, or press Enter.

   The Windows Vista desktop appears and the Welcome Center window opens.

Welcome Center

Click here to turn off Welcome Center

Did You Know?

The Windows password is case-sensitive. Windows makes a distinction between uppercase and lowercase letters. Your password should be at least seven characters long, the optimal length for encryption, which is the process of logically scrambling data to keep a password secure.

Find Basic Information About Your Computer

1 Click the **Start** button, point to **All Programs**, and then point to **Accessories**.

2 Click **Welcome Center**.

The upper pane display basic information about your computer, including:

◆ **What version of Windows Vista you are running**

◆ **Computer processor name and speed**

◆ **Computer memory (RAM)**

◆ **Computer name**

4 To view more details about your computer, click **Show more details**.

5 When you're done, click the **Close** button.

Did You Know?

You can turn off the Welcome Center at startup. In the Welcome Center window, clear the Run at startup check box at the bottom, and then click the Close button.

You can activate Windows Vista or change the product key. Click the Start button, click Control Panel, double-click the System icon in Classic view. Click the activation link or Change product key.

Basic computer information

Activation information

Using Windows Aero

Introducing Windows Aero

Windows Vista provides two distinct user interface experiences: a "basic" experience for entry-level systems, and a more visually dynamic experience called **Windows Aero** (**New!**). The Windows Aero user experience allows you to view Windows Vista in a whole new way. Windows Vista Aero provides spectacular visual effects, such as glass-like interface elements that you can see through, subtle window animations, window colors, live thumbnails that you can display on the taskbar, and Windows Flip and Windows Flip 3D that you can use to graphical open windows.

Live Taskbar Thumbnails

When you rest the mouse pointer over a taskbar item, Windows Aero displays a Live thumbnail of the window, showing the content of that window. The Live thumbnail (**New!**) is displayed whether the window is minimized or not, and whether the content of the window is a document, photo, or even a running video or process.

Windows Aero

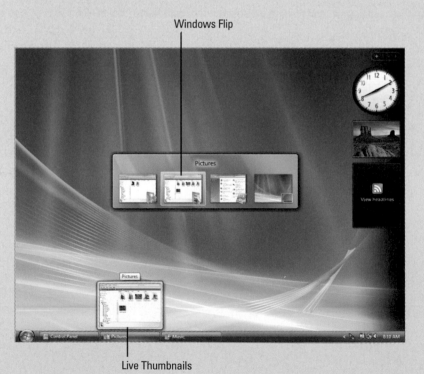

Windows Flip

Live Thumbnails

Windows Flip and Windows Flip 3D

Windows Aero provides two ways to manage windows: Windows Flip and Windows Flip 3D (New!). Flip allows you to flip through open windows (by using Alt+Tab), providing a Live thumbnail of each window, rather than just a generic icon and file name. Live thumbnails make it easier to quickly identify the window you want, particularly when multiple windows of the same kind are open. With Flip 3D, you can use the scroll wheel on your mouse to flip through open windows in a stack, and locate and select the one you want.

Preparing for Windows Aero

Windows Vista can display different features based on the hardware capabilities of the computer it is running on. Computers running Windows Vista Home Basic or those without the hardware needed to run Windows Aero use the basic user interface. If your computer meets the minimal hardware requirements to be **Windows Vista PC Capability Ready**, you see the Windows Vista Basic user experience. If your computer meets the increased hardware requirements to be **Windows Vista PC Premium Ready**, you see the Windows Aero user experience. Windows Aero is an environment with an additional level of visual sophistication, one that is even more responsive and manageable, providing a further level of clarity and confidence to Windows users. See *"Preparing to Install Windows Vista"* in Appendix A for the specific hardware requirements to run Windows Aero.

Running Windows Aero

Before you can run Windows Aero, you need to make sure Windows Vista contains the proper settings. Make sure the color is set to 32 bit, the monitor refresh rate is higher than 10 hertz, the theme is set to Window Vista, the color scheme is set to Windows Aero, and the window frame transparency is turned on.

You can follow these instructions to make sure your computer is set to run Windows Aero:

- **Color.** To set the color to 32 bit, open Personalization in the Control Panel, click Display Settings, select Highest (32 bit) under Colors, and then click OK.

- **Monitor.** To set the monitor refresh rate, open Personalization in the Control Panel, click Display Settings, click Advanced Settings, click the Monitor tab, click a refresh rate that is higher than 10 hertz, and then click OK.

- **Theme.** To change the desktop theme, open Personalization in the Control Panel, click Theme, select Windows Vista in the Themes list, and then click OK.

- **Color scheme.** To change the color scheme, open Personalization in the Control Panel, click Window Color and Appearance, select Windows Aero in the Color Scheme list, and then click OK.

- **Transparency.** To turn on window frame transparency, set the color scheme to Windows Aero, open Personalization in the Control Panel, click Window Color and Appearance, select the Enable Transparency check box, and then click OK.

Exploring the Windows Desktop

When you first start Windows Vista (**New!**), you see the Windows desktop, or a Welcome screen (a way to identify yourself on the computer), depending on your installation. The **desktop** is an on-screen version of an actual desk, containing windows, icons, files, and programs. You can use the desktop to access, store, organize, modify, share, and explore information (such as a letter, the news, or a list of addresses), whether it resides on your computer, a network, or the Internet. The long vertical bar on the right-side of the desktop is called the **Windows Sidebar** (**New!**). It contains mini-programs called **gadgets** (**New!**), which provide easy access to frequently used tools and information at a glance. The bar at the bottom of your screen is called the **taskbar**; it allows you to start programs and switch among currently running programs. At the left end of the taskbar is the **Start button**,

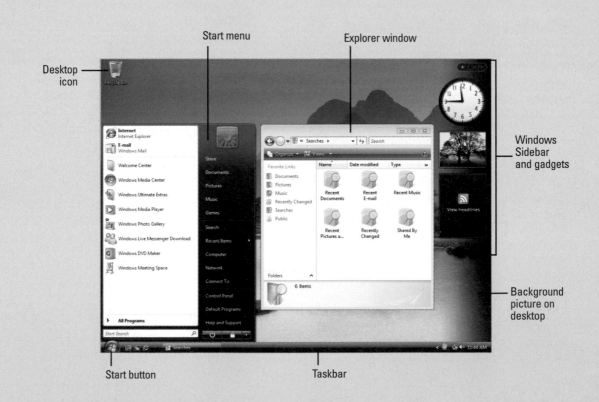

Start menu

Explorer window

Desktop icon

Windows Sidebar and gadgets

Background picture on desktop

Start button

Taskbar

8

which you use to start programs, find and open files, access the Windows Help and Support Center, and much more. Next to the Start button is the **Quick Launch toolbar**, which contains buttons you use to quickly start your Internet browser and media player and show the desktop. At the right end of the taskbar is the **notification area**, which displays the time, the date, and program related icons. If icons in the notification area are not used

for a while, an arrow appears to hide the icons and reduce clutter. You can click the arrow to display and hide the icons. When you use a hidden icon, it reappears in the notification area. If you upgraded your computer to Windows Vista from a previous version of Windows, your desktop might contain additional desktop icons and toolbars.

Open program window

Start button

Quick Launch toolbar

Similar open windows grouped on the taskbar

Notification icons

Using the Mouse

A **mouse** is a handheld input device you roll across a flat surface (such as a desk or a mouse pad) to position the **mouse pointer**, the small symbol that indicates the pointer's relative position on the desktop. When you move the mouse, the mouse pointer on the screen moves in the same direction.

The shape of the mouse pointer changes to indicate different activities. Once you move the mouse pointer to a desired position on the screen, you use the mouse buttons, right or left, to tell your computer what to do.

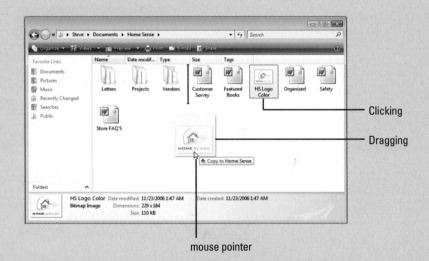

Clicking

Dragging

mouse pointer

Basic Mouse Techniques

Task	What to do
Pointing	Move the mouse to position it over an item on the desktop.
Clicking	Press and release the left mouse button.
Double-clicking	Press and release the left mouse button twice quickly.
Dragging	Point to an item, press and hold the left mouse button, move the mouse to a new location, and then release the mouse button.
Right-clicking	Point to an item, and then press and release the right mouse button.

Using the Mouse for Quick Results

A typical mouse has two mouse buttons. You use the left one to click buttons, select text, and drag items around the screen. When you click an item with the right button, such as an icon, text, or graphic, a shortcut menu appears with a list of commands related to the selected item. For example, when you right-click a file icon, a shortcut menu appears with a list of file commands, such as Open, Explore, Search, Delete, and Rename. Instead of searching for commands on the main menus, you can save time and get quick results by using a shortcut menu.

Use the Shortcut Menu Command

1 Right-click an item.

2 Click a command from the shortcut menu.

Did You Know?

You can swap the functions of the right and left mouse buttons. Click the Start button on the taskbar, click Control Panel, double-click the Mouse icon in Classic view, click the Buttons tab, select the Switch Primary And Secondary Buttons check box, and then click OK.

A mouse wheel can make scrolling fast and easy. If your mouse has a wheel between the two mouse buttons, you can roll it to quickly scroll a few lines or an entire screen at a time.

See Also

See "Changing Mouse Settings" on page 456 for information on changing the way the mouse works.

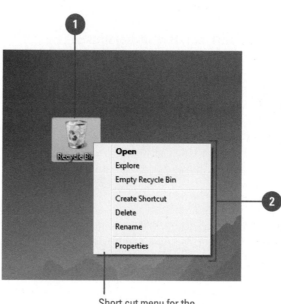

Short cut menu for the Recycle Bin icon.

For Your Information

Using the Mouse with the Web Style

Windows Vista integrates the use of the Internet with its other functions. You can choose to extend the way you click on the Internet with the rest of your computer by single-clicking (known as the Web style) icons to open them, or stay with the default by double-clicking (known as the Classic style). To change from one style to the other, click the Start button, click Control Panel, click Classic View (if necessary), double-click the Folder Options icon, click the Single-click to open an item (point to select), or Double-click to open an item (Single-click to select) option, and then click OK. The steps in this book assume you are using Windows Classic style.

Using the Start Menu

The key to getting started with the Windows desktop is learning how to use the Start button on the taskbar. Clicking the button on the taskbar displays the Start menu, a list of commands that allow you to start a program, open a document, change a Windows setting, find a file, or display support information. The top of the Start menu indicates who is currently using the computer. The left column of the Start menu is separated into two lists: **pinned** items above the separator line and most frequently used items below. The pinned items remain on the Start menu, like a push pin holds paper on a bulletin board. The most frequently used items change as you use programs: Windows keeps track of which programs you use and displays them on the Start menu for easy access.

The right column of the Start menu provides easy access to folders, Windows settings, help information, and search functionality. An arrow next to a menu item indicates a cascading menu, or submenu, which is a list of commands for that menu item. Pointing at the arrow displays a submenu from which you can choose additional commands. As you become more familiar with Windows, you might want to customize the Start menu to include additional items that you use most often and change Windows settings in the Control Panel to customize your Windows desktop.

As you continue to install programs on your computer, finding them on the Start menu can sometimes be difficult. Windows Vista makes it easy with the Instant Search bar (New!), which allows you to search the Start menu to find programs and other Windows items, such as Internet favorites, history, files, contacts, e-mail messages, and appointments. To perform a search, click the Start menu, click in the Search box and start typing the search text you want. As you type, the Start menu shows the possible results with priority given to the programs you use frequently. The search results continue to narrow as you continue to type. If you don't find what you are looking for during a search, you can click Search Everywhere or Search the Internet to use Windows search capabilities.

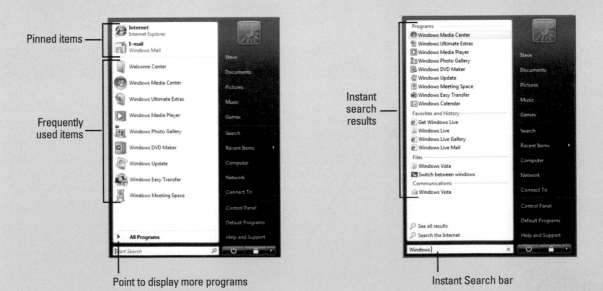

Pinned items

Frequently used items

Point to display more programs

Instant search results

Instant Search bar

Start Menu Commands

Command	Description
Internet	Starts your Internet browser; by default, Internet Explorer
E-mail	Starts your e-mail program; by default, Outlook Express
All Programs	Opens a list of all the programs included on the Start menu
Instant Search (**New!**)	Locates programs, and other Windows items, such as Internet favorites, history, files, contacts, e-mail messages, and appointments
Documents	Opens the Documents folder, where you store and manage files
Pictures	Opens the Pictures folder, where you store and manage photos, images, and graphic files
Music	Opens the Music folder, where you store and manage sound and audio files
Games	Opens the Games folder, where you play Windows Vista games, such as Chess Titans, FreeCell, Hearts, InkBall, Mahjong Titans, Minesweeper, Purble Place, Solitaire, and Spider Solitaire
Search (**New!**)	Allows you to locate programs, files, folders, or computers on your computer network, or find information or people on the Internet
Recent Items	Opens a list of the most recently opened and saved documents
Computer	Opens the Computer window, where you access information about disk drives and other hardware devices
Network	Opens the Network window, where you can connect to a network
Connect To	Opens the Connect to a Network window, where you can connect to a remote network, including wireless, dial-up, and Virtual Private Network (VPN)
Control Panel	Provides options to customize the appearance and functionality of the computer
Default Programs	Displays the Default Programs window, where you can choose default programs for Web browsing, e-mail, playing music, and other activities
Help and Support (**New!**)	Displays Windows Help topics, tutorials, troubleshooting, support options, and tools
Power (**New!**)	Keeps your session in memory and puts the computer in low-power state so you can quickly resume working
Lock (**New!**)	Locks the computer
Arrow (**New!**)	Provides options to shut down the computer, restart the computer, set the computer to sleep or lock, log off the system, or switch to a different users

Using Windows Sidebar

Microsoft
Certified
Application
Specialist

WINV-6.4

Windows Sidebar (New!) is a pane on the side of the Windows Vista desktop that gives you quick access to gadgets such as news headlines and updates, slide shows, weather information, traffic maps, Internet radio streams, and slide shows of online photo albums. **Gadgets** are mini-applications that can connect to Web services, such as an RSS feed (which automatically delivers Web content to your desktop), or integrate with many of your applications, such as viewing your calendar. You can customize Windows Sidebar to suit the way you work—whether you want it always on top or resting below maximized windows. You can also move gadgets off the Windows Sidebar and place them anywhere on your desktop. Windows Vista comes with a set of gadgets to get you started. However, you can easily download more gadgets from an online gadget gallery.

Work with the Sidebar

- **Open the Sidebar**. Right-click the Sidebar icon in the notification area, and then click Open.

- **Close the Sidebar**. Right-click the Sidebar, and then click Close Sidebar.

- **Close a Gadget**. Point to the gadget you want to close, click the Close button, and then click Close Gadget (if requested).

- **Change Gadget Options**. Point to the gadget you want to change, click the Options button (wrench icon), select the options you want, and then click OK.

- **Move a Gadget**. Point to the gadget, and then drag it to another location on the Sidebar or to the desktop.

Did You Know?

You can download more gadgets. Right-click a blank area of the Sidebar, click Properties, and then click Get more gadgets online to open the gadget Web site and download more gadgets.

Point to a gadget to display options

Click to close sidebar

Click to open sidebar

Add a Gadget

1. Point to the plus sign (+) at the top of the Sidebar, and then click the button.

2. Double-click the gadget you want to add.

3. When you're done, click the **Close** button.

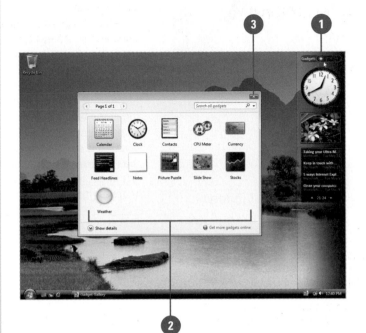

Keep Windows from Covering Sidebar

1. Point to blank area in the Sidebar.

2. Right-click the blank area of the Sidebar, and then click **Properties**.

3. Clear the **Sidebar is always on top of other windows** check box.

4. Click **OK**.

Managing Windows

One of the most powerful things about Windows is that you can open more than one window or program at once. This means, however, that the desktop can get cluttered with many open windows for the various programs. A button appears on the taskbar for each open window. If there isn't enough room on the taskbar to display a button for each open window, Windows Vista groups similar types of windows under one button. You can identify a window by its name on the title bar at the top of the window. To organize your desktop, you must sometimes change the size of a window or move it to a different location. Each window is surrounded by a border that you can use to move or resize the window. Each window has resize buttons in the upper-right corner.

Switch Among Open Windows

1 On the taskbar, click a button. If windows are grouped, a menu appears.

2 Click the window you want from the menu.

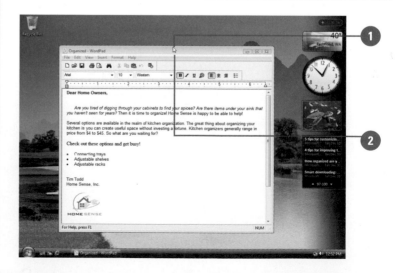

resize button

Move a Window

1 Point to the window's title bar.

2 Drag the window to a new location, and then release the mouse button.

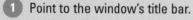

Use Buttons to Resize and Close a Window

All windows contain the same sizing and close buttons:

◆ **Maximize button.** Click to make a window fill the entire screen.

◆ **Restore Down button.** Click to reduce a maximized window.

◆ **Minimize button.** Click to shrink a window to a taskbar button.

◆ **Close button.** Click to close the window.

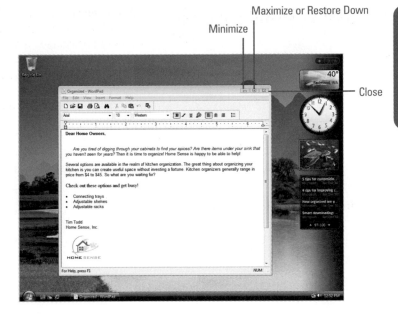

Minimize

Maximize or Restore Down

Close

Use the Mouse to Resize a Window

1. If the window is maximized, click the Restore Down button.

2. Move the mouse over one of the borders of the window until the mouse pointer changes into a two-headed arrow.

   The directions of the arrow-heads show you the directions in which you can resize the window.

3. Drag the window border until the window is the size you want.

Using Menus, Toolbars, and Panes

A **menu** is a list of commands that you use to accomplish certain tasks, such as when you use the Start menu to open the Control Panel. A **command** is a directive that provides access to a program's features. Each Windows program has its own set of menus, which are on the menu bar along the top of the program window. The **menu bar** organizes commands into groups of related operations. Each group is listed under the name of the menu, such as File or Help. To access the commands in a menu, you click the name of the menu. If a command on a menu includes a keyboard reference, known as a **keyboard shortcut**, you can perform the action by pressing the first key, then pressing the second key to perform the command quickly. You can also carry out some of the most frequently used commands

on a menu by clicking a button on a toolbar or command bar. A **toolbar** or **command bar** contains buttons that are convenient shortcuts for menu commands. A **pane** is a frame within a window where you can access commands and navigation controls. You can use menus, toolbar buttons, and commands in a pane to change how the Control Panel window's contents appear. On a menu, a check mark or selected icons identifies a currently selected feature, meaning that the feature is enabled, or turned on. To disable, or turn off the feature, you click the command again to remove the check mark. A bullet mark also indicates that an option is enabled. To disable a command with a bullet mark next to it, however, you must select another command (within the menu section, separated by gray lines) in its place.

Pane   List arrow

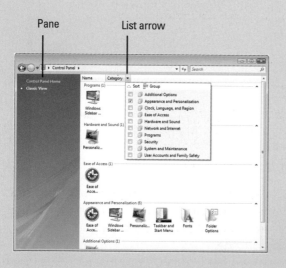

Menu bar   Command bar/Toolbar

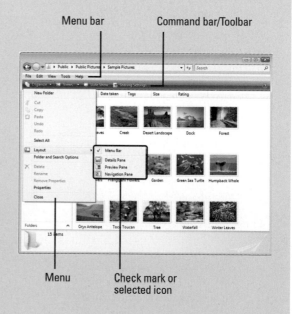

Menu   Check mark or selected icon

Choosing Dialog Box Options

A **dialog box** is a window that opens when you choose a menu command followed by an ellipsis (. . .). The ellipsis indicates that you must supply more information before the program can carry out the command you selected. Dialog boxes open in other situations as well, such as when you open a program in the Control Panel. In a dialog box, you choose various options and provide information for completing the command.

Choose Dialog Box Options

All dialog boxes contain the same types of options, including the following:

◆ **Tabs.** Click a tab to display its options. Each tab groups a related set of options.

◆ **Option buttons.** Click an option button to select it. You can usually select only one.

◆ **Up and down arrows.** Click the up or down arrow to increase or decrease the number, or type a number in the box.

◆ **Check box.** Click the box to turn on or off the option. A checked box means the option is selected; a cleared box means it's not.

◆ **List box.** Click the list arrow to display a list of options, and then click the option you want.

◆ **Text box.** Click in the box and type the requested information.

◆ **Command buttons.** Click a button to perform a specific action or command. A button name followed by an ellipsis (...) opens another dialog box. OK executes the options and closes the dialog box. Cancel ignores the options and closes the dialog box. Apply executes the options and leaves the dialog box open.

◆ **Preview box.** Many dialog boxes show an image that reflects the options you select.

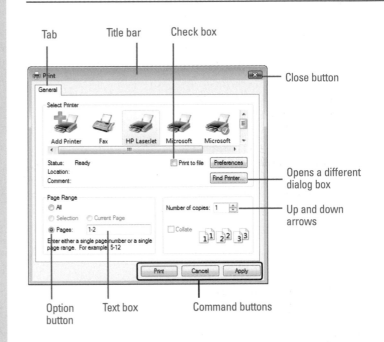

Tab Title bar Check box Close button Opens a different dialog box Up and down arrows Option button Text box Command buttons

For Your Information

Navigating a Dialog Box

Rather than clicking to move around a dialog box, you can press the Tab key to move from one box or button to the next. You can also use Shift+Tab to move backward, or Ctrl+Tab and Ctrl+Shift+Tab to move between dialog box tabs.

Using Windows Help and Support

Microsoft
Certified
Application
Specialist

WINV-7.2.1, WINV-7.2.2
WINV-7.8.4

When you have a question about how to do something in Windows Vista, you can usually find the answer with a few clicks of your mouse. Microsoft Help and Support (**New!**) is a resource of information, training, and support to help you learn and use Windows Vista. Help and Support is like a book stored on your computer with additional links to the Internet, complete with a search feature, and a table of contents to make finding information easier. If you have an Internet connection, you can get online help from a support professional at Microsoft or from other users in Windows communities (an electronic forum where people share information), or you can invite a friend to chat with you, view your screen, and work on your computer to provide remote support.

Use Help and Support

1 Click the **Start** button, and then click **Help and Support**.

2 Click an icon with the type of help you want to use:

- ◆ **Windows Basics.**
- ◆ **Table of Contents.**
- ◆ **Security and Maintenance.**
- ◆ **Troubleshooting.**
- ◆ **Windows Online Help.**
- ◆ **What's New.**

3 Click the item of interest.

4 Read the information.

5 If you can't find the information you need, click the **Search Help** box, type a word or phrase, and then press Enter.

6 If you need additional help, click a link under Ask someone or Information from Microsoft to access resources on the Internet.

- ◆ **Windows Remote Assistance.** Click the link, and then follow the wizard instructions.

7 Click the **Close** button.

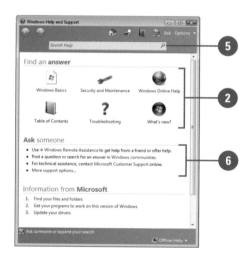

Click to go back

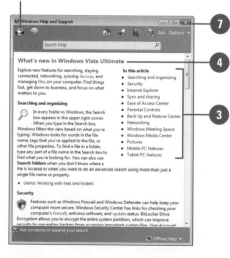

Use Dialog Box or Window Help

1. In a dialog box or window, click the Help button (? icon) or a Help link.

    ◆ In a dialog box, click the item you want information about.

2. Read the Help information.

3. Click the **Close** button.

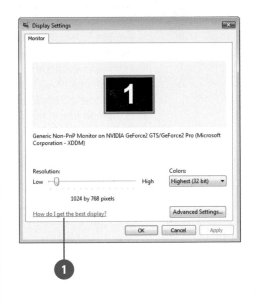

Use Program Help

1. Click the program's Help menu, and then click the Help command to open the Help program.

2. Click the main topic of interest. Click a subtopic, if necessary.

3. Read the Help information.

4. If you can't find the information you need, click the Search box, and get Help information using keywords.

5. Click the **Close** button.

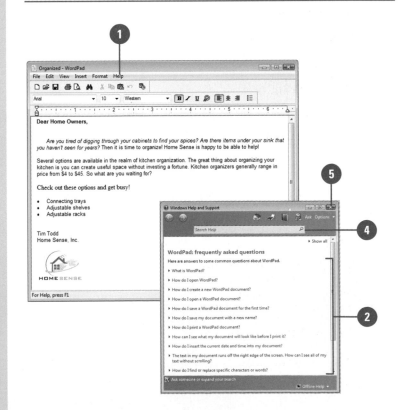

Switching Users

Many users are able to share the same computer. Their individual Windows identities allow them to keep their files completely private and to customize the operating system with their own preferences. Windows manages these separate identities, or accounts, by giving each user a unique user name and password. When a user selects an account and types a password (if necessary), Windows starts with that user's configuration settings and network permissions. When you want to change users, you can log off, (which closes all running programs, saves your settings, and signs you off the computer) or switch users, which quickly switches between users without having to close programs and saves your current settings.

Switch Users Quickly

1. Click the **Start** button, and then point to the arrow next to the Lock button.

2. Click **Switch User** to change users without saving current settings.

   A Welcome screen appears, displaying user accounts.

3. Click your name.

4. If a box for a password appears, type your password.

5. Click the Arrow button or press Enter to log on to Windows Vista.

Start button

Did You Know?

You can change user account options in the Control Panel. Click the Start button, click Control Panel, double-click the User Accounts icon in Classic view, and then select the options you want.

See Also

See "Adding and Deleting User Accounts" on page 312 for information on switching users.

Log Off and Log On Your Computer

1. Click the **Start** button, and then point to the arrow next to the Lock button.

2. Click **Log Off** to close all your programs, save your settings, and sign off the computer.

   A Welcome screen appears, displaying user accounts.

3. Click your name.

4. If a box for a password appears, type your password.

5. Click the Arrow button or press Enter to log on to Windows Vista.

Log Off and Log On a Network Computer

1. Click the **Start** button, and then point to the arrow next to the Lock button.

2. Click **Log Off** to close all your programs, save your settings, and sign off the computer.

3. Press and then release the Ctrl, Alt, and Delete keys at the same time.

4. Click the **Switch User** button, and then click your name or **Other User**.

5. Type your user name. For example: *domain name\user name* or *computer name\user name*

6. Type your assigned password.

7. Click the Arrow button or press Enter to log on to Windows Vista.

Shutting Down Your Computer

When you finish working on your computer, you need to make sure to turn off, or shut down, your computer properly. This involves several steps: saving and closing all open files, closing all open windows, exiting all running programs, shutting down Windows itself, and finally, turning off the computer. However, if you shut down your computer before or while installing Windows updates (download must be complete), Windows will automatically complete the install before shutting down, so you don't have to wait around. Shutting down your computer makes sure Windows and all its related programs are properly closed; this avoids potential problems starting and working with Windows in the future. If you turn off the computer by pushing the power switch while Windows or other programs are running, you could lose important data.

Shut Down Your Computer

1 Click the **Start** button, and then point to the arrow next to the Lock button.

2 Click the option you want:

- ◆ **Restart.** Exits Windows Vista and restarts the computer.

- ◆ **Sleep.** Switches the computer to low-power mode and maintains your session.

- ◆ **Hibernate.** Saves your session, exits Windows, and then restores your session the next time you start Windows.

- ◆ **Shut Down.** Exits Windows Vista and prepares the computer to be turned off.

IMPORTANT *Options vary depending on Windows settings.*

See Also

See "Updating Windows" on page 440 for information on automatically updating Windows.

Shut Down Options	
Option	**When to use it**
Restart	When you want to restart the computer and begin working with Windows again
Sleep	When you want to stop working for a few moments and conserve power (ideal for mobile computers); available when a power scheme is selected in Power Options
Hibernate	When you want to stop working for a while and safely turn off power; restores your session to work again later; available when a power scheme is selected in Power Options
Shut Down	When you finish working with Windows and you want to shut off your computer

Working with Windows Programs

2

Introduction

Now that you know how to work with the graphical elements that make Windows Vista work, you're ready to work with programs. A **program** is software you use to accomplish a specific task, such as word processing or managing files on your computer. This chapter shows you how to access your Windows programs (and to customize this access). It also shows you how to create and edit files in your programs, share information between programs, and what to do when a program is not responding.

Windows comes with several small programs, called **Accessories**, that are extremely useful for completing basic tasks, such as creating a written document or performing basic calculations. Windows Vista also provides a number of ways for you to resolve some common problems. For example, you can use older programs (designed to run on previous versions of Windows) on your Windows Vista computer by changing specific settings using the Accessories menu. You can run commands from a text-based interface (called a command line), and Windows provides an interface for quitting a program that has stopped responding without turning off your computer and losing information in other programs. Other special programs in Windows Vista are games. You can play games on your computer, or with other people over the internet.

Starting and Exiting a Program

The most common way to start a Windows program is to use the Start menu, which provides easy access to programs installed on your computer. Clicking the Start button on the taskbar displays the Start menu, which lists common and recently used programs and the All Programs submenu. The All Programs submenu is the master list of every program on your computer. If you start a program, such as your e-mail program, every time you start Windows, you can save some time by adding the program to the Startup folder. When you're done working with a program, you should exit, or close it, to conserve your computer's resources.

Start a Program from the Start Menu

Windows Vista provides several ways to start a program:

◆ Click the **Start** button, and then click a program.

◆ Click the **Start** button, point to **All Programs**, click a program group if necessary, and then click a program.

◆ Click the **Start** button, click **Computer** or **Documents**, navigate to the folder with the program or file associated with the program you want, and then double-click the icon.

◆ Click the **Start** button, point to **All Programs**, click **Accessories**, click **Run**, type the full path and file name of the program, and then click **OK**.

Documents

Start button   All Programs

Exit a Program

Windows Vista provides several ways to exit a program:

◆ Click the **File** menu, and then click **Exit**.

◆ Click the **Close** button on the program's title bar.

◆ Double-click the Control-menu on the program's title bar.

◆ Right-click the program's taskbar button, and then click **Close**.

Did You Know?

You can display the Programs list in a single column. Right-click the Start button, click Properties, click Customize, click the Advanced tab, select the Scroll Programs check box, and then click OK twice. Point to the black triangle arrows at the top and bottom to scroll through the list.

See Also

See "Using Windows Accessories" on page 29 for information on using Windows built-in programs.

Control menu

Close button

Taskbar button

Changing the Way a Program Starts

If you start a program, such as your e-mail program, every time you start Windows, you can save some time by adding the program to the Startup folder. The contents of the Startup folder appear on the Startup submenu on the All Programs menu. Every time you start Windows, the programs in the Startup folder automatically start. Sometimes a program installs a program to the Startup folder. If you don't want the program automatically starting with Windows, you can remove it from the Startup folder.

Add a Program to the Startup Submenu

① Click the **Start** button, and then locate the program you want to add to the Startup submenu.

② Hold down the Ctrl key, and then drag the program on top of the Startup item on the All Programs submenu.

Using the Ctrl key copies the program to the Startup submenu.

③ When the Startup submenu opens, drag the program onto the submenu, and then release the mouse button and the Ctrl key.

The next time Windows Vista starts, the program will start.

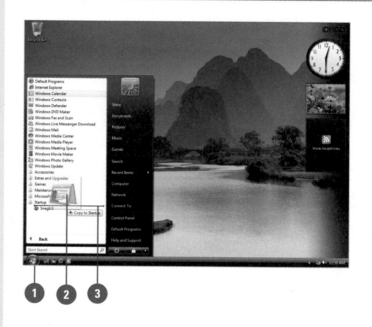

Remove a Program from the Startup Submenu

① Click the **Start** button, point to **All Programs**, and then click **Startup**.

② Right-click the program you want to remove on the Startup submenu.

③ Click **Delete**, and then click **Yes** to confirm the deletion.

Windows deletes the program from the Startup submenu, not from your computer.

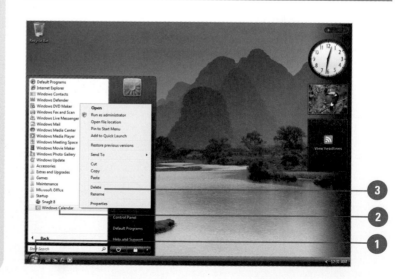

Using Windows Accessories

Windows comes with several accessories, built-in programs that are extremely useful for completing every day tasks.

One of the most useful features Windows offers is the ability to use data created in one file in another file, even if the two files were created in different Windows programs. To work with more than one program or file at a time, you simply need to open them on your desktop. A program button on the taskbar represents any window that is open on the desktop. When you want to switch from one open window to another, click the program button on the taskbar. If you tile, or arrange open windows on the desktop so that they are visible, you can switch among them simply by clicking in the window in which you want to work.

Frequently Used Windows Accessories

Program	Description
Calculator	Performs arithmetic calculations
Internet Explorer	Displays Web (HTML) pages
Notepad	Creates, edits, and displays text only documents
Paint	Creates and edits bitmap pictures
Sound Recorder	Creates and plays digital sound files
Windows Calendar (New!)	Manages appointments and tasks using personal calendars
Windows Contacts (New!)	Stores names, addresses, and other contact information
Windows Defender (New!)	Helps protect your computer from spyware and other harmful intruders
Windows DVD Maker (New!)	Burns pictures and videos to DVDs
Windows Fax and Scan (New!)	Sends and receives faxes or scanned pictures and documents
Windows Live Messenger	Sends and receives instant messages to online contacts; you need to download the program
Windows Mail (New!)	Provides e-mail, newsgroup, and directory services
Windows Media Center (New!)	Provides entertainment options for digital and on-demand media
Windows Media Player	Plays sound, music, and video
Windows Meeting Space (New!)	Provides an online place to share files, programs, or your desktop
Windows Movie Maker	Creates movies using audio and video files
Windows Photo Gallery (New!)	Views, edits, organizes, and shares photos and videos
WordPad	Creates, edits, and displays text, Rich Text Format, and Word documents

Creating a Document

A **document** is a file you create using a word processing program, such as a letter, memo, or resume. When you start WordPad, a blank document appears in the work area, known as the document window. You can enter information to create a new document and save the result in a file, or you can open an existing file and save the document with changes. As you type, text moves, or **wraps**, to a new line when the previous one is full.

Create a Document

1. Click the **Start** button, point to **All Programs**, click **Accessories**, and then click **WordPad**.

   If WordPad is already open, click the **New** button on the toolbar, click **Rich Text Document**, and then click **OK**.

2. Type your text.

3. Press Enter when you want to start a new paragraph.

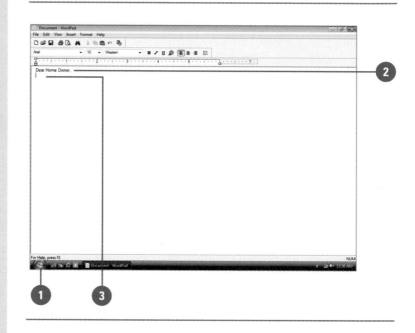

Change the Page Setup

1. Click the **File** menu, and then click **Page Setup**.

2. Specify the paper size and source.

3. Specify the page orientation, either portrait or landscape.

4. Specify the page margins.

5. Click **OK**.

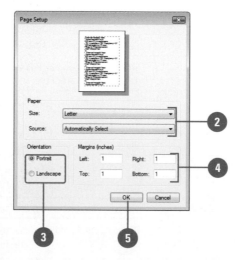

Open an Existing Document from Within a Program

① Click the **Open** button on the toolbar.

② Click the **Files name** list arrow, and then click the file type you want to open.

③ Click an icon on the Favorites Links to open a frequently used folder.

④ If desired, click the **Look in** list arrow, and then click the drive or folder from where you want to open the file.

⑤ Double-click the folder from which you want to open the file.

⑥ Click the document you want to open.

⑦ Click **Open**.

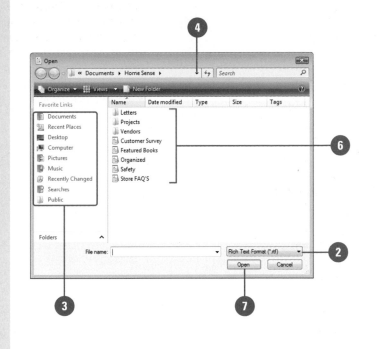

Open a Recent Document from the Start Menu

① Click the **Start** button.

② Point to **Recent Documents**.

③ Click the recently opened document you want to re-open.

Did You Know?

You can remove all recently used documents from the Recent Items submenu. Right-click the Start button, click Properties, click the Start Menu tab, clear the privacy related check boxes, and then click OK.

Editing Text

One of the advantages of using a word processing program is that you can edit a document or change the contents without re-creating it. In the WordPad work area, the mouse pointer changes to the I-beam pointer, which you can use to reposition the insertion point (called navigating) and insert, delete, or select text. Before you can edit text, you need to highlight, or select, the text you want to modify. Then you can delete, replace, move (cut), or copy text within one document or between documents even if they're different programs. When you cut or copy an item, it's placed on the Clipboard, which stores only a single piece of information at a time. You can also move or copy selected text without storing it on the Clipboard by using drag-and-drop editing.

Select and Edit Text

1. Move the I-beam pointer to the left or right of the text you want to select.

2. Drag the pointer to highlight the text.

   TIMESAVER *Double-click a word to select it; triple-click a paragraph to select it.*

3. Perform one of the following editing commands:

   ◆ To replace text, type your text.

   ◆ To delete text, press the Backspace key or the Delete key.

Insert and Delete Text

1. Click in the document to place the insertion point where you want to make the change.

   ◆ To insert text, type your text.

   ◆ To delete text, press the Backspace key or the Delete key.

Move or Copy Text

① Select the text you want to move or copy.

② Click the **Cut** button or **Copy** button on the toolbar.

③ Click where you want to insert the text.

④ Click the **Paste** button on the toolbar.

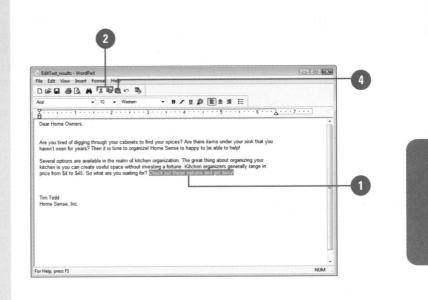

Move or Copy Text Using Drag and Drop

① Select the text you want to move or copy.

② Point to the selected text, and then click and hold the mouse button.

If you want to copy the text to a new location, also press and hold the Ctrl key. A plus sign (+) appears in the pointer box, indicating that you are dragging a copy of the selected text.

③ Drag the selected text to the new location, and then release the mouse button (and the Ctrl key, if necessary).

④ Click anywhere in the document to deselect the text.

Dear Home Owners,

Are you tired of digging through your cabinets to find your spices? Are there items under your sink that you haven't seen for years? Then it is time to organize! Home Sense is happy to be able to help!

Several options are available in the realm of kitchen organization. The great thing about organizing your kitchen is you can create useful space without investing a fortune. Kitchen organizers generally range in price from $4 to $45. So what are you waiting for? Check out these options and get busy

Tim Todd
Home Sense, Inc.

Dear Home Owners,

Are you tired of digging through your cabinets to find your spices? Are there items under your sink that y haven't seen for years? Then it is time to organize! Home Sense is happy to be able to help!

Several options are available in the realm of kitchen organization. The great thing about organizing your kitchen is you can create useful space without investing a fortune. Kitchen organizers generally range in price from $4 to $45. So what are you waiting for?

Check out these options and get busy!

Tim Todd
Home Sense, Inc.

Formatting Text

You can change the format or the appearance of text and graphics in a document so that the document is easier to read or more attractive. A quick and powerful way to add emphasis to parts of a document is to format text using bold, italics, underline, or color. For special emphasis, you can combine formats, such as bold and italics. In addition, you can change the font style and size. A **font** is a set of characters with the same typeface or design that you can increase or decrease in size, such as Arial or Times New Roman.

Format Text

1. Select the text or click in the paragraph you want to format.

2. Use any of the formatting tools to style text:
   - Font list arrow
   - Font Size list arrow
   - Font Script list arrow; a language type
   - Bold button
   - Italic button
   - Underline button
   - Color button

3. Use any of the formatting tools to adjust text spacing:
   - Alignment buttons
   - Bullet button

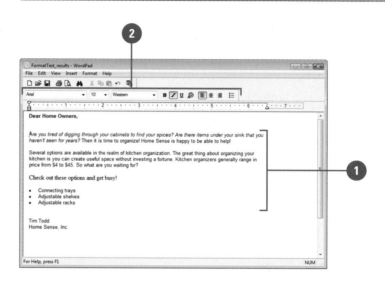

Did You Know?

Font size is measured in points. One point is 1/72 of an inch high.

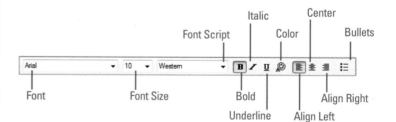

Setting Paragraph Tabs

Tabs set text or numerical data alignment in relation to the edges of a document. A **tab stop** is a predefined stopping point along the document's typing line. Default tab stops are set every half-inch on the ruler, but you can set multiple tabs per paragraph at any location. Each paragraph in a document contains its own set of tab stops. The default tab stops do not appear on the ruler, but the manual tab stops you set do appear. Once you place a tab stop, you can drag the tab stop to position it where you want. If you want to add or adjust tab stops in multiple paragraphs, simply select the paragraphs first.

Create and Clear a Tab Stop

1. Select the text or click in the paragraph you want to format.

2. Click the ruler where you want to set the tab stop.

3. To move a tab, drag the tab stop to position it where you want.

4. To clear a tab stop, drag it off the ruler.

See Also

See "Setting Paragraph Indents" on page 36 for information on changing the text alignment.

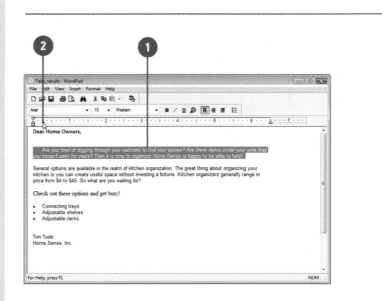

For Your Information

Changing the Word Wrap Display

As you type a complete line of text, it wraps to the next line. Depending on your preference, you can change the Document window to display text wrapped to the window or ruler. To change word wrap options, click the View menu, click Options, click the tab with your text format, click the word wrap option you want, and then click OK. In the Options dialog box, you can set different word wrap options for each of the text formats in which you can save documents, such as Text, Rich Text, Word, and Write. The wrapping options affect only how text appears on your screen. When printed, the document uses the margin settings specified in Page Setup.

Setting Paragraph Indents

When you indent a paragraph, you move its edge in from the left or right margin. You can indent the entire left or right edge of a paragraph or just the first line. The markers on the ruler control the indentation of the current paragraph. The left side of the ruler has three markers. The top triangle, called the **first-line indent marker**, controls where the first line of the paragraph begins. The bottom triangle, called the **hanging indent marker**, controls where the remaining lines of the paragraph begin. The small square under the bottom triangle, called the **left indent marker**, allows you to move the first-line Indent marker and the left indent marker simultaneously. When you move the left indent marker, the distance between the hanging indent and the first-line indent remains the same. The triangle on the right side of the ruler, called the **right indent marker**, controls where the right edge of the paragraph ends.

Change Paragraph Indents

Select the text or click in the paragraph you want to format.

- ◆ To change the left indent of the first line, drag the First-Line Indent marker.

- ◆ To change the indent of the second and subsequent lines, drag the Hanging Indent marker.

- ◆ To change the left indent for all lines, drag the Left Indent marker.

- ◆ To change the right indent for all lines, drag the Right Indent marker.

As you drag a marker, the dotted guideline helps you position the indent accurately.

Hanging indent marker

Left indent marker

First-line indent marker

Right indent marker

Previewing and Printing a Document

Before printing, you should verify that the page looks the way you want. You save time, money, and paper by avoiding duplicate printing. Print Preview shows you the exact placement of your text on each printed page. Printing a paper copy is a common way to review and share a document. You can use the Print button on the toolbar to print a copy of your document using the current settings, or you can open the Print dialog box and specify the print options you want.

Preview a Document

1. Click the **Print Preview** button on the toolbar.

2. Use the toolbar buttons to preview the document:

   - To change the view size, click **Zoom In** or **Zoom Out**.

   - To view other pages, click **Next Page** or **Prev Page**.

   - To view two pages at a time, click Two Pages.

   - To print the document, click Print.

3. When you're done, click **Close**.

Print All or Part of a Document

1. Click the **File** menu, and then click **Print**.

2. Click a printer.

3. Specify the range of pages you want to print.

4. Specify the number of copies you want to print.

5. Click **Print**.

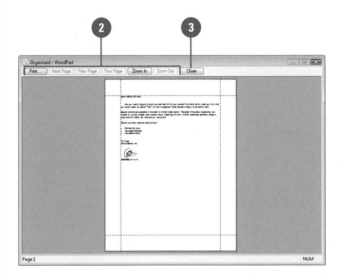

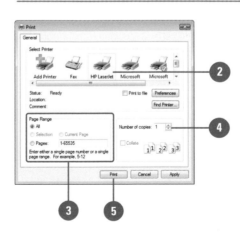

Saving and Closing a Document

Saving your files frequently ensures that you don't lose work during an unexpected power loss. The first time you save, specify a file name and folder in the Save As dialog box. The next time you save, the program saves the file with the same name in the same folder. If you want to change a file's name or location, you can use the Save As dialog box again to create a copy of the original file. To conserve your computer's resources, close any file you are not working on.

Save a Document

1. Click the **File** menu, and then click **Save As**.

2. Click an icon on the Favorites Links to open a frequently used folder.

3. If desired, click the **Save in** list arrow, and then click the drive or folder where you want to save the file.

4. Double-click the folder in which you want to save the file.

5. Type a name for the file, or use the suggested one.

6. To change the format of a file, click the **Save as type** list arrow, and then click a file format.

7. Click **Save**.

New folder button

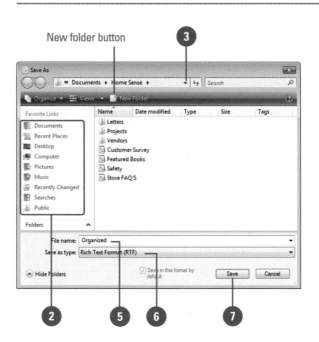

Did You Know?

You can save a file in a new folder. In the Save As dialog box, click the New Folder button, type the new folder name, click Open, and then click Save.

You can close a document. Click the Close button in the program window or click the File menu, and then click Close. If necessary, click Yes to save your changes.

Sharing Information Among Programs

Windows makes it easy to insert a file or part of a file created in one program into a file created in a different program. The ability to share files and information among different programs is called **object linking and embedding (OLE)**. With OLE, you can work with a document in WordPad and at the same time take advantage of the specialized tools in another program, such as Paint or Microsoft Excel. By using OLE, you'll be able to access features from other programs, edit data easily, update to the latest information, and save space.

Information shared between two programs is an **object**, which can be a picture from a graphics program, a chart from a spreadsheet program, a video clip, text, or almost anything else you can create on a computer. The program that creates the object is called the **source program**; the program that creates the file into which you want to insert the object is called the **destination program**. Likewise, the file that originally contained the object is the **source file**, and the file where you want to insert the object is the **destination file**. Both embedding and linking involve inserting an object into a destination file; they differ in where they store their respective objects. With **embedding**, a copy of the object becomes part of the destination file. If you want to edit the object, you make changes in the destination file, and the original file remains intact. With **linking**, a representation of the object appears in the destination file, but the object is stored in the source file. If you want to edit the linked object, you make changes in the source file or its representation in the destination file, and the other file will reflect the changes the next time you open it.

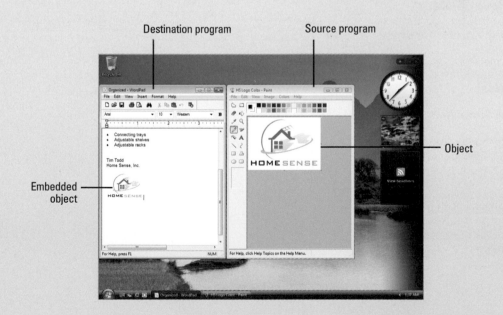

Destination program   Source program

Embedded object

Object

Inserting and Editing Information

Instead of switching back and forth between programs to copy and paste information, you can insert, or embed, the information. Embedding inserts a copy of one document into another. Once you embed data, you can edit it using the menus and toolbars of the source program without leaving the program in which it's embedded (that is, the destination program). For example, you can create a picture in a program, such as Paint, or select an existing picture and insert it into a WordPad document. The inserted picture is an object you can resize.

Embed an Existing Object

1. Click where you want to embed the object.

2. Click the **Insert** menu, and then click **Object**.

3. Click the **Create from File** option.

4. Click **Browse**, and then double-click the file with the object you want to embed.

5. Click **OK**.

Embed a New Object

1. Click where you want to embed the object.

2. Click the **Insert** menu, and then click **Object**.

3. Click the **Create New** option.

4. Double-click the type of object you want to create.

5. Enter information in the new object using the menus and toolbars in the source program.

6. Click outside the object to close the object.

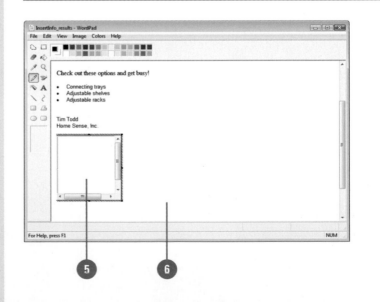

Edit an Object

1. Open the document with the object you want to edit.

2. Double-click the object.

3. Edit the object using the menus and toolbars in the source program.

4. Click outside the object to close the object.

Did You Know?

You can use Paste Special to embed part of a file. Select and copy the information, click where you want to embed the copied information, click the Edit menu, click Paste Special, click the Paste option to embed, select a format, and then click OK.

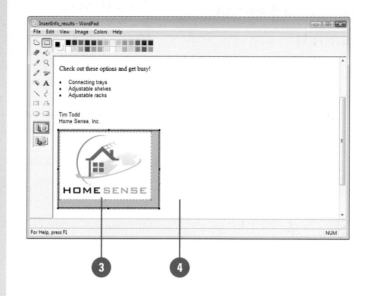

Resize an Object

1. Click the object to select it.

2. Drag a sizing handle to change the size of the object.

   ◆ Drag a corner sizing handle to change height and width simultaneously.

   ◆ Drag the top or bottom middle sizing handle to change height.

   ◆ Drag the left or right middle sizing handle to change width.

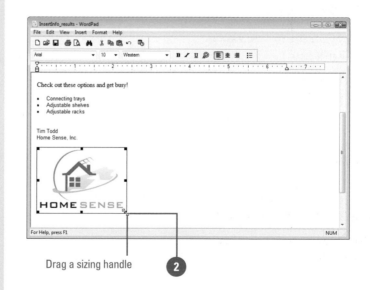

Drag a sizing handle

Linking and Updating Information

When you want to keep source and destination files in sync with each other, you can link the source file that created the object with the destination file that displays the object. Linking displays information stored in one document (the source file) into another (the destination file). You can edit the linked object from either file, although changes are stored in the source file. Only a representation of the object appears in the destination file; any changes made to the object are done in the source file, whether you access it by double-clicking the object in the destination file or by opening it in the source program.

Link an Object Between Programs

1. Click where you want to embed the object.

2. Click the **Insert** menu, and then click **Object**.

3. Click the **Create from File** option.

4. Click **Browse**, and then double-click the file with the object you want to link.

5. Select the **Link** check box.

6. Click **OK**.

Did You Know?

You can use Paste Special to link part of a file. Select and copy the information, click where you want to link the copied information, click the Edit menu, click Paste Special, click the Paste Link option to link, select a format, and then click OK.

Linked object

Update a Linked File

1 Open the file with the source program.

2 Edit the file using the source program's commands.

3 Click the **Save** button on the toolbar.

4 Click the **Close** button to exit the source program.

5 Open the linked file with the destination program.

The object automatically updates.

6 Click the **Save** button on the toolbar.

7 Click the **Close** button to exit the destination program.

Did You Know?

You can change a link to update manually. In the destination program, select the object, click the Edit menu, click Links, click the Manual option button, and then click Close.

For Your Information

Finding, Changing, and Breaking a Linked Object

Instead of opening a linked object from the source file to make changes, you can open a linked object from the destination file using the Open Source button in the Links dialog box. The Open Source button finds the source file containing the linked object and opens that file. After making changes, you exit and return to the destination file. The Links dialog box keeps track of the source file location. You can change the linked source to a different file by using the Change Source button. If you want to disregard a link and change it to an embedded object, select the linked object in the destination file, click Edit on the menu bar, click Object Properties, click the Link tab, click Break Link, click Yes in the message box, and then click OK. On the Link tab in the Object Properties dialog box, you can also open or change the source file, change update options, and update the source for the selected object.

Inserting Special Characters

When you need to insert special characters such as ©, ™, or ® that don't appear on your keyboard, you can use a special accessory program called Character Map to do the job. Character Map displays all the characters that are available for each of the fonts on your computer.

Insert a Special Character

1. Click the **Start** button, point to **All Programs**, click **Accessories**, click **System Tools**, and then click **Character Map**.

2. Click the **Font** list arrow, and then click a font.

3. Double-click the character you want to insert.

   TIMESAVER *Click a character to see an enlarged view of it.*

4. Click **Copy** to place the character on the Clipboard.

5. Click the **Close** button.

6. Click in the document to place the insertion point.

7. Click the **Edit** menu, and then click **Paste**.

   TIMESAVER *Press Ctrl+V to quickly paste the contents from the Clipboard.*

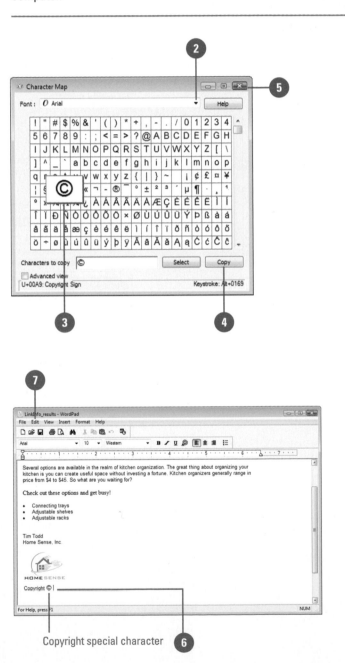

Copyright special character

44

Calculating Numbers

If you don't have a handheld calculator handy, you can use the Calculator program provided by Windows Vista to perform standard calculations or even more complex ones. Calculator performs basic arithmetic, such as addition and subtraction, as well as functions found on a scientific calculator, such as logarithms and factorials.

Use the Calculator

1 Click the **Start** button, point to **All Programs**, click **Accessories**, and then click **Calculator**.

2 Click the **View** menu, and then click **Standard** or **Scientific**.

3 Enter a number, or click the number buttons.

4 Click a function button.

5 Enter another number.

6 When you've entered all the numbers you want, click the equals (=) button.

7 Click the **Edit** menu, and then click **Copy** to copy the result to the Clipboard to paste in a document.

8 When you're done, click the **Close** button.

Did You Know?

You can use the numeric keypad on your keyboard with the Calculator. Press the number, +, -, *, /, and Enter keys to quickly enter numbers and use the calculator.

You can find out the purpose of a key. Right-click the key, and then click What's this?

Running Commands

Microsoft
Certified
Application
Specialist

WINV-7.4.1,
WINV-7.4.2

Besides running Windows Vista programs, you can also enter commands and run programs written in MS-DOS. **MS-DOS** stands for Microsoft Disk Operating System. MS-DOS, or DOS, employs a **command-line interface** through which you must type commands at a **command prompt** to run different tasks. A character such as a > or $ appears at the beginning of a command prompt. Each DOS command has a strict set of rules called a **command syntax** that you must follow when expressing a command. Many commands allow you to include switches and parameters that give you additional control of the command.

Run a Command

1. Click the **Start** button, point to **All Programs**, click **Accessories**, and then click **Command Prompt**.

2. At the prompt, type a command including any parameters, and then press Enter.

3. When you're done, click the **Close** button, or type **exit**, and then press Enter.

Find a Command

1. Click the **Start** button, point to **All Programs**, click **Accessories**, and then click **Command Prompt**.

2. At the prompt, type **help**, and then press Enter.

3. Read the list of commands. Use the scroll bar or scroll arrows to display additional information.

4. When you're done, click the **Close** button, or type **exit**, and then press Enter.

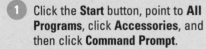

prompt

Get Information About a Command

1 Click the **Start** button, point to **All Programs**, click **Accessories**, and then click **Command Prompt**.

2 At the prompt, type a command followed by a space and **/?**, and then press Enter.

3 Read the information about the command. Use the scroll bar or scroll arrows to display additional information.

4 When you're done, click the **Close** button, or type **exit**, and then press Enter.

Did You Know?

You can use a wildcard character to change more than one file. An asterisk is a wildcard and represents any number of characters. For example, the command *dir at*.doc* matches atback.doc, ati.doc, and atlm.doc.

You can change the appearance of the Command Prompt window. Right-click the Command Prompt window title bar, and then click Properties.

You can ping a connection to make sure it works and find out an IP address. Ping is a diagnostic network tool that verifies whether an IP address is accessible. To test a connection, type **ping *IP address*** at the command prompt, and then press Enter. To find an IP address, type **ipconfig /?** or type **ipconfig /all**, and then press Enter. To get a new IP address, type **ipconfig/release**, press Enter, type **ipconfig/renew**, and then press Enter.

Common DOS Commands

Command	Purpose
cd *foldername*	Changes to the specified folder
cls	Clears the screen
copy	Copies the specified files or folder
dir	Lists the contents of the current folder
c: (where c is a drive)	Switches to the specified drive
exit	Closes the Command Prompt window
rename	Renames the specified file or files
more *filename*	Displays the contents of a file, one screen of output at a time
type *filename.txt*	Displays the contents of the text file

Playing Games

If you have some free time, you can play some fun and exciting games. Windows provides several games you can play against the computer—Chess Titans (**New!**), FreeCell, Hearts, InkBall (**New!**), Mahjong Titans, (**New!**), Minesweeper, Purble Place (**New!**), Solitaire, and Spider Solitaire.

Play a Game

1. Click the **Start** button, and then click **Games**.

2. Double-click the game you want.

3. Play the game.

4. When you're done, click the Game menu, and then click a command to start a new game with the same or different players, or exit the game.

See Also

See "Playing Internet Games" on page 50 for information on playing games over the Internet against other players.

Playing the Game

Game	Object is to
Chess Titans	Put your opponents' king in checkmate. Each player has one king. As you capture your opponent's pieces, strategize a way to capture the opposing king.
FreeCell	Stack the cards in the cells at the top in descending order, starting from any card, alternating the red and black cards.
Hearts	Score the lowest number of points, one point for each heart and 13 points for the Queen of Spades. You play a card to follow suit or a heart or the Queen of Spades when you can't follow suit.
InkBall	Use the mouse or tablet pen, draw ink strokes to guide the balls into holes of the same color and to block balls from entering holes of a different color.
Mahjong Titans	Remove all the tiles from the board by finding matching pairs of free tiles. Mahjong is a form of solitaire that is played with tiles instead of cards.
Minesweeper	Uncover all the squares that don't contain mines in the shortest amount of time. You use the numbers in the uncovered squares to determine which adjacent squares contain mines.
Purble Place	Teach colors, shapes, and pattern recognition.
Solitaire	Reveal all the cards that are turned face down by stacking them in descending order (alternating the red and black cards) on the lower piles, and stack them in ascending order from Ace through King by suit in the upper piles. You use the mouse to drag one card on top of another.
Spider Solitaire	Stack the cards by suit in one column in descending order.

Playing Internet Games

Windows XP provided several games you can play against players over the Internet—Backgammon, Checkers, Hearts, Reversi, and Spades. These and other games are still available on the MSN Games Web site, but you can no longer access them from the Start menu in Windows Vista. When you start an Internet game, the game server finds players matched to your skill level and language from around the world. You can't select the players or locations of your opponents, but you can communicate with them by using the Chat controls.

Play an Internet Game

① Open your Web browser, and then go to *www.zone.msn.com*.

② Follow the online instructions and game Help to play the game you want.

See Also

See "Sending and Receiving Instant Messages" on page 218 for information on playing games over the Internet using Windows Messenger.

Running Older Programs

Microsoft Certified Application Specialist   WINV-3.1.5

Some older programs are designed to run on earlier versions of Windows and don't work properly on Windows Vista. You can set the compatibility of Windows Vista to act like an earlier version of Windows to run an older program. In addition, you can also set display resolution and color settings, and user privilege levels to provide the best level of compatibility for the program and the Windows Vista operating system. You set options in the Compatibility tab in the program's Properties dialog box.

Set Compatibility for an Older Program

1. Click the **Start** button, and then locate the older program.

2. Right-click the program you want to run, and then click **Properties**.

3. Click the **Compatibility** tab.

4. Select the **Run this program in compatibility mode for** check box.

5. Click the list arrow, and then click the version of Windows in which the program was designed.

6. Select the check boxes for applying the appropriate settings to the display, based on the program's documentation.

7. Click **OK**.

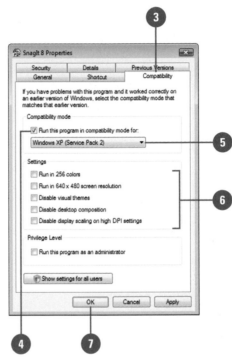

> ### Did You Know?
>
> **You can test your program using the Program Compatibility Wizard.** Click the Start button, click Help and Support, click the Get your programs to work on this version of Windows link, read the Help topic, and then follow the instructions to start the Program Compatibility Wizard.

Quitting a Program Not Responding

Microsoft
Certified
Application
Specialist

WINV-7.5.1

If a program stops responding while you work or freezes up, Windows provides you with the option to end the task (**New!**). When you end a task, you'll probably lose any unsaved work in the problem program. If the problem persists, you might need to reinstall the program or contact product support to fix the problem. Pressing Ctrl+Alt+Delete or clicking the Close button closes the non responsive program and opens the Task Manager, where you can stop the program. You can also use the Task Manager to view system performance and log off users.

End a Task Not Responding

1. Right-click the taskbar, and then click **Task Manager**.

   If Windows doesn't respond when you right-click, press Ctrl+Alt+Delete, and then click **Task Manager**.

2. Click the **Applications** tab.

3. Select the program not responding.

4. Click **End Task**. If you're asked to wait, click **End Now**.

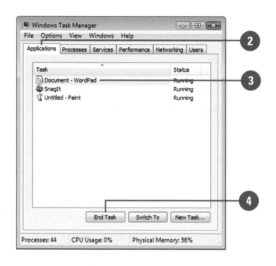

End a Program Not Responding

1. If a program is not responding, click the **Close** button on the program's title bar. Click several times, if necessary.

2. If you see a dialog box telling you the program is not responding, click **End Now**.

3. When a message appears, click **Send Information** to send information about the error over the Internet to Microsoft, or click **Cancel** to continue.

Managing Files and Folders

3

Introduction

File management is organizing and keeping track of files and folders, helping you stay organized, so information is easily located. A **folder** is a container for storing programs and files, similar to a folder in a file cabinet. As with a file cabinet, working with poorly managed files is like looking for a needle in a haystack—it is frustrating and time-consuming to search through irrelevant, misnamed, and out-of-date files to find the one you want. Windows Vista allows you to organize folders and files in a file hierarchy, imitating the way you store paper documents in real folders. Just as a file cabinet contains several folders, each containing related documents with dividers grouping related folders together, so the Windows file hierarchy allows you to organize your files in folders, and then place folders in other folders. At the top of each hierarchy is the name of the hard drive or main folder. This drive or folder contains several files and folders, and each folder contains related files and folders.

Using the file management tools, you can save files in folders with appropriate names for easy identification, quickly and easily create new folders so you can reorganize information and delete files and folders that you no longer need. You can also search for a file when you cannot remember where you stored it, create shortcuts to files and folders for quick and easy access, and even compress files and folders to save space.

A folder can hold different types of files, such as text, spreadsheets, and presentations. The Documents folder is the main location in Windows Vista where you store your files. However, there are some special folders, such as Pictures and Music, designed with specialized features to store specific types of files.

Using the Explorer Window

The Explorer windows (**New!**) are powerful easy-to-use tools for working with files consistently across Windows Vista. Explorers give you more information and control while simplifying how you work with your files. The experience is easy and consistent, whether you're browsing documents or photos or even using the Control Panel. Key elements of the Explorer windows in Windows Vista are designed to help you get to the information you need, when you need it. Each Explorer window includes the following elements:

◆ **Back and Forward buttons.** Use to navigate between previously viewed folders.

◆ **Address bar.** Use to navigate directly to a different location, including local and network disks, folders, and Web locations.

◆ **Search box.** Use to perform instant searches, which show only those files that match what you typed in the Search box for the current folder and any of its subfolders.

◆ **Toolbar/Command bar.** Use to perform file related commands. Toolbar/Command bars display only the task buttons that are appropriate for the files being displayed. There are two consistent buttons on every Toolbar/ Command bar: Organize and Views.

◆ **Navigation pane.** Use to display common folders, such as Documents, Pictures, Music, the Folders list, and other favorite links, such as recently changed files, saved searches, and public folders.

◆ **Folders list.** Use to access additional folders using a folder tree structure similar to the previous version of Windows. To open or close the Folders list, click Folders at the bottom of the Navigation pane.

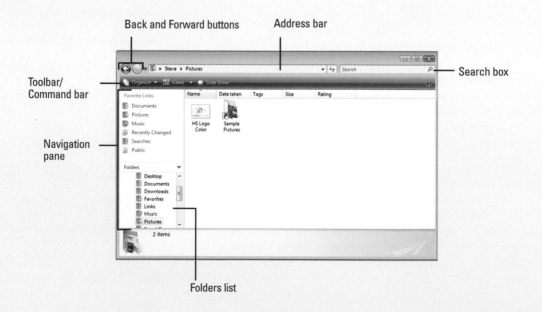

Back and Forward buttons

Address bar

Search box

Toolbar/ Command bar

Navigation pane

Folders list

Changing the Explorer Window View

Windows Vista displays the contents of a drive or folder in different ways to help you find the information you are looking for about a file or folder. The available views include Extra Large, Large, Medium and Small Icons (**New!**), List, Details, and Tiles.

Icons view displays icons in different sizes (Extra Large, Large, Medium, and Small), sorted alphabetically in horizontal rows, with the name of the file or folder below each icon. When you view files using one of the Icon views, Live icons (**New!**)—thumbnails—display the first page of documents, the image of a photo, or the album art for individual songs, making it easier to find exactly what you are looking for.

List view displays small icons, sorted alphabetically into vertical columns, with the name of the file or folder next to each icon.

Details view displays small icons, sorted alphabetically in a single vertical column, with the name of the file or folder and additional information, such as file size, type, and date, in columns to the right.

Tiles view displays icons, sorted alphabetically into vertical columns, with information about the file next to each icon.

Switching Between Views

You use the Views button on the toolbar in an Explorer window to quickly switch between window views. When you click the Views button, the view switches between the following four views: List, Details, Tiles, and Large Icons. If you want to select a different view, you can click the arrow next to the Views button to display a menu, where you can click a view or drag the slider. When you drag the slider, you can position it anywhere within the range, not just the main positions.

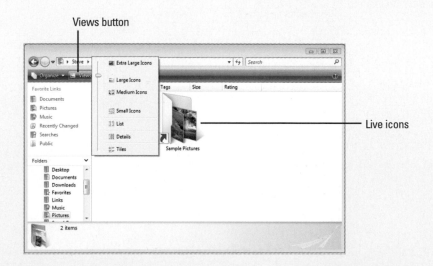

Views button

Live icons

Opening and Viewing the Computer

The Computer window is the starting point to access every disk, folder, and file on your computer. You can access the Computer window from the Start menu. The Computer window displays several types of local, removable, and network drives. Drives and folders are represented by icons. Each drive is assigned a drive letter, denoted with parentheses and a colon, such as Local Disk (C:), to make it easier to identify. Typically, the floppy is drive A, the hard (also known as local) disk is drive C, and the CD or DVD is drive D. If your computer includes additional drives, your computer assigns them letters in alphabetical order. Once you open more than one drive or folder, you can use buttons on the Command bar to help you move quickly between folders.

Open and View the Computer

1. Click the **Start** button, and then click **Computer**.

2. Click a drive to select it.

3. Review the drive details in the Details pane.

4. Double-click the drive to open it.

5. Click the **Back** button or **Forward** button on the toolbar to return or move to a previously visited window.

   TIMESAVER *You can press the Backspace key to go back to a previous folder you visited.*

6. When you're done, click the **Close** button.

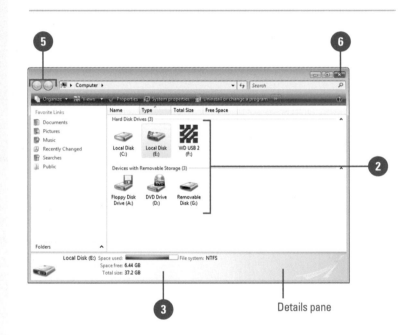

Details pane

Did You Know?

You can add the Computer icon to the desktop. Right-click the desktop in a blank area, click Personalize, click Change desktop icons in the left pane, select the Computer check box, and then click OK.

You can find Windows system information in Computer. Click the Start button, click Computer, click System properties on the toolbar.

You can find drive or device properties in Computer. Click the Start button, click Computer, click the drive or device, click Properties on the toolbar, and then click the General tab.

See Also

See "Changing the Explorer Window View" on page 55 for information on changing the display of a folder's contents.

Typical Disk Drives on a Computer

Icon	Type Description
Local	A hard magnetic disk (or hard disk) on which you can store large amounts of data. The Local Disk (C:) stores all the files on your computer.
Floppy	A soft removable magnetic disk that comes in a 3½-inch size, which stores up to 1.44 MB of data. Floppy disks are slower to access than a hard disk, but are portable and much less expensive.
Removable	A removable magnetic disk on which you can store computer data, such as a Zip disk (requires software). Another is a Flash memory card the size of a large stamp that holds128, 256, 512 MB or greater. Flash drives connect directly into a USB plug without software.
CD-ROM	**Compact Disc-Read-Only Memory** An optical disk on which you can stamp, or burn, up to 1 GB (typical size is 650 MB) of data in only one session. The disc cannot be erased or burned again with additional new data.
CD-R	**Compact Disc-Recordable** A type of CD-ROM on which you can burn up to 1 GB of data in multiple sessions. The disc can be burned again with new data, but cannot be erased.
CD-RW	**Compact Disc-Rewriteable** A type of CD-ROM on which you can read, write, and erase data, just like a hard disk.
DVD	**Digital Video Disc** A type of DVD-ROM that holds a minimum of 4.7 GB, enough for a full-length movie.
DVD-R	**Digital Video Disc-Recordable** A type of DVD-ROM on which you can burn up to 4.7 GB of data in multiple sessions. The disc can be burned again with new data, but cannot be erased.
DVD-RW	**Digital Video Disc-Rewriteable** A type of DVD-ROM on which you can read, write, and erase data, just like a hard disk.

Viewing and Opening Documents

Windows makes it easy to manage the personal and business files and folders you work with every day. You can access your Documents folder from the Start menu. In the Documents folder, you can view file information, organize files and folders, and open files and folders. Once you open more than one folder, you can use buttons on the Command bar to help you move quickly between folders. Depending on previous installation, devices installed, or other users, your personal folders might differ.

View and Open Documents

1. Click the **Start** button, and then click **Documents**.

2. Click a file to select it.

3. Review the document details in the Details pane.

4. Double-click the file to open it.

5. Use the scroll bars to view additional documents. Drag the scroll box, or click the scroll arrows.

6. When you're done, click the **Close** button.

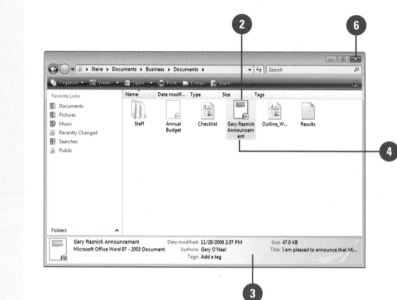

Open Any Folder and Switch Between Folders

1. Click the **Start** button, and then click the user account name, or any other Explorer window, such as **Documents**, **Pictures**, or **Music**.

2. Double-click the folder to open it.

3. Click the **Back** button or **Forward** button to return or move to a previously visited window.

4. When you're done, click the **Close** button.

Did You Know?

Windows stores music and picture files in separate folders in your personal folder. Windows stores music files in the Music folder and pictures in the Pictures folder, which you can access from the Start menu.

See Also

See "Changing the Explorer Window View" on page 55 for information on changing the display of a folder's contents.

For Your Information

Opening a Document with a Different Program

Most documents on your desktop are associated with a specific program. For example, if you double-click a document whose file name ends with the three-letter extension ".txt," Windows automatically opens the document with Notepad, a text-only editor. There are situations, though, when you need to open a document with a program other than the one Windows chooses, or when you want to choose a different default program. For example, you might want to open a text document in WordPad rather than Notepad so that you can add formatting and graphics. To do this, right-click the document icon you want to open, point to Open With, and then click the application you want to use to open the document, or click Choose Program to access more program options. Once you open a text file using WordPad, this option is automatically added to the Open With menu.

Opening Recently Used Documents

Windows Vista makes it easy to find and open recently used files. You can use the Recent Items option on the Start menu, or the Recently Changed folder (**New!**) in the Navigation pane of an Explorer window. To quickly open a recently used file, click the Start menu, point to Recent Items, and then click the file you want to open. To view recently changed files, open an Explorer window, such as Documents, and then click Recently Changed in the Navigation pane. If you want to open a file, simply double-click it.

Open a Recently Used Documents

1. Click the **Start** button, and then point to **Recent Items**.

2. Click the file you want to open from the submenu.

   The program associated with the file starts and opens the file.

3. When you're done, click the **Close** button.

Open a Recently Changed File

1. Click the **Start** button, and then open an Explorer window, such as **Username**, **Documents**, **Pictures**, or **Music**.

2. Click the **Recently Changed** link.

3. To open a file, double-click the file icon.

   The program associated with the file starts and opens the file.

4. When you're done, click the **Close** button.

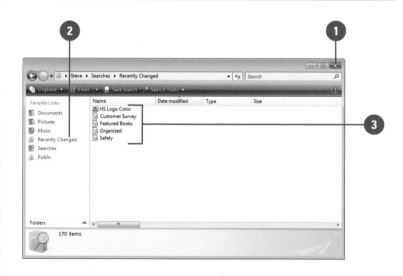

Working with Personal Folders

Windows Vista comes with a personal folder that store your most frequently used folders in one location. The personal folder appears on the Start menu with the name of the person logged on to the computer. The personal folder only contains files and folder associated with a user account and are unique for each user on the computer. The personal folder (**New!**) includes a variety of folders: Contacts, Desktop, Documents, Favorites, Links, Music, Pictures, Saved Games, Searches, and Videos. You can access these folders using the personal folder or by name on the Start menu.

View and Open a Personal Folder

1. Click the **Start** button, and then click the user account name at the top of the right column on the Start menu.

2. Double-click a folder to open it.

3. When you're done, click the **Close** button.

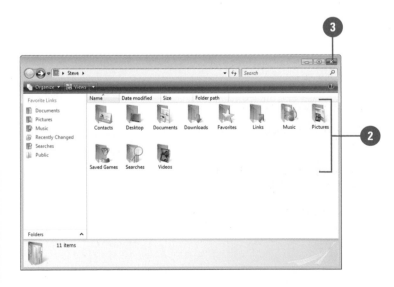

Navigating Between Folders

The Address bar (**New!**) appears at the top of every Explorer window and displays the current location on your computer or network. The location appears as a series of links separated by arrows. You can change your current location by either typing a new location—even a Web address on the Internet—or selecting one using the Address bar. You can also use the Back and Forward buttons to the left of the Address bar to switch between locations you have previously visited.

Navigate to a Location

- **Click a location**. Use either of the following methods:

  - **Visible folder location**. To go directly to a location visible in the Address bar, click the location name.

  - **Visible subfolder location**. To go to a subfolder of a location visible in the Address bar, click the arrow to the right, and then click the location name.

- **Type a location**. Click a blank space (to the right of text) in the Address bar, and then type the complete folder name or path to the location, and then press Enter.

  You can type common locations and then press Enter. The common locations include: Computer, Contacts, Control Panel, Documents, Favorites, Games, Music, Pictures, Recycle Bin, and Videos.

  If you type a Web address (URL) in the Address bar, the Explorer window switches to Internet Explorer.

Address bar   Click a location

Navigation pane

Viewing the Folders List

Windows Vista offers a useful feature for managing files and folders, called the **Folders list**. The Folders list displays the window in two panes, or frames, which allows you to view information from two different locations. The left pane of the Folders list displays the file hierarchy of all the drives and folders on the computer, and the right pane displays the contents of the selected drive or folder. This arrangement enables you to view the file hierarchy of your computer and the contents of a folder simultaneously making it easy to copy, move, delete, and rename files and folders. Using the non filled arrow and the filled arrow to the left of an icon in the Folders list allows you to display different levels of the drives and folders on your computer without opening and displaying the contents of each folder.

View the Folders List

1. Open any folder window.

2. In the Navigation pane, click the **Folders** link.

   TIMESAVER *Press the Windows key+E to open the Computer window with the Folders list.*

3. Perform the commands you want to display folder structure and contents:

   ◆ To show the file and folder structure, click the non filled arrow.

   ◆ To hide the file and folder structure, click the filled arrow.

   ◆ To display the contents of a folder, click the folder icon.

4. In the Navigation pane, click the **Folders** link again to close the Folders list.

> ### Did You Know?
>
> **You can quickly determine if a folder contains folders.** When an arrow doesn't appear next to an icon in the Folders list, the item has no folders in it.

Changing the Explorer Layout

Microsoft
Certified
Application
Specialist

WINV-4.1.4

Windows Vista gives you the option to customize the layout for each Explorer window depending on the information the window contains. The layout (**New!**) for each Explorer window includes a Menu Bar, Details pane, Preview pane, and Navigation pane. The Details and Navigation panes appear by default. Some Explorer windows, such as the personal folder labeled with your user account name, also include a Search Pane, which you can use. The Organize menu shows or hides the layout elements. If you prefer working with menus like the previous version of Windows, you can show the Menu Bar and use traditional menus.

Change the Explorer Layout

① Open the folder window you want to change.

② Click the **Organize** button, and then point to **Layout**.

③ Select the layout item you want to show or hide: **Menu Bar**, **Search Pane**, **Details Pane**, **Preview Pane**, or **Navigation Pane**.

Layout options vary depending on the type of Explorer window.

TIMESAVER *To quickly display the Menu bar, press the Alt key, and then release it. Press the Alt key again to remove it.*

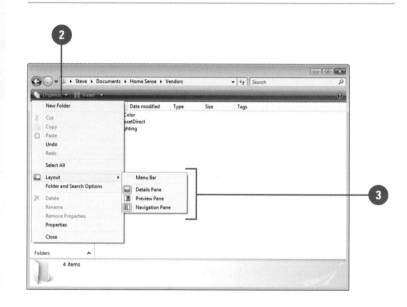

Customizing the Navigation Pane

Microsoft Certified Application Specialist

WINV-4.2.4

The Navigation pane (**New!**) provides links to commonly used folders and saved searches to reduce the number of clicks it takes to locate a file or folder. Windows Vista provides a default list of favorite links including Documents, Pictures, Music, Recently Changed, and Searches. You can customize the Navigation pane to include the folders or saved searches you want for your everyday use. You can move current links, add or rename folders or save searches, or remove an item. If the Navigation pane gets cluttered, you can restore it back to the original default items and start from there.

Customize the Navigation Pane

◆ **Move a link.** Drag an item in the Navigation pane to a higher or lower position.

◆ **Add a link.** Drag an item from its original location to a position on the Navigation pane. This includes folders from the Folder list at the bottom of the Navigation pane.

◆ **Rename a link.** Right-click the item, and then click **Rename**. Type a new name, and then press Enter. The original folder or search is not renamed, only the Navigation link.

◆ **Remove a link.** Right-click the item, and then click **Remove Link**. The original folder or search is not removed, only the Navigation link.

◆ **Restore default links.** Right-click a blank area of the Navigation pane, and then click **Restore Default Favorite Links**.

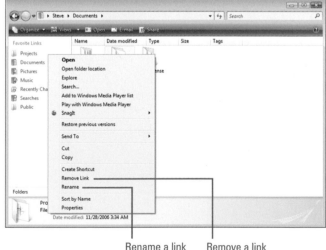

Navigation pane   Move a link

Rename a link   Remove a link

Organizing Files by Headings

Microsoft
Certified
Application
Specialist

WINV-4.5.3, WINV-4.5.4,
WINV-4.5.5

In Explorer windows, files appear in lists with headings at the top. You can use the headings to change how files are displayed in the window. There are several ways to organize your files by using file list headings and they include filtering, stacking, and grouping. Filtering (**New!**) displays only files with the properties you select by heading type. Stacking (**New!**) displays all of the files in the view into piles by heading type. After you stack files into piles, you can open individual ones to view the contents of the stack. Grouping (**New!**) displays a sequential list of all of the files by heading type. Grouping and stacking are similar organizational tools. Grouping organizes files into visible groups, while stacking organizes files into hidden groups within an icon.

Organize Files Using Filtering

1. Open the folder that contains the files you want to filter.

2. Point to the heading you want to filter by.

3. Click the arrow to the right of the heading you want to filter by.

4. Select the property check boxes you want to filter by.

5. Click in a blank area to close the search menu.

   ◆ To cancel the search, press Esc.

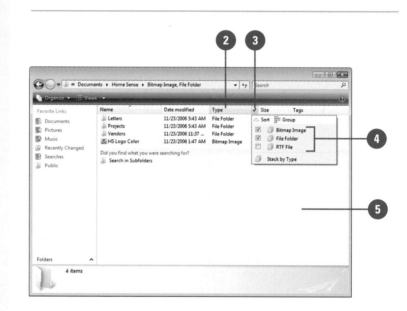

Did You Know?

You can sort files using headings.
Open the folder that contains the files you want to sort, point to the heading you want to sort by, click the arrow to the right, and then click Sort. Click in a blank area to close the search menu. To quickly sort files by headings, click the heading title. Either method, the sort toggles between ascending and descending.

Organize Files Using Stacking

① Open the folder that contains the files you want to stack.

② Point to the heading you want to stack by.

③ Click the arrow to the right of the heading you want to stack by.

④ Click **Stack by <heading name>**.

⑤ Click in a blank area to close the search menu.

◆ To cancel the search, press Esc.

⑥ To view the files within an individual stack, double-click the stack.

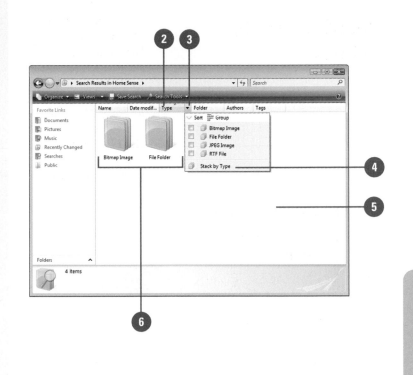

Organize Files Using Grouping

① Open the folder that contains the files you want to group.

② Point to the heading you want to group by.

③ Click the arrow to the right of the heading you want to group by.

④ Click **Group**.

⑤ Click in a blank area to close the search menu.

◆ To cancel the search, press Esc.

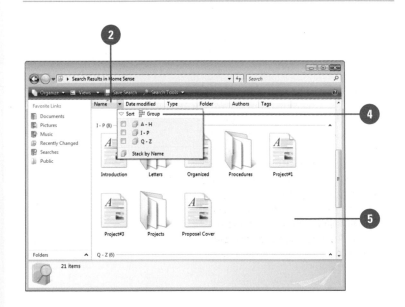

Searching for Files and Folders

Sometimes remembering precisely where you stored a file can be difficult. Windows provides a Search folder (**New!**) to help you find and view all of your files or folders in one place. The Search folder provides easy access to all of your most common files, such as documents, pictures, music, and e-mail, in a single view. If you don't find the file or folders you're looking for, you can perform an advanced search. An advanced search gives you the option to find files or folders by type, name, title, location, date (taken, modified, or created), size, or property tag. The search locates files and programs stored anywhere in indexed locations, which includes personal folders, e-mail, offline files, and Web sites in the History list for your Web browser. The Search folder is accessible from the Start menu (or any folder window) to help you locate files and folders.

Create a Simple Search by Type

1. Click the **Start** button, and then click **Search**.

2. Click the type of file you want to locate: **All**, **E-mail**, **Document**, **Picture**, **Music**, or **Other**.

   ◆ To search for folders, click All.

3. Click in the Search box.

4. Type a word or part of a word.

   As you type, programs and files that match your text appear on the Start menu. You don't have to press Enter.

   TROUBLE? *In the Search box, you must press Enter to start a search for files in non-indexed locations.*

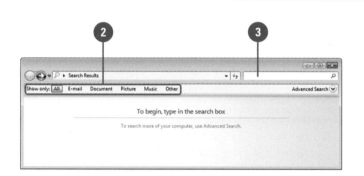

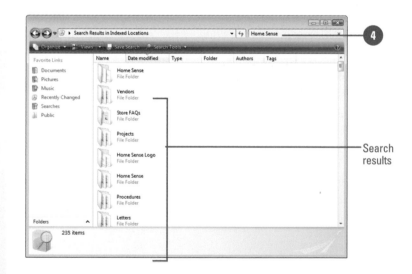

Search results

Did You Know?

You can search everywhere on your computer. If you can't find a file, you can search everywhere on your computer. In the Advanced Search pane, specify any search criteria, click the Locations arrow, click Everywhere, and then click Search. This might take a long time.

Create an Advanced Search

1. Click the **Start** button, and then click **Search**.

2. Click the type of file you want to locate: **All**, **E-mail**, **Document**, **Picture**, **Music**, or **Other**.

3. Click the **Advanced Search** button.

4. Specify the search options you want:

   ◆ **Name.** Type a file name.

   ◆ **Tags.** Type a property tag.

   ◆ **Title.** Type the author name.

   ◆ **Location.** Click the list arrow, and then select a search location.

   ◆ **Date.** Click the first list arrow, select the date type you want to find, click the second list arrow, select a search criteria, and then specify a value.

   ◆ **Size.** Click the list arrow, select a search criteria, and then specify a value.

5. Select or clear the **Include non-indexed, hidden, and system files (might be slow)** check box.

6. Click **Search**.

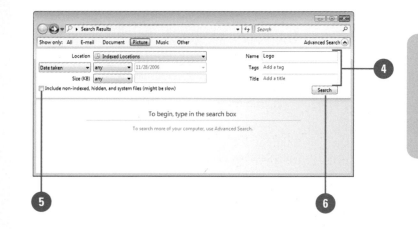

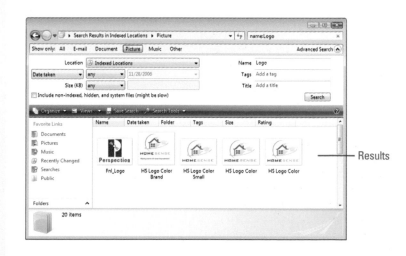

Results

Saving a Search

If you frequently perform the same search, you can save your search results (**New!**) like any file and perform or modify the search again later. When you save a search, the search is saved by default in the Searches folder, which you can open by clicking the Searches folder link in the Navigation pane. Like any link, you can move a saved search from the Searches folder to the Favorite links section in the Navigation pane to make it more accessible. To run a saved search, display the saved search link, and then double-click it.

Save a Search

1. Click the **Start** button, and then click **Search**.

2. Specify the criteria you want, and then perform the search.

3. Click the **Save Search** button on the toolbar.

4. Type a name for the search.

5. Click **Save**.

6. To use a saved search, click the **Searches** link in the Favorite Links pane, and then double-click the saved search.

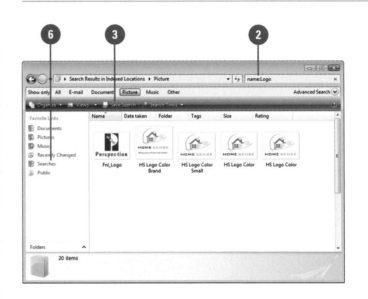

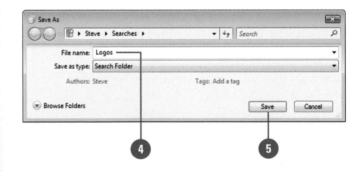

Changing Search Options

Microsoft Certified Application Specialist WINV-4.4.1

When you perform a search for files or folders, Windows Vista uses the search options (**New!**) to help customize the search results. You can specify whether you want to search for file names and content or just for file names and whether to include subfolders or find partial matches. For non-indexed searches, you can set options to include system directories or compressed files (ZIP, CAB...). The search options are available in the Folder Options dialog box under the Search tab.

Change Search Options

1. Click the **Start** button, and then click **Search**.

2. Click the **Organize** button on the toolbar, and then click **Folder and Search Options**.

   TIMESAVER *After a search, click Search Tools on the toolbar, and then click Search Options.*

3. Click the **Search** tab.

4. Select the What to search option you want.

5. Select or clear the check boxes under How to search:

   ◆ **Include subfolders when typing in the Search box.**

   ◆ **Find partial matches.**

   ◆ **Use natural language search.**

   ◆ **Don't use the Index when searching the file system (might be slow).**

6. Select or clear the check boxes under When searching non-indexed locations:

   ◆ **Include system directories.**

   ◆ **Include compressed files (ZIP, CAB, ...)**

7. Click **OK**.

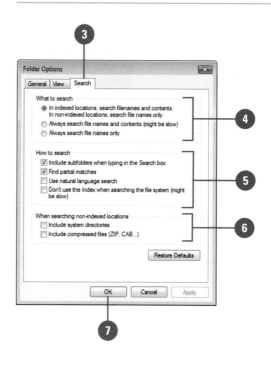

Performing an Instant Search

Microsoft
Certified
Application
Specialist

WINV-4.4.3,
WINV-4.4.4

You can also find files and programs using the Search box at the bottom of the Start menu and at the top of every Explorer window. The Search box (**New!**) filters out items that don't match the text you type. The search includes text in the file name, text in the file, tags (a custom file property), and other file properties. The search locates files and programs stored anywhere in indexed locations, which includes personal folders, e-mail, offline files, and Web sites in the History list for your Web browser.

Find a File or Program Using the Search Box on the Start Menu

1. Click the **Start** button.

2. Click in the **Search** box.

3. Type a word or part of a word.

   As you type, programs and files that match your text appear on the Start menu. You don't have to press Enter.

   TROUBLE? *In the Search box, you must press Enter to start a search for files in non-indexed locations.*

Did You Know?

You can display search properties.
Right-click the heading in an Explorer window that you want to see properties for, and then click More.

Find a File or Folder Using the Search Box From a Folder

1. Click the **Start** button, and then open the Explorer window where you want to start looking, such as **Documents**, **Pictures**, or **Music**.

2. Click in the **Search** box.

3. Type a word or part of a word.

   As you type, programs and files that match your text appear on the Start menu. You don't have to press Enter.

   TROUBLE? *In the Search box, you must press Enter to start a search for files in non-indexed locations.*

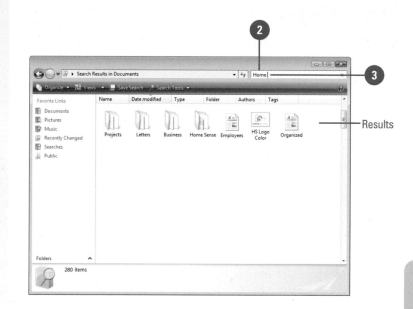

Results

Did You Know?

You can use wildcards to expand a search. Use the * (asterisk) wildcard symbol in a file name when you're unsure of the entire name. For example, type **S*rs** to find all files beginning with "S" and ending with "rs," such as Stars and Sports cars.

Performing an Advanced Search

The Search box (**New!**) at the bottom of the Start menu and at the top of every Explorer window filters out items that don't match the text you type. The search includes text in the file name, text in the file, tags (a custom file property), and other file properties. In the Search box, you can perform advanced searches by specifying properties and using boolean filters. For example, *Name:Agenda* finds only files that have the word *agenda* in the file name. In addition, you can use boolean filters, such as AND, NOT, OR, Quotes, Parentheses, >, or <. For example, *Agenda* AND *Report* find files that contain both words *agenda* and *report*. When you type boolean filters, you need to use all capital letters. You can also combine properties and boolean filters together to create a more specific search.

Find Files and Folders Using the Search Folder

1. Turn off natural language search. (default off).

    ◆ Click the **Start** button, click Control Panel, double-click the **Folder Options** icon in Classic view, click the **Search** tab, clear the **Use natural language search** check box, and then click **OK**.

2. Click in the **Search** box at the bottom of the Start menu or at the top of an Explorer window.

3. Type an advanced search. See the table for some examples.

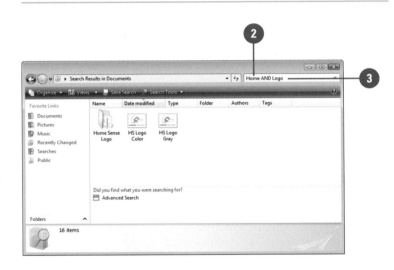

Search Examples

Example	Description
agenda AND report	Finds files that contain both *agenda* and *report*.
agenda NOT report	Finds files that contain agenda, but not *report*.
agenda OR report	Finds files that contain either *agenda* or *report*.
"Agenda Report"	Finds files that contain the exact phrase "Agenda Report" in quotes.
(agenda report)	Finds files that contain both words agenda and report in any order.
date: >10/10/08	Find files that are later than 10/10/08.
size: < 100 MB	Find files that are less than 100 MB.
subject: agenda AND report	Find files with the subject agenda and any files that contain the word report.

Performing Natural Language Searches

If using properties and boolean filters seems a little to much for you to handle, you can find files using natural language search (**New!**), which allows you to perform the same property or boolean search, yet use a form that is easier to use. Instead of *kind: document author: (Steve AND Holly)*, you can type *documents by Steve and Holly*. Before you can use natural language in a Search box, you need to turn it on under the Search tab in Folder Options in the Control Panel.

Turn On Natural Language Search

1. Click the **Start** button, and then **Control Panel**.

2. Double-click the **Folder Options** icon in Classic view.

3. Click the **Search** tab.

4. Select the **Use natural language search** check box.

5. Click **OK**.

Perform a Natural Language Search

1. Click in the **Search** box at the bottom of the Start menu or at the top of an Explorer window.

2. Type a natural language search. Some examples include:

   ◆ documents modified today

   ◆ e-mail from holly sent this week

   ◆ music by Mozart

   ◆ videos of family created December 2007

Adding Properties and Tags to Files

WINV-4.6.1,
WINV-4.6.2

When you create a file, Windows automatically adds properties to the files, such as name, creation date, modified date, and size. These properties are important to Windows, however, they may not be useful when you are searching for a file. You can add or modify common files properties and create or modify custom tag properties (**New!**) to make it faster and easier to locate files in the future. You can add or modify properties for most files. However, there are some exceptions, such as plain text (.txt) or rich text format (.rtf) files. You can add or modify properties using the Details pane in an Explorer window, the Details tab in the Properties dialog box, or in the Save As dialog box. If you want to remove some or all of the property information in a file, you can quickly remove it using the Properties dialog box.

Add or Modify Properties

1. Click the **Start** button, and then click **Documents**.

2. Click the file you want to add or modify properties.

3. In the Details pane, click the tag you want to change, and then type the new tag.

   ◆ If the Details pane is not available, right-click the file, click Properties, click the Details tab. When you're done, click Apply.

4. To add more than one tag, separate each entry with a semicolon.

5. To rate a file using the rating property, click the star that represents the rating you want to give the file.

6. Click **Save**.

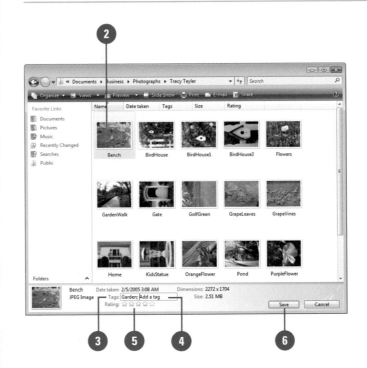

Add or Modify Properties While Saving a File

1. Click the **File** menu in the program you are using, and then click **Save As**.

2. Type tags and other properties in the boxes provides.

3. To add more than one property, separate each entry with a semicolon.

4. Type the name of the file.

5. Click **Save**.

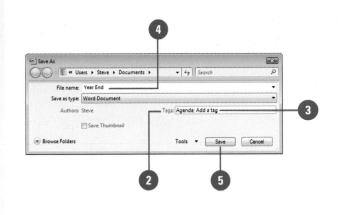

Remove Properties

1. Click the **Start** button, click **Documents**, and then locate the file in which you want to remove properties.

2. Select the file you want to remove properties.

3. Click the **Organize** button on the toolbar, and then click **Remove Properties**.

4. Click the **Create a copy with all possible properties removed** option or click the **Remove the following properties from this file:** option.

5. Select or clear the check boxes for each property.

6. Click **OK**.

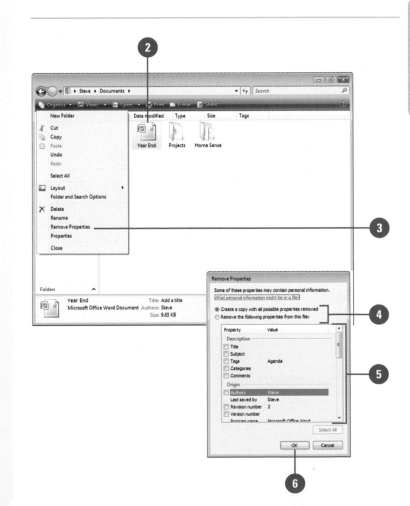

Modifying the Index to Improve Searches

WINV-4.4.1

Windows keeps track of files in indexed locations (**New!**) and stores information about them in the background using an index, like the one found in the back of this book, to make locating files faster and easier. You can use Indexing Options in the Control Panel to view, add, remove, and modify indexed locations, indexed file types, and other advanced index settings. For example, if a file type is not recognized by the index, you can add it, or if you're having problems with the search index, you can rebuild or restore it.

View, Add, or Remove Indexed Locations

1. Click the **Start** button, and then click **Control Panel**.

2. Double-click the **Indexing Options** icon.

   TIMESAVER *After a search, click Search Tools on the toolbar, and then click Modify Index Locations.*

3. Click **Modify**.

4. If you don't see all the locations, click **Show all locations**.

5. If a folder location contains subfolders, you can double-click the folder to expand it.

6. Select or clear the check box next to the folder locations you want to add or remove from the index.

7. Click **OK**.

8. Click **Close**.

Did You Know?

You can index file attributes for a folder. Right-click the folder, click Properties, click the General tab, click Advanced, select the Index this file for fast searching check box, and then click OK twice.

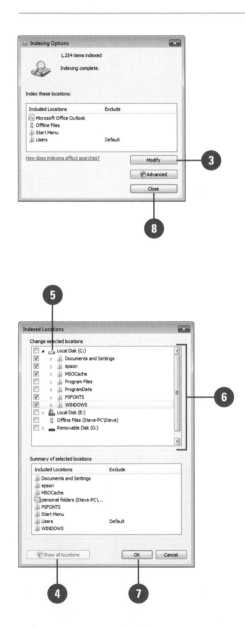

Set Advanced Indexing Options

1. Click the **Start** button, and then click **Control Panel**.

2. Double-click the **Indexing Options** icon.

3. Click **Advanced**.

4. Click the **Index Settings** tab.

5. Select or clear the following check boxes:

   ◆ **Index encrypted files.**

   ◆ **Treat similar words with diacritics as different words.**

6. For index troubleshooting, use either of these buttons:

   ◆ To re-index selected locations, click **Rebuild**.

   ◆ To restore your index to its original settings, click **Restore Defaults**.

7. If you need to change the Index Location, specify a new location or click **Select new**.

8. Click the **File Types** tab.

9. Select or clear the check boxes with the file types you want to include or exclude in the index.

10. For each selected file type, click the option to specify how the file should be indexed.

11. Click **OK**.

12. Click **Close**.

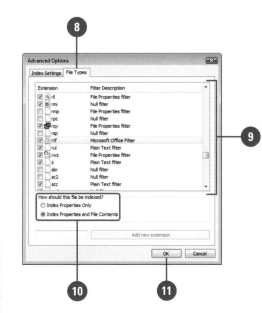

Creating and Renaming Files and Folders

Microsoft Certified Application Specialist

WINV-4.2.1, WINV-4.2.2, WINV-4.6.3

The keys to organizing files and folders effectively within a hierarchy are to store related items together and to name folders informatively. Creating a new folder can help you organize and keep track of files and other folders. In order to create a folder, you select the location where you want the new folder, create the folder, and then lastly, name the folder. You should name each folder meaningfully so that just by reading the folder's name you know its contents. After you name a folder or file, you can rename it at any time.

Create a Folder

1. Open the drive or folder where you want to create a folder.

2. Click the **Organize** button on the toolbar, and then click **New Folder**.

   TIMESAVER *Right-click a blank area of the window, and then click New Folder.*

3. With the New Folder name selected, type a new name.

4. Press Enter.

Did You Know?

File names can be up to 255 characters. You can use spaces and underscores in names, but you can't use the following characters: @ * : < > | ? " \ or /. Remember the best way to keep your files organized is with a consistent naming convention.

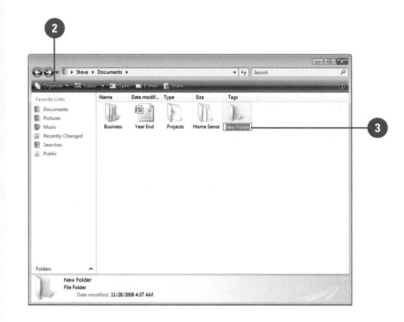

Rename a File or Folder

1. Click the file or folder to select it.

2. Click the **Organize** button on the toolbar, and then click **Rename**.

3. With the name selected, type a new name, or click to position the insertion point, and then edit the name.

4. Press Enter.

> **TIMESAVER** *Right-click the file or folder you want to rename, click Rename, type a name, and then press Enter. You can also select the file, click the file name, type a name, and then press Enter.*

Did You Know?

You can rename a group of files. Select all the files you want to rename, right-click one of the selected files, click Rename from the shortcut menu, type a name, and then press Enter. The group name appears with numbers in consecutive order.

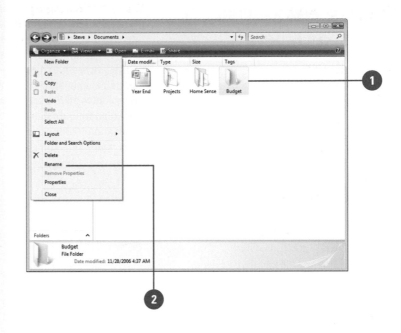

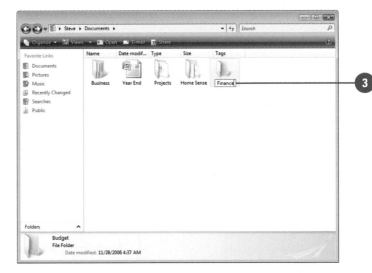

Copying and Moving Files and Folders

Microsoft Certified Application Specialist

WINV-4.6.3

Sometimes you will need to move a file from one folder to another, or copy a file from one folder to another, leaving the file in the first location and placing a copy of it in the second. You can move or copy a file or folder using a variety of methods. If the file or folder and the location where you want to move it are visible in a window or on the desktop, you can simply drag the item from one location to the other. Moving a file or folder on the same disk relocates it whereas dragging it from one disk to another copies it so that it appears in both locations. When the destination folder or drive is not visible, you can use the Cut (to move), Copy, and Paste commands on the Edit menu to move or copy the items.

Copy a File or Folder

① Open the drive or folder containing the file or folder you want to copy.

② Select the files or folders you want to copy.

③ Click the **Organize** button on the toolbar, and then click **Copy**.

④ Display the destination folder where you want to copy the files or folder.

⑤ Click the **Organize** button on the toolbar, and then click **Paste**.

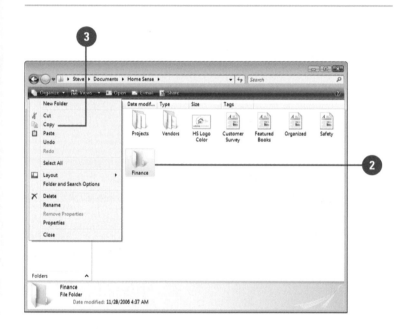

Did You Know?

You can arrange files and folders in an Explorer window by using Auto Arrange or Align to Grid. The Auto Arrange option keeps icons in a window organized so they don't overlap each other, while the Align to Grid option aligns icons in a window according an invisible grid to keep them organized. To turn either of these options on, click the View menu in folder you want to modify, and then click Auto Arrange or Align to Grid. To display the menu bar, click Organize on the toolbar, point to Layout, and then click Menu Bar.

For Your Information

Sending Files and Folders

When you right-click most objects on the desktop or in Computer or Windows Explorer, the Send To command, located on the shortcut menu, lets you send, or move, a file or folder to a new location on your computer. For example, you can send a file or folder to a removable disk to make a quick backup copy of the file or folder, to a mail recipient as an electronic message, or to the desktop to create a shortcut. You can also use the Send To command to move a file or folder from one folder to another. To send a file or folder, right-click the file or folder you want to send, point to Send To on the shortcut menu, and then click the destination you want.

Move a File or Folder

1. Open the drive or folder containing the file or folder you want to move.

2. Select the files or folders you want to move.

3. Click the **Organize** button on the toolbar, and then click **Cut**.

4. Display the destination folder where you want to move the files or folder.

5. Click the **Organize** button on the toolbar, and then click **Paste**.

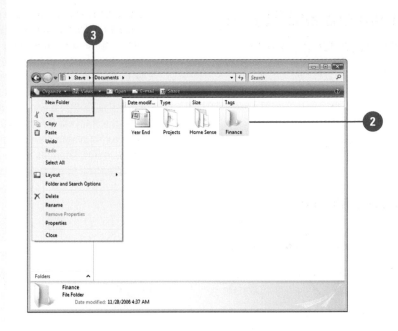

Copy or Move a File or Folder Using Drag and Drop

1. Open the drive or folder containing the file or folder you want to copy or move.

2. Select the files or folders you want to copy or move.

3. Click the **Folders** link in the Navigation pane.

4. Click the arrows to display the destination folder, and then click the destination folder.

5. Right-click the selected files or folders, drag to the destination folder, and then click **Copy Here** or **Move Here**.

   TIMESAVER *To move the selected items, drag them to the destination folder. To copy the items, hold down the Ctrl key while you drag.*

Deleting and Restoring Files and Folders

Microsoft
Certified
Application
Specialist

WINV-4.6.3

When you organize the contents of a folder, disk, or the desktop, you might find files and folders that you no longer need. You can delete these items or remove them from the disk. If you delete a file or folder from the desktop or from the hard disk, it goes into the Recycle Bin. The **Recycle Bin**, located on your desktop, is a temporary storage area for deleted files. The Recycle Bin stores all the items you delete from your hard disk so that if you accidentally delete an item, you can remove it from the Recycle Bin to restore it. Be aware that if you delete a file from a removable disk, it is permanently deleted, not stored in the Recycle Bin. The files in the Recycle Bin do occupy room on your computer, so you need to empty it to free up space.

Delete Files and Folders

1. Select the files and folders you want to delete.

2. Click the **Organize** button on the toolbar, and then click **Delete**.

   TIMESAVER *Press the Delete key to delete selected items.*

3. Click **Yes** to confirm the deletion and place the items in the Recycle Bin.

4. On the desktop, right-click the **Recycle Bin** icon, and then click **Empty Recycle Bin**.

   Your computer permanently removes the items.

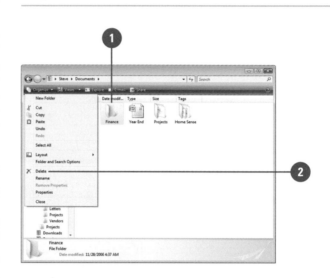

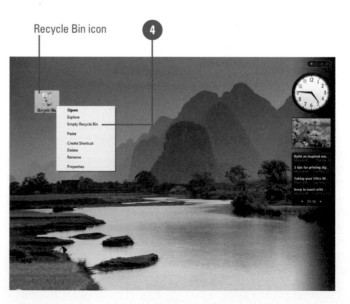

Recycle Bin icon

Restore Files and Folders

1 Double-click the **Recycle Bin** icon on the desktop.

2 Select the item or items you want to restore.

3 Click the **Restore this item** or **Restore all items** button on the toolbar.

For Your Information

Changing Recycle Bin Properties

You can adjust several Recycle Bin settings by using the Properties option on the Recycle Bin shortcut menu. For example, if you want to delete files immediately rather than place them in the Recycle Bin, right-click the Recycle Bin, click Properties, and then select the Do Not Move Files To The Recycle Bin check box. Also, if you find that the Recycle Bin is full and cannot accept any more files, you can increase the amount of disk space allotted to the Recycle Bin by moving the Maximum size of Recycle Bin slider to the right. The percentage shown represents how much space the contents of the Recycle Bin takes on the drive.

Creating a Shortcut to a File or Folder

Microsoft Certified Application Specialist

WINV-4.2.3

Create a Shortcut to a File or Folder

1. Open the drive or folder containing the file or folder in which you want to create a shortcut.

2. Right-click the file or folder, and then click **Create Shortcut**.

3. To change the shortcut's name, right-click the shortcut, click **Rename** from the shortcut menu, type a new name, and then press Enter.

4. Drag the shortcut to the desired location.

Did You Know?

You can improve performance by limiting desktop items. To improve performance on your computer and find files more easily, it's better to create desktop shortcuts rather than store files in the Documents folder.

It could take you a while to access a file or folder buried several levels down in a file hierarchy. To save some time, you can create shortcuts to the items you use frequently. A **shortcut** is a link that you can place in any location to gain instant access to a particular file, folder, or program on your hard disk or on a network just by double-clicking. The actual file, folder, or program remains stored in its original location, and you place an icon representing the shortcut in a convenient location, such as in a folder or on the desktop.

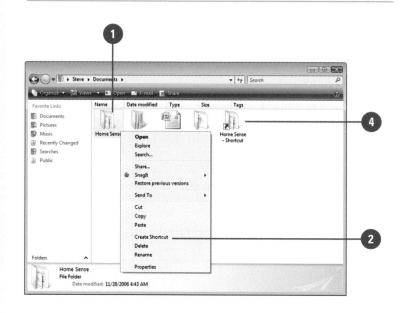

For Your Information

Placing Shortcuts on the Start Menu and Taskbar

You can place shortcuts to frequently used files, folders, and programs on the Start menu or toolbar on the taskbar. To do this, simply drag the shortcut file, folder, or program to the Start button, wait until the Start menu opens, drag to the All Programs submenu, wait until the submenu opens, and then drag the shortcut to the appropriate place on the menu. You can also drag a shortcut to a toolbar on the taskbar using the same method. When you release the mouse, the item appears on the menu or toolbar.

Hiding Files and Folders

Microsoft
Certified
Application
Specialist

WINV-4.1.3

If you want to hide files and folder for added privacy purposes, you can do it by setting two separate options: one to set the option to hide specific files and folders, and the other to set a general folder option to show or hide files and folders. If you set the option to hide specific files and folders and the Show hidden files and folders option is set, the hidden files and folder appear transparent. If the general option is set to Do not show hidden files and folder, the hidden files and folder are actually hidden. The only way to view them again is to set the general option to Show hidden files and folders again. Anyone can show hidden files and folders, so it shouldn't be used for security purposes.

Show or Hide Hidden Files and Folders

1. Right-click the file or folder you want to hide or unhide, and then click **Properties**.

2. Select or clear the **Hidden** check box.

3. Click **OK**.

   The files or folders appear transparent or hidden.

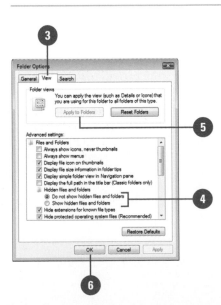

Show or Hide Hidden Files and Folders

1. Click the **Start** button, and then click **Control Panel**.

2. Double-click the **Folder Options** icon.

3. Click the **View** tab.

4. Click the **Do not show hidden files and folders** or **Show hidden files and folders** option.

5. To set the current view to all folders, click **Apply to Folders**.

6. Click **OK**.

Changing Folder Options

Microsoft Certified Application Specialist WINV-4.1.1, WINV-4.1.2, WINV-4.1.3

When you work with files and folders, Windows displays folder contents in a standard way, known as the **default**. The default folder view settings are as follows: Tiles view displays files and folders as icons; common task links appear in the left pane; folders open in the same window; and items open when you double-click them. Depending on previous installation or users, your folder view settings might differ. Instead of changing the folder view to your preferred view—Icons, List, or Details—each time you open a folder, you can change the view permanently to the one you prefer. In addition to the defaults, you can change options such as folder settings to show or hide file extensions for known file types, show or hide hidden files and folders, show or hide protected operating system files, and show pop-up descriptions of folders and desktop items.

Change the Way All Folders Work

1. Click the Start button, and then click **Control Panel**.

2. Double-click the **Folder Options** icon.

3. Click the **General** tab.

4. Select a Tasks option to display frequently used tasks or the contents of the folder.

5. Select a Browse folders option to display each folder in the same window or its own window.

6. Select a Click items as follows option to single-click or double-click items.

7. Click **OK**.

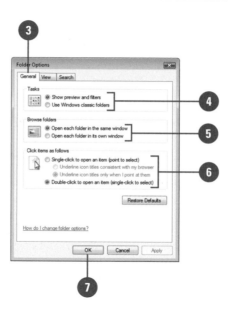

Did You Know?

You can restore all folder options to default Windows settings. On the General tab in the Folder Options dialog box, click Restore Defaults.

Change the Folder View

1 Click the Start button, and then click **Control Panel**.

2 Double-click the **Folder Options** icon.

3 Click the **View** tab.

4 To set the current view to all folders, click **Apply to Folders**.

5 Select the check boxes for the options you want, and clear the check boxes for the ones you don't. Some common options include:

- ◆ **Always show menus (New!)**.

- ◆ **Hidden files and folders**. Click an option to show or hide them.

- ◆ **Hide extensions for known file types**.

- ◆ **Hide protected operating system files (Recommended) (New!)**.

- ◆ **Show encrypted or compressed NTFS files in color (New!)**.

- ◆ **Show pop-up description for folder and desktop items**.

6 Click **OK**.

Did You Know?

You can reset folder views to original Windows settings. On the View tab in the Folder Options dialog box, click Reset Folders.

For Your Information

Understanding File Extensions

The program Windows uses to open a document depends on a three-letter extension to the document's file name, called a **file extension**. You might have never seen a document's file extension because your system might be set up to hide it. The file extension for simple text files is ".txt" (pronounced "dot t-x-t"), and many graphic files have the extension ".bmp". This means that the full name for a text file named Memo is Memo.txt. If you double-click a document whose file name ends with the three-letter extension ".txt," Windows automatically opens the document with Notepad, a text-only editor. If you want to display or change file extension settings, click the Start button, click Control Panel, and then double-click the Folder Options icon. If you want to display file extensions in dialog boxes and windows, click the View tab, and then clear the Hide extensions for known file types check box in the Advanced settings list box. If you want to change the program Windows automatically starts with a given file extension, click the Start button, point to All Programs, click Default Programs, click Associate a file type or protocol with a program, select the file type, and then click Change Program to see the list of the file extensions Windows recognizes and the programs associated with each of them, and make changes as appropriate.

Changing File and Folder List Views

Microsoft
Certified
Application
Specialist
WINV-4.5.2

You can display files and folders in a variety of different ways, depending on what you want to see and do. When you view files and folders in Details view, a default list of file and folder information appears, which consists of Name, Size, Type, and Date Modified. If the default list of file and folder details doesn't provide you with the information you need, you can add and remove any file and folder information from the Details view. If you need to change the way Windows sorts your files and folders, you can use the column indicator buttons in the right pane of Details view. Clicking one of the column indicator buttons, such as Name, Size, Type, or Date Modified, in Details view sorts the files and folders by the type of information listed in the column.

Change File Details to List

1. Open the folder you want to change.

2. Right-click a column title, and then click **More**, or click the **View** menu, and then click **Choose Details**.

   TIMESAVER *Right-click a column title in Details view, and then click the detail you want to show or hide.*

3. Select the check boxes with the details you want to include and clear the ones you don't.

4. Click the **Move Up** or **Move Down** buttons to change the order of the selected items.

5. Click the **Show** or **Hide** button to show or hide the selected items.

6. Specify the width in pixels of the column for the selected items.

7. Click **OK**.

Did You Know?

An ellipsis indicates information is hidden. To show the information, drag the edge of the column indicator button to resize the column.

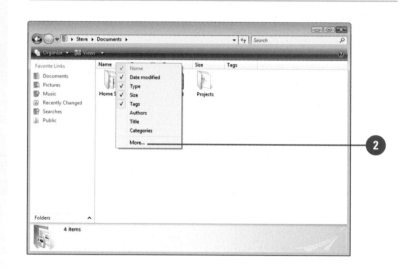

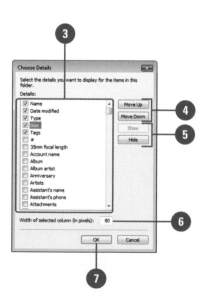

90

Customizing Personal Folders

In your personal folders, you can create your own folders and customize view options based on the contents. In the toolbar of the Pictures and Music folders, Windows provides buttons with file management activities specifically related to the contents of the folder, such as Slide Show in the Pictures folder, or Play All in the Music folders. When you create a new folder, you can customize it for pictures, music, and videos by applying a folder template, which is a collection of folder task links and viewing options. When you apply a template to a folder, you apply specific features to the folder, such as specialized task links and viewing options for working with pictures, music, and videos.

Change the Folder Look

1. Open the folder you want to change.

2. Click the **Organize** button on the toolbar, and the click **Properties**.

3. Click the **Customize** tab.

4. Click the list arrow, and then select the type of folder you want: **All Items**, **Documents**, **Pictures and Videos**, **Music Details**, or **Music icons**.

5. Select the **Also apply this template to all subfolders** check box to apply the option.

6. To select a picture for display on the this folder icon, click **Choose File.**

7. To restore the default picture for the this folder, click **Restore Default**.

8. Click **OK**.

See Also

See "Customizing the Taskbar" on page 118 for information on modifying the taskbar.

Sharing Folders or Files with Others

Microsoft
Certified
Application
Specialist

WINV-4.3.1,
WINV-4.3.2

Windows Vista maintains a set of personal folders and options for everyone on your computer to make sure the contents of each user's personal folders remain private. The contents of your personal folders are private, unless you decide to share the contents with others who use your computer. If you want the other users on your computer to have access to files, you can place those files in a shared folder called the Public folder (**New!**) that each user can access. The Public folder contains subfolders to help you organize the files you are sharing, and include Documents, Downloads, Music, Pictures and Videos. If you're connected to a network, the files in the public folder are available to network users. You can also share files from any folder on your computer that you want to designate as a shared folder. When you specify a shared folder, you can also set access permission levels for a person or group.

Share a File or Folders from the Public Folder

1. Open the drive or folder containing the files or folders you want to share.

2. Select the files or folders you want to share.

3. Click the **Folders** link to display the Folders list.

4. Click the arrow next to the Public folder to display the Public subfolders.

5. Drag the selected items onto the Public folder or subfolder where you want to share files.

See Also

See "Setting Network Sharing Options" on page 374 for information on controlling access to a public folder over a network.

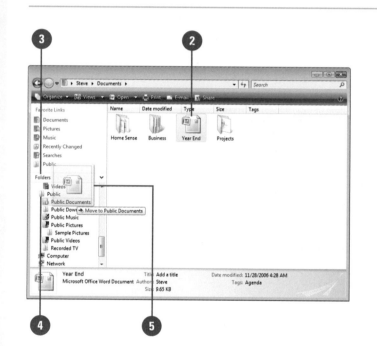

Share Any Folder on Your Computer

1. Open the drive or folder containing the files or folders you want to share.

2. Select the folders you want to share.

3. Click the **Share** button on the toolbar.

4. Do any of the following:

   ◆ Type the name of the person with whom you want to share files, and then click **Add**.

   ◆ Click the arrow to the right of the text box, click the person's name, and then click **Add**.

   ◆ Click the arrow to the right of the text box, and then click **Create a new user** to create a new user account.

5. Click the arrow next to the permission level for the person or group, and then select a sharing permission:

   ◆ **Reader.** Allows viewing only.

   ◆ **Contributor.** Allows viewing and adding files, and changing or deleting files they add.

   ◆ **Co-owner.** Allows viewing, adding, changing, and deleting all files.

   ◆ **Remove.** Deletes the current permission setting.

6. Click **Share**, and the wait while Windows sets up sharing.

7. If you want, click the e-mail or copy link to notify people you have shared this folder and files.

8. Otherwise, click **Done**.

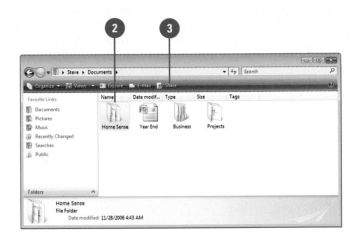

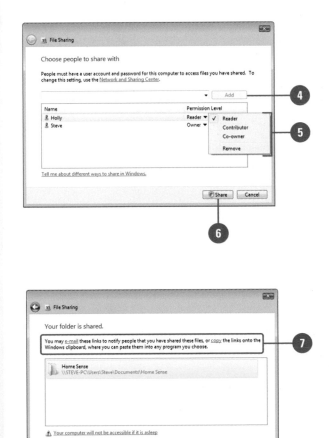

Compressing Files and Folders

You can compress files in special folders that use compressing software to decrease the size of the files they contain. Compressed folders are useful for reducing the file size of one or more large files, thus freeing disk space and reducing the time it takes to transfer files to another computer over the Internet or network. A compressed folder is denoted by a zippered folder icon. You can compress one or more files in a compressed folder by simply dragging them onto the compressed folder icon. When a file is compressed, a copy is used in the compression, and the original remains intact. You can uncompress, or extract, a file from the compressed folder and open it as you normally would, or you can open a file directly from the compressed folder by double-clicking the Compressed File icon. When you open a file directly, Windows extracts the file when it opens and compresses it again when it closes.

Compress Files and Folders

1. Select the files and folders you want to copy to a compressed folder.

2. Right-click one of the selected items, point to **Send To**, and then click **Compressed (Zipped) Folder**.

3. If you want, rename the compressed folder.

4. To copy additional files or folders to the compressed folder, drag the files onto the compressed folder.

Did You Know?

You can also compress file attributes in a folder. Right-click the folder, click Properties, click the General tab, click Advanced, select the Compress contents to save disk space check box, and then click OK twice.

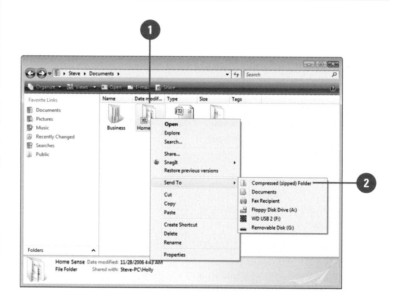

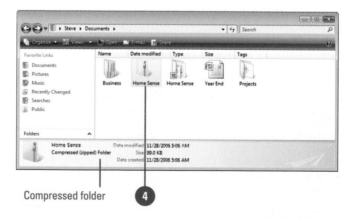

Compressed folder

View Compressed Files

① Double-click the compressed folder to open it.

② Double-click an item in the folder to open it using its associated program.

Decompress Files

① Double-click the compressed folder to open it.

② Select the files you want to decompress.

③ Do one of the following:

   ◆ **Single file or folder.** Double-click the compressed folder to open it, and then drag the file or folder from the compressed folder to a new location.

   ◆ **All files.** Right-click the compressed folder, and then click **Extract All**, and then step through the Extraction Wizard.

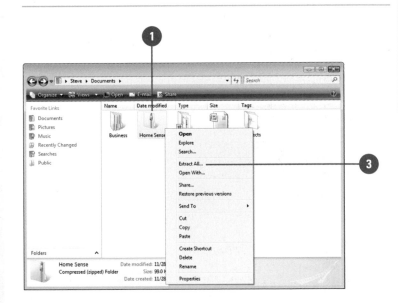

Managing Files Using a CD or DVD

WINV-4.6.4

The low cost and large storage size of discs, either CD or DVD (**New!**), makes creating and using CDs or DVDs an effective way to back up information or transfer large amounts of information to another computer without a network. Before you can create a CD or DVD, you must have a blank writeable CD or DVD and a recorder (also known as a writer or burner) installed on your computer. You can copy, or write, files and folders to either a writeable disc (CD-R or DVD-R) or a rewriteable disc (CD-RW or DVD-RW). With writeable discs, you can read and write files and folders many times, but you can't erase them. With rewriteable discs, you can read, write, and erase files and folders many times, just like a hard disk. When you burn a disc, Windows needs disk space on your hard disk equal to the capacity of the disc. For a typical CD, this is between 650 and 740 megabytes (MB) and for a DVD, this is about 4.7 gigabytes (GB). Do not copy more files and folders to the CD or DVD than it will hold; anything beyond the limit will not copy. With Windows Vista, you can burn a disc using one of two formats: Live File System or Mastered. The **Live File System (New!)** format allows you to copy files to a disc at any time, like a USB drive, while the **Mastered** format needs to copy them all at once. If you need a disc for Windows XP or later and want the convenience of copying files at any time, the Live File System is the best choice. When you need a compatible disc for older computers, the Mastered format is the better choice.

Burn a Disc Using the Mastered Format

1. Insert a writeable CD or DVD into your CD or DVD recorder.

2. Click **Burn files to disc**.

3. Type a name for the disc.

4. Click **Show/Hide formatting options**.

5. Click the **Mastered** option.

6. Click **Next** to continue.

7. Open the folder that contains the files you want to burn, and then drag the files onto the empty disc folder.

8. Click **Burn to disc** on the toolbar.

   The selected files are copied to the disc. The disc recorder tray opens when the disc is complete.

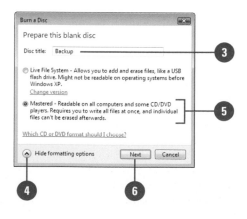

Burn a Disc Using the Live System Format

1. Insert a writeable CD or DVD into your CD or DVD recorder.

2. Click **Burn files to disc**.

3. Type a name for the disc.

4. Click **Show/Hide formatting options**.

5. Click the **Live File System** option, click **Change version**, and then select the version you want.

6. Click **Next** to continue.

   Windows names, formats, and prepares the disc for use.

7. Upon completion, open the folder with the files you want to burn.

8. Drag the files into the disc folder.

   As you drag files into the disc folder, they are copied automatically to the disc.

9. To close the session and prepare the disc for use, press the Eject button on your disc drive or right-click the writeable drive, and then click **Close session**.

   After you close a session, you can still add files to the disc. However, you need to close the session.

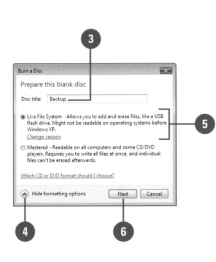

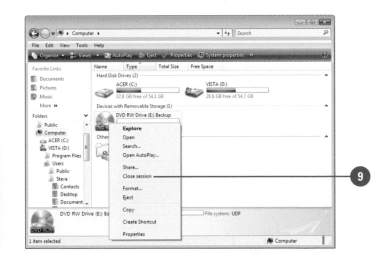

Did You Know?

You can erase some or all of the files on a disc. Insert the writeable disc with the Live File System format, click the Start button, click Computer, click the writeable drive, and then click Erase this disc on the toolbar to erase all the files. Double-click the writeable drive, select the files you want to delete, and then press Delete.

Live File System Versions

Version	Compatible with
1.02	Windows 98 and many Apple Computers; also works if you need to format DVD-RAM or MO (Magneto-optical) discs
1.5	Windows 2000, Windows XP, and Windows Server 2003
2.01	Windows XP and Windows Server 2003
2.5	The latest version of Windows; Windows Vista

Customizing Windows Using the Control Panel

Introduction

Windows Vista gives you the ability to customize your work environment (your computer's desktop and other settings) to suit your personal needs and preferences. You can adjust most Windows features through the Control Panel, a central location for changing Windows settings. From the **Control Panel** you access the individual programs for changing the **properties**, or characteristics, of a specific element of your computer, such as the desktop, the taskbar, or the Start menu. Each icon in the Control Panel represents an aspect of Windows that you can change to fit your own working habits and personal needs. For example, you can use the Display icon to change the background picture or color of the desktop, or the Taskbar and Start Menu icon to customize the taskbar and Start menu. Some Control Panel settings are vital to how you work (such as the Date and Time, or the Language settings) and others are purely aesthetic (such as the background picture, or which screen saver you use).

The Control Panel also includes icons to setup user accounts and maintain security (see Chapter 11), and setup and manage local-area, wide-area, and wireless networks (see Chapter 12). You can access printers and faxes (see Chapter 13), add and remove programs and automatically update Windows (see Chapter 14). You can also work with hardware, such as a scanner, digital camera, modem, audio and speakers, mouse, and keyboard (see Chapter 15).

What You'll Do

View the Control Panel

Change the Desktop Background

Customize the Desktop and Windows Sidebar

Use a Screen Saver

Change the Display

Use Multiple Monitors

Change the Desktop Appearance

Set the Date and Time

Change Regional and Language Options

Work with Fonts

Display and Arrange Toolbars

Customize the Taskbar and Start Menu

Change the Way a CD or DVD Starts

Use the Ease of Access Tools

Use the Ease of Access Center

Listen to the Computer

Recognize Your Speech

Viewing the Control Panel

The Control Panel is a collection of utility programs that determine how Windows Vista looks and works on your computer. The Control Panel displays utilities in two different views: Control Panel Home and Classic View. Control Panel Home displays utilities in functional categories based on tasks with some direct links, while Classic view displays an icon for each utility program as in previous versions of Windows. You can change views by using the Control Panel task pane.

View the Control Panel in Classic View

1. Click the **Start** button, and then click **Control Panel**.

2. In the Navigation pane, click **Classic View**.

> ### See Also
>
> See "Customizing the Start Menu" on page 120 for information on changing the Start menu to directly open Control Panel programs.

View the Control Panel Home

1. Click the **Start** button, and then click **Control Panel.**

2. In the Navigation pane, click **Control Panel Home**.

3. Click a Control Panel icon or task link.

4. Click the **Back** button on the toolbar to return to Control Panel Home.

Changing the Desktop Background

WINV-6.3.1

The desktop **background**, or wallpaper, is a picture that serves as your desktop's backdrop, the basic surface on which icons and windows appear. You can select a background picture and change how it looks using the Desktop Background dialog box. Once you select a background picture, you can display it on the screen three different ways: **Tile** displays the picture consecutively across the screen; **Center** displays the picture in the center of the screen; and **Stretch** enlarges the picture and displays it in the center of the screen. Instead of selecting a background picture, which can sometimes make icons on the desktop difficult to see, you can also change the background to a color.

Select a Desktop Background

1. Right-click a blank area on the desktop, and then click **Personalize**.

2. Click **Desktop Background**.

3. Click the **Picture Location** list arrow and select a location, or click **Browse**, select a picture in the location you want, and then click **Open**. The default picture locations include:

   ◆ **Windows Wallpapers**.

   ◆ **Pictures**.

   ◆ **Sample Pictures**.

   ◆ **Public Pictures**.

   ◆ **Solid Colors**.

4. Select the picture you want to use.

5. Select the position option you want.

6. Click **OK**.

7. Click the **Close** button.

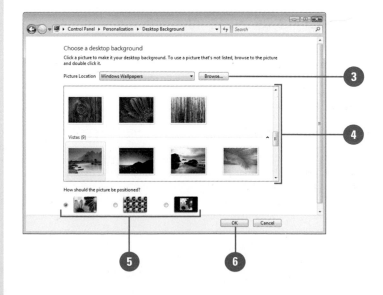

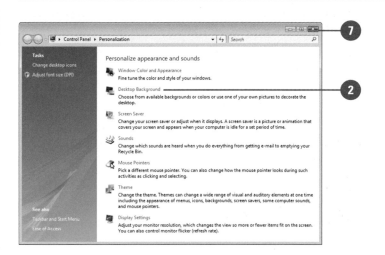

Customizing the Desktop

The icons on the desktop provide easy access to programs, folders, and system related shortcuts. If your desktop is getting cluttered, you can quickly show or hide the desktop icons. In addition, you can customize the desktop to show or hide the familiar icons Computer, User's Files, Network, Recycle Bin, or Control Panel. You can also quickly sort, resize, and rearrange desktop icons by right-clicking the desktop, and then using commands on the View and Sort By submenus.

Display or Hide Desktop Icons

1 Right-click a blank area on the desktop, and then click **Personalize**.

> **TIMESAVER** *To show or hide all desktop icons, right-click the desktop, point to View, and then click Show Desktop Icons.*

2 In the left pane, click **Change desktop icons**.

3 Select or clear the check boxes to show or hide desktop icons.

4 To change the appearance of an icon, select the icon, click **Change Icon**, select an icon, and then click **OK**.

5 Click **OK**.

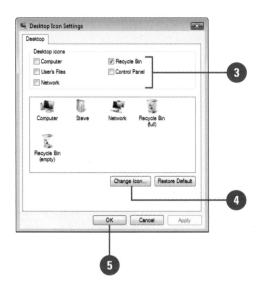

Did You Know?

You can resize desktop icons. Right-click the desktop, point to View, and then click Large Icons, Medium Icons, or Classic Icons. Classic icons are the smallest size.

You can arrange desktop icons. The Auto Arrange option keeps icons organized so they don't overlap each other, while the Align to Grid option aligns icons in a window according an invisible grid to keep them organized. Right-click the desktop, point to View, and then click Auto Arrange or Align to Grid.

6 Click the **Close** button.

Customizing the Windows Sidebar

Microsoft Certified Application Specialist WINV-6.4.2

Windows Sidebar (**New!**) is a pane on the side of the Windows Vista desktop that gives you quick access to mini-applications called gadgets that can connect to Web services, such as news headlines, or integrate with many of your applications, such as viewing your calendar. You can customize Windows Sidebar to suit the way you work—whether you want it always on top or resting below maximized windows. If you are having problems with a gadget, you can stop it from running. If the gadget was installed with Windows Vista, you can restore it.

Change Windows Sidebar Properties

① Right-click a blank area of the Sidebar, and then click **Properties**.

② Select or clear the **Start Sidebar when Windows starts** check box.

③ Select or clear the **Sidebar is always on top of other windows** check box.

④ Click the **Right** or **Left** option to display select a desktop location.

⑤ If you have more than one monitor, click the list arrow, and then select a monitor.

⑥ To stop a gadget from running, click **View list of running gadgets**, select the gadget you want to stop, click **Remove**, and then click **Close**.

⑦ To restore default Windows gadgets, click **Restore gadgets installed with Windows**.

⑧ Click **OK**.

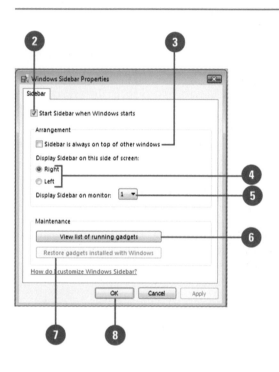

Using a Screen Saver

Microsoft Certified Application Specialist

WINV-1.4.1, WINV-6.3.4

In the past, you needed a screen saver, a continually moving display, to protect your monitor from burn in, which occurs when the same display remains on the screen for extended periods of time and becomes part of the screen. Those days are gone with the emergence of new display technology. Screen savers are more for entertainment than anything else. When you leave your computer idle for a specified wait time, a screen saver displays a continuous scene, such as an aquarium, until you move your mouse to stop it.

Select a Screen Saver

1. Right-click a blank area on the desktop, and then click **Personalize**.

2. Click **Screen Saver**.

3. Click the list arrow, and then click a screen saver.

4. Click **Settings**.

5. Select the options you want for the screen saver, and then click **OK**.

6. Click **Preview** to see the screen saver in full-screen view, and then move your mouse to end the preview.

7. Specify the time to wait until your computer starts the screen saver.

8. Select or clear the **On resume, display logon screen** check box.

9. Click **OK**.

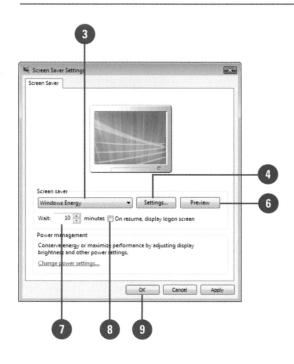

Did You Know?

You can turn off a screen saver. On the Screen Saver tab, click (None) from the Screen Saver list arrow.

Changing the Display

Microsoft Certified Application Specialist WINV-3.4.1, WINV-3.4.2, WINV-3.4.3

If you find yourself frequently scrolling within windows as you work or squinting to read small text, you might want to change the size of the desktop on your monitor. A monitor displays pictures by dividing the display screen into thousands or millions of dots, or pixels, arranged in rows and columns. The pixels are so close together that they appear connected. The **screen resolution** refers to the number of pixels on the entire screen, which determines the amount of information your monitor displays. A low screen resolution setting, such as 640 by 480 pixels (width by height), displays less information on the screen, but the items on the screen appear relatively large, while a high setting, such as 1024 by 768 pixels, displays more information on the screen, but the items on the screen appear smaller. You can also change the color quality. The higher the color quality, the more colors the computer displays, which requires greater system memory. The most common color quality settings are as follows: 16-bit, which displays 768 colors, and 24-bit and 32-bit, both of which display 16.7 million colors.

Change the Display Size

1. Right-click a blank area on the desktop, and then click **Personalize**.

2. Click **Display Settings**.

3. Drag the slider to specify a screen size.

4. Click the **Colors** list arrow, and then click a color quality.

5. Click **OK**.

6. If a message alert appears, click **Yes** or **No** to accept or decline the new settings.

   Windows reverts to original settings after 15 seconds.

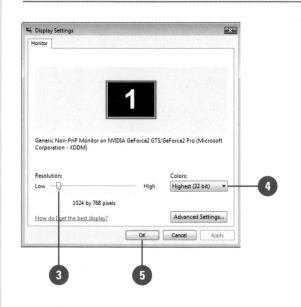

Did You Know?

You can eliminate flicker on your monitor. On the Monitor tab, click Advanced, click the Monitor tab, and then increase the screen refresh rate. 60 Hertz is the default setting.

Using Multiple Monitors

You can increase the size of your workspace on the desktop and your productivity by adding another monitor to your computer. For example, you can work on a document in WordPad on one monitor and search for Web content in your Web browser on the other monitor. One monitor is the primary monitor, which displays the dialog boxes that appear when you start your computer and most programs; the other monitor is the secondary monitor, which displays windows, icons, and programs you drag to it from the primary monitor. Before you can use more than one monitor, you need to install another **display adapter**, a hardware device that allows a computer to communicate with its monitor, on your computer that supports multiple monitors. After you install the display adapter according to the manufacturer's instructions

and restart the computer, Windows automatically detects the new device and applied the video settings best suited to the display. In the Control Panel, double-click the Display icon in Classic View, click the Settings tab, click the monitor icon that represents the secondary monitor that you want to use, select the Extend the desktop onto this monitor check box, and then click Apply to activate the secondary monitor. To arrange multiple monitors, click the monitor icons and drag them in the preview window to the positions you want. You can set different screen resolutions and color settings for each monitor. See *"Adding a Secondary Monitor"* on page 462 for more information on using multiple monitors.

Selected monitor

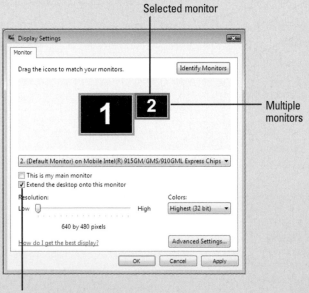

Multiple monitors

Select to extend desktop

Changing Text Size on the Screen

WINV3.4.4

If text and other items, such as icons, on the screen are not large enough for you to comfortably view, you can customize the screen to display items larger. Windows Vista allows you to increase the Dots Per Inch (DPI) scale (**New!**), which is the number of dots that a device can display or print per linear inch. The greater the number, of dots per inch, the better the resolution. DPI is a standard measurement used to specify screen and printer resolution. 96 DPI is the default screen option and 120 DPI is the other available standard option. However, you can set a custom DPI setting, which is not recommended unless you are an experienced user. After you change the DPI, you need to restart Windows to see the change.

Change the DPI Scaling Options

1. Right-click a blank area on the desktop, and then click **Personalize**.

2. In the left pane, click **Adjust font size (DPI)**.

3. Click the **Default scale (96 DPI) - fit more information** or **Larger scale (120 DPI) - make text more readable** option.

4. To create a custom DPI scale, click **Custom DPI**, enter the percentage you want, and then click **OK**.

5. Click **OK**.

   To see the changes, close all of your programs, and restart Windows.

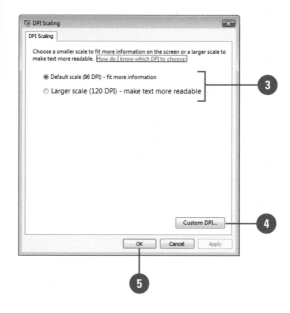

Changing the Desktop Appearance

You can change the entire appearance of the desktop by using desktop themes. A desktop **theme** changes the desktop background, screen saver, mouse pointers, sounds, icons, and fonts based on a set theme, such as baseball, science, sports, travel, or underwater. You can even change your desktop to the classic Windows look. You can use one of the predefined desktop themes or create your own. If a theme isn't exactly what you want, you can change the appearance of colors, fonts, and sizes used for major window elements such as title bars, icons, menus, borders, and the desktop itself.

Select a Desktop Theme

1. Right-click a blank area on the desktop, and then click **Personalize**.

2. Click **Theme**.

3. Click the **Theme** list arrow, and then click a theme.

   ◆ **Use a theme file.** In the Theme list, click **Browse**, select the theme file you want, and then click **Open**.

4. Click **OK**.

Did You Know?

You can save a theme. In the Theme Settings dialog box, click Save As, name the theme, specify a location, and then click Save.

3

Theme Settings

Themes

A theme is a background plus a set of sounds, icons, and other elements to help you personalize your computer with one click.

Theme:

Modified Theme ▾   Save As...   Delete

Sample:

Active Window
Window Text

OK   Cancel   Apply

4

Customize the Desktop Appearance

1 Right-click a blank area on the desktop, and then click **Personalize**.

2 Click **Window Color and Appearance**.

3 Click the color scheme you want.

4 Click **Advanced** if you want to change the color, size, or font for individual items for a Windows Classic color scheme.

5 To set appearance effects, click **Effects**, and then set one or more of the following effects:

◆ Smooth edges of screen fonts; use ClearType.

◆ Show shadows under menus.

◆ Show window contents while dragging.

6 Click **OK**.

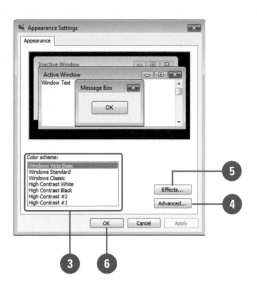

Frequently Asked Questions

What's ClearType

ClearType is a font technology that improves the display on a computer monitor. ClearType makes on-screen text more clear, smooth, and detailed, which can reduce eye strain. ClearType is turned on by default in Windows. This is useful and most effective when you use LCD devices, including flat-panel monitors, mobile computers, and smaller hand-held devices. ClearType is optimized for use with some fonts, including Constantia, Cambria, Corbel, Candara, Calibri, and Consolas. To set the ClearType setting, you open the Personalize window in the Control Panel, open the Appearance Settings dialog box, and then open the Effects dialog box.

Setting the Date and Time

The date and time you set in the Control Panel appear in the lower-right corner of the taskbar. When you click or hover over the taskbar clock, the data appears. Programs use the date and time to establish when files and folders are created and modified. To change the date and time, you modify settings in the Date and Time dialog box. When you modify the time, it's important to also verify or update the time zone setting in the Time Zone Settings dialog box, which is used to accurately display creation and modification dates in a different time zone. With an Internet connection, you can set options on the Internet tab to make sure the time is accurate. If you need to know the time in other time zones, you can display additional clocks, which you can display by clicking or hovering over the taskbar clock.

Change the Date or Time

1 Click the time on the taskbar in the notification area, and then click **Change date and time settings**.

2 Click the **Date and Time** tab.

3 If needed, click **Change time zone**, click the list arrow, select a time zone, and then select or clear the **Automatically adjust clock for Daylight Saving Changes** check box, and then click **OK**.

4 Click **Change date and time**.

5 Click the date arrows to select the month and year.

6 Click a day, and then specify a time.

7 Click **OK**.

8 Click **OK**.

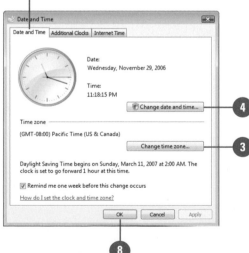

Keep the Time Accurate

1 Click the time on the taskbar in the notification area, and then click **Change date and time settings**.

2 Click the **Internet Time** tab.

3 Click **Change settings**.

4 Select the **Synchronize with an Internet time server** check box.

5 Click the **Server** list arrow, and then click a time server.

6 Click **Update now**, and then wait for the time to update.

7 Click **OK**.

8 Click **OK**.

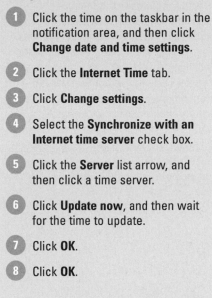

Add Clocks

1 Click the time on the taskbar in the notification area, and then click **Change date and time settings**.

2 Click the **Additional Clocks** tab.

3 Select the **Show this clock** check box.

4 Click the **Select time zone** list arrow, and then select a time zone.

5 Type a name.

6 If you want another clock, perform steps 3 through 5 for Clock 2.

7 Click **OK**.

Changing Language Options

You can also install multiple input languages on your computer and easily switch between them. An **input language** is the language in which you enter and display text. When you install additional languages on your computer, the language for the operating system doesn't change, only the characters you type on the screen. Each language uses its own keyboard layout, which rearranges the letters that appear when you press keys. When you install Text services or another language, the Language Bar toolbar appears on your desktop and in the Toolbars menu. Text services are text-related add-on programs for a second keyboard layout, handwriting recognition, speech recognition, and an Input Method Editor (IME), which is a system that lets you input Asian language characters with a standard 101-keyboard. You can switch between different language keyboard layouts using the Language bar or keyboard shortcuts.

Change Text Services and Input Languages

1. Click the **Start** button, click **Control Panel**, and then double-click the **Regional and Language Options** icon in Classic view.

2. Click the **Keyboards and Languages** tab, and then click **Change keyboard**.

3. Click the **Language** list arrow, and then click a language to use when you start your computer.

4. Click **Add** to add an input language.

5. Select an input language, and then click **Remove** to delete it, or click Properties to modify it.

6. Click the **Language Bar** tab to change the look and behavior of the Language bar.

7. Click the **Advanced Key Settings** tab to define keyboard shortcuts to switch between input language.

8. Click **OK**.

9. Click **OK**.

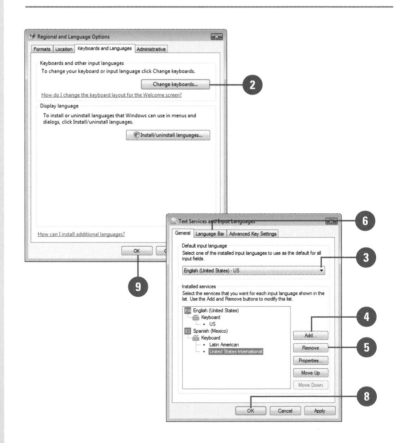

Change the Language Bar Settings

1. Click the **Start** button, click **Control Panel**, and then double-click the **Regional and Language Options** icon in Classic view.

2. Click the **Keyboards and Languages** tab.

3. Click **Change Keyboards**.

4. Click the **Language Bar** tab.

5. Select the options you want.

6. Click **OK**, and then click **OK** again.

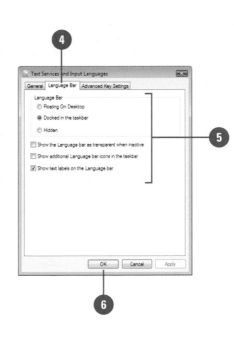

Use the Language Bar

◆ To switch languages, click the **Language bar**, and then click a language.

◆ To change Language bar settings, right-click the **Language bar**, and then click an option, such as transparency, vertical (orientation), and minimize.

◆ To change Text Services and Input Languages, right-click the **Language bar**, and then click **Settings**.

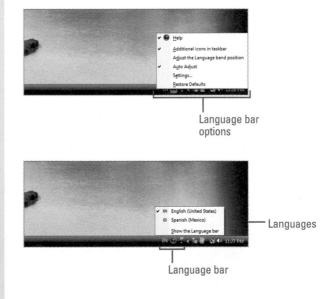

Language bar options

Languages

Language bar

Changing Regional Options

For those who work in international circles, you can change the format of the date, time, currency, and number into almost any form. For example, you can change the decimal symbol and list separator, the format used for negative numbers and leading zeros, and the measurement system (U.S. or metric).

Change the Display for Dates, Times, Currency, and Numbers

1. Click the **Start** button, click **Control Panel**, and then double-click the **Regional and Language Options** icon in Classic view.

2. Click the **Formats** tab.

3. Click the **Format** list arrow, and then click a locale with the settings you want.

4. Click **Customize this format** to change individual settings.

5. Select the format options you want on the different tabs.

6. Click **OK**.

7. Click **OK**.

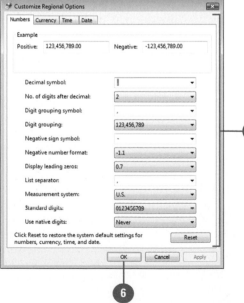

Did You Know?

You can change regional format by language and country. On the Location tab, click the Current language list arrow, and then click a language.

See Also

See "Changing Language Options" on page 112 for information on working with different languages.

Working with Fonts

Everything you type appears in a **font**, or typeface, a particular design set of letters, numbers, and other characters. The height of characters in a font is measured in points, each point being approximately 1/72 inch, while the width is measured by **pitch**, which refers to how many characters can fit in an inch. You might have heard common font names, such as Times New Roman, Arial, Courier, or Symbol. Windows comes with a variety of fonts for displaying text and printing documents. Using the Fonts window, you can view these fonts, see a sample of how a font appears when printed, and even install new fonts.

View or Install Fonts

1. Click the **Start** button, click **Control Panel**, and then double-click the **Fonts** icon in Classic view.

   The currently installed fonts on your computer appears in the Fonts window.

2. Click the **File** menu, and then click **Install New Font**.

   ◆ To quickly display the menu bar, press the Alt key.

3. Navigate to the drive and folder containing the font you want to install.

4. Select the font. To select more than one font, hold down the Ctrl key while you click each font.

5. Click **OK**.

6. Click the **Close** button.

See Also

See "Formatting Text" on page 34 for information on using fonts.

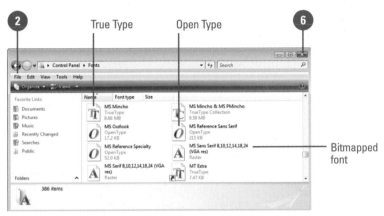

True Type   Open Type

Bitmapped font

Frequently Asked Questions

What's the Difference Between the Fonts?

Everything you type appears in a font, a particular typeface design and size for letters, numbers, and other characters. Usually, each typeface, such as Times New Roman, is made available in four variations: normal, bold, italic, and bold italic. There are two basic types of fonts: scalable and bitmapped. A **scalable font** (also known as **outline font**) is based on a mathematical equation that creates character outlines to form letters and numbers of any size. The two major scalable fonts are Adobe's Type 1 PostScript and Apple/Microsoft's TrueType or OpenType. Scalable fonts are generated in any point size on the fly and require only four variations for each typeface. A **bitmapped font** consists of a set of dot patterns for each letter and number in a typeface for a specified type size. Bitmapped fonts are created or prepackaged ahead of time and require four variations for each point size used in each typeface. Although a bitmapped font designed for a particular font size will always look the best, scalable fonts eliminate storing hundreds of different sizes of fonts on a disk.

Displaying and Arranging Toolbars

Toolbars provide easy access to commonly used tasks. Windows Vista comes with a set of toolbars you can use to access programs, folders, documents, and Web pages right from the taskbar. You can rearrange, resize, and move the toolbars to compliment your working style. When you move a toolbar, you can attach or dock it, to any of the sides on the desktop or you can float it in a window anywhere within the desktop.

Show or Hide a Toolbar

1. Right-click a blank area on the taskbar.

2. Point to **Toolbars**, and then click a toolbar without a check mark.

   A toolbar with a check mark is already displayed.

Did You Know?

You can display hidden buttons on a toolbar. Click the double-arrow at the end of the toolbar.

You can display buttons on the taskbar. Click the up or down arrow on the taskbar to scroll through the taskbar buttons.

You can also show or hide toolbars using the Taskbar and Start Menu Properties dialog box. Right-click the taskbar, click Properties, click the Toolbars tab, select or clear the toolbar check boxes, and then click OK.

See Also

See "Customizing the Taskbar" on page 118 for information on modifying the taskbar.

Toolbars on the Taskbar

Toolbar	Description
Address	Opens Web pages, network locations, files, and folders using the Address bar from Internet Explorer
Windows Media Player	Opens the Windows Media Player to play music and videos
Links	Opens links using the Links toolbar from Internet Explorer
Tablet PC Input Panel	Opens the Table PC Input Panel to use ink as an input device
Language bar	Switches between languages
Desktop	Opens windows to files, folders, and shortcuts on the desktop
Quick Launch	Starts Internet Explorer and other programs, switch between windows,or minimizes all the windows
New Toolbar	Adds a new toolbar to Windows

Unlock or Lock the Taskbar

1. Right-click a blank area on the taskbar.

2. Click **Lock the Taskbar**.

   ◆ Toolbars on the taskbar are locked when a check mark is displayed.

   ◆ Toolbars on the taskbar are unlocked when a check mark isn't displayed.

Move a Toolbar

1. Right-click a blank area on the taskbar, and then click **Lock the Taskbar** to remove the check mark, if necessary.

2. Point to the dotted bar or name of the toolbar, and then drag it to a new location on the desktop docked to the side or floating in the middle.

Did You Know?

You can resize a toolbar. Unlock the taskbar, and then drag the small vertical bar at the beginning of the toolbar.

You can expand or collapse a toolbar. Unlock the taskbar, and then double-click the small vertical bar at the beginning of the toolbar.

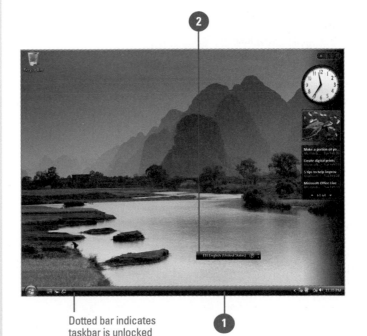

Dotted bar indicates taskbar is unlocked

Customizing the Taskbar

Microsoft
Certified
Application
Specialist

WINV-6.2

The taskbar is initially located at the bottom of the Windows desktop and is most often used to switch from one program to another. As with other Windows Vista elements, you can customize the taskbar; for example, you can change its size and location, customize its display, or add or remove toolbars to help you perform the tasks you need to do. If you need more room on the screen to display a window, Auto-hide can be used to hide the taskbar when it's not in use. You can also group similar windows (such as several WordPad documents) together on the taskbar to save space. If icons in the notification area are hidden when you want to see them, you can customize the notification area to always show the icons you want to use. In addition, you can also choose whether to show or hide common system icons, including Clock, Volume, Network, and Power.

Customize the Taskbar

1. Right-click a blank area on the taskbar, and then click **Properties**.

2. Click the **Taskbar** tab.

3. Select the **Auto-hide the taskbar** check box to hide the taskbar when you're not using it.

   The taskbar appears when you move the mouse to where the taskbar would appear.

4. Select the **Keep the taskbar on top of other windows** check box to keep the taskbar available.

5. Select the **Group similar taskbar buttons** check box to have similar windows grouped together in one button when the taskbar is crowded.

6. Select the **Show Quick Launch** check box to display the Quick Launch toolbar.

7. Click **OK**.

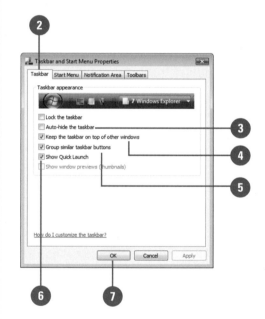

Customize the Notification Area

1 Right-click a blank area on the taskbar, and then click **Properties**.

2 Click the **Notification Area** tab.

3 Select the **Hide inactive icons** check box to hide seldom-used icons in the notification area.

4 Select or clear the system icons you want to show or hide on the notification area.

5 Click **Customize**.

6 Specify which icons are always displayed, which are never displayed, and which are hidden when inactive.

7 Click **OK**.

8 Click **OK**.

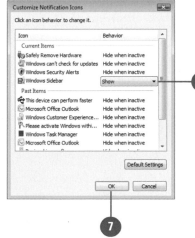

Did You Know?

You can access taskbar and Start menu settings in the Control Panel. Double-click the Taskbar and Start Menu icon in the Control Panel in Classic view.

You can move the taskbar. Unlock the taskbar, and then drag a blank area on the taskbar to a new location on any side of the desktop.

See Also

See "Displaying and Arranging Toolbars" on page 116 for information on working with toolbars on the taskbar.

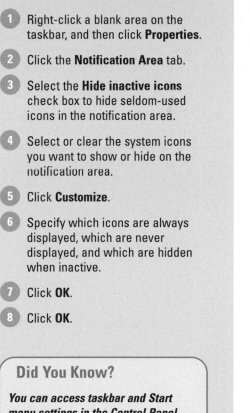

Customizing the Start Menu

The left column of the Start menu is separated into two lists (**New!**): pinned items above the separator line and most frequently used items below. The pinned items remain on the Start menu, like a push pin holds paper on a bulletin board, until you unpin them. The right column of the Start menu provides easy access to folders, Windows settings, help information, and search functionality. You can add shortcuts to programs, files, or folders to the Start menu or customize the way the Start menu looks and functions.

Choose a Start Menu Style

1. Right-click the **Start** button, and then click **Properties**.

2. Click the **Start menu** or **Classic Start menu** option.

3. Click **OK**.

Did You Know?

You can rearrange Start menu items. Click the Start button, point to All Programs, locate the item you want to move, and then drag the item to a new location. A thick, black line indicates the new location of the item.

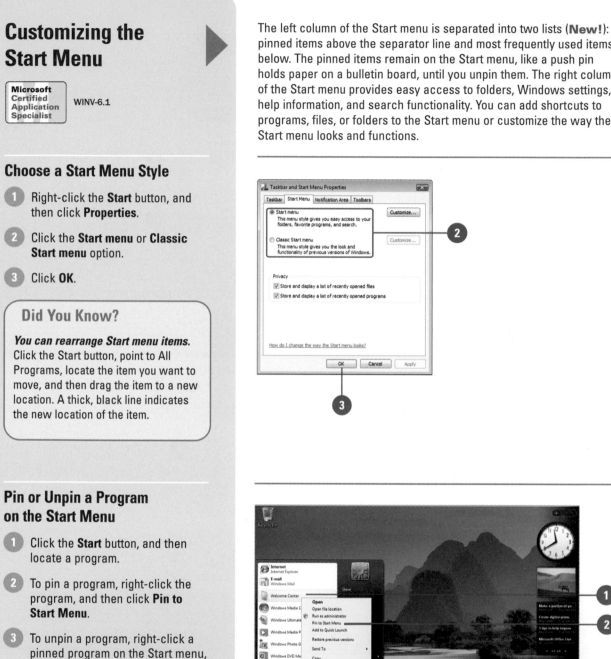

Pin or Unpin a Program on the Start Menu

1. Click the **Start** button, and then locate a program.

2. To pin a program, right-click the program, and then click **Pin to Start Menu**.

3. To unpin a program, right-click a pinned program on the Start menu, and then click **Unpin from Start Menu**.

Customize the Start Menu

1. Right-click the Start button, click **Properties**, and then click **Customize**.

2. Select check boxes and click options to specify the items you want (as a menu or link) or don't want included on the Start menu.

3. Click the up or down arrow to specify the number of recently used programs on the Start menu.

4. To show an Internet or E-mail link on the Start menu, select the **Internet link** or **E-mail link** check boxes, and then select the program you want to use.

5. Click **OK**.

6. Select or clear the privacy check boxes to store and display a list of recently opened files or programs.

7. Click **OK**.

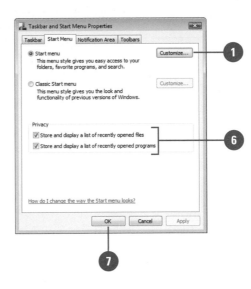

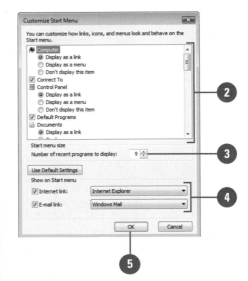

Did You Know?

You can add a shortcut to an item to the Start menu. Right-click the item, point to Send To, and then click Desktop. Drag the shortcut from the Desktop onto the Start button, and then drag it to a new location on the All Programs submenu.

You can run a program automatically when Windows starts. Create a shortcut for the program, and then drag the shortcut into the Startup folder. Click the Start button, point to All Programs, click Access, right-click Startup, and then click Open.

Setting Default Programs

When you double-click an audio or video file, or click a Web link, a default program associated with that file type automatically starts and opens the file. The Set Programs Access and Computer Defaults icon in the Control Panel provides an easy way to change the default program used for specific file types. Types such as .bmp or .jpg, and common activities, such as Web browsing, sending e-mail, playing audio and video files, and using instant messaging. You can also specify which programs are available from the Start menu, the desktop, and other locations. To change default options , you need to have administrator privileges for your computer. The options you set apply to all users on your computer.

Set Your Default Programs

1. Click the **Start** button, and then click **Control Panel**.

   TIMESAVER *Click the Start button, point to All Programs, and then click Default Programs.*

2. Double-click the **Default Programs** icon in Classic View.

3. Click **Set your default programs**.

4. Select a program.

5. Click **Set this program as default**, or **Choose defaults for this program**.

6. If you select Choose defaults for this program, select the extension you want this program to open by default, and then click **Save**.

7. When you're done, click **Close**.

8. Click **OK**.

9. Click the **Close** button.

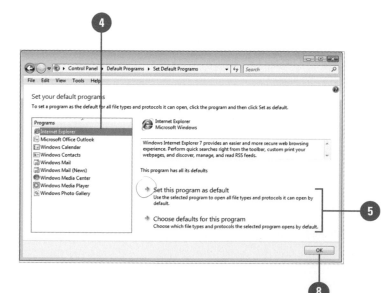

Set Program Access and Computer Defaults

① Click the **Start** button, and then click **Control Panel**.

② Double-click the **Default Programs** icon in Classic View.

③ Click **Set program access and computer defaults**, and then enter administrator permissions, if requested.

④ Click the option for the type of program you want to set: **Computer Manufacturer** (if available), **Microsoft Windows**, **Non-Microsoft**, or **Custom**.

⑤ Click the option or select from a list the defaults you want to set.

⑥ Click **OK**.

⑦ Click the **Close** button.

Change File Type Program Association

① Click the **Start** button, and then click **Control Panel**.

② Double-click the **Default Programs** icon in Classic View.

③ Click **Associate a file type or protocol with a program**.

④ Click the extension.

⑤ Click **Change program**.

⑥ Select the program you want to use; click **Browse** if necessary to locate it.

⑦ Click **OK**.

⑧ When you're done, click **Close**.

⑨ Click the **Close** button.

Changing the Way a CD or DVD Starts

When you insert a CD or DVD into your computer, you can specify how you want Windows Vista to respond. You can have Windows detects the type of content on the disc and automatically start, or prompt you each time to choose an action. If you have CDs or DVDs with music files, pictures, video files, or mixed content, you can change the action Windows takes when it detects the content on the disc. You can have Windows play or rip a CD or DVD using Windows Media Player, open the first folder to view files using Windows Explorer, or take no action. Windows Vista allows you to set AutoPlay options for a wide-variety of CDs and DVDs, including an audio or enhanced audio CD, DVD or enhanced DVD movie, Software and games, pictures, video and audio files, blank CD or DVD, mixed content, HD DVD or Blu-ray Disc movie, Video or Super Video CD.

Set AutoPlay Options

1. Click the **Start** button, and then click **Control Panel**.

2. Double-click the **Auto Play** icon in Classic View.

3. To display the AutoPlay dialog box everytime you insert a CD or DVD, select the **Use AutoPlay for all media and devices** check box.

4. For each of the different media types, click the list arrow, and then select the default action you want; options vary depending on the type of CD or DVD.

   ◆ To turn off AutoPlay for a specific media type, click Take no action.

5. To reset defaults, click **Reset all defaults**.

6. Click **Save**.

Did You Know?

You can stop Windows from performing an action on a CD or DVD. Hold down the Shift key while you insert the CD or DVD.

Using Ease of Access Tools

If you have difficulty using a mouse or typing, have slightly impaired vision, or are deaf or hard of hearing, you can adjust the appearance and behavior of Windows Vista to make your computer easier for you to use. The Ease of Access Center helps you configure Windows for your vision, hearing, and mobility needs. You can also answer a few questions about your daily computer use that can help Windows recommend accessibility settings and programs for you. To open the Ease of Access Center, click the Start button on the taskbar, click Control Panel, and then double-click the Ease of Access icon. To use the Ease of Access questionnaire, click Get recommendations to make your computer easier to use. The Ease of Access Center provides utilities to adjust the way your keyboard, display, and mouse function to suit various vision and motor abilities. Some of the accessibility tools available include Magnifier, On-Screen Keyboard, Narrator, and High Contrast. You can also set accessibility options, such as StickyKeys, FilterKeys, ToggleKeys, Sound-Sentry, ShowSounds, and MouseKeys, that automatically turn off accessibility features, provide warning sounds, and determine when to apply the settings. The accessibility tools in Windows Vista are intended to provide a low level of functionality for those with special needs. If these tools do not meet your daily needs, you might need to purchase a more advanced accessibility program.

Ease of Access Center Tools

Option	Description
Magnifier	Displays a separate window with a magnified portion of the screen; this is designed to make the screen easier to read for users who have impaired vision.
On-Screen Keyboard	Displays an on-screen keyboard; this is designed to use the computer without the mouse or keyboard.
Narrator	Use the computer without a display; this is a text-to-speech utility program designed for users who are blind or have impaired vision.
High Contrast	Sets the desktop appearance to high contrast to make the computer easier to see; this is designed to make the screen easier to read for users who have impaired vision.
StickyKeys	Enables simultaneous keystrokes while pressing one key at a time, such as Ctrl+Alt+Del.
FilterKeys	Adjusts the response of your keyboard; ignores repeated characters or fast key presses.
ToggleKeys	Emits sounds when you press certain locking keys, such as Caps Lock, Num Lock, or Scroll Lock.
SoundSentry	Provides visual warnings for system sounds.
ShowSounds	Instructs programs to provide captions.
MouseKeys	Enables the numeric keypad to perform mouse functions.

Using the Ease of Access Center

The Ease of Access Center (**New!**) allows you to check the status of and start or stop the Magnifier, Narrator, and On-Screen Keyboard accessibility programs. Magnifier is a utility that enlarges an area of the screen. Narrator is a text-to-speech utility that gives users who are blind or have impaired vision access to the computer. On-Screen Keyboard is a utility that displays a keyboard on the screen where users with mobility impairments can type using a mouse, joystick, or other pointing device. If you have administrator access to your computer, you can specify how the accessibility programs start when you log on, lock the desktop, or start the Ease of Access Center.

Use the Ease of Access Center

1. Press ⊞+U to start the Ease of Access Enter.

   TIMESAVER *The Windows key ⊞ is located in the lower-left corner of the keyboard.*

   - You can also start the Ease of Access Center in the Control Panel. Double-click the Ease of Access icon.

2. To get recommendations on what to use, click **Get recommendations to make your computer easier to use**, and then follow the instructions.

3. To provide quick access to common tools, select the **Always read this section aloud** and **Always scan this section** check boxes.

4. Click the utility program or the settings you want to manage.

5. Select or clear the check boxes you want to specify how you want the selected program to start or a setting to be applied.

6. Click **Save** or exit the window.

7. When you're done with the Ease of Access Center, click the **Close** button.

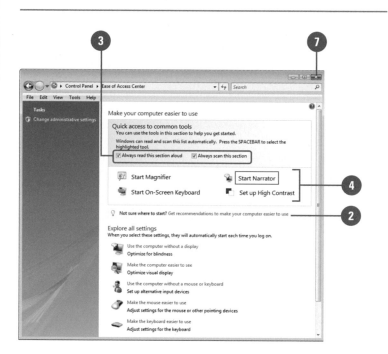

Use the Magnifier

1. Click the **Start** button, point to **All Programs**, click **Accessories**, click **Ease of Access**, and then click **Magnifier**.

2. Click the **Scale factor** list arrow, and then click a level.

3. Select or clear the check boxes with the presentation options to invert colors, start minimized, or show Magnifier.

4. Select or clear the check boxes with the tracking options to follow the mouse cursor, keyboard focus, or text editing.

5. Click **Hide** to use the Magnifier program, or click the **Close** button to close the program. (Restore the Magnifier window, if necessary.)

Use the On-Screen Keyboard

1. Open the program in which you want to type.

2. Click the **Start** button, point to All Programs, click **Accessories**, click **Ease of Access**, and then click **On-Screen Keyboard**.

3. Position the cursor, if necessary.

4. Type the text you want, or type keyboard commands.

5. When you're done, click the **Close** button.

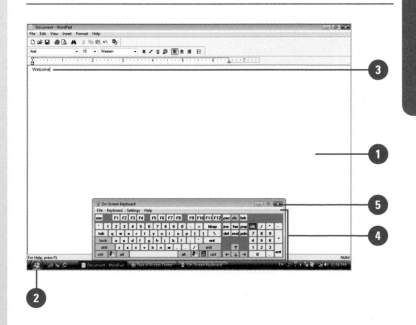

Listening to the Computer

Windows Vista comes with an accessibility tool called Narrator that reads aloud what appears on your screen, such as window items, menu options, and typed characters. Windows uses Text-to-Speech (TTS) technology to recognize text and play it back as spoken words using a synthesized voice, which is chosen from several pre-generated voices. Narrator is designed for those who are blind or have impaired vision and works with the Windows desktop and setup, Control Panel, Notepad, WordPad, and Internet Explorer. Narrator supports only the English language and might not read words aloud correctly in other programs. You can adjust the speed, volume, or pitch of the voice in Narrator and change other Text-to-Speech options using Speech properties in the Control Panel.

Change Text-To-Speech Options

1. Click the **Start** button, click **Control Panel**, and then double-click the **Text to Speech** icon in Classic view.

2. Click the **Voice selection** list arrow, and then select a synthesized voice.

3. Drag the **Voice speed** slider to adjust the speed of the voice.

4. Click **Preview Voice**.

5. To set a preferred audio device as output for TTS playback, click **Advanced**, make a selection, and then click **OK**.

6. To adjust settings for your audio output devices, click **Audio Output**, specify the options you want on the Playback, Recording, or Sounds tabs, and then click **OK**.

7. Click **OK**.

> ### See Also
>
> *See "Recognizing Your Speech" on page 130 for information on speech capabilities.*

Use the Narrator

1. Click the **Start** button, point to **All Programs**, click **Accessories**, click **Ease of Access**, and then click **Narrator**.

2. Select the Narrator check box options you want:

   ◆ To hear what you type, select the **Echo User's Keystrokes** check box.

   ◆ To hear background events, select the **Announce System Messages** check box.

   ◆ To hear an announcement when the screen scrolls, select the **Announce Scroll Notifications** check box.

   ◆ Select the **Start Narrator Minimized** check box to minimize the Narrator dialog box.

3. Click **Voice Settings**.

4. Select a voice and adjust the voice speed, volume, and pitch.

5. Click **OK**.

6. Click the **Minimize** button to use the Narrator program or click **Exit** to close the program. (Restore the Narrator window, if necessary.) Click **Yes**, if necessary.

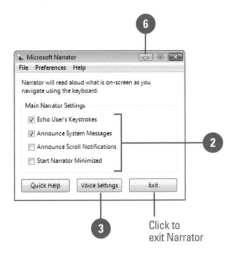

Click to exit Narrator

Common Narrator Shortcuts	
Action	**Result**
Ctrl+Shift+Enter or Alt+Home	Get information about the current item
Ctrl+Shift+Spacebar	Read the entire selected window
Ctrl+Alt+Spacebar	Read the selected window layout
Alt+End	Get a summary of the current item
Ctrl	Stop Narrator from reading text
Insert+F2	Select all of the text with the current text pattern
Insert+F3	Read the current character
Insert+F4	Read the current word
Insert+F5	Read the current line
Insert+F6	Read the current paragraph
Insert+F7	Read the current page
Insert+F8	Read the current document

Recognizing Your Speech

If you have a speech-enabled program, you can initialize and customize speech recognition options using Speech properties in the Control Panel. **Speech recognition (New!)** is the ability to convert a spoken voice into electronic text. Windows Vista adapts to your speech, and speech recognition increases over time. You can use the speech recognition properties to select a language, create a profile to accommodate your speaking style and environment, and train your computer in as little as ten minutes to recognize and adapt to the sound of your voice, word pronunciation, accent, speaking manner, and new or distinctive words. Some programs use speech differently, so you need to check the speech-enabled program for details. Speech Recognition is not available in all languages.

Set Up Speech Recognition

1 Click the **Start** button, click **Control Panel**, and then double-click the **Speech Recognition Options** icon in Classic view.

2 Click **Set up microphone**, and then follow the wizard instructions to adjust the microphone.

3 Click **Take Speech Tutorial**, and then follow the instructions to take the 30 minute training tutorial to teach you the commands used with speech recognition.

4 Click **Train your computer to recognize your speech**, and then follow the wizard instructions to train your voice.

5 When you're done, click the **Close** button.

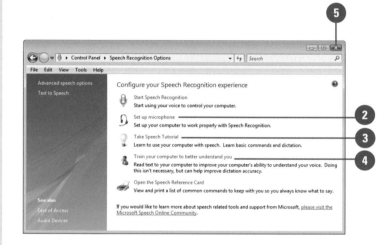

Did You Know?

You can view and print a Speech Recognition reference card. Click the Start button, click Control Panel, double-click the Speech Recognition Options icon in Classic view, and then click Open and Speech Reference Card.

Set Speech Recognition Options

1. Click the **Start** button, click **Control Panel**, and then double-click the **Speech Recognition Options** icon in Classic view.

2. In the left pane, click **Advanced speech options**.

3. Click the **Speech Recognition** tab.

4. Click the list arrow, and then select a language.

5. To start the Profile Wizard, click **New**, type your name, click OK, follow the wizard instructions to create a profile, adjust the microphone, and train your voice, and then click **Finish**.

6. Select or clear the User Settings check boxes you do or don't want.

7. Click **OK**.

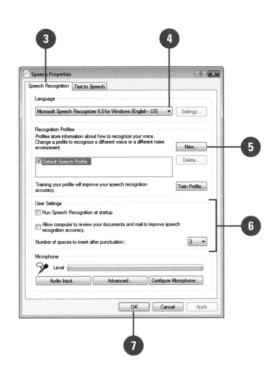

Start Speech Recognition

1. Click the **Start** button, click **Control Panel**, and then double-click the **Speech Recognition Options** icon in Classic view.

2. Click **Start Speech Recognition**.

3. If requested, follow the wizard instructions to create a profile, adjust the microphone, and train your voice, and then click **Finish**.

4. Click the **Speech Recognition** button to toggle between Sleeping and Listening mode.

   TIMESAVER *Right-click the Speech Recognition button to select command options.*

5. When you're done, click the **Close** button.

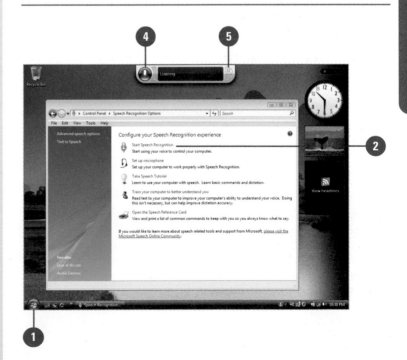

Exploring the Internet

Introduction

The **Internet** is a global collection of more than a billion computers (and growing) linked together to share information. The Internet's physical structure includes telephone lines, cables, satellites, and other telecommunications media. Using the Internet, computer users can share many types of information, including text, graphics, sounds, videos, and computer programs. The **World Wide Web** (also known as the Web) is a part of the Internet that consists of Web sites located on different computers around the world.

History of the Internet and the World Wide Web

The Internet has its roots in the Advanced Research Projects Agency Network (ARPANET), which the United States Department of Defense started in 1969. In 1986, the National Science Foundation formed NSFNET, which replaced ARPANET. NSFNET expanded the foundation of the U.S. portion of the Internet with high-speed, long-distance data lines. In 1991, the U.S. Congress expanded the capacity and speed of the Internet further and opened it to commercial use. The Internet is now accessible in almost every country in the world. The Web was developed in Switzerland in 1991 to make finding documents on the Internet easier. Software programs designed to access the Web, known as Web browsers, use point-and-click interfaces. The first such Web browser, Mosaic, was introduced at the University of Illinois in 1993. Since the release of Mosaic, Microsoft Internet Explorer and Fire Fox have become two popular Web browsers.

What You'll Do

Understand Web Sites and Browsers

Connect to the Internet

Create an Internet Connection

Set Up Windows Firewall

Start Internet Explorer

View the Internet Explorer Window

Browse the Web

Change a Home Page

Modify the Links Bar

Add a Web Page to the Favorites List

View and Maintain a History List

Read and Subscribe to Feeds

Search the Web

Preview and Print a Web Page

Save Pictures or Text from a Web Page

Download Files from the Web or FTP

Save a Web Page

Use Another Web Browser

Understanding Web Sites and Browsers

A **Web site** contains Web pages linked together to make searching for information on the Internet easier. **Web pages** are documents that contain highlighted words, phrases, and graphics, called **hyperlinks** (or simply **links**) that open other Web pages when you click them. Some Web pages contain frames. A frame is a separate window within a Web page that lets you see more than one Web page at a time. **Web browsers** are software programs that you use to "browse the Web," or access and display Web pages. Browsers make the Web easy to navigate by providing

a graphical, point-and-click environment. Microsoft Internet Explorer 7 is a popular browser from Microsoft that is built-in to Windows Vista. With a Web browser, you can display Web pages from all over the world, display Web content on the desktop, view Web feeds (**New!**), use links to move from one Web page to another, play audio and video clips, search the Web for information, make favorite Web pages available offline (when you're not connected to the Internet), and print text and graphics on Web pages.

Web browser   Web site

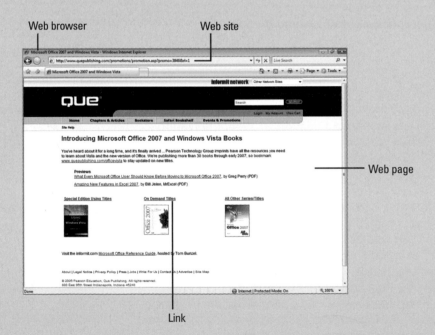

Web page

Link

Connecting to the Internet

Universities and large companies are most likely connected to the Internet via high-speed wiring that transmits data very quickly. As the Internet continues to explode around the world, several high-speed connection options are becoming more available and affordable for business and home use: DSL (Digital Subscriber Lines), wires that provide a completely digital connection; and cable modems, which use cable television lines. DSL and cable modems, also known as broadband connections, are continually turned on and connected and use a network setup. If a broadband connection is not available, you need to establish a connection over a phone line using a dial-up modem. Data travels more slowly over phone lines than over digital lines and cable modems. Whether you use a phone line, a DSL line, or a cable modem, Windows can help you establish a connection between your computer and the Internet using the Connect to the Internet wizard. First, you need to select an ISP (Internet Service Provider), which is a company that sets up an Internet account for you and provides Internet access. ISPs maintain servers connected directly to the Internet 24 hours a day. You pay a fee, sometimes by the hour, but more often a flat monthly rate. To connect to the Internet, you need to obtain an Internet account and connection information from your ISP or your system administrator. For details, see "Creating an Internet Connection" on page 136. If you are working on a network, you can also share one Internet connection with everyone. For information on creating an Internet Connection Sharing (ICS), see "Sharing an Internet Connection" on page 378.

Protecting your Computer with a Firewall

When you connect to the Internet, you can access Web sites on the Internet, but other users on the Internet can also access information on your computer and potentially infect it with harmful viruses and worms. For more information, see "Avoiding Viruses and Other Harmful Attacks" on page 330.

You can prevent this by activating Windows Firewall, another security layer of protection. A **firewall** is a security system that creates a protective barrier between your computer or network and others on the Internet. Windows Firewall monitors all communication between your computer and the Internet and prevents unsolicited inbound traffic from the Internet from entering your computer. Windows Firewall blocks all unsolicited communication from reaching your computer unless you specifically allow it (unblock) to come through, known as an exception. For example, if you run a program, such as Windows Messenger that needs to receive information from the Internet or a network, Windows Firewall asks if you want to block or unblock the connection. If you choose to unblock it, Windows Firewall creates an exception so the program can receive information. For details, see "Setting Up Windows Firewall" on page 137.

If you send and receive e-mail, Windows Firewall doesn't block spam or unsolicited e-mail or stop you from opening e-mail with harmful attachments. To protect your computer from these attacks, see "Protecting Against E-mail Attacks" on page 345. Windows Firewall helps block viruses and worms from reaching your computer, but it doesn't detect or disable them if they are already on your computer or come through e-mail. To protect your computer, you need to install antivirus software.

Creating an Internet Connection

Sometimes connecting your computer to the Internet can be the most difficult part of getting started. The Connect to the Internet wizard simplifies the process, whether you want to set up a new connection using an existing account or select an Internet service provider (ISP) to set up a new account. In either case, you will need to obtain connection information from your ISP or your system administrator.

Create an Internet Connection

1. Click the **Start** button, point to **All Programs**, click **Welcome Center**, and then double-click **Connect to the Internet**.

2. Click **Set up a new a connection**, or **Set up a new connection anyway** to set up a second connection.

3. Click the option with the way you want to connect: **Wireless**, **Broadband (PPPoE)**, or **Dial-up**.

   ◆ For a wireless connection, select a network, and then go to Step 8.

4. Type the name and password your ISP gave you. For a dial-up connection, type a dial-up phone number.

5. For the password, select or clear the **Show characters** or **Remember this password** check boxes.

6. Type a connection name.

7. Select or clear the **Allow other people to use this connection** check box.

8. Click **Connect**.

See Also

See "Connecting to a Wireless Network" on page 364 for information on wireless Internet connection.

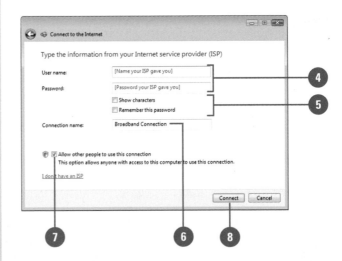

Setting Up Windows Firewall

If your computer is directly connected to the Internet, you need Windows Firewall to protect your computer from unauthorized access from others on the Internet. Windows Firewall is enabled by default for all Internet and network connections. However, some computer manufacturers and network administrators might turn it off, so you need to check it. When Windows Firewall is enabled, you might not be able to use some communication features, such as sending files with a messaging program or playing an Internet game, unless the program is listed on the Exceptions tab in Windows Firewall. If you use multiple Internet and networking connections, you can use the Advanced tab to enable or disable individual connections.

Set Up Windows Firewall

1. Click the **Start** button, click **Control Panel**, double-click the **Windows Firewall** icon in Classic view.

2. In the left pane, click **Turn Windows Firewall on or off**, and then click the **General** tab.

    IMPORTANT *If you're part of a network, options are grayed out.*

3. Click the **On (recommended)** option.

4. To set maximum protection, select the **Block all incoming connections** check box or clear it to make exceptions.

5. To make program exceptions, click the **Exceptions** tab.

6. Select the check boxes with the exceptions you want; if necessary, click **Add program** to add it.

7. Click **OK**, and then click the **Close** button.

Did You Know?

You can restore Windows Firewall default settings. In Windows Firewall, click the Advanced tab, click Restore Defaults, and then click OK.

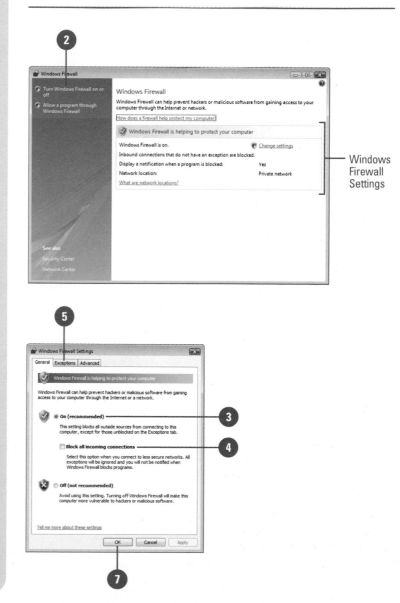

Windows Firewall Settings

Starting Internet Explorer

Internet Explorer is a Web browser that you use to search the Web. You can start Internet Explorer using the Start menu, the Internet Explorer icon on the desktop, or the button on the Quick Launch toolbar on the taskbar. After you start Internet Explorer, you might need to connect to the Internet by selecting a dial-up or broadband service and entering a user name and password. If you have problems running Internet Explorer—sudden shutdowns—due to add-on programs, you can start Internet Explorer with no add-ons (**New!**), and then turn off individual add-ons to determine the problem. The elements of the Internet Explorer window allow you to view, print, and search for information on the Internet. Once you establish a connection to the Internet, you are ready to explore Web pages on the Internet.

Start Internet Explorer

1 Click the **Start** button, and then click **Internet**.

◆ To start Internet Explorer without Add-ons, click the **Start** button, point to **All Programs**, click **System Tools**, and then click **Internet Explorer (Non Add-ons)**.

2 If necessary, click **Connect** to dial your ISP. You might need to type your user name and password before Internet Explorer will connect to the Internet.

The Internet Explorer window opens.

Did You Know?

You can find Internet Explorer on the All Programs submenu. If Internet Explorer doesn't appear on the left column of the Start menu, it's available on the All Programs submenu.

See Also

See "Customizing the Start Menu" on page 120 for information on showing Internet Explorer on the Start menu.

For Your Information

Browsing with Protected Mode

Internet Explorer 7 includes protected mode (**New!**), which makes it difficult for hackers using a Web site to install malicious software on your computer, yet makes it easy for you to installed wanted software using the Standard user account (with security enabled) instead of the Administrator user account (with security disabled). Protected mode is turned on by default. When a Web page tries to install unwanted software, a warning message appears on the Status bar. If you need to disable or enable it, click the Tools button, click Internet Options, click the Security tab, clear or select the Enable Protected Mode (requires restarting Internet Explorer) check box, and then click OK.

Viewing the Internet Explorer Window

Quick Tabs
Displays multiple Web sites in a single browser window

Address bar
Displays the address of the current Web page or document you are viewing or trying to access

Title bar
Displays the name of the Web page you are viewing

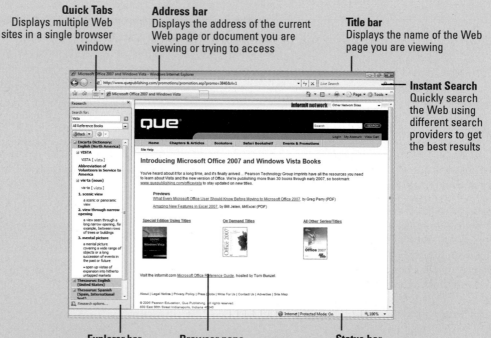

Instant Search
Quickly search the Web using different search providers to get the best results

Explorer bar
Displays links to web pages from Search results, Favorites list, and History list. The Explorer bar is only visible when you click the corresponding button on the toolbar.

Browser pane
Displays the current Web page, document, or folder contents

Status bar
Indicates the progress of loading a Web page, as well as other messages about selected actions

Browsing the Web

A **Web address** (also known as a URL, which stands for Uniform Resource Locator) is a unique place on the Internet where you can locate a Web page. With Internet Explorer, you can browse sites on the Web with ease by entering a Web address or by clicking a link. Each method is better at different times. For example, you might type an address in the Address bar to start your session. Then you might click a link on that Web page to access a new site. As you open Web sites, Internet Explorer creates separate tabs for each one, so you can view multiple Web sites in a single window. When you type an Internet address in the Address bar, Internet Explorer tries to find a recently visited page that matches what you've typed so far. If Internet Explorer finds a match, it fills in the rest of the address. You can also use **AutoComplete** to fill out forms on the Web, including single-line edits, and user names and passwords.

View a Web Page

Use any of the following methods to display a Web page:

◆ In the Address bar, type the Web address, and then press Enter.

   If you have recently entered the Web page address, AutoComplete remembers it and tries to complete the address for you. The suggested match is highlighted. Click the correct address or continue to type until the address you want appears in the Address list.

◆ Click any link on the Web page, such as a picture or colored, underlined text. The mouse pointer changes to a hand when it is over a link.

> **Did You Know?**
>
> *You can have AutoComplete quickly complete a Web address.* In the Address bar, type the name of the Web site, such as *perspection*, and then press Ctrl+Enter. AutoComplete adds the "www." and ".com".

Type a Web address

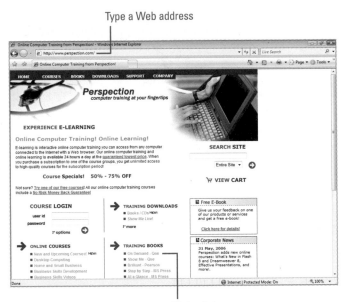

Click a link

Turn Off AutoComplete Options

1 Click the **Tools** button, and then click **Internet Options**.

2 Click the **Content** tab.

3 Click **Settings**.

4 Clear the AutoComplete options you want to turn off.

  ◆ **Web address.**

  ◆ **Forms.**

  ◆ **User names and password on forms.**

5 Click **OK**.

6 Click **OK**.

Did You Know?

You can browse folders and run programs from the Address bar. Click anywhere in the Address bar, type the location of the folder or program, press Enter, and then click Allow. For example, typing **C:\Windows** opens the Windows folder.

You can display the menu bar and toolbar using the Tools button. If you want to display the menu bar and any toolbars that you liked to use from earlier releases of Internet Explorer, click the Tools button, and then click Menu Bar or point to Toolbars and click a toolbar.

You can work offline. If connection time is an issue, you can download and display a Web page and then work offline to read it. Click the Tools button, and then click Work Offline. When you choose to work offline, Internet Explorer starts in offline mode until you click the Tools button, and then click Work Offline again to clear the check mark.

For Your Information

Understanding a Web Address

The address for a Web page is called a URL. Each Web page has a unique URL that is typically composed of four parts: the protocol (a set of rules that allow computers to exchange information), the location of the Web site, the name that maintains the Web site, and a suffix that identifies the type of site. A URL begins with a protocol, followed by a colon, two slashes, the location of the Web site, a dot, the name of the Web site, a dot, and a suffix. The Web site is the computer where the Web pages are located. At the end of the Web site name, another slash may appear, followed by one or more folder names and a file name. For example, in the web site address, http://*www*.perspection.com/downloads/main.htm, the protocol is *http* (HyperText Transfer Protocol), the location of the Web site is *www* (World Wide Web), the name of the Web site is *perspection*, and the suffix is *com* (a commercial organization); a folder at that site is called */downloads*; and within the folder is a file called *main.htm*.

Browsing with Tabs

As you open Web sites, Internet Explorer creates separate tabs (**New!**) for each one, so you can view multiple Web sites in a single window, which reduces the number of items on the taskbar. You can open Web pages on new tabs and quickly switch between them. If you prefer a visual way to switch between tabs, you can use Quick tabs (**New!**), which displays thumbnails, to open and close Web pages. The list arrow to the right of the Quick Tabs button displays a list of all open Web pages, and you can use it to open a Web page as an alternate method. After you have opened a set of tabs, you can save them as a group, so you can quickly view them again later.

Use Tabbed Browsing

Use any of the following methods to use tabbed browsing:

- **Open a new tab.** Press Ctrl+click a link (in the background) or Ctrl+Shift+click a link (in the foreground). If you have a mouse with a wheel or middle button, you can click a link with the wheel or middle button to open a link.

    TIMESAVER *Press Alt+Enter to open a new tab in the foreground from the Address bar.*

- **Open a blank tab.** Click the **New Tab** button, or press Ctrl+T.

- **Open or close Quick Tabs.** Click the **Quick Tabs** button, or press Ctrl+Q. To open the Web page, click a thumbnail. To close a Web page, click the **Close** button in the corner of the thumbnail.

- **Switch between tabs.** Click a tab, or press Ctrl+Tab.

- **Close a tab.** Click the **Close** button on the tab, or press Ctrl+W.

- **Close Internet Explorer and save tabs.** Close Internet Explorer, click **Show Options**, select the **Open these the next time I use Internet Explorer** check box, and then click **Close Tabs**.

Quick Tabs   Close Tab   New Tab

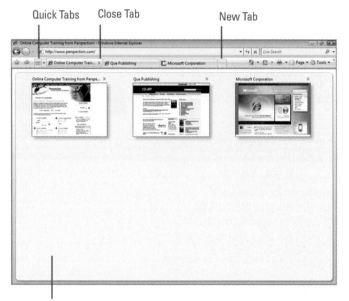

Quick Tabs view

Save a Group of Tabs

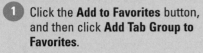 Click the **Add to Favorites** button, and then click **Add Tab Group to Favorites**.

2 Type a name for the group.

3 Click **Add**.

Open a Group of Tabs

1 Click the **Favorites Center** button.

2 Click the **Favorites** button.

3 Click the folder that you want to open.

4 Click the arrow to the right of the folder name.

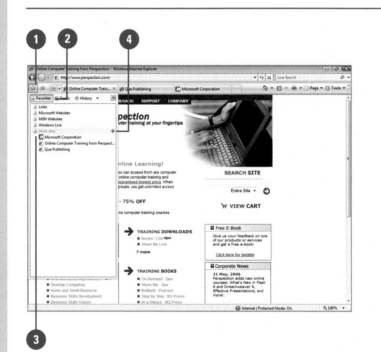

Did You Know?

You can turn off tabs. In Internet Explorer, click the Tools button, click Internet Options, click the General tab, click Settings in the Tabs section, clear the Enable Tabbed Browsing check box, and then click OK.

You can display pop-ups in a window or tab. In Internet Explorer, click the Tools button, click Internet Options, click the General tab, click Settings in the Tabs section, specify the option you want in the When a pop-up is encountered section, and then click OK.

Navigating Basics

As you browse the Web or your local hard disk, you may want to retrace your steps and return to a Web page, document, or hard disk you've recently visited. You can move backward or forward one location at a time, or you can jump directly to any location from the Back list or Forward list, both of which show locations you've previously visited in this session. After you start to load a Web page, you can stop if the page opens too slowly or if you decide not to access it. If a Web page loads incorrectly or you want to update the information it contains, you can reload, or **refresh**, the page. If you get lost on the Web, you can start over with a single click of the Home button. You can also resize your toolbars so you can see more of the Web address or Links bar.

Move Back or Forward

◆ To move back or forward one Web page or document at a time, click the **Back** button or the **Forward** button on the Address bar.

   TIMESAVER *To move back, press Alt+left arrow. To move forward, press Alt+right arrow.*

◆ To move back or forward to a specific Web page or document, click the list arrow next to the Back and Forward buttons on the Address bar, and then select the Web page or document you want to visit.

Back button

Forward button

Back/Forward list arrow

Stop, Refresh, or Go Home

◆ Click the **Stop** button on the Address bar.

   TIMESAVER *Press Esc.*

◆ Click the **Refresh** button on the Address bar.

   TIMESAVER *Press F5.*

◆ Click the **Home** button on the toolbar.

Refresh button

Home button   Stop button

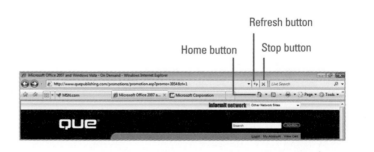

Zooming the View In and Out

Working with the Zoom tools (**New!**) gives you one more way to control exactly what you see in a Web page. Unlike changing text size in previous versions of Internet Explorer, the Zoom tools allow you to enlarge or reduce everything on the page, including text and images. You can adjust the zoom from 10% to 1000%. The Zoom tools are located in the bottom-right corner of the window or available on the Zoom submenu on the Page button. If you have a mouse with a wheel, hold down the Ctrl key, and then scroll the wheel to zoom in or out.

Change the View

1. Use any of the following zoom options available on the Status bar (**New!**):

   ◆ **Zoom In or Out.** Click the **Change Zoom Level** button arrow on the Status bar, and then click a zoom percentage.

   TIMESAVER *Press Ctrl+(+) to zoom in by increments of 10%, or press Ctrl+(-) to zoom out by increments of 10%. Press Ctrl+0 to restore the zoom to 100%.*

   ◆ **Zoom Level.** Click the **Change Zoom Level** button on the Status bar to cycle through 100%, 125%, and 150%.

   ◆ **Zoom Custom.** Click the **Change Zoom Level** button arrow on the Status bar, click **Custom**, type a zoom value, and then click **OK**.

2. To change the view to full screen, click the **Tools** button, and then click **Full Screen**. To change back, press F11.

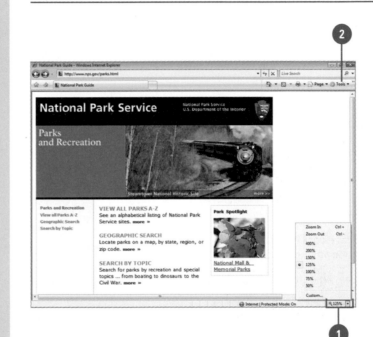

Did You Know?

You can change Web page text size to make it easier to read. Click the Page button, click Text Size, and then click the size you want. When you change the text size, graphics and controls remain unchanged, so you can focus on the text.

Changing Your Home Page

Your **home page** in Internet Explorer is the page that opens when you start the program. When you first install Internet Explorer, the default home page is the Microsoft Network (MSN) Web site. If you want a different page to appear when you start Internet Explorer and whenever you click the Home button, you can change your home page. With the introduction of tabbed browsing, you can display multiple home pages in tab sets (**New!**). You can choose one of the millions of Web pages available through the Internet, or you can select a particular file on your hard drive.

Change the Home Page

1. Open the Web page or multiple Web pages you want to be the new home page.

2. Click the **Home** button arrow, and then click **Add or Change Home Page**.

3. Click one of the following options:

   ◆ **Use this webpage as your only homepage.**

   ◆ **Add this webpage to your homepage tabs.**

   ◆ **Use the current tab set as your home page.**

4. Click **Yes**. Otherwise, click **No**.

5. To remove a Web page as one of your home pages, click the **Home** button arrow, point to **Remove**, and then click the Web page you want to remove, or **Remove All**, and then click **Yes** to confirm.

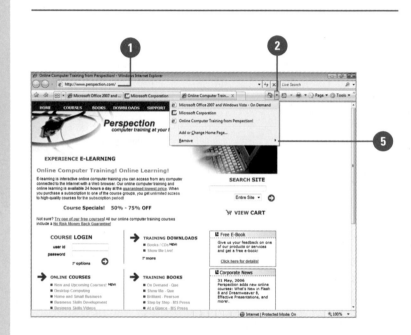

Modifying the Links Bar

The Links bar, located below the Address bar when displayed, provides one-click access to Web pages and favorites. You can add or remove buttons on the Links bar to customize it to meet your needs. The Links bar is also available on the Taskbar (**New!**) when you are not using Internet Explorer.

Display and Hide the Links Bar

1. Click the **Tools** button, and then point to **Toolbars**.

2. Click **Links**.

Did You Know?

You can add a favorite to the Links bar. Click the Favorites Center button, and then drag a favorite shortcut to a new location in the Links folder.

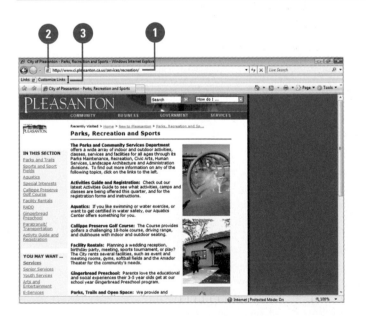

Add a Link Button to the Links Bar

1. Open the Web page or display the folder you want to add to the Links bar.

2. Drag the Web page in the Address bar to the Links bar.

3. Release the mouse button to position the new item.

Did You Know?

You can quickly remove a link button from the Links bar. Right-click the button you want to delete, click Delete, and then click Yes to confirm.

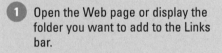

Adding a Web Page to the Favorites List

Rather than memorizing URLs or keeping a handwritten list of Web pages you want to visit, you can use the Favorites Center (**New!**) to store and organize the addresses. When you display a Web page that you want to display again at a later time, you can add the Web page to your the Favorites Center; you can also manage feeds and history. Once you add the Web page to the Favorites Center, you can quickly return to the page. To open all the favorites in a folder at the same time, click the blue arrow to the right of the folder (**New!**). If your list of favorites grows long, you can delete favorites you don't visit anymore or move favorites into folders.

Create a Favorites List

1. Open the Web site you want to add to your Favorites list.

2. Click the **Add to Favorites** button, and then click **Add to Favorites**.

3. Type the name for the site, or use the default name supplied.

4. Click **Create In** arrow, and then select a location on the Favorites menu to place the site.

5. If you want to create a new folder, click **New Folder**, type a folder name, and then click **OK**.

6. Click **Add**.

   Use the Favorites Center button to quickly return to a favorite location.

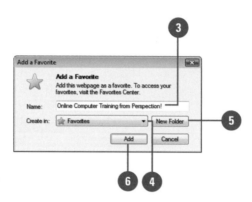

Access Favorites

① Click the **Favorites Center** button.

The Favorites Center pane appears, displaying your current favorites list, like a menu. The pane is not pinned to the window.

② To pin the pane to the window, click the **Pin the Favorites Center** button (green arrow).

When the pane is pinned, the Close button appears on the pane.

③ Click a folder, if necessary.

④ To open all the favorites in a folder at the same time, click the blue arrow to the right of the folder.

⑤ Click the page you want.

⑥ Click off the pane or click the **Close** button.

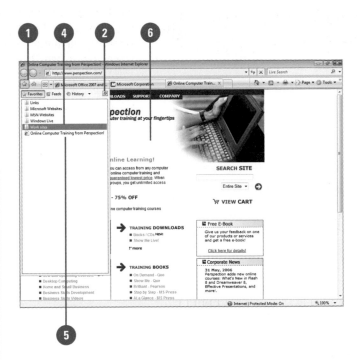

Organize Favorites

① Click the **Add to Favorites** button, and then click **Organize Favorites**.

② Select one or more favorites from the list you want to work with.

③ Do any of the following:

- ◆ **New Folder.** Click **New Folder**, type the new folder name, and then press Enter.

- ◆ **Move.** Click **Move**, select a folder, and then click **OK**.

- ◆ **Rename.** Click **Rename**, type a new name, and then press Enter.

- ◆ **Delete.** Click **Delete**, and then click **Yes**.

④ When you're done, click the **Close** button.

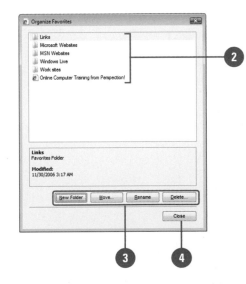

Viewing and Maintaining a History List

Sometimes you run across a great Web site and simply forget to add it to your Favorites list. With Internet Explorer there's no need to try to remember all the sites you visit. The History feature keeps track of where you've been by date, site, most visited, or order visited today. To view the History list, click the History button in the Favorites Center, and then click a day or week in the pane to expand the list of Web sites visited. Because the History list can grow to occupy a large amount of space on your hard drive, it's important to control the length of time you retain Web sites in the list. Internet Explorer deletes the History list periodically, based on the settings you specify.

View and Change the History List

1. Click the **Favorites Center** button on the toolbar.

2. Click the **History** button.

3. To change the history view, click the **History** button arrow, and then select the view option you want.

4. If view By Date, click a week or day to expand or compress the list of Web sites visited.

5. If necessary, click the folder for the Web site you want to view, and then click a page within the Web site.

6. Click off the pane or click the **Close** button.

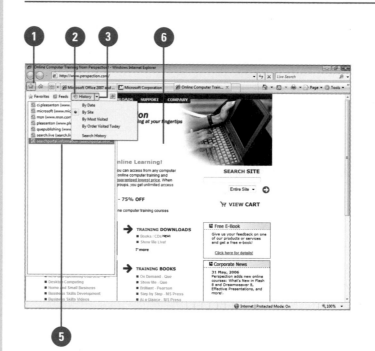

Clear the History List

1 Click the **Tools** button, and then click **Delete Browsing History**.

 ◆ You can also open this dialog by clicking Delete on the General tab in the Internet Options dialog box.

2 Click **Delete History**, and then click **Yes** to confirm the operation.

3 Click **Close**.

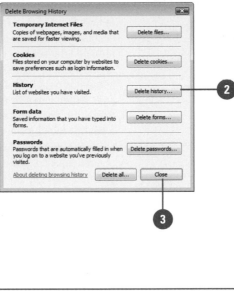

Change the Number of Days Pages Are Saved

1 Click the **Tools** button, and then click **Internet Options**.

2 Click the **General** tab.

3 In the Browsing history section, click **Settings**.

4 Specify the total number of days you want to keep links listed in history.

5 Click **OK**.

6 Click **OK**.

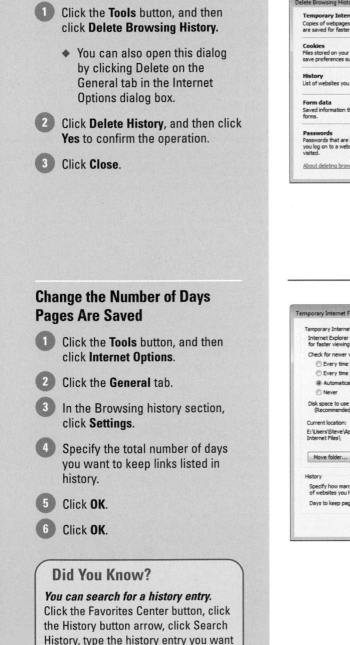

Did You Know?

You can search for a history entry.
Click the Favorites Center button, click the History button arrow, click Search History, type the history entry you want to find, and then click Search Now.

Reading and Subscribing to Feeds

A **feed** (**New!**) delivers frequently updated Web content to your browser on a continuous basis. A feed, also known as RSS (Really Simple Syndication) feed, XML feed, syndicated content, or Web feed, is usually offered on a subscription basis and typically free of charge. A feed can deliver text content in the form of news headlines or blogs, or digital content in the form of pictures, audio, and video. When audio content is delivered usually in the MP3 format, it's referred to as a pod-cast. When you visit a Web site, Internet Explorer checks for available feeds. If it discovers a feed, the Feeds button changes color and plays a sound. You can view an individual feed or subscribe to one to get content automatically. When you subscribe to a feed, Internet Explorer checks the Web site and downloads new content so you always stay updated with the latest site content. Internet Explorer manages a common feeds list, which allows other programs, such as Windows Sidebar or e-mail, to use them.

View and Subscribe to a Feed

1. Visit a Web site with a feed.

   The Feeds button changes color and plays a sound.

   TIMESAVER *You can also press Alt+J to check for feeds.*

2. Click the **Feeds** button.

   If multiple feeds are available, a list of feeds appears.

3. If available, click the feed you want to see.

   A Web page opens, displaying a lists of topics, articles, and other elements you can read and subscribe to.

4. Click the **Subscribe to this Feed** button, and then click **Subscribe to this Feed**, if necessary.

5. Type a name for the feed, and then select a folder location for the feed.

6. Click **Subscribe**.

View Subscribed Feeds

1 Click the **Favorites Center** button.

2 Click **Feeds**.

3 If needed, click a folder to display related feeds.

4 Click the feed to visit the Web site for the feed.

5 Click off the pane or click the **Close** button.

Did You Know?

What formats are feeds available in? The most common formats are RSS and Atom. All Web feed formats are based on XML. XML (Extensible Markup Language) is a platform-independent universal language that enables you to create documents in which data is stored independently of the format so you can use the data more seamlessly in other forms. XML is a markup language just like HTML. You mark up a document to define the structure, meaning, and visual appearance of the information in the document.

You can change feed settings. Click the Tools button, click Internet Options, click the Content tab, click Settings in the Feeds section, specify the options you want, and then click OK twice.

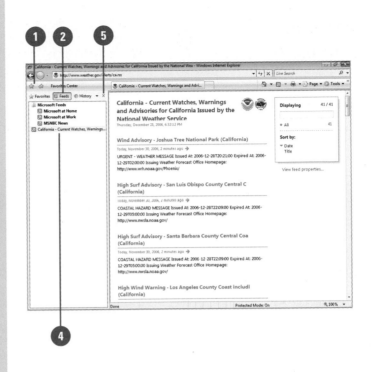

Searching the Web

You can find all kinds of information on the Web using the Instant Search box (**New!**) from the Address bar. The best way to find information is to use a search engine. A **search engine** is a program you access through a Web site and use to search through a collection of Internet information to find what you want. Many search engines are available on the Web, such as Windows Live Search, Lycos, Google, AOL, and Yahoo. When performing a search, the search engine compares keywords with words that if finds on various Internet Web sites. **Keywords** are words or phrases that best describe the information you want to retrieve. If the search engine finds your keywords in the stored database, it lists the matched sites on a Web page. These matched sites are sometimes called **hits**. The company that manages the search engine determines what information its database stores, so search results of different search engines vary.

Search the Web

1. Click in the **Search** box.

   TIMESAVER *Press Ctrl+E to go to the Search box without using the mouse.*

2. To use a specific search provider for this session only, click the **Search** box arrow, and then click the provider you want.

3. Type the information you want to find. Use specific words, eliminate common words, such as "a" or "the", and use quotation marks for specific phrases.

4. Press Enter or press Alt+Enter to display the search results in a new tab.

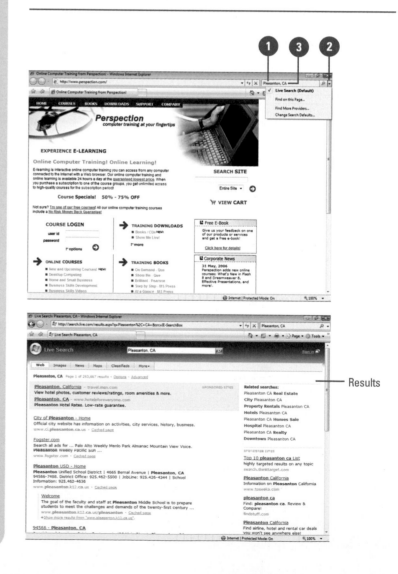

Results

Did You Know?

You can use the Address bar to search for information. In the Address bar, type **go**, **find**, or **?** followed by a space and a word or phrase, and then press Enter. To turn off or change Address bar searches, click the Tools button, click Internet Options, click the Advanced tab, select options under Search from the Address bar, and then click OK.

Change Search Providers

① Click the **Search** box arrow, and then click **Change Search Defaults**.

◆ To add more search providers, click the Search box arrow, click Find More Providers, and then follow the Web site instructions.

② Click the search provider you want to set as the default.

③ Click the button with the option you want to perform:

◆ To set as the default provider, click **Set Default**.

◆ To remove a provider, click **Remove**.

④ Click **OK**.

Did You Know?

You can add search providers discovered on Web pages. Some Web pages offer search providers (**New!**). If one does, click the Search box arrow, click Add Search Providers to open a list of providers discovered by Internet Explorer, and then follow the instructions. A discovered search provider is marked with a gold star on the Search box menu.

You can start an Internet search from the Start menu. Click the Start button, click in the Search box, type search criteria, click Search the Internet, and then perform the search (**New!**).

You can find specific text on a Web page. Click the Search box arrow, click Find (On This Page), type the text you want to find, select find options, and then click Find Next.

Available search providers

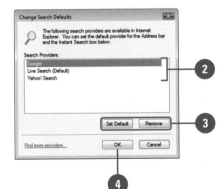

Previewing and Printing a Web Page

Web pages are designed for viewing on a computer screen, but you can also print all or part of one. Before you print, you should verify that the page looks the way you want. You save time, money, and paper by avoiding duplicate or wasteful printing. Printing now scales Web pages to fit the paper you're using. Print Preview shows you exactly how the Web page will look on the printed page, and gives you more control over margins and scaling (**New!**). This is especially helpful when you have multiple pages to print. When you are ready to print, Internet Explorer provides many options for printing Web pages. For Web pages with frames, you can print the page just as you see it, or you can elect to print a particular frame or all frames. You can even use special Page Setup options to include the date, time, or window title on the printed page. You can also choose to print the Web addresses from the links contained on a Web page.

Preview a Web Page

1. Click the **Print** button arrow, and then click **Print Preview**.

2. Use the Print Preview toolbar buttons to preview or print the Web page:

   ◆ **Print the document.**

   ◆ **Portrait** or **Landscape.** (**New!**)

   ◆ **Page Setup.** Opens the Page Setup dialog box.

   ◆ **Turn headers and footers on and off.** (**New!**)

   ◆ **View Full Width** or **View Full Page.**

   ◆ **Show Multiple Pages.**

   ◆ **Change the Print Size.**

3. Use options at the bottom of the Print Preview to specify the page to display or switch between pages.

4. Drag a margin adjust handle to fine tune the page margins (**New!**).

5. When you're done, click the **Close** button.

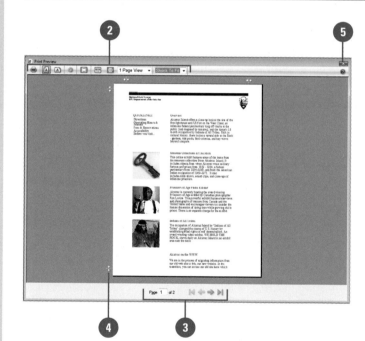

Print a Web Page

1 Click the **Print** button arrow, and then click **Print**.

TIMESAVER *To print the current page with the current print settings, click the Print button.*

2 Click a printer.

3 Specify the range of pages you want to print.

4 Specify the number of copies you want to print.

5 Click the **Options** tab.

6 If the page contains frames, select the print frames option you want.

7 Select or clear the **Print all linked documents** and **Print table of links** check boxes.

8 Click **Print**.

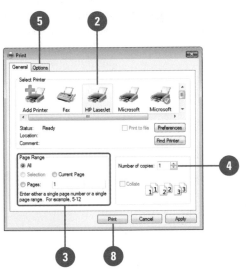

See Also

See Chapter 14 "Printing and Faxing" on page 397 for information on installing and using a printer.

See "Previewing and Printing a Document" on page 37 for more information on using the Preview window and the Print dialog box.

For Your Information

Setting Up the Page Format

When you print a Web page, you can use the Page Setup dialog box to control the printing of text and graphics on a page. To open the Page Setup dialog box, click the Print button arrow, and then click Page Setup. The Page Setup dialog box specifies the printer properties for page size, orientation, and paper source; in most cases, you won't want to change them. From the Page Setup dialog box, you can also change header and footer information. In the Headers and Footers text boxes, you can type text to appear as a header and footer of a Web page you print. In these text boxes, you can also use variables to substitute information about the current page, and you can combine text and codes. For example, if you type **Page &p of &P** in the Header text box, the current page number and the total number of pages print at the top of each printed page. Check Internet Explorer Help for a complete list of header and footer codes.

Saving Pictures or Text from a Web Page

If you find information on a Web page that you want to save for future reference or share with others, you can copy and paste it to another document or save it on your computer. When you copy information from a Web page, make sure you're not violating any copyright laws.

Save a Picture from a Web Page

1. Open the Web page with the picture you want to save.

2. Point to the picture you want to save to display a toolbar on the graphic, and then click the **Save** button.

    If the toolbar doesn't appear, right-click the picture, and then click **Save Picture As**.

3. Select the drive and folder in which you want to save the file.

4. Type a name for the file, or use the suggested name.

5. To change the format of a file, click the **Save as type** arrow, and then click a file format.

6. Click **Save**.

Did You Know?

You can save a page or picture without opening it. Right-click the link for the item you want to save, and then click Save Target As.

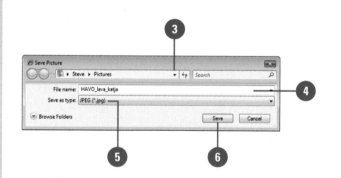

Set a Picture from a Web Page as the Background Picture

1. Open the Web page with the picture you want to use.

2. Right-click the picture, and then click **Set As Wallpaper** or **Set As Background**.

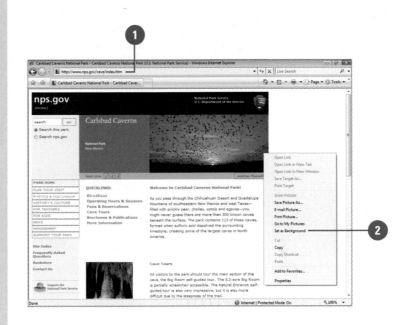

Copy Text from a Web Page

1. Open the Web page with the text you want to copy.

2. Select the text you want to copy.

    TROUBLE? *The I-beam cursor may or may not appear. You can still select the text.*

3. Right-click the selected text, and then click **Copy**, or press Ctrl+C.

4. Switch to where you want to paste the text.

5. Click the **Edit** menu, and then click **Paste**, or press Ctrl+V.

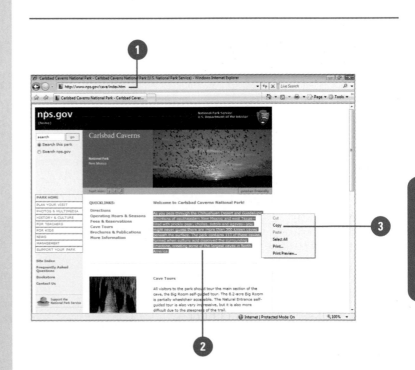
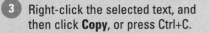

Did You Know?

You can create a desktop shortcut to the current Web page. Right-click in the Web page, click Create Shortcut, and then click OK.

Downloading Files from the Web

There are thousands of sites on the Internet offering all sorts of files you can download to your computer, from trailers to the latest game demos. You can download files from any Web site by finding the file you want, right-clicking the link, and telling Internet Explorer where you want to save the file. Some Web sites are designed with specific links to make it easier to download files. When you click a download link, a Security Warning dialog box opens, asking you to run or don't run the file from the Internet or save the file to your computer. Internet Explorer checks to see whether there are any irregularities with the file or a potential for harm based on the file type, and provides strong warning and guidance to help you understand more about the file you are downloading.

Download a File from a Web Page

1 Open the Web page from which you want to download a file.

2 Click the download link, and then click **Save**, or right-click the link pointing to the actual file, and then click **Save Target As**.

3 Select the folder in which you want to save the file.

4 Type a name for the file, or use the suggested name.

5 Click **Save**.

The File Download dialog box displays the estimated time to download the file, along with the estimated transfer time.

6 When the download is complete, click **Open** or **Run** to open or run the file, or click **Close**.

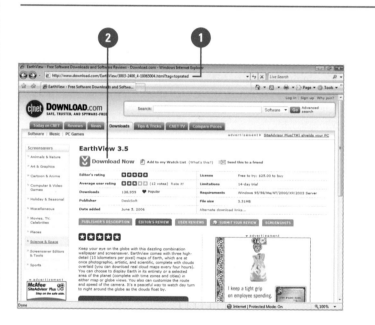

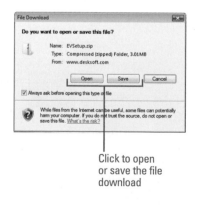

Click to open or save the file download

> ### Did You Know?
>
> *You can access a site with lots of files to download.* Try these sites to find plenty of files to download: *http://www.download.com* and *http://www.shareware.com*. Just beware of viruses which can come from downloaded files off the Internet.

Downloading Files from an FTP Site

Sometimes you'll need to connect directly to a File Transfer Protocol (FTP) site to download or transfer a file to a remote computer. Internet Explorer allows you to easily access and download files from any FTP site, public or private. Public FTP sites allow you to access files without requiring that you have an account on the server. Private FTP sites expect you to enter your user name and password in order to see the folders and files. When you are connected to an FTP site, Internet Explorer's view of the files is the same as looking at a folder on your local hard disk. Within this view you can drag onto your desktop or right-click to copy the file in a particular folder on your computer.

Download a File from an FTP Site

1 In the Address bar, type the address for the FTP site, and then press Enter.

2 If necessary, type your user name and password, and then click **Log On**.

> **IMPORTANT** *Before you download files, make sure your antivirus software is up-to-date.*

3 Click the **Page** button, and then click **Open FTP Site in Windows Explorer**.

4 Right-click the file or folder you want to download, click **Copy To Folder**, select a location, and then click **OK**.

> **TIMESAVER** *You can select the items you want to download, and then use the Copy and Paste commands. Select the files, press Ctrl+C, display the destination folder, and then press Ctrl+V.*

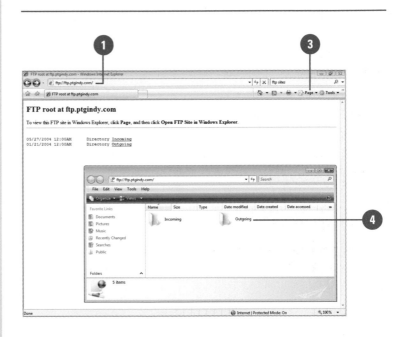

Saving a Web Page

You can save a Web page you want to view offline even if you don't need to share it with others or update its content, such as a published article whose content will not change. There are several ways you can save the Web page, from saving just the text to saving all of the graphics and text needed to display that page as it appears on the Web. When you save a complete Web page, Internet Explorer saves all the graphic and text elements in a folder. If you need to send a Web page to a friend or co-worker, you can save all the elements of the Web page in a single file to make the process easier.

Save a Web Page

1 Open the Web page you want to save.

2 Click the **Page** button arrow, and then click **Save As**.

3 Select the drive and folder in which you want to save the file.

4 Type a name for the file, or use the suggested name.

5 Click the **Save as type** arrow, and then click one of the following:

◆ **Web Page, complete** to save the formatted text and layout with all the linked information, such as pictures, in a folder.

◆ **Web Archive, single file** to save all the elements of the Web page in a single file.

◆ **Web Page, HTML only** to save the formatted text and layout without the linked information.

◆ **Text File** to save only the text.

6 Click **Save**.

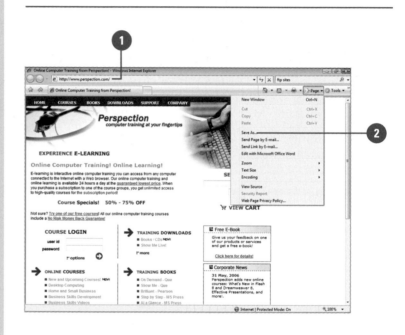

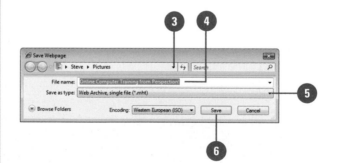

See Also

See "Saving and Closing a Document" on page 38 for more information on using the Save As dialog box.

Sending a Page or Link by E-mail

If you come across a Web page that you want to share with a friend or co-worker, you can send the page or a link to the page directly from Internet Explorer using your default E-mail program. When you use the Send Page by E-mail and Send Link by E-mail commands on the Page button, Internet Explorer automatically opens your default E-mail program and creates a new message with the Web page or link.

Send a Page or Link by E-mail

1. Open the Web page with the picture you want to send.

2. Click the **Page** button arrow, and then click **Send Page by E-mail** or **Send Link by E-mail**.

   Internet Explorer opens your mail program, and creates a new message.

3. Address and send the message.

Searching for Research Material

With the Research task pane (**New!**), you can access data sources and insert research material right into your text without leaving Internet Explorer. The Research task pane can help you access electronic dictionaries, thesauruses, research sites, and proprietary company information. You can select one reference source or search in all reference books. This research pane allows you to find information and quickly and easily incorporate it into your work. To open the Research task pane, click the Research button on the toolbar. If the button is not visible, click the double-arrow to the right first, and then the button should appear.

Using Another Web Browser

Windows Vista comes with Internet Explorer as the default Web browser. If you prefer to use another browser, you can remove Internet Explorer from your computer using the Programs and Features utility in the Control Panel, install another browser, and set it as your default Internet program on the left column of the Start menu.

Use Another Web Browser

1. If you want, remove Internet Explorer using the Programs and Features utility in the Control Panel.

2. Install another browser according to the manufacturer instructions.

3. Right-click the **Start** button, and then click **Properties**.

4. Click **Customize**.

5. Click the **Internet link** arrow, and then select your browser.

6. Click **OK**, and then click **OK** again.

Did You Know?

You can turn off the alert asking to make Internet Explorer the default. In Internet Options, click the Programs tab, clear the Tell me if Internet Explorer is not the default web browser check box, and then click OK.

You can use the same procedure to use another e-mail program. Windows Vista also comes with Windows Mail as the default e-mail program. You can use the same basic procedure to use another e-mail program.

See Also

See "Adding or Removing Windows Components" on page 437 for information on adding or removing Windows components.

For Your Information

Resetting Internet Explorer Settings

If you installed another Web browser after installing Internet Explorer, some of your Internet Explorer settings may have changed. You can reset your Internet Explorer settings to their original defaults, including your home page and search pages, and choice of default browser, without changing your other browser's settings. To reset Internet Explorer settings, click the Tools button, click Internet Options, click the Advanced tab, click Reset, read the dialog box carefully, and then click Reset again.

Exchanging Messages and Information

Introduction

If you're like many people today who are using the Internet to communicate with friends and business associates, you probably have piles of information (names, e-mail addresses, phone numbers, etc.) that you need often. Unless this information is in one convenient place, and can be accessed immediately, the information becomes ineffective and you become unproductive. Microsoft Windows Mail (the successor to Outlook Express) solves these problems by integrating management and organization tools into one simple system. Windows Vista includes Microsoft Windows Mail, a powerful program for managing **electronic mail** (known as e-mail), and contact information like names, and e-mail addresses.

Using Windows Mail with an Internet connection allows you to accomplish several tasks:

◆ Create and send e-mail messages

◆ Manage multiple e-mail accounts

◆ Use the Windows Contacts (**New!**) to store and retrieve e-mail addresses

◆ Create stationery or add a personal signature to your e-mail messages

◆ Attach a file to an e-mail message

◆ Set junk e-mail options and mark e-mail messages as block or safe

◆ Join any number of newsgroups, which are collections of e-mail messages on related topics

◆ Use the Windows Calendar (**New!**) to make and manage appointments and tasks

◆ Send invitations to meeting participants from within Windows Meeting Space (**New!**)

Starting Windows Mail

Whether you want to exchange e-mail with colleagues and friends or join newsgroups to trade ideas and information, Windows Mail provides you with the tools you need. When you install Windows Vista, a menu item for Windows Mail appears in the left column of the Start menu and the All Programs submenu. The first time you start Windows Mail, you need to set up an e-mail account. The Connect to the Internet wizard walks you through the process. You can set Windows Mail as your default e-mail program so that whenever you click an e-mail link on a Web page or choose the mail command in your Web browser, Windows Mail opens. You can also set Windows Mail as your default news reader so that when you click a newsgroup link on a Web page or choose the news reader command in your Web browser, Windows Mail opens.

Start Windows Mail

1. Click the **Start** button.

2. Click **Windows Mail**.

   TROUBLE? *If Windows Mail doesn't appear in the left column of the Start menu, it's available on the All Programs submenu.*

   If the Connect to the Internet wizard opens, follow the step-by-step instructions to set up your e-mail account.

See Also

See "Setting Up an Account" on page 168 for information on creating an e-mail account.

166

Set Options to Start Windows Mail from Your Web Browser

1. Click the **Start** button, and then click **Control Panel**.

2. Double-click the **Default Programs** icon.

3. Click **Set your default programs**.

4. Click **Windows Mail** or **Windows Mail (News)**.

5. Click **Set this program as default**.

6. Click **OK**.

7. Click the **Close** button.

Did You Know?

You can get Help in Windows Mail. If you want to connect to the Internet to get mail or learn how to use Windows Mail features, you can get help from several different sources. To get Windows Mail Help, you can use the Help system that comes with the program, or you can view Windows Mail Web sites on the Internet. To open Windows Mail Help, click the Help menu, and then click View Help. To browse through a list of questions and answers on a discussion Web site, click the Help menu, and then click Questions & Answers from Communities. Your browser starts and displays the Windows Mail discussion Web site.

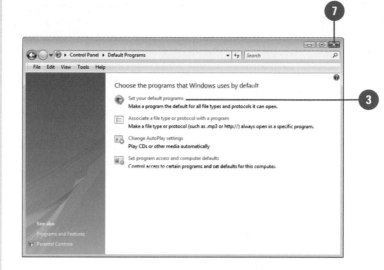

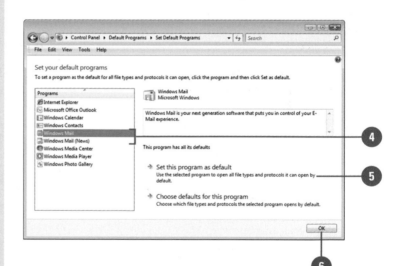

Setting Up an Account

Before you can set up an e-mail account, you need your account name, password, e-mail server type, and the names of your incoming and outgoing e-mail servers from your ISP or network administrator. The Connect to the Internet wizard helps you connect to one or more e-mail servers. Windows Mail allows you to send and retrieve e-mail messages from different types of e-mail servers, which are the locations where your e-mail is stored before you access it. Windows Mail supports three types of accounts: mail, newsgroups, and directory services. A **newsgroup** is an electronic forum where people with a common interest can share ideas, ask and answer questions, and comment on and discuss any subject. **Directory services** are online address books that are typically provided by large organizations. You can set up multiple accounts in Windows Mail.

Set Up an Account

1. Click the **Tools** menu, click **Accounts**, and then click **Add**.

   ◆ If Windows Mail starts for the first time, and the Connect to the Internet wizard begins.

2. If prompted, click **E-mail Account**, and then click **Next** to continue.

   ◆ You can also set up an account for a newsgroup or Directory Service; the wizard steps vary depending on the account type.

   The Connect to the Internet wizard begins.

3. Type your name, and then click **Next** to continue.

4. Enter your e-mail address, and then click **Next** to continue.

5. Click the **Mail Server** arrow, and then select the incoming mail server you want to use.

6. Enter the name of the incoming mail server.

7. Enter the name of the outgoing mail server, and then click **Next** to continue.

Your Name

When you send e-mail, your name will appear in the From field of the outgoing message. Type your name as you would like it to appear.

Display name: [   ]

For example: John Smith

Where can I find my e-mail account information?

Internet E-mail Address

Your e-mail address is the address other people use to send e-mail messages to you.

E-mail address: [   ]

For example: someone@microsoft.com

Set up e-mail servers

Incoming e-mail server type:

[POP3   ▾]

Incoming mail (POP3 or IMAP) server:

[   ]

Outgoing e-mail server (SMTP) name:

[   ]

☐ Outgoing server requires authentication

Where can I find my e-mail server information?

[Next] [Cancel]

8 Enter your account name and a password, and then click **Next** continue.

9 Click **Finish**.

10 If Windows Mail detect previously installed e-mail software, select an the option you want, and follow the import instructions.

Internet Mail Logon

Type the account name and password your Internet service provider has given you.

E-mail username:

Password:

☑ Remember password

8

Windows Mail Import

Import Messages

Windows Mail has detected previously installed e-mail software. You can choose to have Windows Mail import your messages, so you can use them with Windows Mail.

⦿ Import from:

Microsoft Exchange or Outlook or Windows Messaging

○ Do not import at this time

< Back   Next >   Cancel

10

Frequently Asked Questions

How Do I Choose an E-mail Server?

Windows Mail supports two types of incoming e-mail servers: **POP3** (Post Office Protocol), and **IMAP** (Internet Message Access Protocol). Windows Mail doesn't support **HTTP** (Hypertext Transfer Protocol). A protocol is a set of rules and standards that control the transmission of content, format, sequencing, and error management for information over the Internet or network much like rules of the road govern the way you drive. POP3 servers allow you to access e-mail messages from a single Inbox folder, while IMAP servers allow you to access multiple folders. HTTP servers are used on Web sites, such as Windows Live Mail (formerly Hotmail), and allow you to send and receive e-mail messages on a Web site. If you need HTTP support, you can use Windows Live Mail (which you can download from the Microsoft Web site) instead of Windows Mail with Windows Vista. When you use POP3 or IMAP e-mail servers, you also need to provide an outgoing e-mail server. **SMTP** (Simple Mail Transfer Protocol) is generally used to send messages between e-mail servers.

Viewing the Windows Mail Window

Menu bar
The Menu bar gives you access to all Windows Mail commands.

Toolbar
The Toolbar contains buttons for the most commonly used commands you need to work with mail messages.

Folders list
The Folders list contains all the folders in which Windows Mail stores e-mail messages.

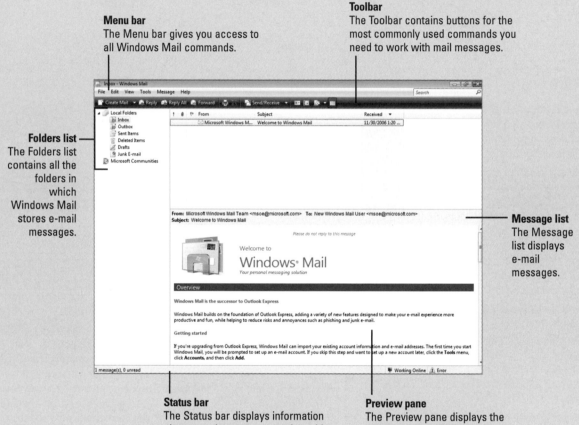

Message list
The Message list displays e-mail messages.

Status bar
The Status bar displays information about your Internet connection with a mail or newsgroup server.

Preview pane
The Preview pane displays the contents of the current message selected in the Message list.

Frequently Asked Questions

How Do You Customize The Layout?

You can use the Layout command on the View menu to customize the Windows Mail window to suit your needs. You can show or hide different parts of the window, customize the Preview pane display, and customize the toolbar.

Importing and Exporting Information ▶

Windows Mail can import contacts, mail messages, and account settings from many of the most popular e-mail programs. You can also export your messages or Windows Contacts information from Windows Mail to work with other programs.

Import an Windows Contacts

1. Click the **File** menu, point to **Import**, and then click **Windows Contacts**.

2. Click an import file type. CSV is a common text file type.

3. Click **Import**.

4. Follow the additional instructions, and then click **OK**.

5. Click **Close**.

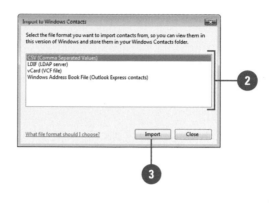

Export Your Windows Contacts

1. Click the **File** menu, point to **Export**, and then click **Windows Contacts**.

2. Click an export file type. CSV is a common text file type.

3. Click **Export**.

4. Type a file name, and then click **Next** to continue.

5. Select the fields for exporting.

6. Click **Finish**.

7. Click **OK**, and then click **Close**.

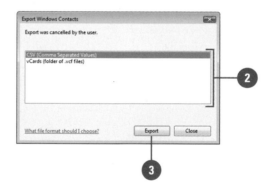

Did You Know?

You can import mail messages from another e-mail program. Click the File menu, point to Import, and then click Messages. Select the e-mail program, and then follow the wizard instructions to import the e-mail messages.

Adding a Contact to Windows Contacts

A **contact** is a person or company that you communicate with. One contact can often have several mailing addresses, phone numbers, or e-mail addresses. You can store this information in Windows Contacts (**New!**) along with other detailed information, such as job title, cell phone number, and Web page addresses. You can organize your contacts into folders or into **contact groups**, which are groups of related people with whom you communicate regularly.

Add or Edit a Contact

1. Click the **Contacts** button on the toolbar.

   ◆ You can also click the Start button, point to All Programs, and then click Windows Contacts.

2. Click the **New Contact** button on the toolbar to create a new contact or select a contact, and then click **Edit** on the toolbar to edit one.

3. Enter the contact's name.

4. Enter the e-mail address.

5. Click **Add**.

6. Click the other available tabs to enter additional information.

7. Click **OK**.

8. Click the **Close** button.

Did You Know?

You can add an address from an e-mail message. In the Inbox, open the message with the e-mail address you want, right-click the address, and then click Add Sender to Contacts.

You can automatically add a reply address to Windows Contacts. Click the Tools menu, click Options, click the Send tab, select the Automatically put people I reply to in my Contacts list check box, and then click OK.

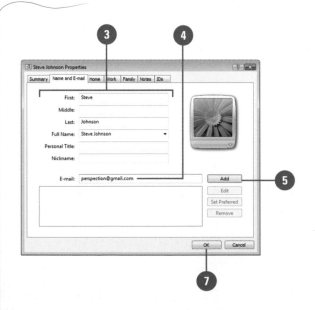

Create a Contact Group

1. Click the **Contacts** button on the toolbar.

2. Click the **New Contact Group** button on the toolbar.

3. Type a name for the new group.

4. Click **Add to Contact Group** to display your current list of contacts.

5. Click each member in the list of contacts you want to add. Press Ctrl to select multiple contacts.

6. Click **Add**.

   Repeat this step to add more contacts.

7. To add a contact just to the group and not to your Contacts list, type the contact and e-mail address, and then click **Create for Group Only**.

8. To remove a contact from the group, click the contact, and then click **Remove Selected Contacts**.

9. Click **OK**.

10. When you're done, click the **Close** button.

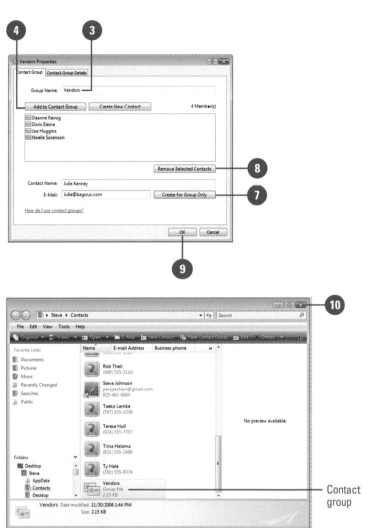

Contact group

Did You Know?

You can sort your Windows Contacts. In Windows Contacts, point to the heading by which you want to sort, click the arrow, and then click Sort. You can switch the sorting method from ascending to descending by clicking the same column heading again.

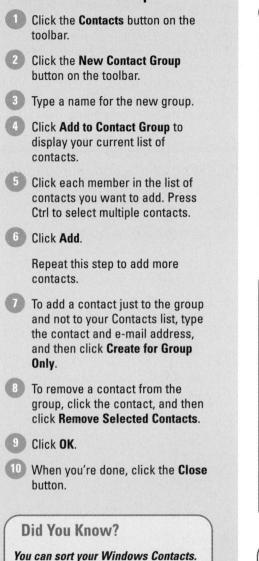

For Your Information

Printing Contacts from Windows Contacts

You can print your contact information in a variety of formats, such as Memo, Business Card, and Phone List. The Memo style prints all the information you have for a contact with descriptive titles. The Business Card style prints the contact information without descriptive titles. The Phone List style prints all the phone numbers for a contact or for all your contacts. To print contact information, open Windows Contacts, select the contacts you want to print, click Print on the toolbar, select a print range, print style, and the number of copies you want to print, and then click Print in the Print dialog box.

Composing and Sending E-mail

E-mail is becoming the primary form of written communication for many people. E-mail messages follow a standard memo format, with fields for the sender, recipient, date, and subject of the message. To send an e-mail, you need to enter the recipient's e-mail address, type a subject, then type the message itself. For a personal touch, you can also create an e-mail message with stationery designs. You can send the same e-mail to more than one individual, to a contact group, or to a combination of individuals and groups. Before you send the e-mail, you can set a priority flag (high, normal, or low) to convey the message's importance.

Compose and Send an E-mail

1. Click the **Create Mail** button on the toolbar.

   ◆ To create an e-mail with stationery, click the Create Mail button arrow, then click a stationery.

2. Click the **To** button to select contacts.

   TIMESAVER *Type the recipient's name in the To box.*

3. Click a recipient or group.

4. Click one of the following:

   ◆ The **To** button if you want the recipient to receive the message and to see the addresses in the To and Cc fields.

   ◆ The **Cc** button if you want the recipient to receive a copy of the message and to see the addresses in the To and Cc fields.

   ◆ The **Bcc** button if you want the recipient to receive a copy of the message but not be listed as a recipient on any other copy of the message.

5. Click **OK**.

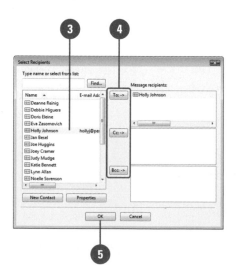

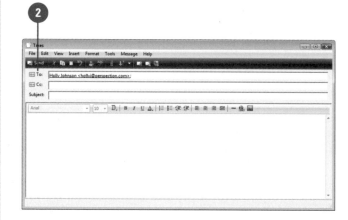

6 Click in the **Subject** box, and then enter a brief description of your message.

7 Click in the **message** box, and then type the text of your message.

8 If you want, use the commands on the Formatting toolbar to format your message.

9 If you want, click the **Set Priority** button arrow on the toolbar, and then select a priority level.

10 To encrypt or digitally sign a message, click the **Encrypt** or **Digitally Sign** button on the toolbar.

11 Click the **Send** button on the toolbar. Or click the **File** menu, click **Send Later**, and then click **OK** to confirm that the message has been placed in your Outbox folder.

12 If you chose Send Later, click the **Send/Receive** button on the toolbar to contact the mail server and deliver your message.

> **TIMESAVER** *Press Ctrl+M to send and receive e-mail for all accounts.*

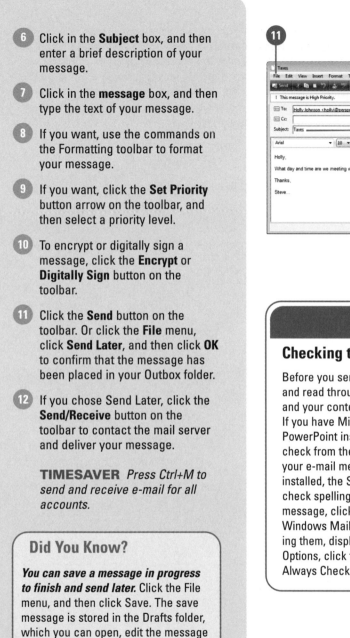

Did You Know?

You can save a message in progress to finish and send later. Click the File menu, and then click Save. The save message is stored in the Drafts folder, which you can open, edit the message and send later.

You can send and receive e-mail from a specific account. Click the Send/Receive button arrow, and then click the account you want.

For Your Information

Checking the Spelling in E-mail

Before you send an e-mail message, you should spell check the text and read through the content to make sure your spelling is accurate and your content conveys the message you want to the recipient(s). If you have Microsoft Word, Microsoft Excel, or Microsoft PowerPoint installed on your computer, Windows Mail uses the spell check from the Microsoft Office program to check the spelling of your e-mail messages. If you do not have one of these programs installed, the Spelling command is not available, and you need to check spelling manually. To start the spell check, type an e-mail message, click the Tools menu, and then click Spelling. To have Windows Mail spell check all of your e-mail messages before sending them, display the Outlook window, click the Tools menu, click Options, click the Spelling tab in the Options dialog box, select the Always Check Spelling Before Sending check box, and then click OK.

Creating E-mail Stationery

If you're tired of the typical bland, unexciting look of e-mail, Windows Mail has the answer—Windows Mail stationery. This feature allows you to create e-mail messages with their own colorful background and font styles. You can also customize your messages with a signature or by attaching your business card. A **signature** is any file, text file with your signature, or photo of yourself that you choose. Several stationery styles are included with Windows Mail.

Create a Signature

1. Click the **Tools** menu, and then click **Options**.

2. Click the **Signatures** tab.

3. Click **New** to create a new signature.

4. Type the information for the signature. If available, select the file that contains your signature.

5. To enter more than one signature, repeat steps 3 and 4.

6. Select the signature you want to use most of the time, and then click **Set as Default**.

7. If you have multiple accounts, click **Advanced**, select the check boxes for the accounts you want to use, and then click **OK**.

8. If you want, select the **Add signatures to all outgoing messages** check box, or select the **Don't add signatures to Replies and Forwards** check box.

9. Click **OK**.

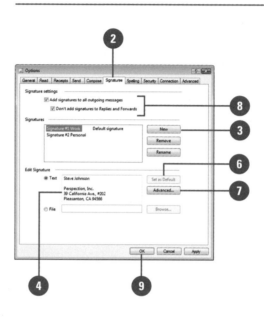

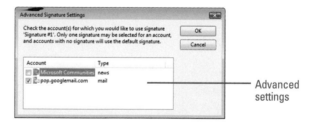

Advanced settings

Did You Know?

You can add your signature to e-mail quickly. In an e-mail message, click where you want the signature, click the Insert menu, and then click Signature. If you have more than one signature, point to Signature, and then click the signature you want to use.

Create Stationery Using the Stationery Setup Wizard

1 Click the **Tools** menu, and then click **Options**.

2 Click the **Compose** tab.

3 Click **Create New**, and then click **Next** to begin the Stationery Setup Wizard.

4 Select a picture and color, and then click **Next**.

5 Choose the font, font size, and color, and then click **Next**.

6 Choose the left and top margin, and then click **Next**.

7 Type a name for your stationery, and then click **Finish**.

8 Select the **Mail** check box to always include stationery with your e-mail messages.

9 Click **Select** to choose the standard stationery, and then click **OK**.

10 Click **OK**.

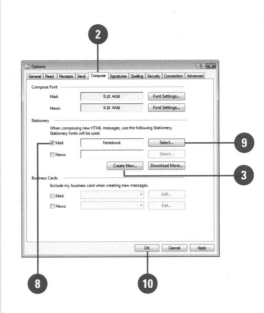

Did You Know?

You can create a message using other or new stationery. Click the New Mail button arrow on the toolbar, and then select a stationery, or click Select Stationery to select from other choices or to create a new one.

You can select a stationery for every new message. Click the Tools menu, click Options, click the Compose tab, select the Mail check box, click Select, click a stationery file, click OK, click the Send tab, click the HTML option, and then click OK.

Reading and Replying to E-mail

You can receive e-mail anytime—even when your computer is turned off. You can retrieve your e-mail manually or set Windows Mail to do so automatically. When you start Windows Mail, the program checks for new e-mail. It continues to check periodically while the program is open. New messages appear in boldface in the Inbox along with any messages you haven't moved or deleted. Message flags may appear next to a message, which indicate a certain priority, the need for follow up, or an attachment. Windows Mail blocks images and other potentially harmful content from automatically downloading in an e-mail message from unknown people. Blocked items are replaced with a red "x". You can use the Information Bar or modify the e-mail to view the blocked content. You can respond to a message in two ways: reply to it, which creates a new message addressed to the sender(s) and other recipients; or forward it, which creates a new message you can send to someone else. In either case, the original message appears in the response.

Open and Read an E-mail

1. Click the **Inbox** icon in the folder list for the mail account you want.

2. Open an e-mail message.

   ◆ Click an e-mail message to read it in the Preview pane.

   ◆ Double-click an e-mail message or press Enter for a selected message to open it in its own window.

3. To download blocked pictures and other content, click the Information Bar at the top of the message.

4. Click the **Previous** or **Next** button on the Message toolbar to read additional e-mail messages.

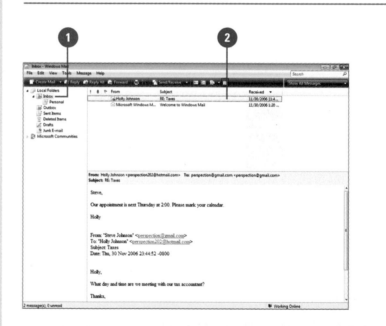

See Also

See "Avoiding Viruses and Other Harmful Attacks" on page 330 for information on viruses.

See "Protecting Against E-mail Attacks" on page 345 for information on how to protect your computer against viruses from an e-mail.

For Your Information

Reading E-mail in Plain Text To Avoid Viruses

If you're unsure of the source of an e-mail, yet still want to protect your computer from viruses, you can securely view the e-mail in plain text, instead of HTML which can contain potentially harmful content, such as viruses and worms. To read all e-mail in plain text, click the Tools menu, click Options, click the Read tab, select the Read All Messages In Plain Text check box, then click OK.

Reply to an E-mail

1. Open the e-mail message you want to reply to.

2. Click the **Reply** button to respond to the sender only, or click the **Reply All** button to respond to the sender and to all other recipients.

   TIMESAVER *Press Ctrl+R to reply to the message author.*

3. Add or delete names from the To or the Cc box.

4. Type your message.

5. Attach any files to send.

6. Click the **Send** button on the toolbar.

Forward an E-mail

1. Open the e-mail message you want to forward.

2. Click the **Forward** button on the toolbar.

3. Type the name(s) of the recipient(s), or click the **To** button, and then select the recipient(s).

4. Type your message.

5. Attach any files to send.

6. Click the **Send** button on the toolbar.

Did You Know?

Attachments aren't sent on replies.
When you reply to a message that had an attachment, the attachment isn't returned to the original sender. You can forward the message to the original sender if you need to send the attachment back.

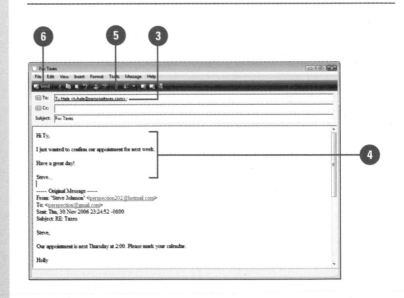

Sending and Retrieving a File

You can use e-mail to easily share a file, such as a picture or a document by attaching it to an e-mail. Upon receiving the e-mail, the recipient can open the file in the program that created it or save it. Make sure you know and trust the sender before you open it, because it might contain a virus or other security threat. It's important to keep your antivirus software up-to-date. The Attachment Manager provides security information to help you understand more about the file you are downloading. If an attachment is considered safe, Windows Mail makes it completely available to you. Examples of safe attachments are text files (.txt) and graphic files, such as JPEGs (.jpg) and GIFs (.gif). If an attachment is potentially unsafe, such as an executable program (.exe), screensavers (.scr) or script files (including .vbs), Windows Mail displays a notice on the Information Bar and blocks it so you will not be able to open it without taking explicit action. If Windows Mail can't determine the safety of an attachment, it displays a security warning (when you try to move, save, open, or print the file) with information about the file.

Send a File in an E-mail

1. Compose a new message or reply to an existing message.

   IMPORTANT *Some ISPs have trouble sending attachments over 3 MB; check with your ISP.*

2. Click the **Attach File** button on the toolbar.

3. Select the drive and folder that contains the file you want to attach.

4. Click to select the file.

5. Click **Open**.

6. Click the **Send** button on the toolbar.

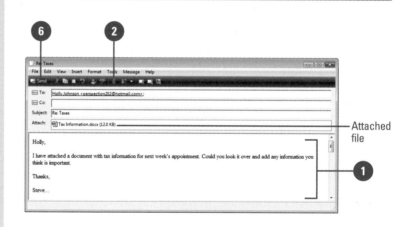

Attached file

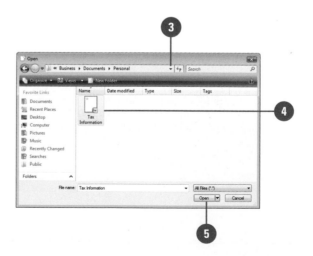

Open a File in an E-mail

1. Select the message with the attached file.

   IMPORTANT *If you're not sure of the source of an attachment, don't open it, because it might contain a virus or worm. Be sure to use anti-virus software.*

2. Click the **Attachment** icon, and then click the file name.

3. Click **Open**.

See Also

See "Avoiding Viruses and Other Harmful Attacks" on page 330 for information on how to avoid getting a virus and other harmful threats.

See "Protecting Against E-mail Attacks" on page 345 for information on how to avoid getting a virus from an attached file in an e-mail.

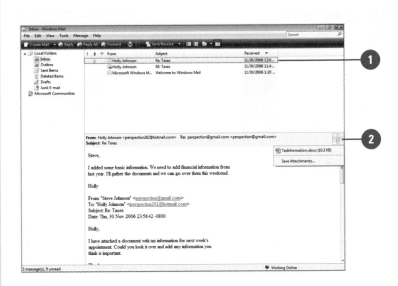

Save Files in an E-mail

1. Select the message with the attached file.

2. Click the **Attachment** icon, and then click **Save Attachments**.

3. Select the attached file you want to save or click **Select All** to select all the attached files.

4. Click **Browse**, select the drive and folder where you want to save the file, and then click **Open**.

5. Click **Save**.

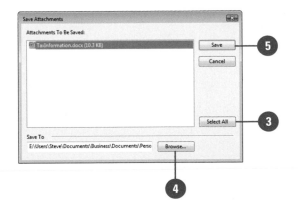

Managing E-mail

A common problem with using e-mail is an overcrowded Inbox. To keep your Inbox organized, you should move messages you want to save to other folders and subfolders, delete messages you no longer want, and create new folders as you need them. Storing incoming messages in other folders and deleting unwanted messages make it easier to see the new messages you receive and to keep track of important messages. If you can't find a message, you can use the Search box (**New!**) to quickly find it. If you have not finished composing a message, you can save it in the Drafts folder and work on it later.

Create a New Folder

1. Click the **File** menu, point to **New**, and then click **New Folder**.

2. Type a name for the new folder.

3. Click the folder in which you want to place the new folder.

   ◆ Click Local Folders to place the folder in the folder list.

   ◆ Click one of the other folders in the list to make the new folder a subfolder.

4. Click **OK**.

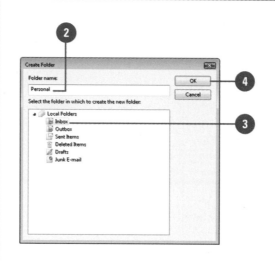

Organize E-mail in Folders

1. Select the e-mail message you want to move. If necessary, press and hold the Ctrl key, and click to select multiple e-mail messages.

2. Drag the e-mail message(s) to the new folder.

Did You Know?

You can sort messages quickly.
To sort messages by sender, subject, date, priority or flag, click a header in the Preview pane.

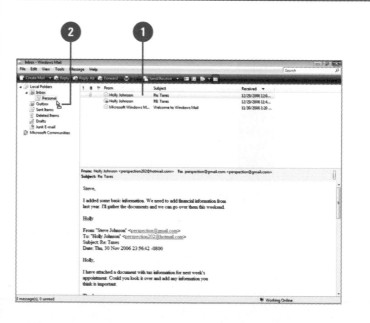

Find an E-mail or News Message

 Click in the **Search** box.

2 Type a word or part of a word in the message.

   As you type, the message list narrows and displays messages that match the search text.

3 When you see the message you want, double-click the message to open it.

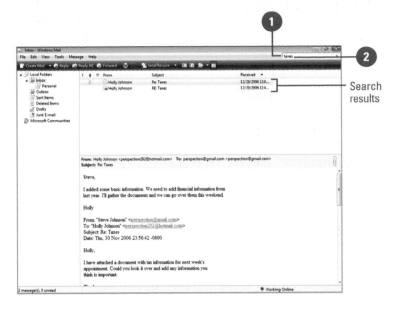

Search results

Did You Know?

You can flag an important message that need attention later. Select the e-mail message, click the Message menu, and then click Flag Message.

Work on a Draft E-mail

1 Open a new or a reply to an existing e-mail message, and then type a message.

2 Click the **File** menu, and then click **Save**, and then click **OK**.

3 Close the e-mail message.

4 Click the **Drafts** folder in the folder list.

5 Double-click the e-mail message to view it.

6 When you're done with the message, click the **Send** button.

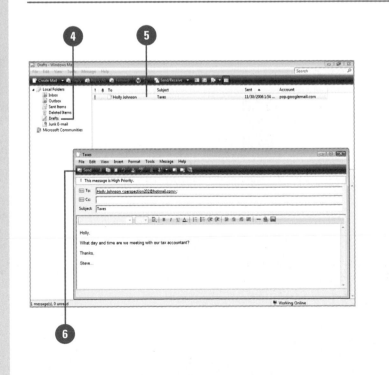

Deleting E-mail

When you delete an e-mail message, Windows Mail simply moves it into the Deleted Items folder. If you want to recover a deleted message, you just have to retrieve it from the Deleted Items folder. To get rid of a message permanently, you need to open the Deleted Items folder, select the message, and click Delete. Windows Mail automatically places e-mail messages in the Sent Items folder every time you send them. You will want to periodically open the Sent Items folder and delete messages so your mail account doesn't get too large. You can also use maintenance options to help you clean up.

Delete Unwanted E-mail

1. Click a folder icon in the folder list with the e-mail you want to delete.

2. Click the e-mail you want to delete.

3. Click the **Delete** button on the toolbar.

   TIMESAVER *Press Delete or Ctrl+D to delete the selected message(s).*

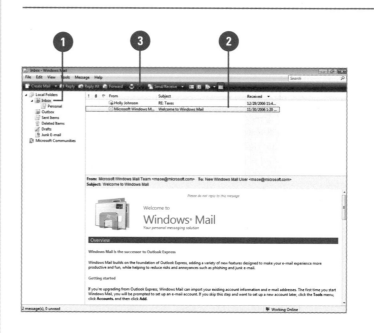

Recover E-mail from the Deleted Items Folder

1. Click the **Deleted Items** folder in the folder list to open the folder.

2. Select the e-mail message you want to retrieve.

3. Drag the e-mail message to another folder.

Change E-mail Maintenance Options

1. Click the **Tools** menu, and then click **Options**.

2. Click the **Advanced** tab.

3. Click **Maintenance**.

4. Select the maintenance options you want.

   ◆ Delete messages on exit or after a certain number of days.

   ◆ Compact messages to save space.

5. Click **Close**.

Setting Junk E-mail Options

Junk e-mail can seem like a never ending battle. It keeps piling up. Windows Mail provides the Junk E-mail Options dialog box to help you reduce the amount of junk e-mail you receive. You can set a junk e-mail protection level that makes sense to you, from no filtering to only the safe senders list. If you receive junk e-mail from international domains or languages, you can quickly and easily block them. E-mail has become the new way to commit fraud using spoof sites and addresses. These types of e-mail are called phishing. You can set options in Windows Mail that can help protect you again potential phishing attacks.

Change Junk E-mail Options

① Click the **Tools** menu, and then click **Junk E-mail Options**.

② Click the **Options** tab.

③ Click the level of junk e-mail protection option you want.

④ Select or clear the **Permanently delete suspected junk e-mail instead of moving it to the junk E-mail folder** check box.

IMPORTANT *You should only select this option if you selected the Low option above to avoid deleting regular e-mail.*

⑤ Click **OK**.

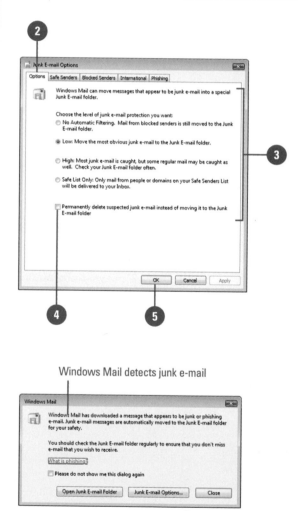

Windows Mail detects junk e-mail

Guard Against Phishing

1. Click the **Tools** menu, and then click **Junk E-mail Options**.

2. Click the **Phishing** tab.

3. Select the **Protect my Inbox from messages with potential Phishing links** check box.

4. Select the **Move phishing E-mail to the Junk Mail folder** check box.

5. Click **OK**.

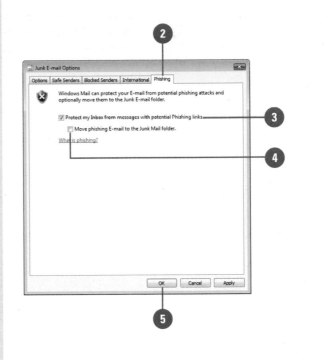

Block International Junk E-mail

1. Click the **Tools** menu, and then click **Junk E-mail Options**.

2. Click the **International** tab.

3. Click **Blocked Top-Level Domain List**.

4. Select the individual check boxes with the domains you want to block or click **Select All**.

5. Click **OK**.

6. Click **OK**.

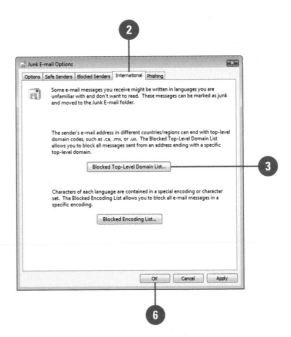

Marking an E-mail Blocked or Safe

If you receive unwanted e-mail from a specific address or domain, you can block all messages from that sender. On the other hand, if you find a wanted e-mail in the Junk E-mail folder, you can mark it as safe and not as junk. When you mark a message as junk, Windows Mail moves the message into the Junk E-mail folder, where you can browser through or delete it later. You can mark individual or groups of messages as blocked or safe. If you want to add, edit, or remove addresses or domains from the Safe or Block Senders list, you can use the Junk E-mail Options dialog box, which you can access from the Tools menu.

Mark an E-mail Blocked or Safe from a Sender

1. Select the e-mail you want to block.

2. Click the **Message** menu, and then point to **Junk E-mail**.

3. Click the Junk E-mail option you want:

   ◆ **Block.** Click **Add Sender to Block Senders List** or **Add Sender's Domain to Blocked Senders List.**

   ◆ **Safe. Add Sender to Safe Senders List** or **Add Sender's Domain to Safe Senders List.**

4. Click **OK** to alert message.

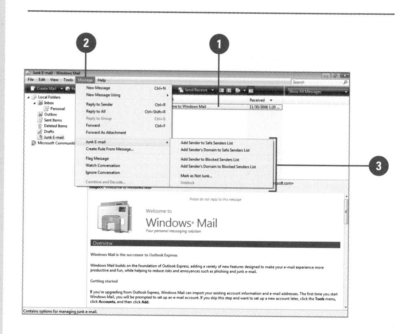

Did You Know?

You can mark e-mail not as junk. In the Junk E-mail folder, select the e-mail you want to change, click the Message menu, point to Junk E-mail, and then click Mark as Not Junk. The e-mail is moved back to the Inbox.

You can add, remove, and change blocked or safe sender in the Junk E-mail Options dialog box. Click the Tools menu, click Junk E-mail, click the Safe Senders or Blocked Senders tab, and then make the changes you want.

Diverting Incoming E-mail to Folders

Windows Mail can direct incoming messages that meet criteria to other folders in the Folders list rather than to your Inbox. For example, your friend loves sending you funny e-mail, but you often don't have time to read it right away. You can set message rules to store any messages you receive from your friend in a different folder so they won't clutter your Inbox. When you are ready to read the messages, you simply open the folder and access the messages just as you would messages in the Inbox. If you receive unwanted e-mail from a specific address, you can block all messages from that sender.

Set Rules for Incoming E-mail

1. Click the **Tools** menu, point to **Message Rules**, and then click **Mail**.

   If no rules are set, skip to step 3.

2. Click **New** to create a new rule, or select a rule and click **Modify** to edit an existing one.

3. Click the appropriate conditions and actions for your rule.

4. Click a link to enter the underlying information for that condition or action.

5. Specify the criteria for your rule in the Selection dialog box that appears, and then click **OK**.

6. Repeat steps 4 and 5 for each condition and action you have set.

7. Type a name for this rule.

8. Click **OK**.

9. Click **OK**.

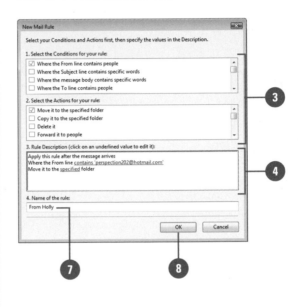

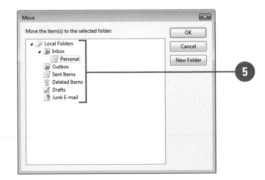

Did You Know?

You can apply rules right now. Click the Tools menu, point to Message Rules, and then click Mail. Click Apply Now. Select the rule(s) you want to apply and the folder that contains the messages, and then click Apply Now.

Selecting a News Server

A newsgroup is an electronic forum where people from around the world with a common interest can share ideas, ask and answer questions, and comment on and discuss any subject. You can find newsgroups on almost any topic. Before you can participate in a newsgroup, you must select a news server. A **news server** is a computer located on the Internet, which stores newsgroup messages, also called **articles**, on different topics. Each news server contains several newsgroups from which to choose. The Internet Connection Wizard walks you through the process of selecting a news server. This wizard also appears the first time you use Windows Mail News. To complete the wizard process, you might need an account name and password, and you need to choose a news server that you want to use.

Set up a News Server Using the Connect to the Internet Wizard

1. Click the **Tools** menu, click **Accounts**, and then click **Add**.

2. Click the **Newsgroup Account**, and then click **Next** to continue.

3. Type your name, and then click **Next** to continue.

4. Read the information in each wizard dialog box, type the required information, and then click **Next** to continue.

5. In the final wizard dialog box, click **Finish**.

6. If prompted, click a subscribe to newsgroups option.

7. Click **OK**.

Did You Know?

You can change the news server. Right-click the news server in the Folders list, click Properties, change settings, and then click OK.

You can remove a news server. Right-click the news server in the Folders list, click Remove Account, and then click Yes.

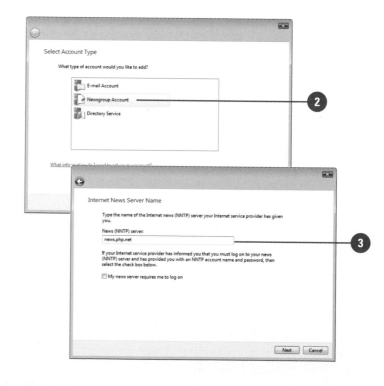

Subscribing to a Newsgroup

When you add a news server account, Windows Mail retrieves a list of newsgroups available on that server. Once you select a newsgroup, you can view its contents, or, if you expect to return to the newsgroup often, you can subscribe to it. Subscribing to a newsgroup places a link to the group in the Folders list, providing easy access to the newsgroup. If you find that you are no longer interested in a newsgroup, you can unsubscribe from it. You can also view a newsgroup without subscribing to see if you might want to add it to your Folders list.

Subscribe to a Newsgroup

1. Click the **Tools** menu, and then click **Newsgroups**.

2. Type the word or phrase for which you want to search. As you type, the results appear in the Newsgroup list.

3. Scroll through the list of available newsgroups.

4. Click the newsgroup you want to subscribe to.

5. Click **Subscribe**.

6. Click **Go to** to see the posted messages.

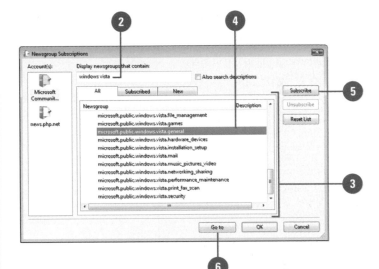

Click to view subscribed newsgroups

Did You Know?

You can unsubscribe from a newsgroup. If you no longer want to see a newsgroup in your Folders list, right-click the newsgroup name, click Unsubscribe on the shortcut menu, and then click OK.

Reading the News

Once you have subscribed to a newsgroup, you will want to view its messages. Click the newsgroup to display messages, and then click the message you want to read. Newsgroup messages appear in the Preview pane, just as e-mail messages do. If a plus sign (+) appears to the left of a newsgroup message, then the message contains a conversation thread. A **conversation thread** consists of the original message on a particular topic along with any responses that include the original message. Icons appear next to the news messages to indicate whether a conversation thread is expanded or collapsed, and whether or not it has been read.

Open and Read News Messages

1 Click the newsgroup in the Folders list whose message you want to read.

2 Scroll through the list to see the posted messages.

3 Find the message you want to read using the following methods:

◆ To display all the responses to a conversation thread, click the plus sign (+) to the left of a message.

◆ To hide all the responses to a conversation thread, click the minus sign (-) to the left of a message.

◆ To view only unread messages, click the **View** menu, point to **Current View**, and then click **Hide Read or Ignored Messages**.

◆ To sort the messages based on type, click the column button you want to sort by. The column button toggles between sorting the column in ascending and descending order.

4 To read a message, click its header in the message list.

5 Read the message in the Preview pane.

News server

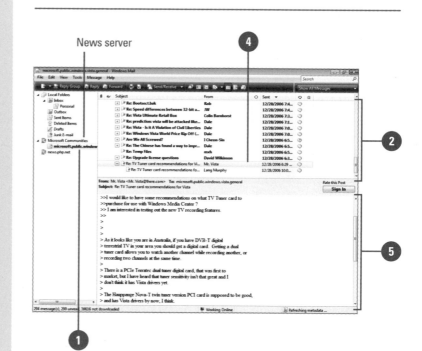

Filtering the News

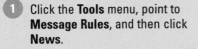

After you become familiar with a newsgroup, you might decide that you don't want to retrieve messages from a particular person, about a specific subject, of a certain length, or older than a certain number of days. This is called **filtering** newsgroup messages.

Filter Unwanted Messages

1. Click the **Tools** menu, point to **Message Rules**, and then click **News**.

2. If necessary, click **New**.

3. Select the conditions for your rule.

4. Select the actions for your rule.

5. Click any undefined value, such as the e-mail address you want to divert and the folder where you want to store the unwanted messages, and then provide information.

6. Type a name.

7. Click **OK**.

8. Click **OK**.

Did You Know?

You can ignore or watch a conversation. Select the conversation you want to ignore or watch, click the Message menu, and then click Ignore Conversation or Watch Conversation.

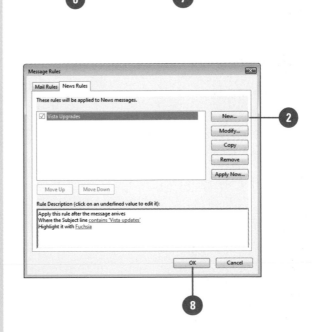

Posting a News Message

Part of the fun of newsgroups is that you can participate in an ongoing discussion, respond privately to a message's author, or start a new thread yourself by posting your own message on a topic of interest to you. If you post a message to a newsgroup and then change your mind, you can cancel the message. Keep in mind that if someone has already downloaded the message, canceling the message will not remove it from that person's computer.

Post a News Message

1. Click the newsgroup in the folder list to which you want to post a message.

2. Click the **New Post** button on the toolbar.

3. Type a subject for your message.

4. Type your message.

5. Select a post type option.

6. Click the **Send** button on the toolbar.

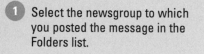

Cancel a Message

1. Select the newsgroup to which you posted the message in the Folders list.

2. Select the message you want to cancel. You will need to wait until the newsgroup posts the message.

3. Click the **Message** menu, click **Cancel Message**, and then click **OK**.

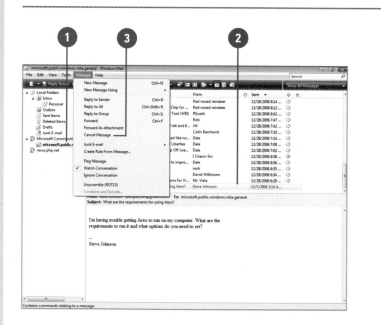

Did You Know?

You need to think before you post. Respond to personal questions posted to a newsgroup directly to the author, not to the entire newsgroup. Remember to click the Reply button.

Reply to a Message

1. Click the message to which you want to reply.

2. Select the appropriate command.

   ◆ Click the **Reply Group** button on the toolbar to post your response to the newsgroup.

   ◆ Click the **Reply** button on the toolbar to send the message's author a private e-mail message.

   ◆ Click the **Forward** button to send an e-mail message to some other recipient.

3. Type your message, and if you want, delete parts of the original message that are unrelated to your reply.

4. Click the **Send** button on the toolbar.

Did You Know?

You should name your messages carefully. When you compose a message, choose a subject that accurately reflects the content of your message so that people can decide whether they want to read it. When you reply to a message, don't change the subject line so that the conversation will remain threaded.

Viewing the Windows Calendar

Windows Calendar (**New!**) is an electronic version of the familiar paper daily planner. You can schedule time for completing specific tasks, meetings, vacations, holidays, or for any other activity with the Calendar. You can change the Calendar to show activities for the Day, Work Week (five business days), Week (all seven days), or Month. The Appointment area serves as a daily planner where you can schedule activities by the day, work week, full week, or month. Appointments are scheduled activities such as a doctor's visit, and occupy a block of time in the Appointment area. Events are activities that last 24 hours or longer, such as a seminar, and do not occupy blocks of time in your calendar. Instead, they appear in a banner at the beginning of a day. The bottom left pane of Calendar view displays the tasks associated with the days displayed in the calendar.

Open and Change the Calendar View

1. In Windows Mail, click the **Windows Calendar** button on the toolbar.

   ◆ You can also click the **Start** button, point to **All Programs**, and then click **Windows Calendar**.

2. You can change the Calendar view in several ways.

   ◆ Click the **View** menu, and then click the view option you want.

   ◆ Click the **View** button arrow, and then click a view.

   ◆ Click the left arrow or right arrow on the Date Navigator to change the current month.

   ◆ Click a date on the Date Navigator to view that day's schedule. The date highlighted in red is today's date.

   ◆ Click the **View** menu, and then click **Details Pane** to see appointment or task details.

3. View and work with appointment or tasks associated with the current Calendar view.

Date Navigator

Use to change the view

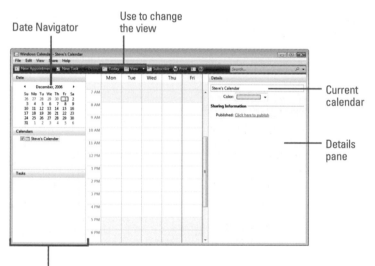

Current calendar

Details pane

Navigation pane

Scheduling an Appointment

In Windows Calendar, an **appointment (New!)** is any activity you schedule that doesn't include other people or resources. An **event** is any appointment that lasts one or more full days (24-hour increments), such as a seminar, a conference, or a vacation. You enter appointment or event information in the same box; however, when you schedule an event, the *All-day appointment* check box is selected; the check box is cleared when you schedule an appointment. If an appointment or event recurs on a regular basis, such as a meeting, you can set the Recurrence option. If you need a reminder, you can also set the amount of time you need.

Schedule an Appointment

1. In Windows Mail, click the **Calendar** button on the toolbar.

2. In Day view, select the day select the time you want for the appointment.

3. Click the **New Appointment** button on the toolbar.

4. In the Details pane, type the name and location of the appointment.

5. Click the **Calendar** button arrow, and then select calendar where you want the appointment to appear.

6. To make an all-day appointment, select the **All-day Appointment** check box.

7. Enter start and end times, as necessary.

8. To make an appointment recur, click the **Recurrence** button arrow, and then select the option you want.

9. To set a reminder, click the **Reminder** button arrow, and then specify a reminder time.

10. To invite someone, type the e-mail address of the person you want, press Enter, click the address, and the click **Invite**.

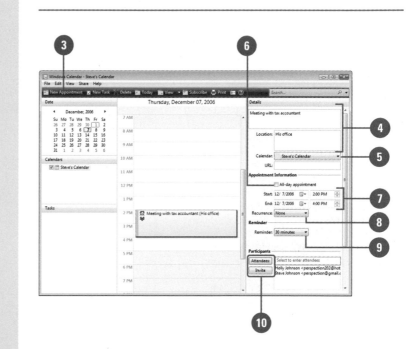

Creating Tasks

A **task** is something you want to accomplish within a specific time. Windows Calendar allows you to create and manage tasks to their completion. You can quickly create a detailed task (**New!**) using the New Task button on the toolbar. In the Details pane, you can set a Start Date, Due Date (the date by which the task must be completed), and Priority (Low, Medium, or High) for a task. If you need a reminder, you can specify a reminder date and time. To manage the completion of a task, you can select or clear the task check box in the Navigation pane or the Complete check box in the Details pane. If you need to add additional information about a task, you can use the Notes area at the bottom of the pane.

Create or Update a Task

① In Windows Mail, click the **Calendar** button on the toolbar.

② Click the **New Task** button on the toolbar.

③ In the Details pane, type the name of the task.

④ Click the **Calendar** button arrow, and then select calendar where you want the task to appear.

⑤ Click the **Priority** button arrow, and then select a priority.

⑥ Enter start and due dates.

⑦ To set a reminder, click the **Reminder** button arrow, click **On date**, and then specify a date.

The task appears in the Navigation pane.

⑧ Enter notes for the task.

⑨ When a task is done, select the check box next to the task in the Navigation pane or the **Complete** check box in the Details pane.

⑩ To edit a task, click the task in the Navigation pane to display it in the Details pane, where you can make the changes you want.

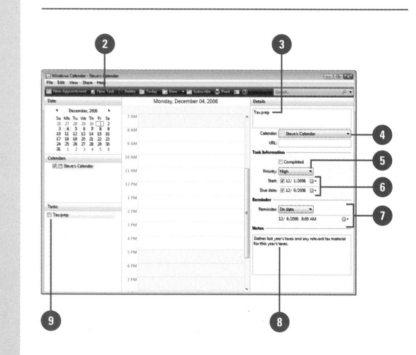

Creating and Sharing Calendars

In Windows Calendar, you can create individual calendars for multiple people who use the program and share them with each other (**New!**). When you have multiple calendars, you can view them individually or all at once, side-by-side, or overlaid to make it easier to compare one calendar with another and check for free time. Appointments for each calendar are displays in a different color to make them easier to tell whose schedule each item belongs to. If you want to add an appointment from another calendar to your calendar, you can drag appointments between the two calendars.

Create and Share a Calendar

1. In Windows Mail, click the **Windows Calendar** button on the toolbar.

2. To create a new calendar, click the **File** menu, click **New Calendar**, type the name you want for the calendar, and then press Enter.

3. To choose the color of your appointments, click the **Color** list arrow in the Details pane, and then select the color you want.

4. To view multiple calendars, select the check boxes next to the calendars you want in the Navigation pane.

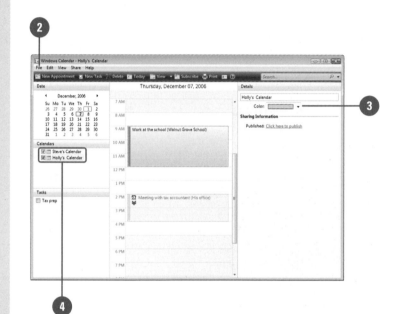

Did You Know?

You can search for an appointment or task. In the Search box, type letters or words from the appointment or task you want to find. As you type, the search results that match what you type continue to appear.

You can print a calendar. Display the calendar you want to print, click the File menu, click Print, select a printer, the print style you want (Day, Work Week, Week, or Month), and a print range (Start and End), and then click OK.

Publishing Calendars Over the Internet

Windows Calendar uses the Internet compatible iCalendar format with the .ics file extension, which allows you to publish and subscribe to calendars over the Internet (**New!**). After you create a calendar, you can publish it to a Web hosting site where you can share it with others over the Internet. If you want to specify who can access and view a published calendar, you can add password protection. In addition to publishing, you can also subscribe to a published calendar on the Web, so you can stay up-to-date with other people.

Publish a Calendar

1. In Windows Mail, click the **Windows Calendar** button on the toolbar.

2. Click the **Share** menu, and then click **Publish**.

3. Type the calendar name you want.

4. Enter the location where you want to publish the calendar, such as a Web site, or click **Browse**.

5. Select or clear the **Automatically publish changes made to this calendar** check box.

6. Select or clear the check boxes for details you want to include: **Notes**, **Reminders**, or **Tasks**.

7. Click **Publish**.

8. If you want to send an e-mail announcement with calendar links, click **Announce**, and then address and send the message.

9. Otherwise, click **Finish**.

10. To unpublish a calendar, click the **Share** menu, click **Stop Publishing**, and then click **Unpublish**.

> ### Did You Know?
>
> *You can subscribe to a calendar.* click the Share menu, click Subscribe, and then follow the wizard instructions. Check out *www.calendardata.com*.

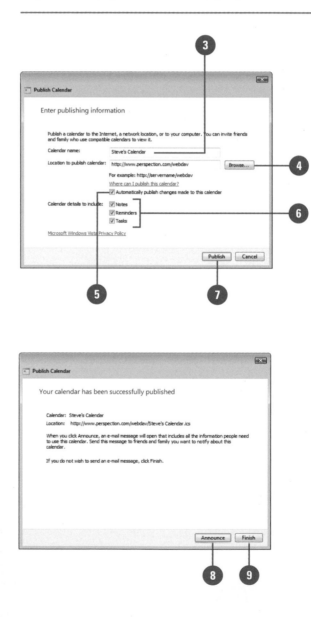

Starting a Windows Meeting

Windows Meeting Space (**New!**) is a program that allows you to set up a meeting with up to ten people and share documents, programs, or your desktop. Before you can hold a meeting, each person attending the meeting needs to be running Windows Vista. To start a new meeting, you give it a name and password for security purposes, and then you invite others to attend. In the meeting, you can share a program or your desktop, and distribute any handout files you want to attendees.

Start a New Meeting with Windows Meeting Space

1. Click the **Start** button, point to **All Programs**, and then click **Windows Meeting Space**.

   The first time you start Windows Meeting Space, select People Near Me options to activate the network to run Meeting Space.

2. Click **Start a new meeting**.

3. Type a name for the meeting.

4. Type a password to create a secure meeting.

5. To show the password, select the **Show characters** check box.

6. To set visibility and network options, click **Options**, select options to allow or not allow people to see this meeting, or to create a private wireless network to use with a meeting, and then click **OK**.

7. Click the **Create a meeting** button (green arrow).

8. To exit or leave a meeting, click the **Meeting** button, and then click **Exit** or **Leave meeting.**

First time set up for People Near Me options

Holding a Windows Meeting

In Windows Meeting Space (**New!**), you invite participants to a meeting and they can individually join in. To invite a person to join a meeting, you send them an e-mail message or an invitation file with meeting information. Participants can join a meeting at any time during the meeting session. For those within your network, you can change meeting participant settings and sign in options to allow people near you to send you invitations. A meeting continues until all participants have left the meeting. To exit or leave a meeting, you use the Meeting button on the Windows Meeting Space window.

Send Invitations to a Meeting

1 In a meeting, click **Invite People**.

2 Select or clear the **Require participants to type the meeting password** check box.

3 Use one of the following:

◆ Select the check box next to the name of each person you want to invite, and then click **Send invitations**.

◆ Click **Invite others**, and then click **Send an invitation in e-mail**.

◆ Click **Invite others**, and then click **Create an invitation file**, save the file, and then give the file to the person you want to invite.

Did You Know?

You can change participant status in a meeting. In a meeting, click the participant name you want to change, click a status option: Available, Busy, Be right back, or Away.

You can select a trusted contact. A trusted contact is someone who sends you their user name and other information in an e-mail message or file that is accompanied by a digital certificate of identity.

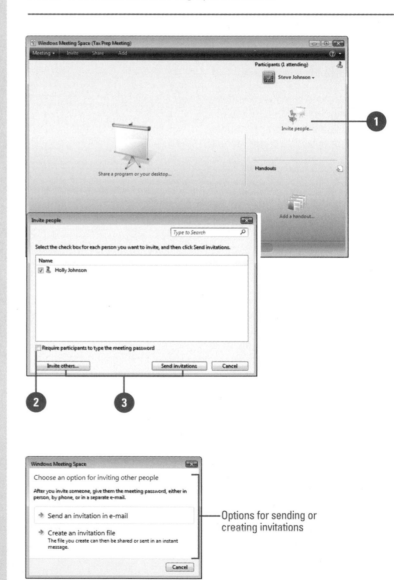

Options for sending or creating invitations

Join a Meeting

1. If necessary, start Windows Meeting Space.

   ◆ Click the **Start** button, point to **All Programs**, and then click **Windows Meeting Space**.

2. If the meeting is already in progress, click **Join a meeting near me**. Or, if you know that someone has sent you an invitation file, click **Open an invitation file**.

3. Type the password you received from the person who calls the meeting.

4. Click the **Join a meeting** button (green arrow).

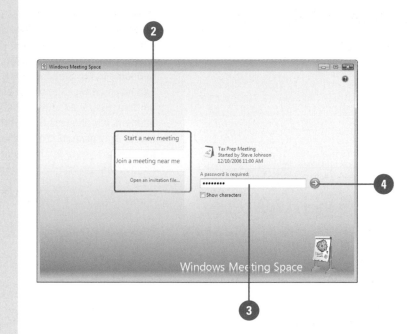

Change Participant Settings

1. In a meeting, click the participant name you want to change, and then click **Personal settings.**

   ◆ You can also open the People Near Me icon in the Control Panel to change these settings.

2. Type the name you want other people to see.

3. Select or clear the **Make my picture available** check box.

4. Click the **Allow invitations from** list arrow, and then select an option. Select or clear the **Display a notification when an invitation is received** check box.

5. Select or clear the **Sign me in automatically when Windows starts** check box.

6. Click **OK**.

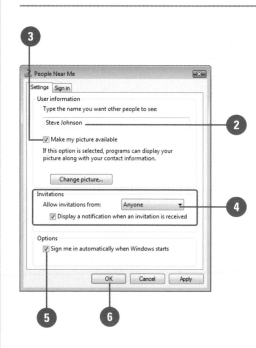

Sharing Information in a Windows Meeting ▶

Windows Meeting Space (**New!**) allows you to share documents, programs, or your desktop with up to ten people running the same version of Windows Vista. When you share documents, programs, or your desktop, participants can view your computer. You can also add handouts to the meeting. Each participant is given a copy of the file and can make changes to the copy one at a time. The changes for each participant are made to all participants' handouts, except the original handout, which stays the same. During a sharing session, you can temporarily give control to another participant to make a change to a file. Since you are in charge of the meeting, you can take control back at any time.

Share a Program or Your Desktop

1. Start the program you want to share in a meeting.

2. In a meeting, click the **Share a program or your desktop** button, and then **OK**, if necessary.

3. Click **Desktop**, the running program you want to share, or **Browse for a file to open and share** to open a program and file.

4. Click **Share**.

5. If necessary, select a file to share, and then click **Open** to start the associated program and file.

6. To add a handout to the meeting, click the **Add a handout** button, select the file, and then click **Open**.

7. If you want, click the **Show me how my shared session looks on other computers** or **Stop sharing**.

8. Minimize the Windows Meeting Space window, and then start using the program or your desktop in the meeting.

9. To stop, pause, or see how the sharing session looks, click the appropriate button at the top of the screen.

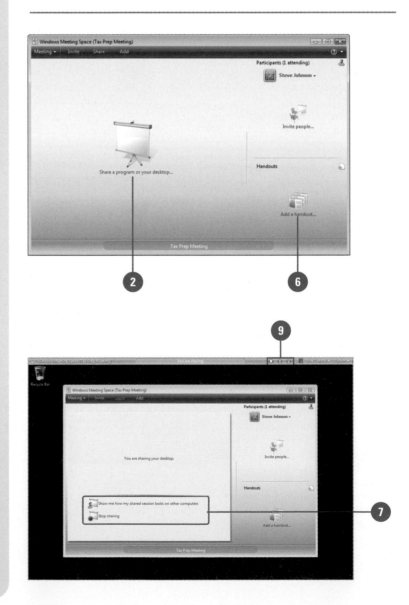

Give and Take Control of a Sharing Session in a Meeting

1. In a meeting with a shared document, program, or your desktop, click the **Give Control** button.

2. To take back control, click **Take Control**.

    TIMESAVER *Press the Windows Logo key+Esc to take control back.*

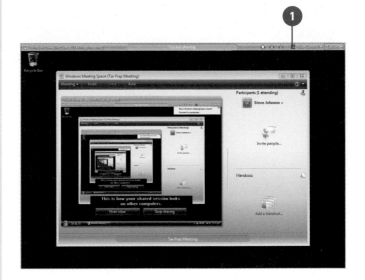

Change Settings During Sharing Session

1. In a meeting with a shared document, program, or your desktop, click the **Options** button.

2. Click the command you want:

    ◆ **Show Windows Meeting Space window.**

    ◆ **Connect to a projector.** Follow the on-screen instructions to connect to a video projector that is connected to a network, which you can control remotely.

Did You Know?

The data shared during a meeting is secure. All the data and communications shared during a meeting are encrypted to provide security for all the participants involved.

Holding Web Discussions and Video Conferences

Introduction

Windows Vista makes communicating with other computers over the Internet easier than ever with Windows Live Messenger (version 8). You can talk to others over the Internet (like you do on a telephone), use video to see and be seen by others while you converse, share programs and files, collaborate on documents, share graphical content on a whiteboard (a drawing canvas), and ask for or get remote online assistance from a contact.

You can use Windows Live Messenger (New!) to exchange instant messages with a designated list of contacts over the Internet. An **instant message** is an online typewritten conversation in real-time between two or more contacts. Unlike an e-mail message, instant messages require both parties to be online, and the communication is instantaneous. With Windows Live Messenger, you can send instant messages to any of your contacts who are online; have conversations with a group of friends; see the latest information about your contacts; see and hear your contacts; send and receive text messages with a mobile device; send a voice clip to express yourself personally; and save your conversations. In addition, you can make PC to telephone or PC to PC calls, share and update files with your friends using the Sharing folder, and connect with your friends who use Yahoo Messenger (New!).

Windows Live Messenger uses different services to exchange messages, files, and other information. The default service is .NET Messenger Service, which individuals mostly use. For those working in a corporate environment, Windows Live Messenger supports Communications Service for networks that use SIP-server technology and Exchange Instant Messaging for networks that use Microsoft Exchange Server. You can set up Windows Live Messenger to access more than one type of messaging service.

Preparing for Windows Live Messenger

Windows Live Messenger (**New!**) is an instant messenging program that allows you to send and receive instant messages, hold video chats, and share files. Windows Live Messenger doesn't come installed with Windows Vista, so you need to download and install it from the Microsoft Web site. Before you can use Windows Live Messenger, you need to get an account ID. You use the ID to sign-in to Windows Live Messenger as well as other Windows Live services, such as Windows Live Mail and Windows Live Spaces. If you already have an MSN Hotmail, MSN Messenger, or Microsoft Passport account, you've already got a Windows Live ID.

Download Windows Live Messenger

1. Click the **Start** button, and then click point to **All Programs**.

2. Click **Windows Live Messenger Download**.

   Your Web browser opens, displaying the Windows Live Messenger Web site.

3. Click the link to download the Windows Live Messenger software.

4. Click **Run** to start the download and the installation, or click **Save** to save the installation files to your hard disk, and then double-click the Setup icon.

5. Follow the online instructions to complete the installation.

Create an Account

1. Click the **Start** button, point to **All Programs**, and then click **Windows Live Messenger**.

   The Windows Live Messenger sign-in windows opens.

2. Click **Get a new account** at the bottom.

   Your Web browser opens, displaying the Get your Windows Live ID Web site.

3. Click the link to sign up for the Windows Live ID.

4. Follow the online instructions to create a Windows Live ID.

Forgot Your Password

1. Click the **Start** button, point to **All Programs**, and then click **Windows Live Messenger**.

   The Windows Live Messenger sign-in windows opens.

2. Click **Forgot your password?** at the bottom.

   Your Web browser opens, displaying the Reset your password Web site.

3. Type your Windows Live ID.

4. Type the security characters in the picture.

5. Click **Continue**.

6. Follow the online instructions to reset your password.

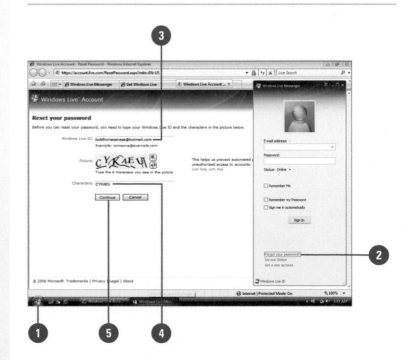

Starting Windows Live Messenger

Windows Live Messenger is an instant messaging program that allows you to exchange instant messages with a designated list of contacts over the Internet. An **instant message** is an online typewritten conversation in real time between two or more contacts. Instant messages require both parties to be online, and the communication is instantaneous. Before you can use Windows Live Messenger, you need a Windows Live ID, which you can get for no charge from Microsoft. After you start Windows Live Messenger, you sign in to let others online know you are connected. When you're done, you sign out.

Start Windows Live Messenger and Sign In and Out

1. Click the **Start** button, point to **All Programs**, and then click **Windows Live Messenger**.

   TIMESAVER *Double-click the Windows Live Messenger icon in the notification area of the taskbar.*

2. If you're not automatically signed in, enter your user name and password. If you want to sign-in with a different ID, click the **E-mail address** list arrow, and then click **Sign in with a different e-mail address**.

3. Select or clear the **Remember Me**, **Remember my Password**, or **Sign me in automatically** check box.

4. Click the **Sign In** button.

5. If you want to stay signed in, yet still close Windows Live Messenger, click the **Close** button.

6. To sign out, click **Tools**, and then click **Sign out**.

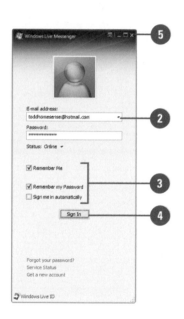

Did You Know?

You can stop signing in automatically. Click Tools, click Sign out, and then clear the Sign me in automatically check box in the Sign-in window.

Configuring Windows Live Messenger

If you are having problems signing into Windows Live Messenger, you might need to add the program (MSNmsgr.exe) to your firewall exceptions list. If that doesn't help, you might need to check the Microsoft .NET Messenger Service status, which is the online service provided by Microsoft that makes it possible for you to use Windows Live Messenger or MSN Messenger. Microsoft is continually updating Windows Messenger with new functionality. When a software update is available, Windows Live Messenger displays a message, where you can download and install the upgrade.

Update Windows Messenger

1. When an update is available, a message appears at the top of the window, click the **Click here** link.

2. Click the **Yes** option.

3. Click **OK**.

4. After the download is complete, click **Run**, and then follow the instructions to download and install the upgrade.

Did You Know?

You might need to configure the firewall. Double-click the Windows Firewall icon in the Control Panel, click Allow a program through Windows Firewall in the left pane, select the Windows Live Messenger check box, and then click OK.

You might need to check the .NET Messenger Service status. Click Service status in the Sign-in window, or click the Help menu, and then click Service status.

You might need to configure your Web browser for sharing. Start Internet Explorer, click the Tools button, click Internet Options, click the Security tab, click Internet, click Custom Level, enable all scripting options, click Medium or lower setting for Reset, click the Privacy tab, drag the slider to Medium or higher, and then click OK.

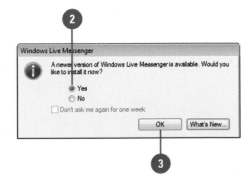

Viewing Windows Live Messenger

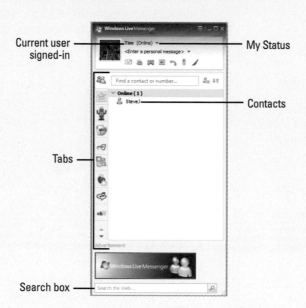

Current user signed-in

My Status

Contacts

Tabs

Search box

Conversation with contact

Toolbar

Conversation participants

Type and send conversation text

Format conversation text

Changing My Status

When you sign in with Windows Live Messenger, the program notifies contacts currently online from your Contacts list that you are available to chat. While you're signed in, you might need to leave your computer for a meeting or lunch. Instead of signing out, you can change your online status to let your contacts know that you'll be right back, or that you're not available at the moment for other reasons.

Change My Status

1. Select **Tools**, and then click a status type:
   - ◆ **Online**
   - ◆ **Busy**
   - ◆ **Be right back**
   - ◆ **Away**
   - ◆ **In a call**
   - ◆ **Out to lunch**
   - ◆ **Appear offline**
   - ◆ **Sign out**

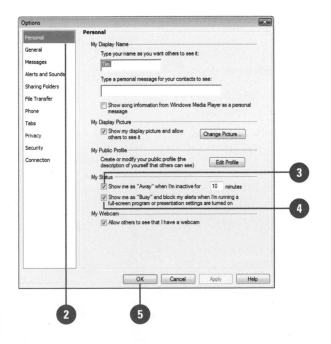

Status types

Change Status Preferences

1. Select **Tools**, and then click **Options**.

2. In the left pane, click **Personal**.

3. Select or clear the **Show me as "Away" when I'm inactive for X minutes** check box, and then enter the number of inactive minutes you want, if necessary.

4. Select or clear the **Show me as "Busy" and block my alerts when I'm running a full-screen program or presentation settings are turned on** check box.

5. Click **OK**.

Personalizing Windows Live Messenger

Before you start using Windows LIve Messenger, you can customize the program to show the menu bar if you prefer, automatically sign in, and display personalized information. You can change your display name, provide a personal message, and select a picture to represent you while you communicate with others online. Instead of selecting a regular static picture, you can select a dynamic display picture (**New!**) or character that provides animation, such as a WeeMee, MeeGos, Quebles, or Kiwee.

Access and Show or Hide Menus

◆ **Access and Show Menus.** Click the **Show Menu** button at the top of the window to display menus, and then click **Show the menu bar**.

◆ **Hide Menus.** Click the **Hide the menu bar** button.

Show Menu button

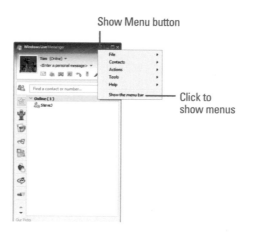

Click to show menus

Change Sign In Preferences

1 Select **Tools**, and then click **Options**.

2 In the left pane, click **General**.

3 Select or clear the check boxes with the sign in options you want to change:

◆ Run this program when Windows starts

◆ Allow automatic sign in when connected to the Internet

◆ Show Windows Live Today

◆ Use the same display picture and personal message

4 Click **OK**.

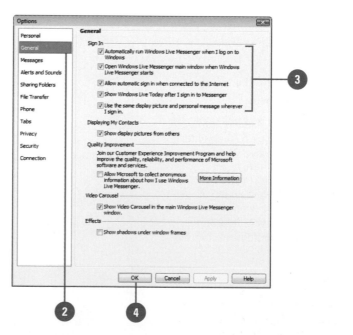

Change Personal Information

1. Select **Tools**, and then click **Options**.

2. In the left pane, click **Personal**.

3. Type the name you want others to see when you are online.

4. Type a personal message for your contacts to see.

5. To show a display picture, select the **Show my display picture and allow other to see it** check box, click **Change Picture**, select a picture, and then click **OK**.

6. Click **OK**.

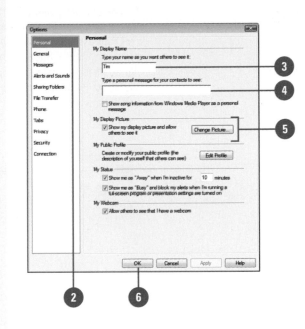

Change Display Picture

1. Select **Tools**, and then click **Change display picture**.

2. Select the picture you want to use using one of the following:

   ◆ **Dynamic Display Pictures.** Click a dynamic display picture link, and then follow the online instructions.

   ◆ **Regular Pictures.** Click the picture you want.

   ◆ **Remove Pictures.** Select the picture, and then click **Remove**.

   ◆ **No Picture.** Select the **Don't show a picture** check box.

3. Click **OK**.

   TIMESAVER *In the Conversation window, click the Options for this person button arrow for you to change your display picture and other options.*

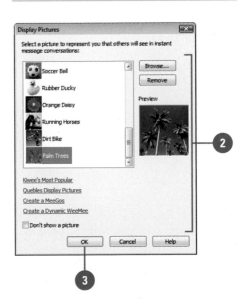

Adding Online Contacts

Before you can send instant messages to other people, they need to be in your Contacts list. You can add a person who has a Windows Live ID or a Yahoo member (**New!**) to your Contacts list by using the Add a contact button. If the person that you want to contact doesn't have Windows Live Messenger or an ID, you can send the person an e-mail with information about getting and installing Windows Live Messenger and obtaining an ID.

Add an Outline Contact

1. Double-click the **Windows Live Messenger** icon in the notification area of the taskbar, and then sign in, if necessary.

2. Click the **Add a contact** button.

3. Type the e-mail address of the person you want to add.

4. If the person doesn't have Windows Live Messenger, type a personal invitation message.

5. Type a nickname that others see during a conversation.

6. To add a contact to a group, click the **Group** button arrow, and then select a group.

7. In the Contact, Personal, Work, and Notes sections, enter the information you want to include.

8. Select or clear the **Subscribe to updates for this contact** check box.

9. Click **Add contact**.

> ### Did You Know?
>
> *You can quickly delete a contact.*
> Right-click a contact, click Delete contact, select or clear the Also block this contact and Also remove from my hotmail contacts check boxes, and then click Delete contact.

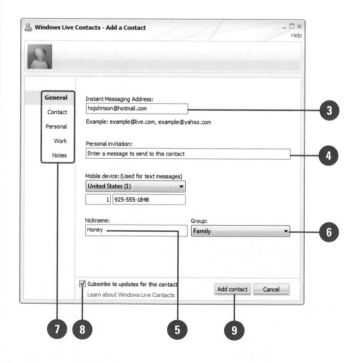

Managing Contacts and Groups

As your Contacts list grows, you may want to organize your contacts into groups or remove the ones you no longer use. Windows Live Messenger makes it easy to organize them into predefined groups and groups that you create. Windows Live Messenger comes with four pre-defined groups by default: Coworkers, Family, Friends, and Other Contacts. Once you have organized your groups, you can select or clear contact check boxes to modify it. You can use the Up and Down buttons next to the group name to hide and display contacts in a group.

Create a Contacts Group

1 Click the **Contacts** menu, and then click **Create a group**.

> **TIMESAVER** *Right-click a group, and then click Create new group.*

2 Type a name for the new group.

3 Select the contacts or type the e-mail addresses you want to add to the group.

4 Click **Save**.

Modify Contacts and Contact Groups

◆ **Edit Contact**. Right-click the contact, click **Edit contact**, make changes, and then click **Save**.

◆ **Edit Contact Group**. Right-click the contact group, click **Edit group**, select or clear contact check boxes, and then click **Save**.

◆ **Rename Contact Group**. Right-click the contact group, click **Rename group**, type a name, and then press Enter.

◆ **Delete Contact Group**. Right-click the contact group, click **Delete group**, and then click **Yes**.

Right-click contacts or groups to perform tasks

Sending and Receiving Instant Messages

An instant message is an online typewritten conversation in real-time between two or more contacts. As you type an instant message, you can format your messages by changing fonts and text color and by inserting backgrounds and color schemes (**New!**). Each message can contain up to 400 characters. If you have a writing input device and Microsoft Windows Journal Viewer installed, you can also draw or handwrite (**New!**) your messages. You cannot send an instant message to more than one person, but you can invite other people using the same messaging service to participate in an existing conversation; you can include up to five people in a conversation.

Send and Receive Instant Messages

1. Double-click the **Windows Live Messenger** icon in the notification area of the taskbar, and then sign in, if necessary.

    When a message arrives, an alert appears. Click the alert to open Windows Live Messenger.

2. Double-click a contact or right-click a contact group and then click **Send an instant message to this group**.

3. Type your message in the box at the bottom of the window.

    To start a new line while typing, press Shift+Enter.

4. If you want to handwrite your message, click the **Handwrite** tab, and then ink your message using the formatting buttons.

5. Click **Send** or press Enter, and then wait for a reply.

6. If you want to add another person to the conversation, click the **Action** menu, click **Invite a contact to join this conversation**, and then double-click the person you want to add.

7. When you're done, click the **Close** button to end the session.

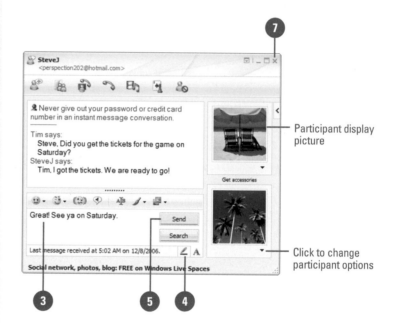

Participant display picture

Click to change participant options

Format Message Text

1. In the Conversation window, click the **Font** button.

2. Specify the font, font style, size, color, and effect you want, and preview the result in the sample box.

3. Click **OK**.

4. Type and send the formatted message.

Apply a Background or Color Scheme to the Conversation Window

◆ **Background.** In the Conversation window, click the **Background** button, and then select a background. To set options or remove a background, click **Show all**.

◆ **Color Scheme.** In the Conversation window, click the **Color Scheme** button, and then select a color or click **More Colors** to select a custom color.

Background button

Color Scheme button

Did You Know?

You can search for contacts. Click in the Find a contact or number box at the top of the main Messenger window, and then start typing to display results. Click the Click here to clear text button to clear the search.

Adding Symbols and Voice to an Instant Message

As you type an instant message, you can format your messages by inserting graphical symbols called **emoticons**, such as a happy face, which help convey your emotions, or graphical animations, such as as a wink (**New!**). If your conversation needs a nudge to get people conversing, you can use the Nudge button (**New!**). If you want to add a little audio to an instant message, you can record a voice clip (**New!**) and send it to others involved in the conversation. The voice clip appears in the conversation window and plays automatically. You need a microphone to record a voice clip and audio speakers to hear a clip.

Insert Emoticons

1. In the Conversation window, click the **Emoticons** button.

2. Click the icon you want to insert into the conversation.

    ◆ To create, modify, or remove an emoticon, click **Show all**.

    TIMESAVER *You can also type a sequence of characters to quickly insert emoticons as you type your message. To find out the characters, point to an icon on the Emoticons menu.*

Did You Know?

You can insert a nudge message to keep a conversation going. In the Conversation window, click the Nudge button.

You can create your own blog. A blog is short for Web log, which is an online journal. In the main Messenger window, click the Get your own space button. In the Create your Windows Live Space Web site, follow the online instructions.

You can save an instant message. In the Conversation window, click the File menu, click Save As, select a folder location, type a file name, and then click Save.

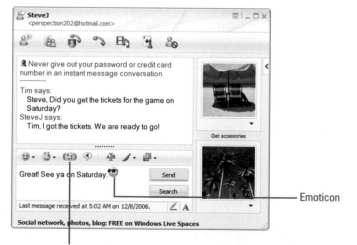

Emoticon

Nudge button

Insert a Wink

1. In the Conversation window, click the **Wink** button.

2. Click the wink icon you want to insert into the conversation.

   ◆ To preview or remove a wink, click **Show all**.

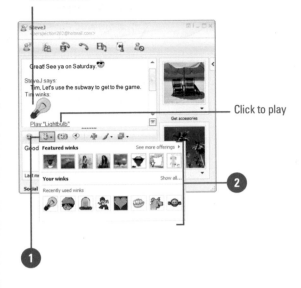

Inserted wink

Click to play

Record and Play a Voice Clip

1. In the Conversation window, point to the **Voice Clip** button.

2. Press and hold down the Voice Clip button or press F2, and then record your voice message.

3. Release the button or key to send the voice message.

4. To play or stop a voice clip, click **Play / Stop** in the Conversation window.

   TIMESAVER *Press Esc to stop the voice clip.*

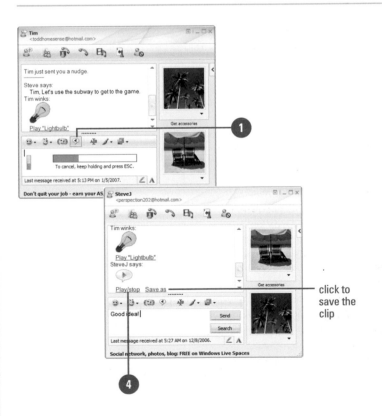

click to save the clip

Did You Know?

You can save a voice clip. In the Conversation window, click Save As or drag it from the conversation window onto your desktop or into a folder.

You reuse a voice clip in another conversation. In the Conversation window, drag a voice clip to another another conversation window.

Blocking a Contact

If you no longer want to receive instant messages from a specific contact, you can block the contact from directly sending you instant messages. When you block a contact, you appear to be offline to the person, who doesn't know blocking is turned on. If another contact invites you and someone you blocked into a conversation, the blocked person can send you messages indirectly. Blocking a contact moves them from your Allow list to your Block list. Deleting a blocked contact from your Contacts list does not remove the block.

Block or Unblock a Contact

1. Select **Tools**, and then click **Options**.

2. In the left pane, click **Privacy**.

3. Select the contacts you want to block, and then click **Block**.

4. Select the contacts you don't want to block, and then click **Allow**.

5. To find out which users have added you to their Contacts list, click **View**, and then click **Close**.

6. Click **OK**.

Did You Know?

You can quickly block or unblock a contact. Right-click the contact, and then click Block contact or Unblock contact. You can also click the Block button during a conversation.

You can block a person not in your Contacts list. Click the Actions menu, and then click Send an instant message, type the person's e-mail address in the results list box, click OK, and then click the Block button.

You can allow others to add you to their Contacts list without seeking your approval. Select Tools, click Options, click Privacy in the left pane, clear the Alert me when other people add me to their contact list check box, and then click OK.

Sending a File During an Instant Message

While you are conversing in Windows Live Messenger, you can send a contact a single file. You can send many different types of files, including documents, photos, and music. When you send a file, a request to transfer the file is sent to your contact. You are notified when your contact accepts or declines your request. Before you receive files over the Internet, make sure you have up-to-date virus protection software on your computer. When you receive a file, the Windows Live Messenger provides security information to help you understand more about the file. If your computer is located on a network behind a firewall, you might not be able to send files to those outside the firewall. If you want to send files to those behind the firewall, you need to manually open the connection; check with your network administrator for details.

Send a Single File

1. Click the **Actions** menu, point to **Send other**, and then click **Send a single file.**

2. Select the contact you want to send the file to.

3. Click **OK**.

4. Select the file you want to send.

5. Click **Open**.

6. To open a file, click the link in the Conversation window to start the transfer.

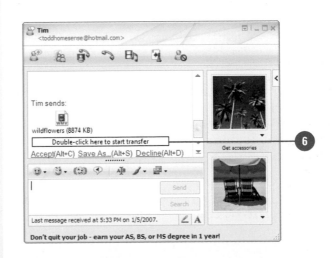

Did You Know?

You can follow up on a conversation with an e-mail. Right-click the contact, point to Send other, and then click E-mail.

You can show or hide your display picture from contacts. Select Tools, click Options, click General in the left pane, select or hide the Show display pictures from others check box, and then click OK.

You can sort or filter contacts. Click the Contacts menu, point to Sort contacts by or Filter contacts, and then select the options you want.

Sharing Files Using Shared Folders

With Sharing Folders (**New!**), you can share the same files with more than one contact and update the content automatically. To share or transfer files, you and your contact must have Windows XP or Windows Vista and Windows Live Messenger 8 or later. You also need to set sharing options in Windows Liver Messenger. After you're set up, you can simply drag files to share them. When you are online with a contact, the files you share are automatically synchronized. When you no longer want to share files with a contact using Sharing Folders, you can remove the contact's shared folder, which doesn't delete them from contacts. To keep your computer safe, you can set options to reject potentially unsafe files and install the free Windows Live OnCare safety scanner to check for viruses, and other disk management operations.

Set Sharing Folders Options

1. Select **Tools**, and then click **Options**

2. In the left pane, click **Sharing Folders**.

3. Select the **Use a sharing folder when I drag a file onto a contact's name in my contact list** check box.

4. Select the **When I drag a file onto a contact's name, automatically create a sharing folder if that contact doesn't already have one** check box.

5. In the left pane, click **File Transfer**.

6. To reject potentially unsafe file types, select the **Automatically reject file transfers for known unsafe file types** check box.

   When you try to share a potentially unsafe file an exclamation point appears over the icon for the file, and a Tooltip describes the security reason for blocking the file.

7. To scan received files, select the **Scan files for viruses using** check box, and click **Browse** or click **Install** to use the free virus scanner for Messenger.

8. Click **OK**.

Share Files Using a Shared Folder

◆ To share files, drag them from your file folder onto the contact in the main Messenger window or drag them onto the message area in the Conversation window.

◆ To add files, pause sharing, or view the Activity log, click the **Sharing Folders** button in the main Messenger window.

IMPORTANT *If a contact deletes a shared file, the local file on your hard drive is permanently deleted. However, if you delete a shared file, you can recover it from the recycle bin.*

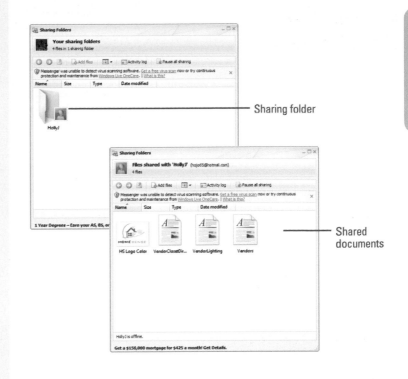

Sharing folder

Shared documents

Stop Sharing Files

① Select **Tools**, and then click **Options.**

② In the left pane, click **Sharing Folders**.

③ Select the contact you want to remove.

④ Click **Remove**.

⑤ Click **OK**.

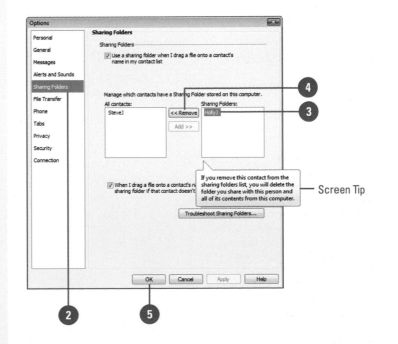

Screen Tip

Making a Video Call with the Internet

When used with Windows Vista and the right hardware, Windows Live Messenger provides state-of-the-art computer communications features. With Windows Live Messenger, you can talk to others over the Internet as you do on a regular phone, and you can use video to see others and let others see you as you converse (**New!**). Once you set up your computer hardware—Webcams, microphones and speakers—and related software, you're ready to communicate over the Internet. You have two communication choices: audio only, and audio and video. With audio only, you speak into a microphone and hear the other person's response over your computer's speakers. With audio and video, you send video to others so they receive live images as well as sound. If the contacts you call don't have a video camera, they will see you, but you won't see them.

Have a Video Conversation

1. Double-click the Windows Live Messenger icon in the notification area of the taskbar, and then sign in, if necessary.

2. Double-click the contact you want to send an instant message.

3. Click the **Video Call** button, and then wait for the other person to accept the invitation.

4. Use the controls to adjust the volume of the speakers or microphone.

5. Start talking.

6. When you're done, click the **Close** button.

> ### Did You Know?
>
> **You can set Webcam video options.** Click the Actions menu in the Conversation window, point to Video, and then select commands to show your Webcam or View a contact's Webcam.

Making a Phone Call with the Internet

Windows Live Messenger allows you to dial regular phones through a voice service provider using the Internet or a modem on your computer. Once the modem connects to the number you are dialing, called the remote party, you can pick up your phone and talk. This feature is useful for people who would otherwise be spending a fortune in long distance calling. It's also helpful for people who spent a lot of time on their computer. When you use Windows Live Messenger, having your modem's speakers on is helpful so you can hear what is actually happening with the connection. If your computer is located on a network behind a firewall, you might not be able to make phone calls; check with your network administrator for details.

Make a Phone Call With Windows Live Messenger

1. Click the **Actions** menu, point to **Call**, and then select one of the following commands:

   ◆ **Call a contact's computer**.

   ◆ **Call a contact's phone**.

   ◆ **Call a phone**.

   TIMESAVER *If you're in a conversation, click Make a phone call button, and then select a phone number.*

2. If you need a voice service provider, follow the instructions to sign up.

3. Select a contact or type a phone number, including the area code (even for local calls), and then type a name after it for easy identification on your list.

4. Click **OK** or **Call**.

   When you call a contact for the first time, click the link for the Windows Live Call Web site to authenticate your ID.

5. Use the controls to adjust the volume of the speakers or microphone.

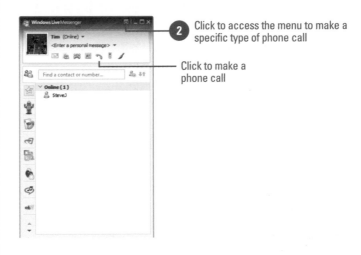

2 Click to access the menu to make a specific type of phone call

Click to make a phone call

Click to start a call while in a conversation

Connected call

Sending a Message to a Mobile Device

If you have a wireless device, such as a Web-enabled cellular phone, a pager, a Smartphone, Pocket PC Phone, or Pocket PC, you can set it up to receive instant messages using Windows Live Messenger (**New!**). When you send a message to a contact's mobile device, the message includes your e-mail address and phone number unless the mobile device doesn't support the feature. If your contact's mobile device is not turned on, the message might be delayed or not arrive at all.

Set Up an Account for a Mobile Device

1. Select **Tools**, and then click **Options**.

2. In the left pane, click **Phone**.

3. Click **Mobile Settings**.

4. Follow the online instructions on the Web site.

5. When you're done setting up a mobile account, close your browser, if necessary.

6. Select the **Allow people on my contact list to send messages to my mobile device** check box.

7. Click **OK**.

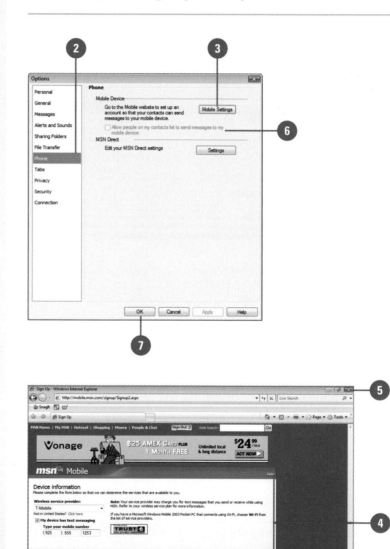

Did You Know?

You can send messages to a SmartWatch using MSN Direct. Select Tools, click Options, click Phone in the left pane, click Settings under MSN Direct, and then follow the online instruction on the Web site to activate and setup an account.

Send a Message to a Mobile Device

1. Double-click the Windows Live Messenger icon in the notification area of the taskbar, and then sign in, if necessary.

2. Right-click the contact you want to send a message, point to **Send other**, and then click **Send a message to a mobile device**.

   ◆ You can also, click the Actions menu, point to Send other, click Send a message to a mobile device, select a contact, and then click OK.

3. Type your message.

4. Click **Send**, and then wait for a reply.

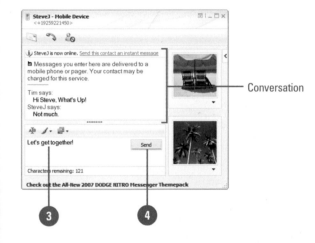

Conversation

For Your Information

Making a Call Using Messenger and Your Phone

You can use use Windows Live Messenger and Windows Live Call to place a call with Windows Live Messenger from your phone. Before you can use Window Live Call, you need to sign up for the service at the Windows Live Call sign up Web page. You also need to place at least one Windows Live Call from your computer before you can use your phone. You can access a phone number in your contacts list or the enter the phone number you want to call. To call a contact, press the # key followed by the number, or enter the number you want to reach from any other PC mode screen. To call a number that isn't in your contact list, switch to PC mode by pressing the Windows Live Messenger or PC connect button on your phone, or select the PC Call softkey, if available.

Getting Remote Assistance

Sometimes the best way to fix a computer problem is to get help from a friend or colleague who knows how to solve it. If your friend or colleague lives too far away to help you in person, you can use Remote Assistance within Windows Live Messenger and an Internet connection to help you get the support and answers you need. You can ask a trusted contact in another location to connect to your computer over the Internet and provide support in real time. After connecting to your computer, you can invite a contact to view your desktop, chat online using instant messages, talk online using a microphone and speakers, and send files. Instead of simply talking about a solution, sometimes you need someone to show you how to perform the steps before you fully understand the procedure. With Remote Assistance, you can give a contact control of your computer whereby he or she can demonstrate how to perform the procedure using his or her mouse and keyboard while you watch in real time. If your computer is located on a network behind a firewall, you might not be able to use remote assistance; check with your network administrator for details.

Ask for Remote Assistance

1. Double-click the Windows Messenger icon in the notification area of the taskbar, and then sign in, if necessary.

2. Double-click the contact you want to send an instant message.

3. Click the **Actions** menu, and then click **Request remote assistance**, and then wait for the other person to accept the invitation.

4. Enter a password twice, and then click **OK**.

5. Click **Yes** to let this person connect to your computer.

6. To have a conversation, type a message to explain your problem, and then press Enter.

7. If the person asks to take control of your computer, click **Yes** or **No**.

8. To take back control of your computer, click **Stop Sharing** on the toolbar.

9. When you're done, click **Disconnect**, and then click **Yes**.

Provide Remote Assistance

1. Sign-in to Windows Messenger, and then wait for an invitation to provide remote assistance.

   ◆ To offer remote assistance, select a contact, click the Actions menu, and then click Request remote assistance.

2. When you receive the invitation, click **Accept**, and then wait for the Remote Assistance window to open.

3. Wait, enter a password from the person asking for assistance, and then click **OK**.

4. To have a conversation, type a message to discuss the problem, and then press Enter.

5. Watch the screen of the person you want to help during the conversation.

6. To take control of the person's computer, click the **Request Control** button on the toolbar, and then wait for the other person's response.

7. To give back control of the other person's computer, click the **Stop Sharing** button on the toolbar.

8. When you're done, click **Disconnect**, and then click **Yes**.

9. If necessary, click Cancel to exit remote assistance and not connection to another person.

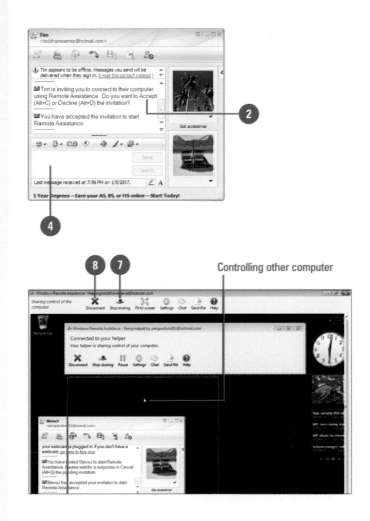

Controlling other computer

For Your Information

Sharing Games and Activities

If you need to share information in a specific program or document with others in a conference, you can use Windows Live Messenger to share your documents and programs. They cannot work with the document until you give them access to it. The user who clicks the program window "takes control" of the program and can then run any menu commands or make changes to the document. If you have a multi-player game, such as Age of Empires II, installed on both computers, you can play the game using Windows Live Messenger. To start an activity or game, click the Actions menu, click Start an activity or Play a game, and then follow the on-screen instructions.

Customizing Windows Live Messenger

Windows Live Messenger allows you to customize the program in many ways, including the display, the sign in process, message delivery, alerts and sounds, file sharing, file transfer, privacy, security, and connection status. To change program options, select a category in the left pane of the Options dialog box, and then select or specify the individual options you want. On the left side of the main Messenger window, tabs provide easy access to commonly used products and services. If the tab you use most often is at the bottom of the list, you can rearrange the tabs to suit your own needs. If the tabs are in the way, you can hide them all together.

Customize Windows Live Messenger

1. Select **Tools**, and then click **Options**.

2. In the left pane, click **Messages**.

3. Select or clear the options to determine how you want messages to appear or be responded to.

4. In the left pane, click **Alerts and Sounds**.

5. Select the alert check boxes you want to use.

6. Click the event you want to set the sound for, click **Browse**, select a sound, and then click **Open**.

7. In the left pane, click **Tabs**.

8. To arrange tabs, select the tab you want to move, and then click **Up** or **Down**.

9. To hide tabs, select the **Hide tabs** check box.

10. Click **OK**.

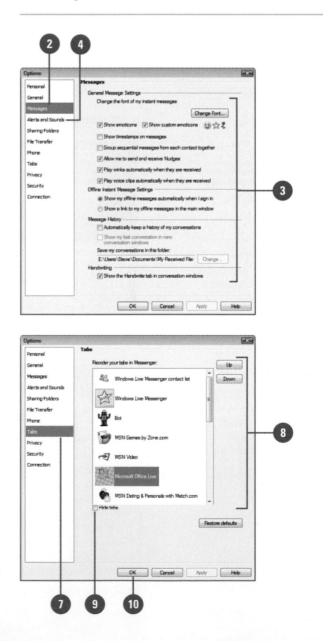

Working with Pictures

Introduction

Windows Vista makes it easy to store and work with your pictures using the Pictures folder. You can quickly access the folder from the Start menu. From the Pictures folder you can view, organize, and share pictures with others on the Internet. When you download and save pictures from your digital camera or scanner to your computer, Windows stores the digital images in the Pictures folder by default. (You can specify an alternative location.) You can view your picture files as a slide show or in the Extra-Large view, which displays a larger image above thumbnail images of the pictures. The Pictures folder also contains links to specialized picture tasks that help you share pictures with others, such as sending pictures in an e-mail, publishing pictures and documents on the Web, printing photographs, and ordering prints from the Internet. You can also create your own pictures or edit existing ones in Paint, a Windows accessory program designed for drawing and painting. Paint is useful for making simple changes to a picture, adding a text caption, or saving a picture in another file format.

Windows Vista introduces Windows Photo Gallery (**New!**), which allows you to view, locate, organize, open, and edit photos and pictures. Windows Photo Gallery shows all the pictures and videos located in the Pictures folder. In Windows Photo Gallery, you can also print photos, order photos through an online service, e-mail photos and pictures using your e-mail program, create CDs or DVDs, and make a movie using Windows Movie Maker.

Drawing a Picture

Paint is a Windows accessory you can use to create and work with graphics or pictures. Paint is designed to create and edit bitmap (.bmp) files, but you can also open and save pictures created in or for other graphics programs and the Internet using several common file formats, such as .tiff, .gif, or .jpeg. A **bitmap** file is a map of a picture created from small black, white, or colored dots, or bits. Paint comes with a set of tools in the Toolbox (located along the left edge of the window) that you can use for drawing and manipulating pictures. A tool remains turned on until you select another tool in the Toolbox. In addition to the drawing tools, you can also add text to a picture. When you create a text box and type the text, you can edit and format it, but once you deselect the text box, the text becomes part of the picture, which you can't edit.

Draw a Picture

1. Click the **Start** button, point to **All Programs**, click **Accessories**, and then click **Paint**.

2. If you want, drag a resize handle on the canvas to resize it.

3. Click a drawing tool.

4. If available, click a fill option for the selected tool.

5. Click the color you want to use with the left mouse button to select the foreground color and the right mouse button to select the background color.

6. Drag the shapes you want by holding down one of the following:

   ◆ The left mouse button to draw with the foreground color.

   ◆ The right mouse button to draw with the background color.

   ◆ The Shift key to constrain the drawing to a proportional size, such as a circle, square, or horizontal line.

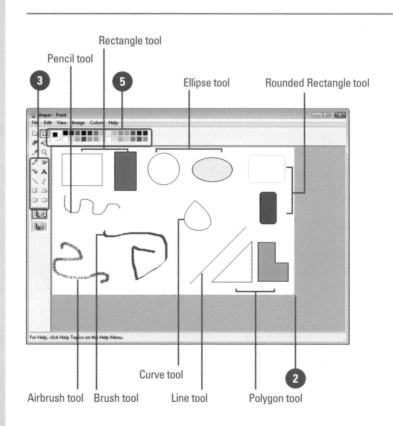

Rectangle tool

Pencil tool

Ellipse tool

Rounded Rectangle tool

Airbrush tool   Brush tool   Curve tool   Line tool   Polygon tool

Add Text to a Picture

1. In Paint, create or open the picture you want to modify.

2. Click the **Text** tool.

3. Drag a text box.

4. Select the font, font size, and any formatting you want to apply to the text.

5. Click in the text box, if necessary, and then type the text.

6. Drag a text box resize handle to enlarge or reduce the text box.

7. Edit and format the text.

8. Click outside the text box to deselect it and change the text to a bitmap.

   IMPORTANT *Once you click outside the text box to place the text in the picture, the text becomes part of the picture.*

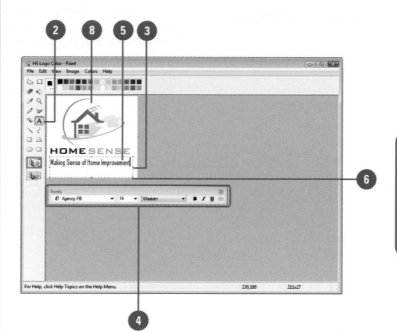

Save a Picture in Different Formats

1. In Paint, create or open the picture you want to save in a different format.

2. Click the **File** menu, and then click **Save As**.

3. Select the drive and folder in which you want to save the file.

4. Type a name for the file, or use the suggested name.

5. Click the **Save as type** list arrow, and then click a file format.

6. Click **Save**.

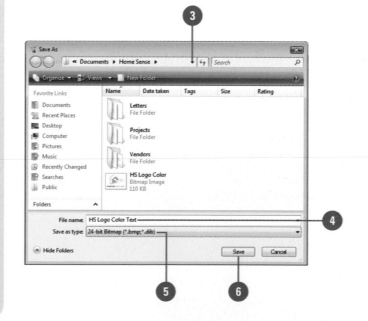

Editing a Picture

After you create or open a picture, you can select all or part of the picture and use commands on the Image menu, such as rotate, stretch, and invert colors, to further modify it in Paint. In addition to the drawing tools, you can also use painting tools, such as Fill With Color, Airbrush, Brush, Pencil, and Pick Color, to transform the picture. The Fill With Color tool is useful if you want to color an entire item or recolor text letter by letter. If you need to remove part of a picture, you can use the Eraser tool, which comes in four different sizes.

Modify a Picture

① In Paint, create or open the picture you want to edit.

② Click the **Free-Form Select** tool to select irregular shapes, or click the **Select** tool to select rectangle shapes.

③ Drag the selection area you want.

④ Click the **Opaque Background** option or the **Transparent Background** option.

⑤ Click the **Image** menu, and then click one of the following:

- ◆ **Flip/Rotate**
- ◆ **Resize/Skew**
- ◆ **Invert Colors**
- ◆ **Attributes**

⑥ Click **OK**.

⑦ Save the picture and exit Paint.

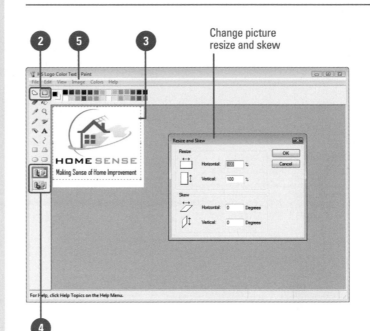

Change picture resize and skew

Did You Know?

You can save part of a picture to a file.
Select the part of the picture you want to save, click the Edit menu, click Copy To, select a folder, type a name, and then click Save.

You can quickly copy a selection.
Hold down the Ctrl key, and then drag the selection.

Fill Part of a Picture

1. In Paint, create or open the picture you want to edit.

2. Click the color you want to fill, or click the **Pick Color** tool and click a color from the picture.

3. Click the **Fill With Color** tool.

4. Point the tip of the paint bucket to the area you want to fill, and then click.

Did You Know?

You can replace any color with the background color. Set the foreground color to the color to be replaced and the background color to the replacement color, and then hold down the right mouse button and drag the Eraser over the area you want to replace.

Erase Part of a Picture

1. In Paint, create or open the picture you want to edit.

2. To magnify an area of the screen, click the Magnifier tool, and then click the area you want to magnify.

3. Click the **Eraser** tool.

4. Click the **Eraser** size.

5. Drag the Eraser over the area you want to erase.

6. If you make a mistake, click the **Edit** menu, and then click **Undo** to restore your last action.

7. To restore the magnification, click the **Magnifier** tool, and then click the area again.

Viewing Pictures

Windows gives you several ways to view pictures. In a folder with pictures, you can use Extra Large Icons view to see a larger view of the pictures. In the Pictures folder, you can use the slide show feature to display pictures in a full screen slide show. If you want to preview picture or open a picture to edit, you can double-click the file icon to use the default program associated with the picture file type, or select the specific program—such as Paint, Windows Photo Gallery, Microsoft Office Document Imaging, or Microsoft Office Picture Manager—you want to use to make changes.

View a Picture

1. Click the **Start** button, and then click **Pictures**.

2. To view sample pictures, double-click the Sample Pictures folder.

3. Click a picture to view information about the picture in the Details pane.

4. Click the **Preview** or **Open** button arrow, and then click the program you want to open the picture.

See Also

See "Understanding Faxes" on page 411 for information on working with faxes.

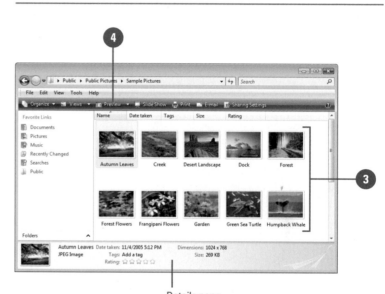

Details pane

Preview in Photo Gallery

View Pictures as Extra Large Icons

1. Click the **Start** button, click **Pictures**, or open any other folder with pictures you want to view.

2. Click the **Views** button arrow, and then click **Extra Large Icons**.

View Pictures as a Slide Show

1. Click the **Start** button, click **Pictures**, or open any other folder with pictures you want to view.

2. Select the pictures you want in the show, or click one picture to see all the pictures.

3. Click the **Slide Show** button, and then watch the show.

4. To manually advance to the next slide, click anywhere in the picture.

5. To control the slide show, right-click the screen, and then click the control you want, including **Shuffle**, **Loop**, or a **Slide Show Speed (Slow, Medium, or Fast)**.

6. To exit the slide show, press Esc or right-click the screen, and then click **Exit**.

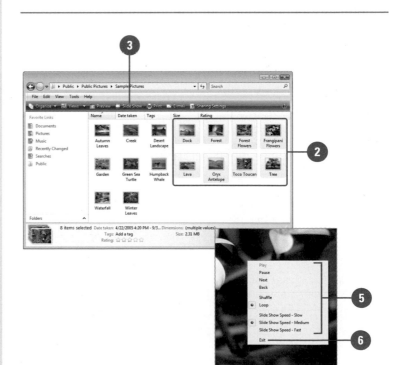

Managing Pictures in the Photo Gallery

Windows Photo Gallery (**New!**) is a program that allows you to view, locate, and edit pictures. Windows Photo Gallery shows all the pictures and videos located in the Pictures folder. However, you can add and view other folders on your computer. The left pane in Windows Photo Gallery displays a tree structure like the Folders list that allows you to display pictures by different criteria, including Pictures, Recently Imported, Tags, Date Taken, Ratings, and Folders. To help you sort and search for pictures, you can add tags, ratings, and captions to pictures. The Search box used in all Explorer windows is also available. You can also use the View button next to the Search box to change the icon thumbnail views, view a table of contents, or display groups and sorts.

View Pictures Using Windows Photo Gallery

1. Click the **Start** button, point to **All Programs**, and then click **Windows Photo Gallery**.

2. To change the view, click the **View** button, and then select a view: **Thumbnails, Thumbnails with Text, Tiles, Group By, Sort By,** or **Table of Contents**.

3. Use the tree structure in the left pane to view the pictures:

   ◆ **Pictures or videos.** Under All Pictures and Videos, click Pictures or Videos.

   ◆ **Imported Pictures.** Under Recently Imported, click Recent Imports.

   ◆ **Tags.** Under Tags, click the tag you want to sort by.

   ◆ **Date.** Under Date Taken, click the date you want to sort by.

   ◆ **Ratings.** Under Ratings, click the rating you want to sort by.

   ◆ **Folders.** Under Folders, click the picture related folder you want to display.

4. Use the controls at the bottom of the window to change the display size, play slide show, delete pictures, and rotate pictures.

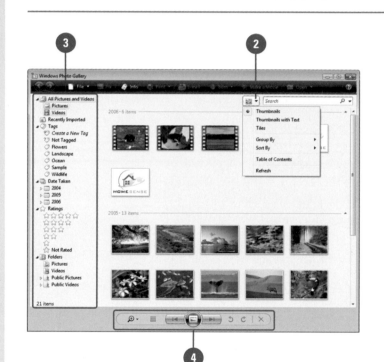

Add Tags, Ratings, or Captions

 Click the **Start** button, point to **All Programs**, and then click **Windows Photo Gallery**.

 Select the photo you want to add tags, a rating, or a caption.

 Click the **Info** button on the toolbar.

 To add a tag, click **Add Tags**, type the tag you want, and then press Enter.

 To add a rating, click the rating star you want.

 To add a caption, click <**Add Caption**>, type the caption you want, and then press Enter.

 When you're done, click the **Close** button in the Info pane.

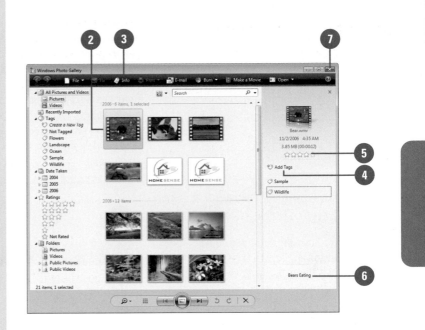

Find Pictures in Windows Photo Gallery

 Click the **Start** button, point to **All Programs**, and then click **Windows Photo Gallery**.

 Click in the Search box.

 Type the work or phrase you want to find associated with the picture.

As you type, the pictures that match the criteria display in the gallery.

 When you're done, click the **Close** button.

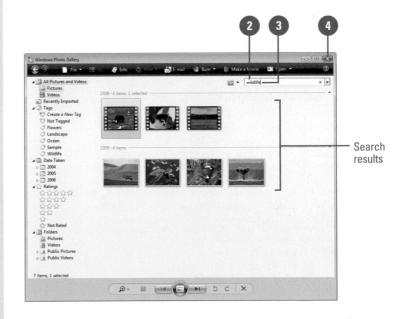

Search results

Fixing Pictures in the Photo Gallery

If you need to edit a picture, you can use Windows Photo Gallery (**New!**) to adjust brightness, contrast, and color, and to remove red eye. You can also crop a picture. If the colors in a picture don't look right, you can use Auto Adjust to enhance picture by changing the brightness (light), contrast (dark), color temperature, tint, or saturation. Color temperature allows you to make the colors warmer (red) or cooler (blue); tint modifies the color cast (add or remove green); and saturation changes color vividness. If you don't like the changes made by Auto Adjust, you can use Adjust Color to change the individual color attributes.

Fix Pictures Using Windows Photo Gallery

1. Click the **Start** button, point to **All Programs**, and then click **Windows Photo Gallery**.

2. Select the photo you want to fix.

3. Click the **Fix** button on the toolbar.

4. Click **Auto Adjust**.

5. To adjust brightness and contrast, click **Adjust Exposure**, and then drag the sliders.

6. To adjust color temperature, tint, or saturation, click **Adjust Color**, and then drag the sliders.

7. To crop a picture, click **Crop Picture**, select a proportion or drag a selection, and move the selection, and then click **Apply**.

8. To fix red eye, click **Fix Red Eye**, and then drag a rectangle around the eye you want to fix.

9. If you don't like the changes, click the **Undo** button arrow, and then select the options you want to undo or click **Undo All**.

10. When you're done, click the **Back To Gallery** button.

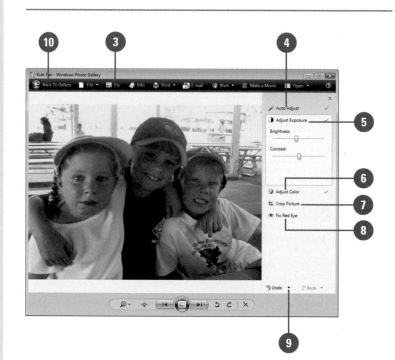

E-mailing a Picture

If you have one or more photos, pictures, or documents that you want to share with others, you can send them in an e-mail as attachments. Before you send photos or pictures in an e-mail as an attachment, you typically need to resize them in a separate graphics program so your recipient can view them with minimal scrolling, open your e-mail program, and then attach the files. With Windows you can send a photo or picture in an e-mail message without having to resize it in a separate graphics program, or even open your e-mail program. Using the E-mail button on the toolbar in Windows Photo Gallery or any Explorer window, Windows simply asks how you want to size the photos and pictures, and then opens an e-mail message window with the attached files from your default e-mail program. All you need to do is address the message, add any message text, and then send it.

E-mail a Photo or Picture

1. In Windows Photo Gallery or an Explorer window, open the folder containing the picture or folder you want to e-mail.

2. Select the pictures or a folder with pictures you want to e-mail.

3. Click the **E-mail** button on the toolbar.

4. Click the **Picture** size arrow, and then select the resolution size you want: **Smaller: 640 x 480, Small: 800 x 600, Medium: 1024 x 768, Large: 1280 x 1024**, or **Original Size**.

5. Click **Attach** to open your e-mail program, displaying an e-mail message with a file attachment.

6. Type an e-mail address.

7. Click **Send**.

See Also

See "Sending and Retrieving a File" on page 180 for information on sending a file in an e-mail message.

Formatting and Printing Photos

Windows makes it easy to format and print photographs from Windows Photo Gallery, which allows you to print photographs. During the process, you can select the photo(s) to print, the paper type, and a page layout, such as full-page prints, contact-sheet prints, 4 x 6-inch prints, 5 x 7-inch prints, 8 x 10-inch prints, 3.5 x 5-inch prints, and wallet size prints. To print a photo from your computer, you need a color printer and special photo paper. In order to get the best results when you print photographs, set your printer resolution to the highest setting for the best quality output, and use high-quality glossy paper designed specifically for printing photographs. Check your printer documentation for the best resolution setting suited to print your photographs. When you print photographs with a high resolution setting, the printing process might take longer. Many printer manufacturers also make paper designed to work best with their printers; check your printer manufacturer's Web site for more information.

Format and Print a Photo

1. In Windows Photo Gallery or an Explorer window, open the folder containing the photo or folder you want to print.

2. Select the photos you want to print.

3. Click the **Print** button on the toolbar, and then click **Print** (in Windows Photo Gallery).

4. Specify the printer options you want:

   ◆ Click the **Printer** arrow, and then select a printer.

   ◆ Click the **Paper size** arrow, and then select a paper size.

   ◆ Click the **Quality** arrow, and then click a resolution.

5. Select photo size you want.

6. Specify the number of copies you want.

7. Select or clear the **Fit picture to frame** check box.

8. Click **Print**, and then follow any printer specify instructions.

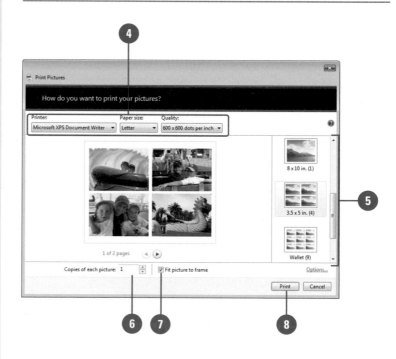

Ordering Photo Prints from the Web

If you have digital photographs taken from a digital camera or scanned into your computer, you can send your digital photographs to an online printing company where they create photo prints and send them to your mailing address. Windows makes the process easy from Windows Photo Gallery, which walks you through the ordering process. You'll need to provide print sizes, quantities, and billing and shipping information to complete the order.

Order Photo Prints from the Web

1. In Windows Photo Gallery, open the folder containing the photo or folder you want to print.

2. Select the photos you want to send to an online printing company.

3. Click the **Print** button on the toolbar, and then click **Order Prints**.

4. Select the printing company you want to send your photos.

5. Click **Send Pictures**.

6. If necessary, click **Send**.

7. Follow the remaining steps to place an order with the specific printing company.

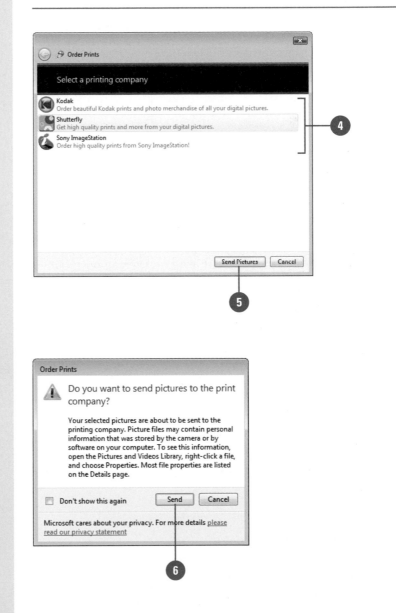

Installing a Scanner or Digital Camera

Windows makes it easy to install a scanner or digital camera on your computer using plug-and-play. In most cases, all you need to do is turn off your computer, plug in the hardware device, and restart your computer. Windows recognizes the new hardware and installs it. If for some reason Windows doesn't recognize the hardware, you can start a wizard, which walks you through the installation process.

Install a Scanner or Digital Camera

1. Plug your scanner or camera into your computer to start the Scanner and Camera wizard.

   If the wizard doesn't open, click the **Start** button, click **Control Panel**, double-click the **Scanners and Cameras** icon, and then click **Add Device**.

2. Click **Next** to continue.

3. Click the manufacturer of the scanner or camera you want to install, click the device name, and then click **Next** to continue.

   TROUBLE? *If your scanner or camera is not listed, try to install it using the Device Manager.*

4. Connect your device to your computer, select a port, and then click **Next** to continue.

5. Type a name for the device, or use the suggested one, and then click **Next** to continue.

6. Click **Finish**.

246

Testing a Scanner or Digital Camera

After you install a scanner or digital camera on your computer, it's a good idea to test the hardware device to make sure it's working properly. When you test a scanner or digital camera, Windows checks to see if the hardware device is communicating with the operating system.

Test a Scanner or Digital Camera

1. Click the **Start** button, click **Control Panel**, and then double-click the **Scanners and Cameras** icon in Classic view.

2. Right-click the scanner or camera you want to test, and then click **Properties**.

3. Click the **General** tab.

4. Click **Test Scanner** or **Test Camera**.

   A message appears with the results of the test.

5. Click **OK**.

6. Click **OK**.

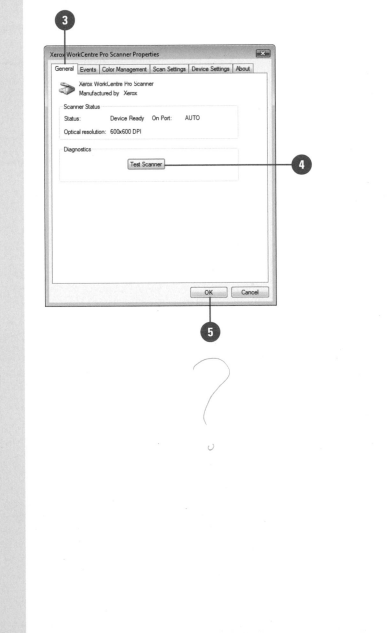

Did You Know?

You can remove a scanner. Click the Start button, click Control Panel, double-click the System icon in Classic view, click Device Manager in the left pane, click the plus sign (+) next to Imaging devices, select the scanner you want to remove, click the Uninstall button on the toolbar, and then follow the on-screen instructions.

Scanning a Picture

Windows Vista makes it easy to scan pictures with Windows Photo Gallery (**New!**) and Windows Fax and Scan (**New!**). A **scanner** is like a photocopy machine on which you can lay photographs, books, and other documents that you want to save in digital form on your computer. In addition to scanning photographs, many high resolution scanners also allow you to scan a negative from a film strip and enlarge it. You use Windows Photo Gallery to start the scanning process and store the scanned photo in the in Pictures folder. With Windows Fax and Scan, you can choose scanning preferences, such as picture type, resolution (the number of dots per inch (dpi), preview the scanned picture, adjust the scan area, and select a graphic format. In order to use the scanner features of Windows, you need to have a scanner attached and installed on your computer.

Scan a Picture
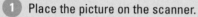

1. Place the picture on the scanner.

2. Click the **Start** button, point to **All Programs**, and then click **Windows Photo Gallery**.

3. Click the **File** button, and then click **Import from Camera or Scanner**.

4. Select the scanner you want to use.

5. Click **Import**.

   The New Scan dialog box from Windows Fax and Scan opens.

   ◆ You can also access this dialog box from Windows Fax and Scan. Click the Start button, point to All Programs, and then click Windows Fax and Scan.

   The default settings for scanning a document are automatically selected.

6. Specify the options you want for the new scan. Some important ones include:

   ◆ Click the **Profile** button arrow, and then click **Photo**.

   ◆ Click the **File type** list, and then click the file type you want.

◆ Click the **Resolution (DPI)** list, and then click the resolution you want.

◆ Adjust the brightness and contrast to the settings you want.

7 Select or clear the **Preview or scan images as separate files** check box.

8 To preview the scan, click **Preview**, and then make any adjustments you want before the final scan.

9 Click **Scan**.

10 Click the **Tag these pictures (optional)** list, type a tag name.

11 Click **Import**.

Windows Photo Gallery displays the scanned picture.

Did You Know?

You can change where Windows Photo Gallery stores scanned pictures. In Windows Photo Gallery, click the File button, click Options, click the Import tab, click the Settings for list, and then click Scanners. Click Browse next to the Import to list, and then select the location you want.

See Also

See "Installing a Scanner or Digital Camera" on page 246 for information on installing a scanner.

See "Installing a Scanner or Digital Camera" on page 246 for information on installing a scanner.

For Your Information

Selecting the Appropriate File Format

Each file type has a different format and recommended use. JPG (Joint Photographic Experts Group; also known as JPEG) and PNG (Portable Network Graphics) are graphic file formats commonly used on web pages, while BMP (Bit-mapped) and TIF (Tagged Image File Format, also known as Tiff) are file formats used in documents. The format specifies how the information in the file is organized internally. JPG and PNG formats are compressible, which means that the file size is smaller and transfers over the Internet faster. Each file format uses a different compression method, which produces different results when you display the graphic files. JPG is designed for photographs and supports millions of colors, but loses some image quality by discarding image data to reduce the file size. PNG is designed for web graphics and supports millions of color without losing image quality, but not all web browsers fully support its capabilities without using a plug-in, which is a software add-on installed on your computer. TIF is designed for all graphics and colors and one of the most widely used graphic formats, but the file size is large. BMP is the standard Windows graphic format and is similar to TIF.

Downloading Digital Camera Pictures

A **digital still camera** stores pictures digitally rather than on film. The major advantage of digital still cameras is that making photos is fast and inexpensive. In order to use the digital camera features of Windows, you need to have a digital still or video camera attached and installed on your computer. When you connect a digital camera to your computer, Windows Vista display the AutoPlay dialog, where you can choose to import or view files in the Camera window. When you import pictures, the files are store and made available in Windows Photo Gallery. If you don't use AutoPlay, you can also use an Import command in Windows Photo Gallery or the Camera window. You can use the Camera window available from the Computer window to view pictures that you have already taken with the camera and copy them in a folder on your computer, or delete pictures from your camera.

Download Pictures from a Camera

1. Connect the digital camera to your computer, and follow instructions to install and recognize the camera.

2. If the AutoPlay dialog box opens, click **Import Pictures** to import the pictures and complete the process.

   If the AutoPlay dialog box doesn't open, continue.

3. Click the **Start** button, and then click **Computer**.

4. Right-click the digital camera icon, and then click **Import Pictures**.

   ◆ You can also click the Start button, point to All Programs, click Windows Photo Gallery, click the File button, and then click Import from Camera or Scanner.

5. To change import settings, click the **Options** link, select the options you want, and then click **OK**.

6. Click **Import**.

   Windows Photo Gallery opens by default to display the pictures.

Manage Pictures on the Camera

1. Connect the digital camera to your computer.

2. If the AutoPlay dialog box opens, click **Open this device to view files**, and then skip to Step 4.

   If the AutoPlay dialog box doesn't open, continue.

3. Click the **Start** button, and then click **Computer**, and then double-click the Camera icon associated with the digital camera.

4. Double-click the removable storage icon, and any folders to display the pictures stored on the digital camera.

5. Click a picture, and then perform any of the following commands:

   ◆ Right-click a picture, and then click **Preview** to display the picture in Windows Photo Gallery.

   ◆ Right-click a picture, and then click **Open** to display the picture the default program.

   ◆ Click the **Edit** menu, click **Copy to Folder**, select a folder, and then click **Copy**.

   ◆ Right-click a picture, and then click **Delete**.

Using Pictures as a Screen Saver

Instead of using standard screen savers provided by Windows, you can use your own pictures to create a slide show screen saver. Windows displays all the pictures, which you have designated in a folder, to create as a full screen slide show. You can add or remove pictures from the folder to modify the slide show.

Use Pictures as a Screen Saver

1. If you want to create a custom folder for pictures, create a folder, and then place the pictures you want to use in the slide show in the folder.

2. Right-click a blank area of the desktop, and then click **Personalize**.

3. Click **Screen Saver**.

   ◆ You can also click the File button in Windows Photo Gallery, and then click Screen Saver Setting to open this dialog box.

4. Click the **Screen Saver** list, and then click **Photos**.

5. Click **Settings**.

6. Select the option to use pictures from the Photo Gallery or your own folder. If necessary, click **Browse**, select the folder with your pictures, and then click **OK**.

7. Click the **Slide Show speed** list, and then select the speed you want.

8. Click **Save**.

9. Click **Preview**, and then click the mouse to stop it.

10. Click **OK**.

Using a Picture as a Desktop Background

Instead of using one of the pictures provided by Windows, you can select a picture on your hard disk or from a web page as the desktop background. You can use Paint or any graphics program to create new background designs or change existing ones. Acceptable formats for background files are Bitmap (the format of a Paint file), JPEG (the format of an Internet graphic file), or HTM (the format of a web page). After you set a picture as the desktop background, Windows adds the picture to the Background list on the Desktop tab in the Display Properties dialog box. When you use a picture from a web page, Windows saves it in the Background list as Internet Explorer Background. Each new picture from a web page you set as a background replaces the previous one.

Set a Picture as the Background

1. Open the folder or the Web page with the picture you want to set as the background.

2. Right-click the picture.

3. Click **Set as Desktop Background** for a picture file, or click **Set as Background** for a Web picture.

   If the picture doesn't appear on your desktop, continue.

4. Right-click a blank area of the desktop, and then click **Personalize**.

5. Click **Desktop Background**.

6. Click the picture you set as the background.

7. Click **OK**.

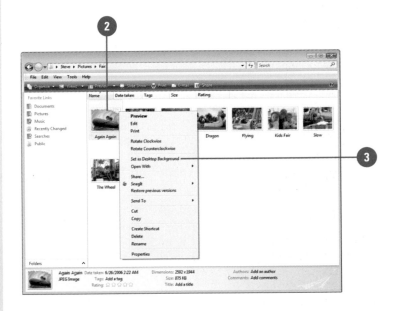

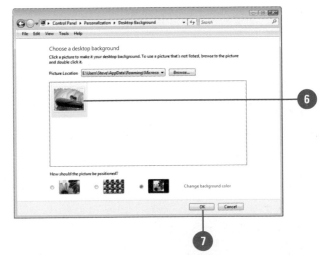

Setting Photo Gallery Options

Windows Photo Gallery allows you to set general and import options. The general options allow you to show pictures and video previews in tooltips, specify how long to keep original photos that are fixed, and whether to get program update alerts. The import options allow you to specify import settings for cameras, CDs and DVDs, or Scanners. The import settings specify where Windows Photo Gallery import pictures based on date and tag criteria. As you specify settings, you can view an example of the criteria, so you can better determine if the import settings are what you want. In addition, you can set other options that allow you to rotate pictures, open Windows Photo Gallery, erase picture from the camera, or receive a prompt to add tags.

Set Windows Photo Gallery Options

1. Click the **Start** button, point to **All Programs**, and then click **Windows Photo Gallery**.

2. Click the **File** button, and then click **Options**.

3. Click the **General** tab.

   ◆ **Tooltips.** Select to show picture and video previews in tooltips.

   ◆ **Save original pictures.** Select a delete option for original pictures.

   ◆ **Check for updates.** Select to get update alerts.

4. Click the **Import** tab.

   ◆ **Settings for.** Select Cameras, CDs and DVDs, or Scanners

   ◆ **Import to.** Select a location.

   ◆ **Folder name.** Select a folder criteria based on date and tag.

   ◆ **File name.** Select an option to preserve tags and file names.

   ◆ **Other options.** Select or clear the check boxes you want.

5. Click **OK**.

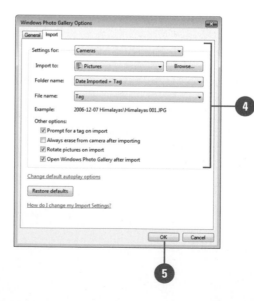

Working with Windows Media Player

Introduction

You can use Windows Media Player (WMP version 11) to play sounds, music, and digital movies on your computer and on the Internet, or listen to radio stations from all over the world. In addition, you can play and copy CDs, rip music from CDs, create your own CDs, play DVDs or VCDs, and copy music and videos to portable devices, such as portable digital audio players and portable PCs. Using Windows Media Player requires a sound card, speakers, and an Internet connection to view the Media Guide and other online stores, look for music licenses, and listen to radio stations on the Internet.

Windows also comes with Sound Recorder, a sound recording utility program you can use to create and modify a sound. You can use the sound to indicate a Windows event, such as starting Windows or if an error has occurred. Using Sound Recorder requires a sound card, speakers, and a microphone.

In addition to Windows Media Player, you can also use Windows Media Center to play media files on your computer or on the Web. Windows Media Center (**New!**) is an entertainment system integrated into your computer that lets you watch live or recorded TV, play video and watch pictures, listen to music and radio using an FM tuner or the Internet, play and burn CDs or DVDs, browse online media, and play games. You can also use Windows Media Center Extenders to add entertainment devices—such as a TV, DVD player, digital camera, or Xbox 360—to your system and control each one from Windows Media Center within a networked environment.

Starting and Updating Windows Media Player

Before you can use Windows Media Player, you need to check to make sure you have the latest version (11 or later) installed on your computer using the About Windows Media Player command on the Help menu for the current player. If it's not, you can download and install it from the Web at *www.microsoft.com/downloads*. You start Windows Media Player like any other Windows program. You can use the Start menu or a button on the Quick Launch toolbar. After you start Windows Media Player, you should check for software updates on the Internet. Microsoft is continually adding features and fixing problems. You can use the Help menu in Windows Media Player to access the updates.

Start and Update Windows Media Player

1. Click the **Start** button, point to **All Programs**, and then click **Windows Media Player**.

2. Click the **Help** menu, and then click **Check for Updates**.

3. Follow the wizard instructions to complete the upgrade.

4. To move around, click the task tabs along the top of the windows. The arrows below the tabs provide access additional task options. You can use the Back and Forward button to retrace previous steps.

Did You Know?

You can show and hide the menu bar. To show or hide the menu bar, click the Layout Options button, and then click Show Classic Menus.

You can automatically check for software updates. Click the Tools menu, click Options, click the Player tab, and then click the Once a day, Once a week, or Once a month option.

You can display Media Player as a button on the taskbar. Right-click a blank area of the taskbar, point to Toolbars, and then click Windows Media Player.

For Your Information

What's New in Windows Media Player 11

Windows Media Player 11 comes with a new streamline design that makes it easier to access top activities and common tasks, such as ripping from CDs, burning to CDs, and syncing to portable devices. WMP now integrates tightly with with URGE, a digital music service from MTV networks. WMP supports more portable devices and improves syncing features to make it easy to take your music with you. Improved functionality lets you create custom CDs. A new media sharing feature lets you stream the contents of your library to networked devices.

Viewing the Media Player Window

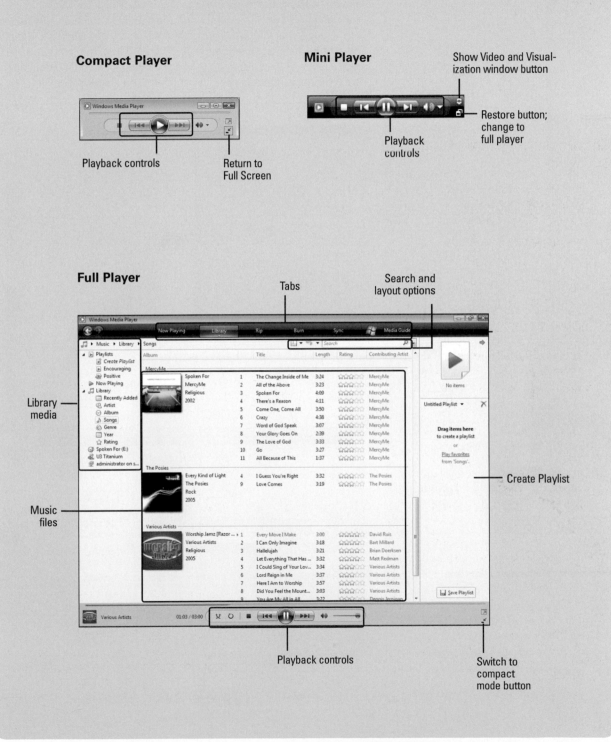

Compact Player

Playback controls

Return to
Full Screen

Mini Player

Show Video and Visual-
ization window button

Restore button;
change to
full player

Playback
controls

Full Player

Tabs

Search and
layout options

Library
media

Music
files

Create Playlist

Playback controls

Switch to
compact
mode button

Playing Music from CDs

Windows allows you to play music on your computer in the background while you work. After you insert a music CD into your CD-ROM drive and the music starts to play, you can minimize Windows Media Player and continue to work with other programs on your computer. If you are connected to the Internet when you play a music CD, Windows Media Player tries to locate information about the CD from the Internet, such as the name of the artist and the songs on the album. If the information is not available, the track number of each song displays instead.

Play a Music CD

1 Insert a music CD into your CD-ROM drive.

2 If the Audio dialog box appears, click **Play audio CD** (using Windows Media Player).

The Windows Media Player window appears, and the CD starts to play on the Now Playing tab.

3 To pause the music, click the **Pause** button.

4 To stop the music, click the **Stop** button.

5 To play a specific song, double-click the song in the list.

6 To play the previous or next song, click the **Previous** or **Next** button.

7 Click the **Minimize** button to continue to listen while you work, or click the **Close** button to exit.

Did You Know?

You can play CD songs in random order. Click the Turn Shuffle On button.

You can stop a song from playing. Right-click the song in the list, and then click Remove from list.

You can play a CD continuously. Click the Play menu, and then click Repeat.

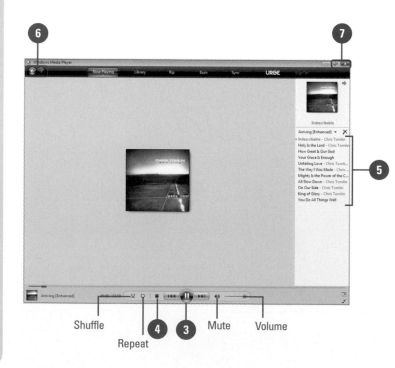

Playing a DVD or VCD Movie

If you have a DVD drive and decoder hardware or software on your computer, you can play DVD movies with Windows Media Player. If you don't have a decoder, you can purchase one from a third party manufacturer. If you only have a CD player, you can play VCD movies. A VCD is similar to a DVD, yet the video quality is not as high. When you play a DVD or VCD movie, a list of titles appear with a section of content from the movie. You can use the titles to browse through the contents of the DVD or VCD.

Play a DVD or VCD Movie

1 Insert a DVD into your DVD drive or a VCD into your CD drive.

2 If the Audio dialog box appears, click the option to play the DVD or VCD, and then click OK.

The Windows Media Player window appears, and the DVD or VCD starts to play.

3 To expand the contents list of the DVD or VCD click the plus sign (+).

4 To pause the movie, click the **Pause** button.

5 To stop the movie, click the **Stop** button.

6 To play a specific title, double-click it in the list.

7 To play the previous or next section of the movie, click the **Previous** or **Next** button.

8 Click the **Close** button to exit.

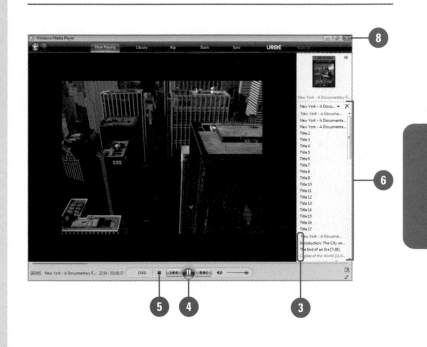

Did You Know?

You can display captions and subtitles for a DVD. Click the Play menu, point to Lyrics, Captions, and Subtitles, and then click Off (toggles on and off) or Default to select the language you want to use.

Controlling the Volume

Windows comes with master volume controls that allow you to change the volume of all devices and applications on the computer at once. You can increase or decrease the volume, or you can mute (turn off) the sound on your computer. The volume control is available by default on the notification area on the taskbar. The Volume icon makes it easy to increase or decrease the volume or mute the sound on your computer. In addition to changing the master volume on your computer, you can also adjust the volume of specific devices, such as a CD or DVD player, without affecting the volume of other devices.

Change the Computer Volume

1 Click the **Volume** icon in the notification area on the taskbar.

2 Drag the slider to adjust the volume to the level you want.

TIMESAVER *Press F9 to increase the volume, press F8 to decrease the volume, or press F9 to mute the volume.*

3 To mute the sound, click the **Mute** button.

4 Press Esc or click off the menu to close the volume controls.

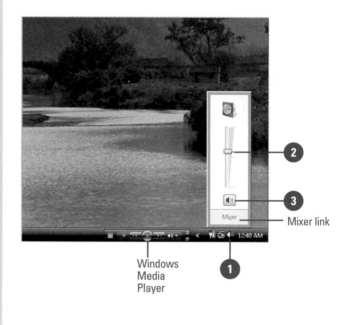

Windows Media Player

Mixer link

Did You Know?

You can display the Volume icon on the taskbar. Right-click the taskbar, click Properties, select the Volume check box, and then click OK.

You can quickly display the Volume. Point to the Volume icon in the notification area.

Troubleshooting

Testing Your Sound Hardware

If your are having trouble hearing the sound from Windows Media Player, the best place to start is to test your sound hardware. Click the Start button, click Control Panel, and then double-click the Sounds icon in Classic view. Next, click the Playback tab, click Configure, click Test, click Next, and then follow the instructions to test the hardware. Once you have tested the hardware, click Finish, and then click OK.

Set Volume Levels for Specific Devices

1 Click the **Volume** icon in the notification area on the taskbar.

2 Click the **Mixer** link.

3 Drag the **Speakers** slider to adjust the settings for the sound level you want.

The volume for the speakers is the main volume control.

4 Drag the other sliders to adjust the settings for the applications you want.

The volume for the speakers is the main volume control.

5 When you're done, click the **Close** button.

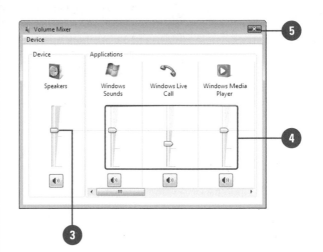

Did You Know?

You can set the recording volume.
Right-click the Volume icon, click Recording Devices, click a device, click Properties, click the Levels tab, adjust the volume level, and then click OK twice.

You can set the playback volume for left and right speakers. Right-click the Volume icon, click Playback Devices, click a device, click Properties, click the Levels tab, adjust the volume level, click Balance, adjust L and R levels, click OK, and then click OK twice.

Browsing the Media Guide and Online Stores

The Windows Media Player comes with a built-in Media Guide that is updated daily with the latest music, movies, and entertainment news from the Internet as well as access to your favorite online media stores, such as URGE, Napster, Emusic, Mixplay, Getmusic, and Satellite Radio, where you can download music and more. WMP provides special integration with URGE, an online music service provided by MTV networks. The Media Guide is a web page that provides links to a variety of media topics ranging from music to sports. Selecting a link opens a web page with more information about the topic, or plays music or movies. Links to media files, such as music or movies, appear with different speeds, which indicate the speed at which the file downloads and plays on your Internet connection.

Use the Media Guide and Online Stores

1. Start Windows Media Player and connect to the Internet, if necessary.

2. Click the **URGE** button to display the URGE online store, or click the button **arrow** below it, and then click **Media Guide** or **Browse all Online Stores**.

   If necessary, follow the on-screen instructions to accept the license agreement and install any updates.

3. Click the links you want on the web page.

4. When you're done, click the **Close** button.

> ## Did You Know?
>
> *You can Automatically hide menus.* To turn on/off Autohide menus, click the View menu, point to Menu Bar Options, and then click Autohide Menu Bar. Point to the menu bar location to show the menu and point away to hide it.

Listening to Radio Stations

You can use Windows Media Player to listen to radio stations around the world that broadcast on the Internet. When you listen to a radio station on the Internet, the audio continuously streams to your computer. The audio is partially downloaded and stored in a buffer, a temporary storage area, before it begins to play. As more audio streams, Windows Media Player continues to buffer it, which minimizes the interruptions to the radio broadcast. When you play a radio station, a web page for the radio station is displayed in your web browser behind Windows Media Player. While you listen to a radio station, you can browse the web or work in other programs.

Listen to the Radio on the Internet

1. Start Windows Media Player and connect to the Internet, if necessary.

2. Click the **arrow** below the **Online Stores** tab, and then click the **Media Guide**.

3. Click the link for **Internet Radio**.

4. Click the name of the radio station you want to play.

5. Click **Play**.

   TROUBLE? *If Play is not available, click Visit Website, and then play the radio station.*

6. To stop playing the radio station, click the **Stop** button.

7. To add the station to your **My Stations list**, click **Add to My Stations**.

8. When you're done, click the **Close** button.

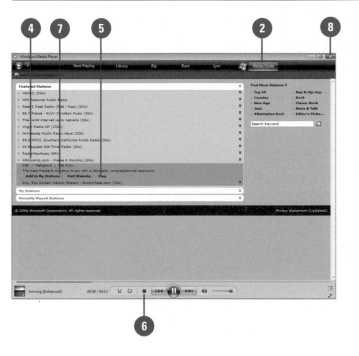

For Your Information

Playing Media Over the Web or Network

When you play music from the Internet, Windows Media Player uses streaming, which is a method of delivering audio and video files across a network or the Internet without downloading an entire file before it plays. All streaming media files buffer before playing. Buffering is the process of sending a certain amount of information to the computer before the content actually plays. Windows Media Player monitors network conditions and makes adjustments to ensure the best reception and playback. If the information in the buffer runs out, you will notice a break in the playback. When a file finishes playing, it is not stored on your computer.

Playing Media Files

With Windows Media Player, you can play sound and video files on your computer. You can find and download sound and video files from the Internet or copy media files from a CD or DVD. The Library makes it easy to organize your media. You can quickly search for media by name or you can browse through the Library and select the media file that you want to play. When you start Windows Media Player for the first time or play a song, the Player automatically searches certain folders on your computer for media files and organize them by category, such as Artist, Album, Genre, Rated Songs, or Year Released.

Perform a Quick Search

1 Click the **Library** tab.

2 Click in the **Search** box.

3 Type the text that you want to search by.

> **TIMESAVER** *Click Search Results in the Library list to display it at any time.*

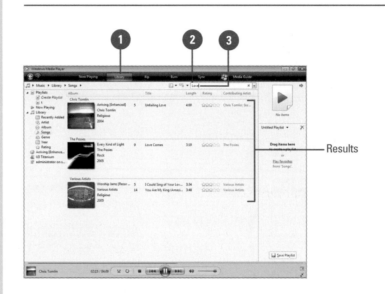

Results

Browse Media Files

1 Click the **Library** tab.

2 Click the **Select a Category** button on the address bar, and then select a category, such as Music, Pictures, Video, Recorded TV, or Other Media.

3 Select a view of that category in the Navigation pane.

4 To change the view:

◆ **View More**. Click the list arrow next to a button on the address bar, and then select a category.

◆ **View Less**. Click a button on the address bar to the left.

Change the Folders Monitored by the Player

1. Click the **Library** tab.

2. To add a currently playing track or playlist to the Library, play it now.

3. Click the **arrow** below the Library tab, and then click **Add to Library**.

4. Select the **My personal folders** or **My folders and those of others that I can access** option to select the folders to monitor.

5. Click **OK**.

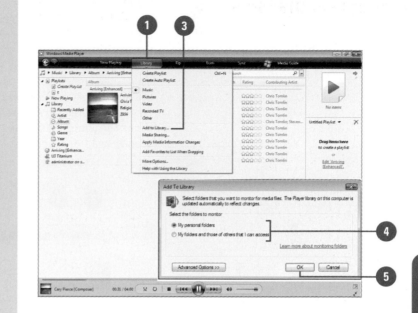

Play Media Files from the Library

1. Click the **Library** tab.

2. Click an arrow next to the category you want to view.

3. Click a category.

4. Double-click the media file to play it.

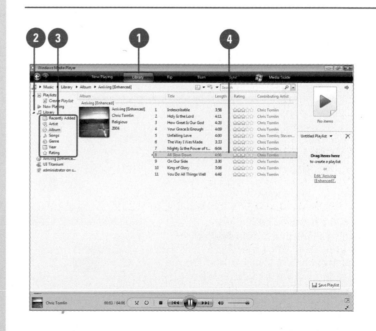

Did You Know?

You can automatically add media files to the Library when played. Click the arrow below the Now Playing tab, click More Options, select the Add media files to library when played check box, and then click OK.

You can delete a file from the library. Click the Library tab, right-click the file you want to remove, click Delete, click the Delete from library only or Delete from library and my computer option, and then click OK.

Playing Media Using a Playlist

Instead of playing digital media files, such as music tracks, video clips, or DVD segments, one at a time or in sequential order from a CD or DVD, you can use Windows Media Player to create a **playlist**. A playlist is a customized list or sequence of digital media that you want to listen to or watch. A playlist allows you to group together media files and specify the order in which you want to play back the media. You can mix and match the media files on your computer, a network, a CD, or the Internet, creating a personal juke box. You can create an easy access general playlist called Now Playing List, create one with a specify name, or specify criteria to create an Auto Playlist.

Create a Now Playing List

1. Click the **Library** tab.

2. Right-click the the media files, point to **Add to**, and then click **Now Playing**.

3. Click the **Now Playing** tab.

4. To clear the Now Playing List, click the **Clear List pane** button.

5. To save the list, click the **Now Playing** button, click **Save Playing List As**, type a name, specify a location, and then click **Save**.

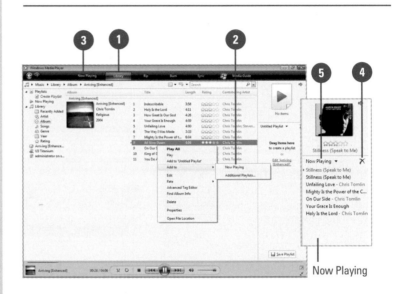

Now Playing

Create a Playlist

1. Click the **Library** tab.

2. Click the **arrow** below the Library tab, and then click **Create Playlist**.

3. Display the media files you want to add to the playlist, and then drag them to the playlist.

4. Type a name for the playlist, and the press Enter.

5. Click **Save Playlist** to save the playlist in the Playlists folder.

   ◆ To save a playlist in a another format, click the **List** button, and then click **Save Playlist As**.

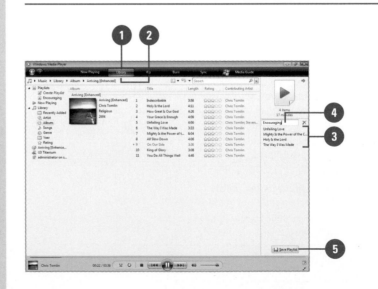

Create an Auto Playlist

 1 Click the **Library** tab.

2 Click the **arrow** below the Library tab, and then click **Create Auto Playlist**.

3 Type a name for the Auto Playlist.

4 Select the criteria options you want.

5 Click **OK**.

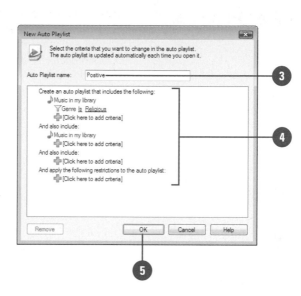

Add Media Files from Your Hard Disk to a Playlist

1 Open the folder window that contains the files or folders you want to add to a playlist.

2 Select the file(s) or folder(s) you want to include in the playlist.

3 Right-click the selection, and then click **Add to 'playlist name'**.

Did You Know?

You can quickly play a playlist. Click th Library tab, and then double-click the playlist in the Navigation pane you want to play.

You can edit playlist. Click the Library tab, right-click the playlist you want to edit, click Edit in Pane, make your changes, and then click Save Playlist.

Ripping CD Music

Windows Media Player (WPM) allows you to **rip**, or copy, one music track or an entire album from a music CD to your computer. When you rip music from a CD or download music from the Web to your computer, Windows copies music by the same artist into one folder in the Music folder and creates subfolders for each album. Windows gives you several ways to play the music on your computer.

Rip Tracks from a Music CD

1. Insert your music CD into the CD-ROM drive.

2. If the Autoplay dialog box appears, click **Rip music from CD** (using Windows Media Player) to burn the entire CD, or click **Play audio CD** (using Windows Media Player) to burn individual tracks.

   The WMP window opens, and plays on the Now Playing tab.

3. Click the **Rip** tab.

4. Clear the check boxes next to the tracks you don't want to copy.

5. Click **Start Rip** (toggles with Stop Rip).

   The music is copied to the Music folder unless you specify a different location.

6. To stop the copy at any time, click **Stop Rip**.

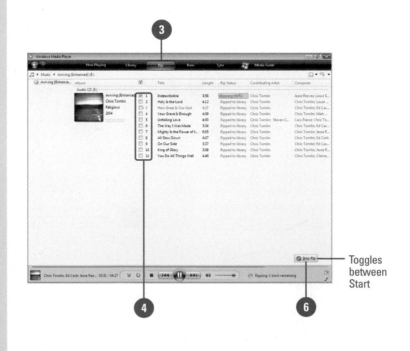

Toggles between Start

Did You Know?

You can use error correction during a copy. Click the Tools menu, click Options, click the Devices tab, select the CD-ROM drive, click Properties, click Digital, select the Use error correction check box, and then click OK.

You can change the folder where you copy media files. Click the Tools menu, click Options, click the Rip Music tab, click Change, select or create a new folder, and then click OK.

Select Rip Music Settings

1 Click the **arrow** below the Rip tab, and then click **More Options**.

2 To change the location where Windows Media Player stores ripped music, click **Change**, select a new folder location, and then click **OK**.

3 Select the format and copy setting you want:

- ◆ **Windows Media Audio.** Most common WMA format with widest range of quality and file size.

- ◆ **Windows Media Audio (variable bit rate).** High quality with variable file size.

- ◆ **Windows Media Audio Lossless.** Quality closest to the original with high file size.

- ◆ **MP3.** Common and flexible format.

4 Drag the slider to adjust audio quality.

5 Click **OK**.

Did You Know?

You can turn off music copy protection. Click the Tools menu, click Options, click the Rip Music tab, and then clear the Copy Protect Music check box, and then click OK.

For Your Information

Getting a License to Copy Music

Most CD music is secured with a license to prevent illegal distribution. A license is a legal agreement that specifies whether the license expires or how you can use the file. The terms of the license are entirely dependent upon the person or company that provided the file. Windows Media Player cannot play licensed files without a license. When you copy music from a CD with the Acquire Licenses Automatically option selected, Windows Media Player searches the Internet for the license and copies it to your computer. If the license is not available, you can still acquire a license by copying the music and selecting the Protect Content check box on the Rip Music tab in the Options dialog box. As you copy the music, the licenses are issued. The license allows you to copy the music to your hard disk, a portable device, or a CD. If you want to view the license information for a file, right-click the file, click Properties, and then click the License Information tab. If you copy music without a license, you could be violating the music's copyright. You can avoid license problems by backing them up. Click the Tools menu, click License Management, click Browse, select a folder, click OK, and then click Backup Now.

Copying Media Files to a CD or Portable Device

Windows Media Player makes it easy to burn (copy) music to a CD using a CD burner or copy the music and video you want to a portable device and keep it in sync. If you have a Portable Digital Media Player, such as an ipod or zune, you can download digital media from an online store and play it on the go. Windows Media Player verifies that there is enough space for the selected files on the portable device and then starts the copying process. As the music copies, the amount of used and free space on the portable device is displayed at the bottom of the Music On Device pane. You can synchronize music, video, and picture files to the device so you can bring your whole library with you. You can choose to automatically or manually sync your digital media between WMP and your device, known as a partnership. Set up Auto Synch once, and everytime you connect your device to your computer, WMP updates the digital media between them, so devices that allow you to rate your music can automatically send them back to WMP.

Copy Music to a CD

1. Click the **Burn** tab, click the **arrow** below the Burn tab, and then click the type of disc you want to burn: audio CD or data CD or DVD.

2. Insert a blank CD or DVD in your CD recorder.

   If the Autoplay dialog box appears, click **Burn an audio CD**.

   If you need to erase your disc, right-click the drive in the Navigation pane, and then click **Erase disc**.

3. If you need to clear the List pane, click the **Clear List pane** button.

4. Drag the files you want to burn from the Details pane to the List pane.

5. To remove a file from the list, right-click the file, and then click **Remove from List**.

6. Drag the files in the list to arrange them in the order you want.

7. Click the **Start Burn** button.

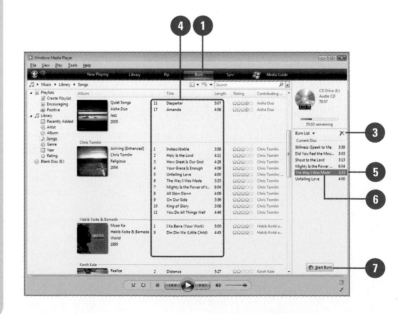

Copy Music to a Portable Device

1. Start Windows Media Player, and then connect the portable device to your computer.

2. If sync setup is needed for the device, follow the wizard instructions, and then click **Finish**.

3. If you setup Auto Sync, synchronization begins, click **Stop Sync**.

4. Click the **Library** tab.

5. If you need to clear the List pane, click the **Clear List pane** button.

6. Display and drag the media files you want to the sync list.

7. Click the **Sync** tab.

8. To change sync priority order, sync method, and other settings, click the arrow below the Sync tab, point to the device name, and then click **Set Up Sync**, specify options, and then click **OK**.

9. To remove a file from the list, right-click the file, and then click **Remove from List**.

10. Click the **Start Synch** button.

11. If you want to stop the sync, click **Stop Sync**.

    Upon completion, status information appears next to files indicating success or failure.

Did You Know?

You can find a list of compatible portable devices on the Windows Media web site. Open your browser, go to *www.windowsmedia.com*, and then click the Music Players link.

Current status of the sync

Adding Functionality to Media Player

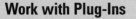

Windows Media Player allows you to add functionality to the player using plug-ins. Plug-ins add or enhance the media experience with audio and video effects, new rendering types, and visualizations. Before you can use a plug-in, you need to download it from the Web and add it to the Media Player. You can find lots of Media Player plug-ins at *www.wmplugins.com*. Before you download a plug-in, read the online information about the plug-in for additional instructions.

Work with Plug-Ins

1. Click the **arrow** below the Now Playing tab, point to **Plug-Ins**, and then click **Options**.

2. To download a plug-in, click **Look for plug-ins on the Web** link, and then follow the instructions on the Web page.

3. Select a plug-in category.

4. Select a plug-in option, if available.

5. To modify a plug-in, click **Properties**.

6. To remove a plug-in, click **Remove**.

7. Click **OK**.

Did You Know?

You can download a creativity fun pack for the Media Player. Open your browser, go to *www.wmplugins.com*, and then search for the Creativity Fun Pack for Windows Media Player download link.

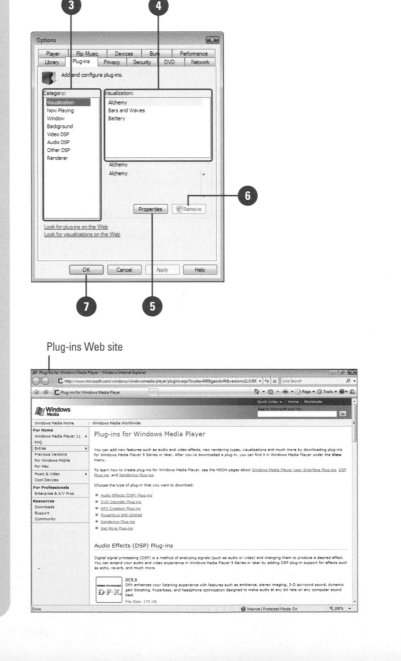

Plug-ins Web site

Enhancing the Media Player Display

Visualizations are plug-ins that display geometric shapes and color on the Now Playing tab when you play music. Visualizations are grouped together into collections. You can add and remove visualizations or download additional collections from the Web. You can also display special enhancement controls to change video settings, play speed, or audio levels with a graphics equalizer, choose color effects, and send a media link in an e-mail.

Select Visualizations

1. Click the **Now Playing** tab.

2. Click the **arrow** below the Now Playing tab, and then point to **Visualizations**.

3. Point to a category, and then click the visualization you want to display.

   TIMESAVER *In Now Playing, right-click the display, point to a category, and then click the visualization you want.*

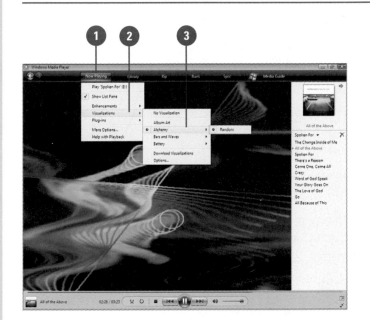

Select Enhancements

1. Click the **Now Playing** tab.

2. Click the **arrow** below the Now Playing tab, and then point to **Enhancements**.

3. Click the enhancement you want to display.

4. Adjust the enhancement controls.

5. When you're done, click the **Close** button in the pane.

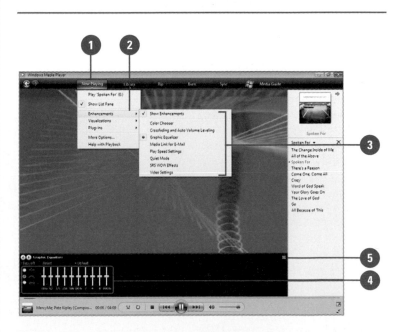

Changing the Media Player Look

Windows Media Player gives you the freedom of expression to change the look, known as the **skin**, of the Media Player. Windows Media Player includes several skins from which you can select the one you like the best. When you select a skin, Windows Media Player changes from full mode to skin mode. You can use skins only when Media Player is in skin mode. Skin mode displays a smaller player, which provides more room on the screen for other programs.

Apply a Skin

1. Click the **View** menu, and then click **Skin Chooser**.

2. Click a design.

3. Click **Apply Skin**.

4. Use the controls to play a media file.

5. To return to the full window, click the **Return To Full Mode** button.

   TIMESAVER *Press Ctrl+1 to return to full mode.*

6. To switch back to skin mode, click the **View** menu, and then click **Skin Mode.**

   TIMESAVER *Press Ctrl+2 to return to skin mode.*

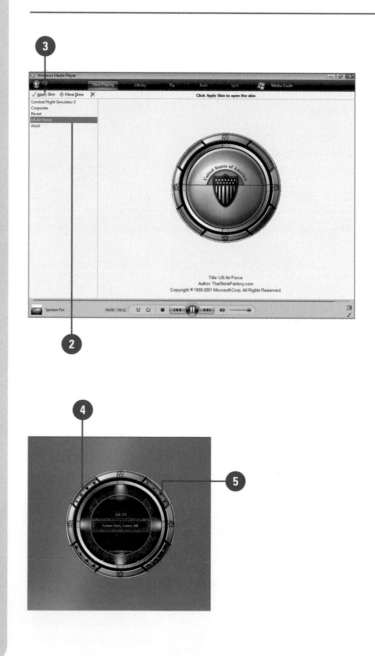

Did You Know?

You can download more skins from the Internet. Click the View menu, click Skin Chooser, click More Skins, click the link to the skin you want to download, follow the instructions, and then click View Now.

You can delete a skin. Click the View menu, click Skin Chooser, select the skin you want to delete, click the Delete Selected Skin button, and then click Yes.

You can access a shortcut menu of commands in skin mode. Press Shift+F10 to display a shortcut menu of convenient commands.

Viewing and Playing Music Files

You can view and play music files with relative ease in the Music folder. The Music folder is a folder specifically designated to play and manage music files. When you copy music files from a CD or download them from the Internet, the files are copied to the Music folder by default unless you specify a different location. The Music folder contains links to specialized music tasks that can help you play the music you store on your computer. In the Music folder, you can click Play All or Play on the toolbar or double-click an individual music file to open and play the music in Windows Media Player. If you click Play All in the Music folder, Windows Media Player opens and plays all the music in your Music folder and subfolder in random order. If you click Play All in a subfolder within your Music folder, Windows Media Player opens and plays all the music in the folder in consecutive order.

View and Play Music Files

1. Click the **Start** button, and then click **Music**.

2. Select the music files or folder you want to play.

3. Click **Play** or **Play all**.

Creating a Sound File

Using Sound Recorder and a microphone, you can record your own sound files. Sound Recorder creates Windows Media Audio files with the .wma file extension. If you are using Windows Vista Home Basic or Business, Sounder Recorder saves files in the .wav format instead of .wma. Sound Recorder doesn't play sounds; you can play your recording in a digital media player, such as Windows Media Player. Before you can use Sound Recorder, you need to have a sound card, speakers, and a microphone installed on your computer.

Record a Sound

1 Click the **Start** button, point to **All Programs**, click **Accessories**, and then click **Sound Recorder**.

2 Click the **Start Recording** button, and then record the sounds you want.

3 When you're done, click the **Stop Recording** button.

4 Select a folder, type a name for the file, and then click **Save**.

5 Click the **Close** button.

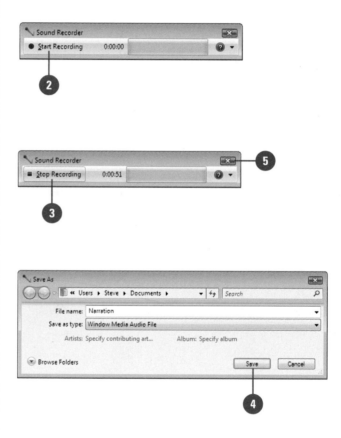

Associating a Sound with an Event

WINV-6.3.3

Besides customizing the desktop appearance of Windows, you can also add sound effects to common Windows commands and functions, such as starting and exiting Windows, printing complete, opening and closing folders, or emptying the Recycle Bin. You can select a sound scheme (a collection of sounds associated with events), or you can mix and match sound files to create your own sound scheme for your computer. You need to use Wave files with the .wav file extension.

Create and Select a Sound Scheme

1. Click the **Start** button, click **Control Panel**, and then double-click the **Sound** icon in Classic view.

2. Click the **Sounds** tab.

3. Click an event to which you want to associate a sound.

4. Click the **Sounds** list arrow, and then select a sound, or click **Browse** and locate the sound file you want to use.

5. Click the **Test** button to preview the sound.

6. Click **Save As**, type a name for the sound scheme, and then click **OK**.

7. To select a sound scheme, click the **Sound Scheme** list arrow, and then select a scheme.

8. Click **OK**.

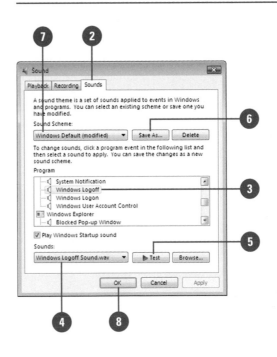

Did You Know?

You can add sounds to the list. If you put WAV files in the Media folder, located in the Windows folder, the sound files appear in the Sounds list.

You can remove a sound associated with an event. On the Sounds tab, click an event, click the Sounds list arrow, and then click (None).

Starting and Navigating Windows Media Center

Windows Media Center (**New!**) is an entertainment system integrated into your computer that lets you watch live or recorded TV, play video and watch pictures, listen to music and radio using an FM tuner or the Internet, play and burn CDs or DVDs, browse online media, and play games. Because Windows Media Center is designed to be used as an entertainment system, the display and navigation are unlike any other Windows program. When you start Windows Media Center, the program uses the entire screen and doesn't use menus or toolbars. You navigate by using the up and down arrows to specify a main category, and then left and right arrows to specify a subcategory. Play, Record, and other VCR/DVD type commands are available in the bottom right corner when you point to them. You can use your mouse or a remote control to navigate the system. Before you can play FM radio or watch TV, you need additional hardware installed on your computer, an FM tuner and a TV tuner card along with a remote control.

Start, Navigate, and Exit Windows Media Center

1 Click the **Start** button, point to **All Programs**, and then click **Window Media Center**.

2 Point to the large icon in the middle of the start screen, and then move the pointer up or down to display an arrow.

3 Point to or click the up or down arrow to scroll the list of categories: **Tasks**, **Online Media**, **Pictures + Videos**, **Music**, **TV + Movies**.

4 When the category you want appears in the middle, point to it to display left and right arrows, if available for the category.

5 Point to or click the left or right arrow to display the subcategory you want, and then click the icon.

6 To get back to the main screen, point to the upper-left corner, and then click the **Back** button.

7 To exit, point to the upper-right corner, and then click the **Close** button.

Changing Windows Media Center Settings

You can set up and customize Windows Media Center (**New!**) by selecting Tasks on the start screen, and then selecting Settings. In the Settings area, you can set general options for Windows Media Center and specific options for each of the media types, including TV, Pictures, Music, and DVD. You can also set options for extenders and libraries. A Windows Media Center Extender is a device you connect to your computer, such as a TV, DVD player, digital camera, or Xbox 360, that you want to control from Windows Media Center within a networked environment. Before you get started with Windows Media Center, it's a good idea to set general options, which include startup and window behavior, visual and sound effects, program library options, Windows Media Center set up, parental controls, automatic download options, optimization, and privacy.

Change Windows Media Center Settings

1. On the Windows Media Center start screen, scroll to **Tasks**.

2. Display and click **settings**.

3. Click the type of settings you want to change: **General**, **TV**, **Pictures**, **Music**, **DVD**, **Extender**, or **Library Setup**.

4. Click the setting type you want to change.

5. Specify the options you want. Use the up and down arrow to display option screens.

6. When you're done, click **Save** or **Cancel**.

7. Click the **Back** button to navigate back to the start screen.

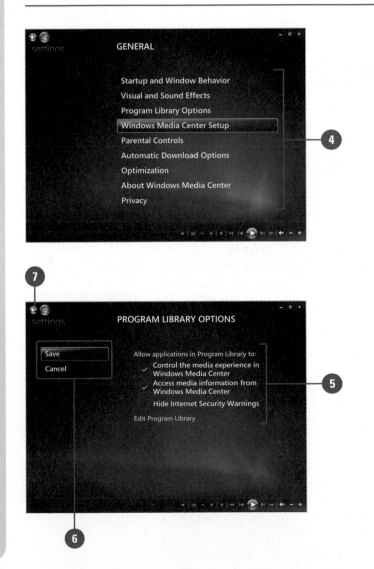

Finding and Viewing Windows Media Center Files

Windows Media Center (**New!**) uses all the media files you already have on your computer and integrates it into an entertainment system. The same video and music files you use with Windows Media Player are available for use with Windows Media Center. For example, when you rip music to your computer, you can play it using Windows Media Player and Windows Media Center. You can choose either one, the preference is yours. As you navigate to a media area, you can select options to find the media you want, and then use the media specific commands and controls to view, play, or change the media files.

Find and View Windows Media Center Files

1. On the Windows Media Center start screen, scroll to to a media type: **Pictures + Videos**, **Music**, or **TV + Movies**.

2. Display and click the media type library you want, such as video library, music library, or picture library.

   ◆ If you know the library and want to play all the media, click **play all**.

3. Navigate to one of the sort criteria and find the file you want to view. You can sort by folders or date taken.

4. Use the available commands for the media you want to view, play or change.

5. Use the controls on the lower-right to pause, play, stop, and navigate through the media.

6. Click the **Back** button to navigate back to the start screen.

   ◆ You can select Now Playing or Now Playing + Queue on the start screen to quickly access and play items in the queue, which is a custom list of all the media you want to play.

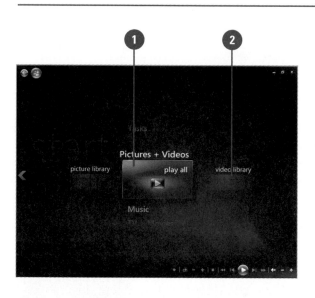

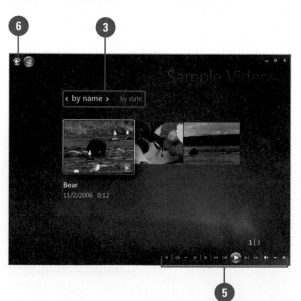

Creating Movies Using Movie Maker

Introduction

Windows Vista comes with an accessory called Windows Movie Maker (version 6) that lets you combine video, audio, and image files with special effects to create movies you can show on your computer or CD, e-mail to others, record on a digital camera, or place on a web page.

In Movie Maker, you create a project that contains the arrangement and timing information of audio and video clips, video transitions, video effects, and titles in a storyboard or timeline. You drag video and audio clips from a collection to the storyboard or timeline. After you arrange the video and audio clips in the sequence you want, you can add video transitions, video effects, titles, and credits. After you preview your project using the monitor, you publish it as a movie file to your computer or to a recordable CD, send it as an attachment in an e-mail message, save and send it to the web, or record your movie to a digital video tape. The movie you create can be watched in a media player, such as Microsoft Windows Media Player, or in a web browser. If you would rather create a DVD, Movie Maker connects you with Windows DVD Maker (**New!**) and automatically imports your movie. In Windows DVD Maker, you can insert additional video, pictures, and audio, add DVD titles and menus, and specify publishing options before you burn the movie to a DVD. Windows DVD Maker is a stand-alone program and can be used separately from Movie Maker.

Before using Movie Maker, you need to connect and install the equipment needed to transfer video content to your computer, such as a digital video or web camera. Movie Maker must detect the video device on your computer, and you must properly connect the device to a USB port, a video capture card, or an IEEE 1394 port. (Check your computer documentation for details.)

What You'll Do

Plan a Movie Maker Project

Start Movie Maker

View the Movie Maker Window

Open an Existing Project

Capture Video and Audio

Import Video and Audio

Add Slides to a Movie

Organize Clips and Collections

Work with Clips

Create a Movie Maker Project File

Trim Clips

Add Transitions Between Clips

Add Video Effects

Add Titles and Credits

Add a Soundtrack and Narration

Use AutoMovie

Save a Project and a Movie

Create a DVD Video

Planning a Movie Maker Project

Movie Maker lets you combine video, audio, and image files to create movies you can show on your computer, e-mail to others, or place on a web page. You save the movie you create as a file, just as you would save a word processing or spreadsheet file, and you can play and view it at any time. However, movies and their accompanying files are larger than most other documents you create—usually exceeding 5 MB. Before you begin, it's a good idea to plan your content.

Decide the purpose of the movie

Your movie might be a promotional piece or catalog for business use, or a vacation movie to share with family and friends. Your purpose determines the subject, type, and quality of the **source material**, which is the video and audio material you will use.

Determine how to share the movie with others

You might want to show your movie on a computer projection screen at a meeting, send it as an attachment in an e-mail message, or place it on a web site. When you place a movie on a web site, viewers might download it, which means to transfer it to their computers and store it for future viewing. If your movie is very long or has many high-quality images, the movie file will be large and will take a long time to download.

Choose source material

If you have a digital video or digital web camera, you can record or capture digital images directly into Movie Maker on your computer. To use existing video or audio segments, called **clips**, you must import them, or bring them into Movie Maker. You can also import clips from videotape, but your computer must have a video capture card to convert clips from analog to digital format. You can start the System Information accessory on the System Tools submenu to determine whether you have a video capture card installed on your computer.

Sketch the movie

Before putting your movie together in Movie Maker, it's important to make a sketch of your movie that shows the order of the audio and video components. What audio clips do you want to play with what video clips?

Review the process used to create a movie

First, you bring clips of source material into a Movie Maker project file. A **project file**, which is the working copy of your movie, is a Movie Maker document with the file name extension .mswmm. You then use the project file to do the following: set the order of your movie segments; **trim** (delete) portions of clips you don't want to use; specify how clips display from one to the next, called **transitions**; add a video special effect to clips; add titles and credits to the beginning and end of the movie or individual clips; and, lastly, preview your work. Finally, you save your project file as a movie with the file name extension .wmv and display the completed movie using the Windows Media Player program.

Starting Movie Maker

Before you start Movie Maker, use Display Properties in the Control Panel to make sure the screen resolution is set correctly. Movie Maker is a Windows accessory program that you can start from the Start menu. You achieve the best results in Movie Maker when the screen resolution is set to 1024 by 768 or higher. When you start Movie Maker, a new untitled movie project is displayed. You can either create a new movie project or open an existing one.

Start Movie Maker

1 Click the **Start** button, and then point to **All Programs**.

2 Click **Windows Movie Maker**.

Did You Know?

You can check online for the latest version of Movie Maker. Click the Start button, point to All Programs, click Windows Update, connect to the Internet, scan for updates, check for a new version of Movie Maker, and then download it.

See Also

See "Changing the Display" on page 105 for information on changing the screen resolution.

For Your Information

Having Fun with Movie Maker

Microsoft Windows provides additional Power Toys in Creativity Fun Packs you can download from the Web. The Creativity Fun pack for Movie Maker includes sound effects, music tracks and transitions, and video titles and end credits that make it fun to create movies. Before you can use the Movie Maker fun pack, you need to download it from the Web and install it. The fun pack movie files are stored in your Videos folder. Click the Help menu, and then click Windows Movie Maker on the Web. The Movie Maker Web site opens in your web browser. Locate and click the link to the Movie Maker Creativity Fun Pack. Download the file, save it to your hard disk, and then double-click to install it. Follow the wizard instructions to complete the installation.

Viewing the Movie Maker Window

Tasks button
The button displays the Movie Tasks pane. The Movie Tasks pane lists the common tasks that you may need to perform when making a movie.

Collections pane
The Collections pane displays your collections, which contains clips.

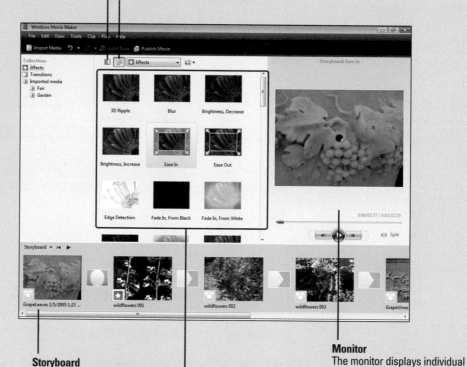

Storyboard
The Storyboard displays a sequence of clips, video effects, and video transitions in your movie project.

Contents pane
The Contents pane displays all of the video, audio, pictures, video transitions, and video effects that can be added to the storyboard/timeline to include in your movie project.

Monitor
The monitor displays individual clips or an entire project.

Opening an Existing Project

After you save a project in Movie Maker, you can open it and continue to work on the project. A Movie Maker project file is saved with a .mswmm file name extension, which you can open using the Open Project button on the toolbar. The project file's extension will change, once the project is finalized.

Open an Existing Project

1. Click the **Start** button, point to **All Programs**, and then click **Windows Movie Maker**.

2. Click the **File** menu, and then click **Open Project**.

3. Select the drive and folder that contains the project you want to open.

4. Select the project file.

5. Click **Open**.

Did You Know?

You can automatically open a project. Click the Tools menu, click Options, click the General tab, select the Open Last Project On Startup check box, and then click OK.

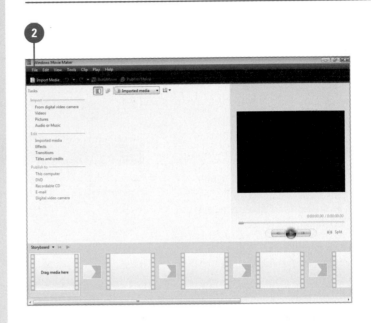

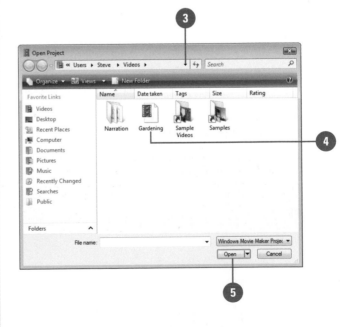

Capturing Video and Audio

You can capture video and audio to your computer from a digital video (DV) or analog camera, web camera, videotape (VCR), or television tuner card directly in Movie Maker. Similarly, you can record audio source material from a microphone, radio, audio or video tape, or a CD. Before you can capture video and audio, a video capture device must be connected properly and detected on your computer by Windows Movie Maker. If you record clips from any commercial source, however, be aware of copyright restrictions that regulate how you may or may not use the content. In the capturing process, Movie Maker converts the material to Windows Media format.

Capture Video from a Video Camera

1. Make sure the digital video camera is connected properly, and then set the camera to play recorded video.

2. Click **From digital video camera** in the Tasks pane.

3. Click the digital video camera, and then click **Next** to continue.

4. Type a file name for your captured video file.

5. Select the location where you want to save the video, and then click **Next** to continue.

6. Specify the video settings you want for capturing video and audio, and then click **Next** to continue.

7. Click **Capture parts of the tape manually**.

8. To separate the video into smaller clips, select the **Create clips when wizard finishes** check box.

9. Click **Start Capture**.

10. To stop capturing video, click **Stop Capture**.

11. Click **Finish**.

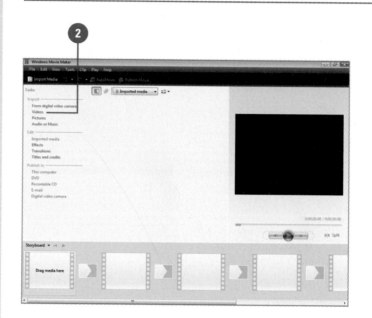

Capture Live Video

① Make sure the digital video camera is connected properly, and then set the camera to play recorded video.

② Click **From digital video camera** in the Tasks pane.

③ Click the digital video camera, and then click **Next** to continue.

④ Type a file name for your captured video file.

⑤ Select the location where you want to save the video, and then click **Next** to continue.

⑥ Specify the video settings you want, and then click **Next** to continue.

⑦ To separate the video into smaller clips, select the **Create clips when wizard finishes** check box.

⑧ To automatically stop the capture, select the **Capture time limit** check box, and then type or select a time limit.

⑨ Click **Start Capture**.

⑩ To stop capturing video, click **Stop Capture**.

⑪ Click **Finish**.

Did You Know?

Twenty hours of video take a gigabyte of hard disk space. You can store more than 20 hours of video for each gigabyte of hard disk space on your computer.

Importing Video and Audio

If you want to use existing video and audio clips in your movie instead of recording them yourself, you can obtain them from various companies that specialize in video processing, or you can download them from the Web. Commercial CDs are excellent sources for audio clips. You can import the video and audio clips into Movie Maker from files on your computer, from your CD drive, or from the Web. If you already imported a video clip and need a still picture of a frame from a video, you can take a picture of the video frame and save it as a file, which you can then import back into Movie Maker.

Import Video or Audio

1. Click the **Import Media** button on the toolbar.

2. Select the folder that contains the video or audio files you want to import.

3. To select a specific media type, click the **Files of type** list arrow, and then select a file type.

4. Select the files you want to import.

   TIMESAVER *To import several files at one time, press and hold down the Ctrl key, and then click each file that you want to import.*

5. Click **Import**.

   Movie Maker creates a new collection for the imported video or audio clips.

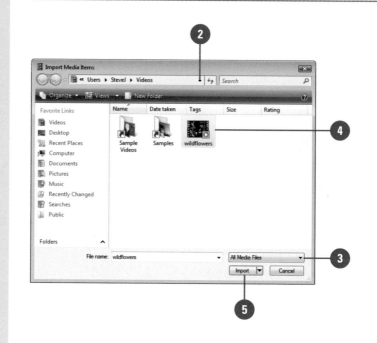

Movie Maker Import File Types

File Type	File Extensions
Video	.asf, .avi, .m1v, .mp2, .mp2v, .mpe, .mpeg, .mpg, .mpv2, .wm, and .wmv
Audio	.aif, .aifc, .aiff, .asf, .au, .mp2, .mp3, .mpa, .snd, .wav, and .wma
Pictures	.bmp, .dib, .emf, .gif, .jfif, .jpe, .jpeg, .jpg, .png, .tif, .tiff, and .wmf

Display Clip Properties

1 Right-click the clip you want, and then click **Properties**.

2 Scroll the list of properties.

3 Click **OK**.

Did You Know?

You can rename a media clip. Click the Collection folder that contains the clip you want to rename, right-click the clip in the Collection area, click Rename, type a name, and then press Enter.

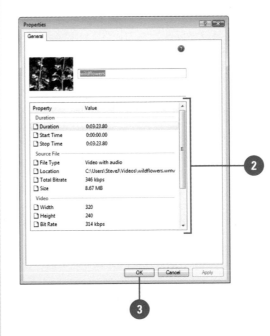

Adding Slides to a Movie

Instead of using video clips, you can create slide shows in Movie Maker with still images that you create using a digital camera, web camera, or scanner. You can import the clips into Movie Maker and create transitions between them, just as you would in a movie. You can change the duration of individual pictures in Timeline view. You can also add sound clips to create a sound track that plays as your pictures appear on the screen. Portrait-oriented pictures in Movie Maker are the same height as landscape-oriented pictures, and Movie Maker inserts a black background on either side of each one.

Set Picture Duration

1. Click the **Tools** menu, and then click **Options**.

2. Click the **Advanced** tab.

3. Specify the picture duration in seconds.

4. Click **OK**.

Import Pictures

1 Click the **Collections** button, and then click the collection where you want to place the imported pictures.

2 Click **Pictures** in the Tasks pane.

3 Select the folder that contains the picture files you want to import.

4 Select the files you want to import.

TIMESAVER *To import several files at one time, press and hold down the Ctrl key, and then click each file that you want to import.*

5 Click **Import**.

Movie Maker adds the imported pictures into the selected collection.

Take a Picture from Video

1 Click the video clip from which you want to take a picture.

2 Drag the **Playback** indicator on the Seek bar to the frame that you want to capture as a picture.

3 Click the **Tools** menu, and then click **Take Picture from Preview**.

4 Select a folder, and then type a name.

5 Click **Save**.

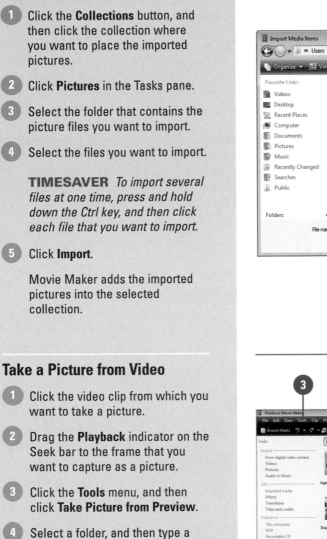

Organizing Clips and Collections

When you bring video clips, audio clips, or pictures into Movie Maker, the program stores them in a collection folder in the **Collections pane**. The contents of the selected collection folder appear in the **Collections area**. As you continue to collect media clips for use in different movie projects, the number of clips in a collection and in Movie Maker can grow rapidly and become hard to manage. You can use the same management techniques you use in Windows Explorer to help you organize and remove clips and collections. Once you have clips in your collections, you can move them around and rename the clips and collections as you would a file or folder and use them to create a movie. When you no longer need individual video and audio clips or entire collections, you can remove them from Movie Maker. When you remove video and sound clips and collections, they are deleted only from Movie Maker; the original video and sound files, which you imported into Movie Maker, are not deleted and remain unchanged on your hard drive.

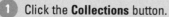

View and Create a Collection

1. Click the **Collections** button.

2. Click the Collection folder you want to view.

3. Click the **Views** button on the toolbar, and then click **Thumbnails** or **Details**.

4. Click the **Views** button on the toolbar, point to **Arrange Icons By**, and then click an arrangement type.

5. To create a new collection, click the **File** menu, click **New Collection Folder**, type a name, and then press Enter.

6. To close the Collection pane, click the **Collections** button.

7. To open the Tasks pane, click the **Tasks** button.

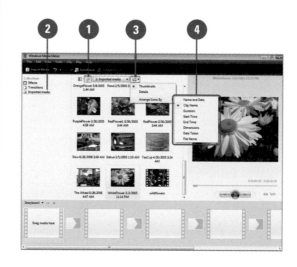

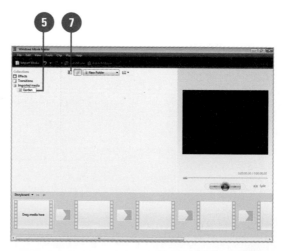

Move a Clip to a Collection

1. Click the **Collections** button.

2. Click the Collection folder that contains the clip you want to move.

3. Drag the clip to another Collection folder.

Did You Know?

You can create a collection folder. Click the Collections button on the toolbar, click the folder where you want the new folder, click the New Collection Folder button on the toolbar, type a name, and then press Enter.

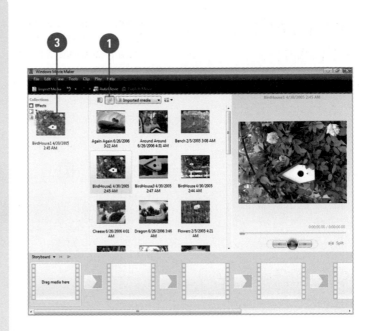

Rename a Collection

1. Click the Collections button.

2. Right-click the Collection folder you want to rename, and then click **Rename**.

3. Type a name, and then press Enter.

Did You Know?

You can delete a media clip. Click the Collection folder that contains the clip you want to delete, click the clip in the Collections area, and then press Delete.

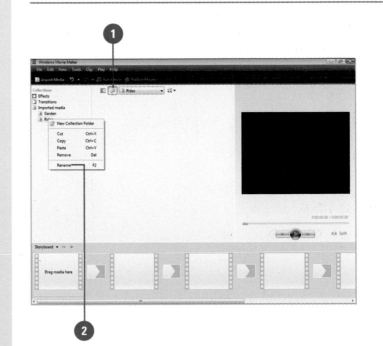

Working with Clips

After you capture or import a video clip or audio clip, you can preview the individual clips within a collection in the monitor. The monitor works similarly to a VCR/DVD. If you have a long clip that you want to divide into smaller clips, you can split the clip on your own or let Movie Maker try to do it. Movie Maker creates clips automatically based on time stamps insert by the digital video camera or significant frame change in the video.

Preview a Clip in a Collection

1 Click the **Collections** button.

2 Click the Collection folder you want to preview.

3 Click the clip you want to preview.

4 Click the **Play** button.

TIMESAVER *Press Spacebar to play or pause a clip quickly.*

5 To pause the clip, click the **Pause** button. Click the **Play** button again to continue.

6 To stop the clip, click the **Stop** button.

Did You Know?

You can drag a clip to play it. You can drag any clip from the Collections area to the monitor to begin playing that clip.

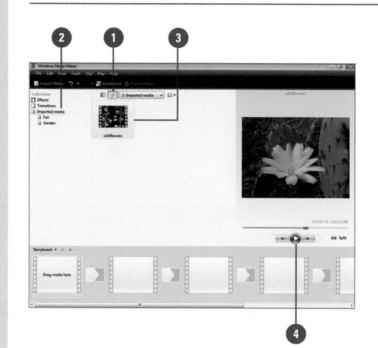

Split a Clip

1. Click the clip from which you want to split.

2. Drag the **Playback** indicator on the Seek bar to the frame where you want to split the clip.

3. Click the **Split the Clip** button.

   TIMESAVER *Press Ctrl+L to split a clip.*

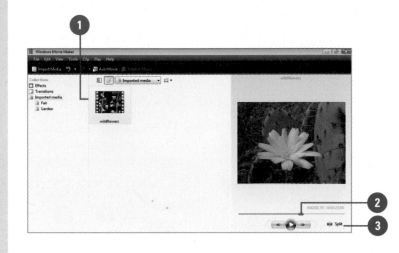

Create Clips Automatically

1. Click the video clip for which you want to detect and create clips.

2. Click the **Tools** menu, and then click **Create Clips**.

> ### Did You Know?
>
> *You can combine clips.* Hold down Ctrl, click the consecutive clips you want to combine, click the Clip menu, and then click Combine.

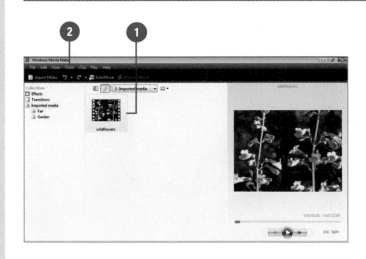

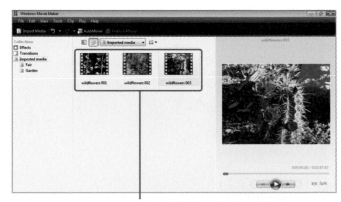

Creates individual clips from one clip

Creating a Movie Maker Project File

When you start Movie Maker, a new, untitled project opens. A project contains the arrangement and timing information of audio and video clips, video transitions, video effects, and titles you have added to the storyboard/timeline. You can view a project in one of two views: **Storyboard view**, which shows the order of your clips, and **Timeline view**, which shows the duration of each clip and the types of transitions between them, as well as, the sound track. To create a movie, drag video and audio clips from your Collections area to the project file's storyboard or timeline, and then rearrange the clips in any order you want. After you preview your project using the monitor and you are satisfied with the results, you can save it as a movie file.

Create a Project

1. Click the **Collections** button.

2. Click the Collection folder that contains the clips you want to use in your project.

3. To switch between the Timeline and the Storyboard, click the **Timeline/Storyboard** button, and then click **Timeline** or **Storyboard**.

   TIMESAVER *Press Ctrl+T to switch between Timeline and Storyboard.*

4. Drag clips from the Collections area to the place in the storyboard or timeline where you want them.

5. To rearrange the order of clips, drag clips on the storyboard or timeline.

Did You Know?

You can delete a clip from the storyboard. If you drag the wrong clip to the storyboard, select it, and then press Delete. The clip remains in the Collections area and on your hard drive.

Preview a Project

1. Click the **Rewind Storyboard** button or click **Rewind Timeline** button.

   The buttons change depending on the view.

2. Click the **Play Storyboard** button or click the **Play Timeline** button.

Change the Preview Monitor Size

1. Click the video you want to preview.

2. Click the **View** menu, and then point to **Preview Monitor Size**.

3. Click **Small (320x240)** or **Large (640x480)**.

   TROUBLE? *This option is available when there is enough room to resize the monitor without resizing the storyboard/timeline.*

Did You Know?

You can play the video using the entire screen. Click the View menu, and then click Full Screen.

Trimming Clips

Frequently, the clips you record or import into Movie Maker run longer than you want them to in your final movie. You can easily trim clips in Timeline view by playing the clip and setting the **trim beginning** point and **trim end** point. The portion between the trim points remains in your movie. The frames before and after the trim points are deleted from your movie, but the original clip in your collection is not affected and retains its original length. You can trim a clip as it plays, or you can pause and set the trim points. You can use the Start Trim Point and End Trim Point commands on the Clip menu or drag the **timeline trim handles** (small triangles at the beginning and end of a selected clip).

Crop a Clip

1. Click the **Timeline/Storyboard** button, and then click **Timeline**.

2. Select the clip you want to crop.

3. Drag the **Seek** bar to the point where you want to start the clip.

4. Click the **Clip** menu, and then click **Trim Beginning**.

    TIMESAVER *Position the pointer on the left edge or right edge of the clip, and then drag the trim handles to crop the clip.*

5. Drag the **Seek** bar to the point where you want to end the clip.

6. Click the **Clip** menu, and then click **Trim End**.

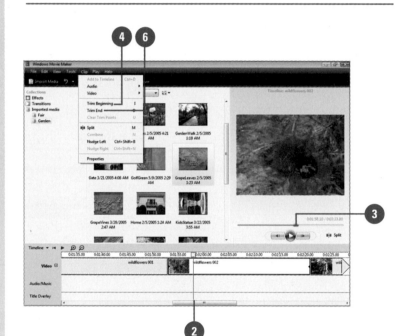

> ### Did You Know?
>
> ***You can restore a clip to its original length.*** Click Clip on the menu bar, and then click Clear Trim Points.

Adding Transitions Between Clips

A **transition** is an effect that provides a smoother, more gradual change between clips in a movie. A transition plays before one clip ends while another starts to play. You can add a transition between two video clips, pictures, or titles on the storyboard or timeline. Movie Maker provides a variety of video transitions that you can quickly add to a movie project, such as Bow Tie, Eye, Diamond, Fan Up, and Shatter In.

Adding a Transition

1. Click the **Locations** list arrow, and then click **Video Transitions**.

2. Click the **Timeline/Storyboard** button, and then click **Timeline** or **Storyboard**.

3. To view the Transition track in the timeline, click the plus sign (+) next to the Video track in the timeline.

4. Drag a transition to the video transition cell in the storyboard or between the two clips in the timeline.

5. To increase the transition duration in the timeline, drag the beginning of the transition towards the beginning of the timeline.

6. To decrease the transition duration in the timeline, drag the beginning of the transition towards the end of the timeline.

Video transitions

Video transition cell

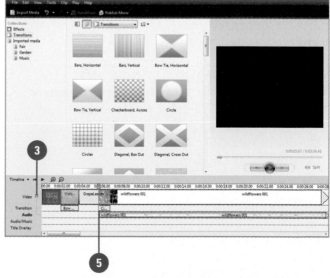

Adding Video Effects

Movie Maker offers a variety of video effects that you can add to a movie project, such as Ease In, Blur, Film Age Old, Mirror Vertical, Speed Up Double, and Watercolor. A video effect is applied for the entire duration of a clip, picture, or title in a movie project. You can add multiple video effects to the same clip, as well as customize the order. If you no longer want to use a video effect, you can remove it.

Add a Video Effects

1. Click the **Locations** list arrow, and then click **Effects**.

2. Click the **Timeline/Storyboard** button, and then click **Timeline** or **Storyboard**.

3. Drag the effect to the video effect cell of the clip in the storyboard or on the clip on the Video track in the timeline.

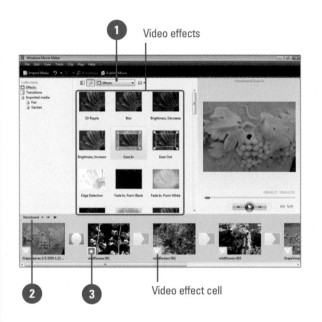

Video effects

Video effect cell

Change Order or Remove Video Effects

1. Right-click the clip with the effects you want to change, and then click **Effects**.

2. Click the displayed effect you want to move or remove.

3. To remove the effect, click **Remove**.

4. To move the effect, click **Move Up** or **Move Down**.

5. When you're done, click **OK**.

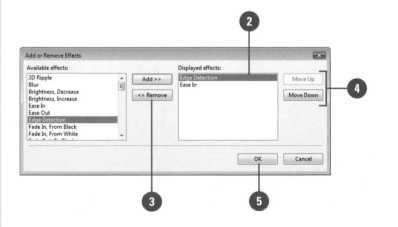

Adding Titles and Credits

You can add titles and credits to your movies just like the professionals. You can add any text you want, such as the title of your movie, your name, captions, and credits at the end. You can add a title at the beginning of a movie, before or after a clip, or overlapping a clip or credits at the end of a movie. You can also change the appearance of the title or credits, and you can add special animation effects, which play for the time you specify in the Title Overlay track in the timeline.

Add Titles and Credits

1. Select the clip you to which you want to add a title.

2. Click the **Tasks** button, if necessary, and then click **Titles or credits** in the Task pane.

3. Click the link to where you want to add a title or credit.

4. Type the text you want to appear as the title.

5. Click **Change the text font and color**.

6. Specify the font, font color, font size, formatting, background color, transparency, and position you want.

7. Click **Change the title animation**, and then select a title animation.

8. Click **Add Title**.

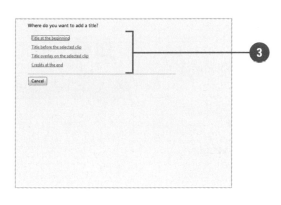

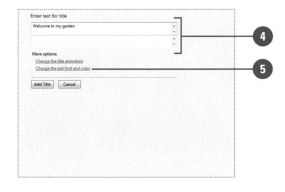

Did You Know?

You can change the title or credit duration. In the timeline, select the title or credit in the Title Overlay track, and then drag the edge to change the duration.

You can remove a title. Select the title in the storyboard or timeline, and then press Delete.

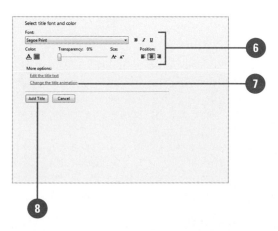

Adding a Soundtrack

With Movie Maker, you can play a video clip sound and soundtrack simultaneously and have one play louder than the other. You can put two types of sounds in your movies: sounds that are part of a video clip, and separate sounds, such as music or narration, that appear on the Audio bar of the timeline. You can import and edit sound clips in the soundtrack the same way you edit video clips using the Audio bar. Remember that if you use a clip from a CD, you must obtain permission from the publisher.

Add a Soundtrack

1. Click the **Tasks** button, if necessary, and then click **Audio or Music**.

2. Select the folder that contains the files you want to **Import**.

3. Select the files you want to import, and then click Import.

4. Click the **Timeline/Story Board** button, and then click **Timeline**, if necessary.

5. Drag the sound clip onto the Audio/Music bar at the location where you want the clip to play.

6. Click the **Tools** menu, and then click **Set Audio Levels**.

7. Click the **Rewind Timeline** button, and then click the **Play Timeline** button.

8. Drag the **Audio Levels** slider to adjust the balance between the video click and the soundtrack.

9. When you're done adjusting the volume, click the **Close** button.

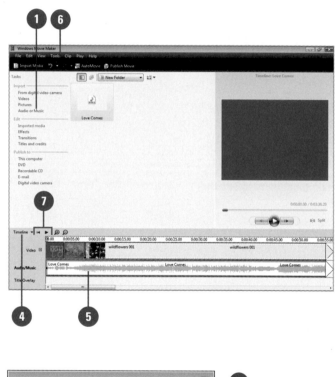

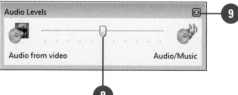

Adding a Narration

If you have a microphone attached to your computer, you can record a narration to accompany your movie. Your narration is saved as a .wav sound file directly in your Collections area so that you can place it in the Audio bar like any other audio clip.

Add a Narration

1. Click the **Timeline/Story Board** button, and then click **Timeline**, if necessary, and then drag the playback indicator to the place where you want to start the narration.

2. Click the **Tools** menu, and then click **Narrate Timeline**.

3. To select an audio device, input source, and other settings, click **Show Options**.

4. Drag the slide to adjust the input levels.

5. Click **Start Narration**.

6. When you're done speaking, click **Stop Narration**.

7. Save the audio file.

8. Click **Close**.

See Also

See "Adding a Soundtrack" on page 270 for information on changing the audio levels.

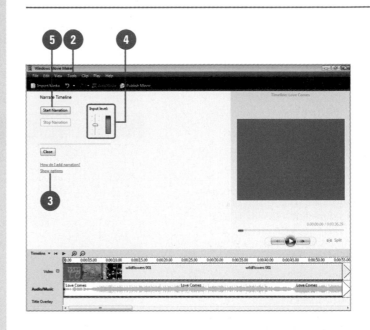

Using AutoMovie

You can use AutoMovie to help you automatically create a movie based on the selected clips or collection. AutoMovie analyzes the selected video clips, pictures, and music and combines them into a movie based on your AutoMovie editing style. To use AutoMovie, the total length of the clips you use need to last for at least 30 seconds; each picture needs to play at least 6 seconds, and an audio clip needs to play at least 30 seconds.

Use AutoMovie

1. Select the clips, pictures, and audio you want in the Collections area.

2. Click the **AutoMovie** button on the toolbar.

3. Click an AutoMovie editing style.

4. Click **Enter a title for the movie**.

5. Type the text you want to appear as the title.

6. Click **Select audio or background music**.

7. To select an audio or music file, click **Browse**, locate and select the audio or music file you want to use, and then click **Open**.

8. Drag the slider to adjust the audio balance level.

9. Click **Create AutoMovie**.

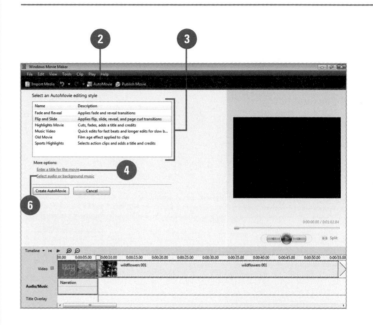

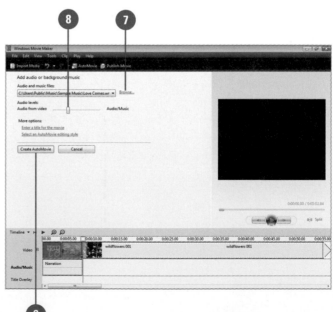

Saving a Project

If you're still working on a project, you can save the project file and open it later to continue working with your movie. A saved project file in Movie Maker has an .mswmm file name extension. Before you save your project, you can include general information about the movie, such as the title, author, copyright, a rating, and a description, that is often displayed during playback by many media players.

Save a Movie Project

1. Click the **File** menu, and then click **Save Project**.

2. Select the folder where you want to save the project file.

3. Type a project name.

4. Click **Save**.

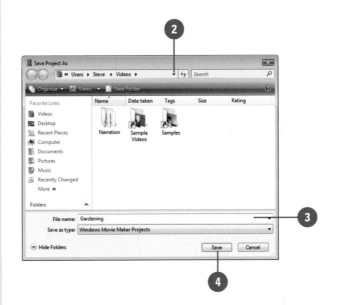

Add Project Properties

1. Click the **File** menu, and then click **Properties**.

2. Type the movie title.

3. Type the author name.

4. Type any copyright information.

5. Type a rating for the movie.

6. Type a description.

7. Click **OK**.

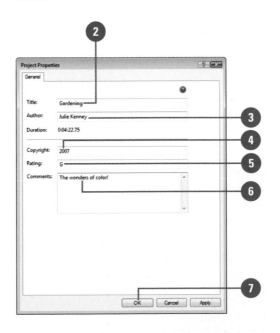

Publishing a Movie

After you preview the final project using the monitor, you can publish the project file as a movie file. Using the Publish Wizard, you can publish the movie file to your computer or a recordable CD, send it as an attachment in an e-mail message, or save and send it to the web. If you have a digital video camera connected to your computer, you can also record your movie to a tape. After you save the movie in the .wmv format, you can play it in a media player, such as Windows Media Player, or in a web browser. If you want to create a DVD, Movie Maker connects you with Windows DVD Maker (**New!**) and imports your movie where you can customize it, and burn the movie to a DVD.

Publish a Movie to Your Computer or Recordable CD

1 Click the **Tasks** button, if necessary.

2 In the Task pane, click **This computer** or **Recordable CD**.

3 Type a file name for the movie.

4 Select a save location or insert a recordable CD.

5 Click **Next** to continue.

6 Click the movie quality option you want: Best quality, Compress, or More settings.

7 Click **Publish**.

Wait while Movie Maker saves the movie file.

8 Click **Finish**.

Did You Know?

You can save a movie to a digital video camera. Turn on your digital camera, and connect it to your computer. In Movie Maker, click the Tasks button, click Digital video camera in the Tasks pane, select your digital camera, click Next, use your video camera controls to cue the tape, click Next, click Yes, and then click Finish.

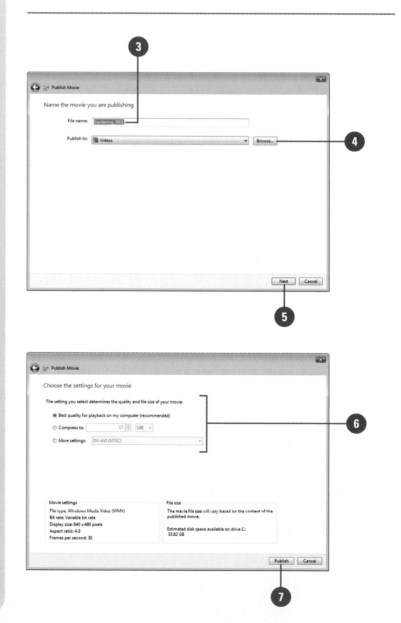

Publish a Movie to a DVD with Windows DVD Maker

① Insert a blank DVD into your DVD-R or DVD-RW drive.

② In Movie Maker, click the **Tasks** button if necessary, click **DVD**, and then click **OK** to burn your movie to a DVD.

③ Click the **Add items** button, locate and select the media you want to insert, and then click **Import**.

④ Select a media item, and then click the **Move up** or **Move down** button to arrange the media on the DVD.

⑤ Click **DVD Burner** list arrow, and then select a DVD burner.

⑥ To set options, click the **Options** button, specify the options you want, and then click **OK**.

⑦ Type a disc title, and then click **Next** to continue.

⑧ Click the **Menu text** button, specify the text you want, and then click **Change Text**.

⑨ Click a menu style in the right pane.

⑩ Click **Burn**.

⑪ Click the **File** menu, click **Save**, specify a location and name, and then click **Save**.

Did You Know?

You can send a movie in e-mail. Click the Tasks button, if necessary, click E-mail in the Tasks pane, click Attach Movie to open a new e-mail message with the attached movie file, type an address and message, and then click Send.

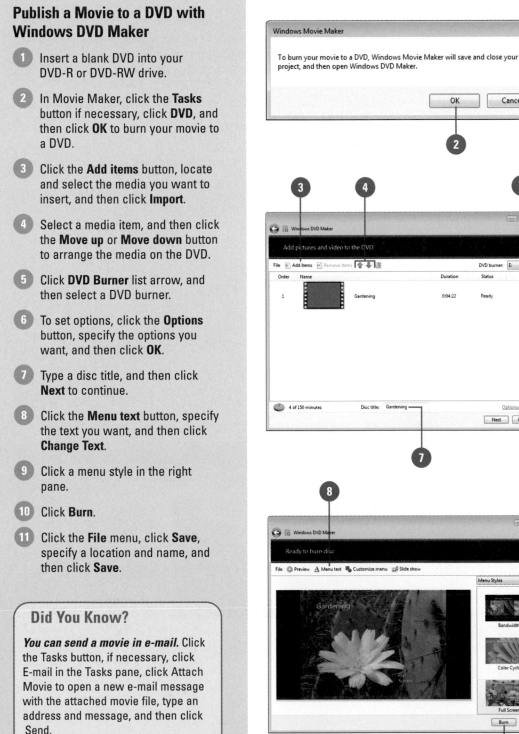

Creating a DVD Video

With Windows DVD Maker (**New!**), you can insert video, pictures and audio, and combine it with titles and predefined menus to create a DVD video disc that you can play on a TV using a DVD player. To create a DVD, you add and arrange your media, add menu text, select a menu style, choose DVD playback options, and then burn it. If you have still photos, you can also create a slide show set to music.

Create a DVD Video Using Windows DVD Maker

1. Click the **Start** button, point to **All Programs**, and then click **Windows DVD Maker**.

2. Click the **Add items** button, locate and select the media you want to insert, and then click **Import**.

3. Select a media item, and then click the **Move up** or **Move down** button to arrange the media on the DVD.

4. Click **DVD Burner** list arrow, and then select a DVD burner.

5. To set options, click the **Options** button, specify the options you want, and then click **OK**.

6. Type a disc title, and then click **Next** to continue.

7. Click the **Menu text** button, specify the text you want, and then click **Change Text**.

8. Click a menu style in the right pane.

9. To customize the menu, click the **Customize menu** button, specify the options you want, and then **Change Style**.

10. Click the **Slide show** button, specify picture length and music, and then **Change Slide Show**.

11. Click **Burn**.

12. Click the **File** menu, click **Save**, specify a location and name, and then click **Save**.

Setting Up Accounts and Maintaining Security

Introduction

With user accounts, you can customize and personalize Windows for each user on your computer. Each user can have their own Documents folder and list of Web favorites, customize computer preferences, and protect private files. When you set up a new user account, the account appears on the Welcome screen, where the new user can log on. You can use User Accounts in the Control Panel to add or delete user accounts, create a guest account, change a user's group or account type, change the way Windows starts, change the account picture, and set, change, and reset an account password.

Keeping your computer safe and secure is a continuing battle. With the Windows Security Center, you can manage computer security from one place. The Security Center makes it easy to find information about the latest virus or security threat, check the status of essential security settings, and quickly get support from Microsoft for a security-related issue.

While you're browsing the Internet or working in your e-mail program, you need to be aware of viruses and other harmful attacks so you can protect your computer from being infected by one. Internet Explorer and Windows Mail include security enhancements to help you make your computer more secure. In Internet Explorer, you can create security zones to designate trusted web sites, set web site ratings to restrict user access, clean up Internet files and information, and manage cookies to protect your personal identity from unauthorized access. If you're tired to closing unwanted pop-up ads, you can use Pop-up Blocker in Internet Explorer to prevent most pop-up windows from appearing. In Windows Mail, you can select a security zone, set options to prevent viruses in attachments and spam, and send secure e-mail using digital IDs and encryption.

Securing a Computer

Windows Vista provides several ways to secure your computer.

Create User Accounts

For a shared or workgroup computer, there are two main types of user accounts: administrator and standard. For a domain network computer, different account types (administrator, standard user, restricted user) provide similar permissions as the ones on a shared or workgroup computer.

The **administrator** account is for the person who needs to make changes to anything on the computer as well as manage user accounts. An administrator account can install programs and hardware, make system-wide changes, access and read all non private files, create and delete user accounts, change other people's accounts, change your own account name and type, change your own picture, and create, change, or remove your own password.

The **standard** account is for the person who needs to manage personal files and run programs. The standard account cannot install software or hardware or change most computer settings.

The **guest** account doesn't have a password for easy access and contains more restrictions than the standard account. The guest account is disabled by default and needs to be turned on.

You can also create a **user group**, which is a collection of user accounts that all have the same security rights. The most common user groups are the standard user and administrator. A single account can be a member of more than one group.

Use Security Center

Use the Security Center to check your security settings— Window Firewall, Automatic Updates, and antivirus software—and learn how to improve the security of your computer.

If a security option displays the Security Center icon (**New!**) next to it, you need to enter the administrator password or provide confirmation when prompted. This adds an additional level of security on your computer.

Icon indicates you need Administrator account privileges to access

Administrator account

Enable Windows Firewall

Windows Firewall is a security system that creates a protective barrier between your computer or network and others on the Internet. Windows Firewall monitors all communication between your computer and the Internet and prevents unsolicited inbound traffic from the Internet from entering your computer. For more information on Windows Firewall, see "Connecting to the Internet" on page 135 and "Setting Up Windows Firewall" on page 137.

Enable Automatic Updates

Windows Automatic Updates allows you to keep your computer up-to-date with the latest system software and security updates over the Internet. For more information, see "Updating Windows" on page 440.

Enable Internet Security Options

Internet Explorer provides security zones to browse secure web sites and a rating system to screen content, protects personal information and your privacy on the Internet, blocks pop-up ads, and displays information to help you make security decisions. For more information, see "Understanding Security on the Internet" on page 332.

Enable E-mail Security Options

Windows Mail provides security zones to help you determine whether or not to run potentially harmful content from inside an e-mail, prevents your e-mail program from sending mail with your e-mail address to contacts in your address book (which is a common way propagate a virus), and stops pictures and other content from automatically downloading inside and e-mail to your computer (which is a common way spammers confirm your e-mail address to send more spam). For more information, see "Sending and Retrieving a File" on page 180 "Reading and Replying to E-mail" on page 178, and "Protecting Against E-mail Attacks" on page 345.

Protect Files and Folders

Another way to protect the files on your computer is to use the built-in security provided by the NTFS file system. The NTFS file system is available for Windows NT-based computers, which doesn't include Windows 95, Windows 98, or Windows Me. You can select your hard disk in My Computer and display Details on the task pane to determine whether your computer uses the NTFS file system.

The NTFS file system provides additional security for your files and folders. You can make a folder private, use the advanced Encrypting File System (EFS) to protect sensitive data files on your computer. If someone tries to gain access to encrypted files or a folder on your computer, a unique file encryption key prevents that person from viewing it. While these security options are more advanced, they could be helpful for securing very sensitive information. For more information, see "Encrypting Files for Safety" on page 328.

Understand the Enemy

Knowing your enemy (harmful intruders) can help you make safe computing decisions that lead to a secure computer rather than unsafe ones that lead to potential disaster. For information, see "Avoiding Viruses and Other Harmful Attacks" on page 330.

Adding and Deleting User Accounts

Microsoft
Certified
Application
Specialist

WINV-1.6

If you have an administrator account or are a member of the Administrators group, you can create a new user account or delete an existing one. When you add a new user to your computer, Windows creates a separate identity, allowing the user to keep files completely private and customize the operating system with personal preferences. The name you assign to the user appears on the Welcome screen and the Start menu. The steps to add and delete user accounts differ, depending on whether your computer is part of a domain network or shared/workgroup computer.

Add an Account

1. Click the **Start** button, and then click **Control Panel.**

2. Double-click the **User Accounts** icon in Classic view.

3. Click **Manage another account**.

4. Click **Create a new account**.

5. Type an account name.

6. Click the **Administrator** option, or click the **Standard** option.

7. Click **Create Account**.

8. Click the **Close** button.

Did You Know?

You can delete an account. In User Accounts, click the account you want to remove, click Delete the account, click Keep Files to save account file to the desktop or click Delete Files, click Delete Account, and then click the Close button.

You may need administrator access to make security changes. If a security option displays the Security Center icon (**New!**) next to it, you need to enter the administrator password or provide confirmation when prompted to make a change.

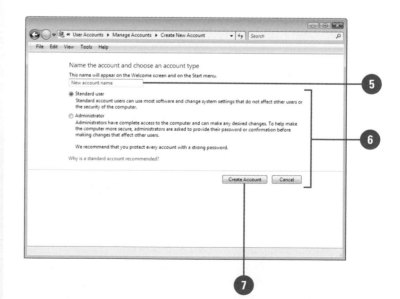

Add an Account on a Domain Network

① Click the **Start** button, and then click **Control Panel**.

② Double-click the **User Accounts** icon in Classic view, and then click **Manage User Accounts**.

③ Click **Add**.

④ Type a user name and domain, and then click **Next** to continue.

⑤ Click a user access level option: **Standard user**, **Administrator**, or **Other**.

⑥ Click **Finish**.

⑦ Click **OK**.

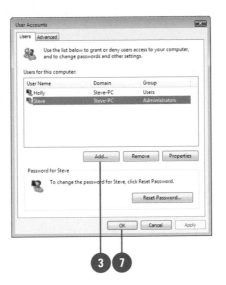

Did You Know?

You can delete an account on a domain network. In the User Accounts dialog box, click the Users tab, select the user you want to delete, click Remove, click Yes to confirm, and then click OK.

You can turn User Account Control on or off. In the User Accounts dialog box, click Turn User Account Control on or off, select or clear the User Account Control (UAC) to help protect your computer check box, click OK, and then click the Close button.

Creating a Guest Account

If you have an administrator account or are a member of the Administrators group, you can create a guest account. A guest account provides access to a computer for anyone who doesn't have a user account. The steps to create a guest account differ, depending on whether your computer is part of a domain network or shared/work-group computer.

Create a Guest Account

1. Click the **Start** button, and then click **Control Panel.**

2. Double-click the **User Accounts** icon in Classic view.

3. Click **Manage another account**.

4. Click the **Guest** icon.

5. Click **Turn On**.

6. Click the **Close** button.

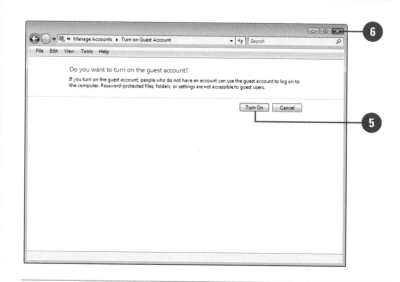

Create a Guest Account on a Domain Network

1. Click the **Start** button, and then click **Control Panel.**

2. Double-click the **User Accounts** icon in Classic view, and then click **Manage User Accounts.**

3. Click the **Advanced** tab, and then click **Advanced.**

4. Click **Users.**

5. Double-click the **Guest** icon.

6. Clear the **Account is disabled** check box.

7. Click **OK**, and then click the **Close** button.

8. Click **OK.**

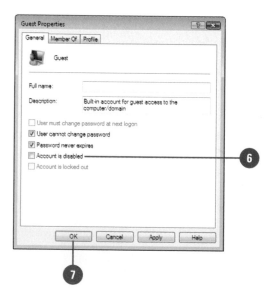

Changing a User's Group or Account Type

If you have an administrator account or are a member of the Administrators group, you can change a user's account type or user group on a domain network. A user account or group grants permissions to a user to perform certain types of tasks based on the account type or user group (domain network). The steps to create a guest account differ, depending on whether your computer is part of a network domain or shared/workgroup computer.

Change a User's Account Type

1. Click the **Start** button, and then click **Control Panel**.

2. Double-click the **User Accounts** icon in Classic view.

3. If you want to change another account, click **Manage another account**, and then click the user's account name.

4. Click **Change your account type** or **Change the account type**.

5. Click an account type option.

6. Click **Change Account Type**.

7. Click the **Close** button.

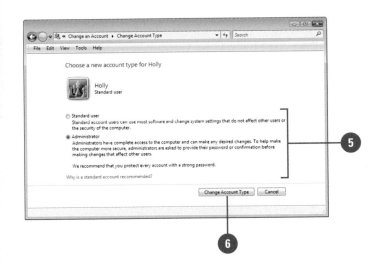

Change a User's Group on a Domain Network

1. Click the **Start** button, and then click **Control Panel**.

2. Double-click the **User Accounts** icon in Classic view, and then click **Manage User Accounts**.

3. Click the **Users** tab.

4. Select the user account name you want to change.

5. Click **Properties**, and then click the **Group Membership** tab.

6. Click the group you want.

7. Click **OK**, and then click **OK** again.

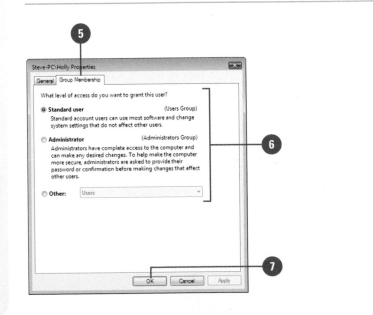

Changing the Start Up Screen

For added security, you can require users to use Ctrl+Alt+Delete (or Ctrl+Alt+Del) before they can select a user account and enter a password. This prevents other programs, such as spyware or a virus, from getting your user name and password as you enter it without your consent. When you lock your computer or switch users, the security option also requires users to press Ctrl+Alt+Delete.

Increase Logon Security on a Domain Network

① Click the **Start** button, and then click **Control Panel**.

② Double-click the **User Accounts** icon in Classic view, and then click **Manage User Accounts**.

③ Click the **Advanced** tab.

④ Select the **Require Users To Press Ctrl+Alt+Delete** check box.

⑤ Click **OK**.

Did You Know?

You can also change the logon security on a workgroup network. Open Advanced User Accounts, click the Advanced tab, select the Require users to press Ctrl+Alt+Delete check box, and then click OK.

Changing an Account Picture

When you log on to Windows, the Welcome screen appears, displaying a list of user accounts with a picture next to each one. When you complete the logon process, the picture associated with your account appears at the top of the Start menu along with your user name. This identifies you as the current user of the computer. You can change the picture to suit your own personality. Changing your account picture is not available for computers on a domain network.

Change an Account Picture

1. Click the **Start** button, and then click **Control Panel**.

2. Double-click the **User Accounts** icon in Classic view.

3. If you want to change another account, click **Manage another account**, and then click the user's account name.

4. Click **Change your picture** or **Change the picture**.

5. Click the picture you want.

6. Click **Change Picture**, or click **Browse for more pictures** and double-click the picture you want.

7. Click the **Close** button.

> ### See Also
>
> *See Chapter 8, "Working with Pictures" on page 233 for information on creating, scanning, and using pictures.*

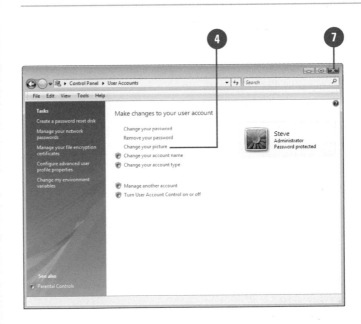

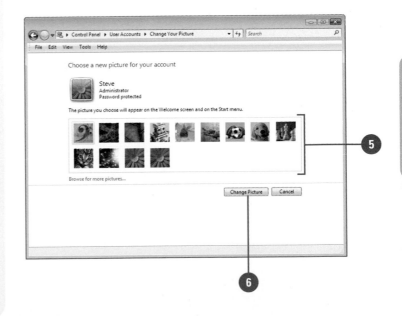

Changing and Setting a Password

Microsoft Certified Application Specialist WINV-1.6

If you don't have a password associated with your user account, anyone can access your files. A password controls who has access to your files. When you create a password, enter one that is easy for you to remember, yet difficult for others to guess. Good passwords are typically at least seven characters and include letters (uppercase and lowercase), numbers, and symbols. Once you create a password, you can always change it.

Change or Create a Password

1. Click the **Start** button, and then click **Control Panel**.

2. Double-click the **User Accounts** icon in Classic view.

3. If you want to change another account, click **Manage another account**, and then click the user's account name.

4. Click **Change your password**, **Change the password**, or **Create a password**.

5. Type a password, and then type it again.

6. Type a hint that reminds you of the password.

7. Click **Change password** or **Create password**.

8. Click the **Close** button.

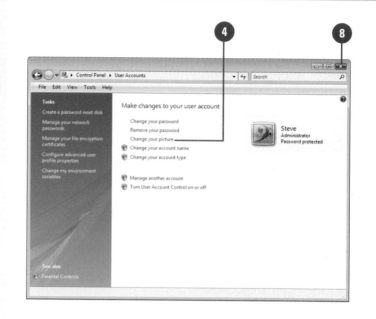

> **Did You Know?**
>
> *You can change a password.* In User Accounts, click the account you want to change, click Change My Password, type your current password, if necessary, type a new password, type it again, type a hint, and then click Change password.

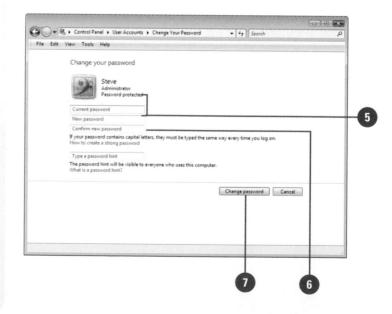

Change an Administrator Password on a Domain Network

① Click the **Start** button, and then click **Control Panel**.

② Double-click the **User Accounts** icon in Classic view, and then click **Manage User Accounts**.

③ Click the **Users** tab.

④ Click the administrator account.

⑤ Click **Reset Password**.

⑥ Type the new password, and then type it again.

⑦ Click **OK**.

⑧ Click **OK**.

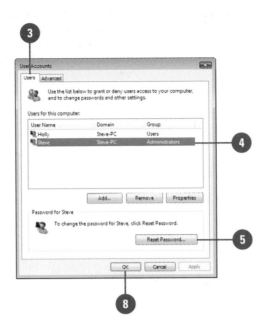

Security Alert

Working Smarter as the Administrator

If you are an administrator, it's recommended that you log out and use another account for general work to avoid harmful damage to your computer by a virus or malicious user. For example, if a hacker received access to your computer with administrator privileges, the attacker could reformat your hard drive, delete files, or create a new administrator account.

Resetting a Password

If you have ever forgotten your password, you understand how important it is to write it down. However, writing down a password is not very secure. You can create a Password Reset disk, either a floppy disk or USB flash drive, to help you log on and reset your password. If you have any security credentials and certificates on your computer, the Password Reset disk restores them. If you have forgotten your password and don't have a Password Reset disk, you can ask your administrator to reset it for you. Resetting your password also erases any security credentials and certificates on your computer.

Create a Password Reset Disk

1. Click the **Start** button, and then click **Control Panel**.

2. Double-click the **User Accounts** icon in Classic view.

3. Insert a blank disk in the Floppy drive or USB Flash drive.

4. In the Tasks pane, click **Create a password reset disk**.

5. Follow the instructions in the Forgotten Password Wizard to create a password reset disk.

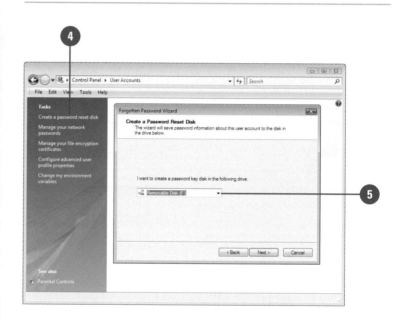

Did You Know?

You can reset your password at the welcome screen. At the Welcome screen, click the Help button to see your password hint, and then type the password if you remember it. If you don't, click the arrow. Click Reset password, and then follow the instructions in the Password Reset Wizard to create a new password. Type your new password, and then press Enter.

Type user account password

Locking the Computer

Microsoft Certified Application Specialist

WINV-1.4.2

If you are working on sensitive material and need to leave your computer unattended for a while, you can lock it so that no one can use it without your permission. While your computer is locked, all your programs continue to run. When you return to your computer, you can access your computer in the same way you started Windows. If the Ctrl+Alt+Del security option is enabled, you are required to press Ctrl+Alt+Del before you can enter a password.

Lock and Unlock the Computer

1. Click the **Start** button, and then click the **Lock** button.

   TIMESAVER Press ⊞+L to lock the computer. T*he Windows key* ⊞ *is located in the lower-left corner of the keyboard.*

2. If the Ctrl+Alt+Del screen appears, press Ctrl+Alt+Del.

3. At the Welcome screen, click your name (if prompted), type your password, and then press Enter.

See Also

See "Starting Windows Vista" on page 4 and "Switching Users" on page 22 for information on logging on to Windows Vista.

Managing Security in One Place

The Windows Security Center provides a single place to manage your four security essentials, Windows Firewall, Automatic Updating, Malware protection (virus and spyware) and Other security settings (Internet security and User Account Controls). The Security Center recommends security settings that you can use to help protect your computer. It also provides links to important information about the latest virus or other security threat, or to get customer support from Microsoft for a security related issue. As you work, Windows Vista uses security alerts and icons in the notification area on the taskbar to help you recognize potential security risks, such as a new virus, out of date antivirus software or an important security option is turned off, and choose appropriate settings.

View Essential Security Settings Using the Security Center

1. Click the **Start** button, and then click **Control Panel**.

2. Double-click the **Security Center** icon in Classic view.

   IMPORTANT *If you're part of a network, options might be grayed out; your security settings are managed by your network administrator.*

3. To find out information on a security area, click the down arrow next to it.

4. To set security settings, click the link (Windows Update, Windows Firewall, Windows Defender, and Internet Options) for the area you want to change.

5. When you're done, click the **Close** button.

Act Upon Security Alerts

1. If the Security Center detects that your computer needs enhanced security, it displays an alert in the notification area.

2. Read the security alert, and then click it.

3. To find out information on a security option, click the down arrow next to it.

4. To find out how to address the problem, click a link or a button, and then follow the instructions.

5. When you're done, click the **Close** button.

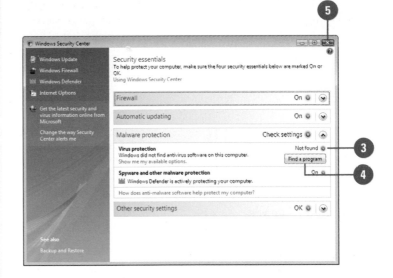

Did You Know?

You can change the way Automatic Updates alerts changes. Click the Start button, click Control Panel, double-click the Windows Update icon in Classic view, click Change settings, select the alert option you want, click OK, and then click the Close button.

Security Icons

Icon	Description
🛡️	**Security Settings:** Indicates important security information and settings that are available, such as the Windows Security Center.
🛡️	**Potential Risk:** Indicates your computer encountered a potential security risk; act upon the security alert.
🛡️	**No Risk:** Indicates your computer is more secure and using recommended security settings; no action needed.
🛡️	**Security Warning:** Indicates your computer encountered a warning alert, which is potentially harmful; consider adjusting security settings.
🛡️	**Security Problem:** Indicates your computer is not using recommended security settings; consider adjusting them.

Defending Against Malicious Software

Microsoft Certified Application Specialist

WINV-1.2

Windows Defender (**New!**) helps you protect your computer from spyware and other potentially harmful software that attempts to install itself or run on your computer. Spyware is software that tries to collect information about you or change computer settings without your consent. Windows Defender alerts you in real-time when unwanted software tries to run on your computer. You can also use Windows Defender to scan your computer and set up a schedule to automatically scan on a regular basis. When you receive an alert of a potential problem, you can use the Microsoft SpyNet community to help you determine if the software is already to run. Windows Defender uses definitions to determine potential problems. Since software dangers continually change, it's important to have up-to-date definitions, which you can get online.

Use Windows Defender

1 If a real-time alert appears with an attempt to:

◆ **Install software.** Click **Ignore**, **Quarantine**, **Remove**, or **Always Allow**.

◆ **Change Windows settings.** Click **Permit** or **Deny**.

2 Click the **Start** button, and then click **Control Panel**.

3 Double-click the **Windows Defender** icon in Classic view.

4 To perform a scan, click the **Scan** button arrow, and then click **Quick Scan** or **Full Scan**.

5 To view or clear history, click the **History** button, and then click an item to view history or click **Clear History** to remove all activities.

6 To go backward and forward to the previously viewed screens, click the **Back** or **Forward** button.

7 When you're done, click the **Close** button.

Status information

Change Windows Defender Options

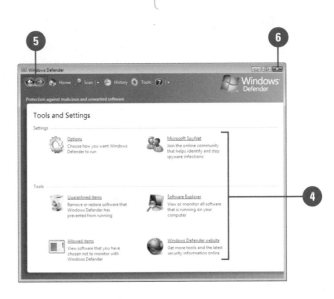

1. Click the **Start** button, and then click **Control Panel**.

2. Double-click the **Windows Defender** icon in Classic view.

3. Click the **Tools** button.

4. Click the links to the tools and settings you want to change:

   ◆ **Options.** Set up a scan schedule and choose default actions when alerts appear.

   ◆ **Microsoft SpyNet.** Allows you to join the SpyNet community.

   ◆ **Quarantined items.** Allows you to remove and restore items.

   ◆ **Allowed items.** Allows you to remove items from the list.

   ◆ **Software Explorer.** Allows you to scan your computer for programs and provide security information about them. You can stop, remove, disable or enable programs.

   ◆ **Windows Defender website.** Access the Windows Defender Web site at Microsoft to get updates and definitions.

5. To go backward and forward to the previously viewed screens, click the **Back** or **Forward** button.

6. When you're done, click the **Close** button.

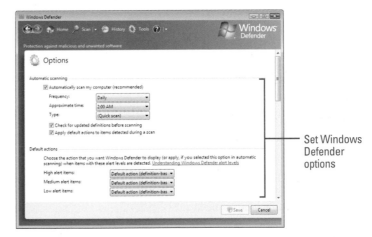

Set Windows Defender options

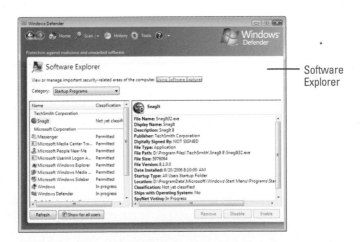

Software Explorer

Setting Parental Controls

Parental Controls (**New!**) help you manage how your children use the computer. Parental Controls allows you to set limits on your children's Web access, the amount of time spent logged on the computer, and which games and programs they can use. You can set different settings for each user account on your computer, so you can adjust the level you want for each child. You can also review activity reports on a periodic basis to see what your children are doing on the computer.

Set Parental Controls

1. Click the **Start** button, and then click **Control Panel**.

2. Double-click the **Parental Controls** icon in Classic view.

3. To select a games rating system, or an activity report reminder option, click an option in the Tasks pane.

4. Click the standard user account for which you want to set controls.

5. Click the **On, enforce current settings** option and then click the **On, collection information about computer usage** option.

6. Click the links to the Windows Settings you want to change:

   ◆ **Web restrictions.** Select a Web restriction level (High, Medium, None or Custom) and options to block or allow websites or file downloads.

   ◆ **Time limits.** Click and drag the hours you want to block or allow.

   ◆ **Games.** Select options to block or allow games based on ratings or specific games.

   ◆ **Allow or block specific programs.** Select an option to use all programs or only the programs I use.

7. Click **OK**, and then click **OK** again.

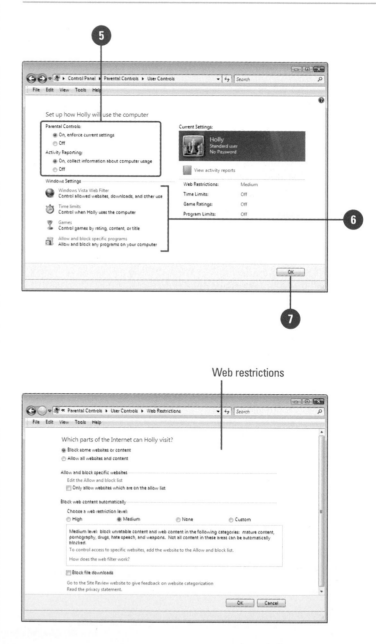

Web restrictions

Sending Secure Information Using Windows CardSpace

With Windows CardSpace (**New!**), you can securely send information in the form of online cards to Web sites or online services. Windows CardSpace is a system for creating relationships with Web sites and online services that provides a consistent way for you to review the identity of a site, manage your information, review information before sending it to a site and for sites to request information from you. Windows CardSpace can replace the user names and passwords that you use to register and log on to Web sites and online services. You can create a personal card or have a business or organization issue you a managed card.

Use Windows CardSpace

1. Click the **Start** button, then click **Control Panel**.

2. Double-click the **Windows CardSpace** icon in Classic view.

3. If necessary, click **OK** to dismiss the introduction screen.

4. To add a card, click the **Add a card** button, click **Add**, click a card type, enter information, and then click **Save**.

5. In the main screen, use task commands to duplicate, delete, back up, and restore cards.

6. To modify a card, double-click the card, and then click any of the following task commands:

   ◆ **Edit card.** Make changes, and then click Save.

   ◆ **View card history.** View the information, and then click OK.

   ◆ **Lock card.** Type a PIN code, type it again, and then click Lock.

7. To go back to the main screen, click the **Back** button.

8. When you're done, click the **Close** button.

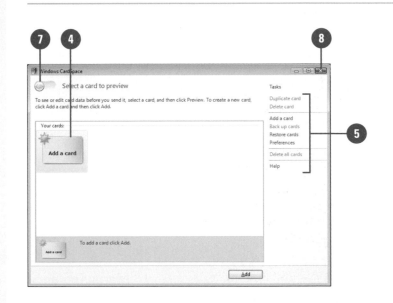

Encrypting Files for Safety

Encrypt or Decrypt a File or Folder

1 Right-click the file or folder you want to encrypt, and then click **Properties**.

2 Click the **General** tab.

3 Click **Advanced**.

4 Select the **Encrypt contents to secure data** check box to encrypt the file or folder or clear the check box to decrypt it.

5 Click **OK**.

6 Click **OK**.

7 If necessary, click an option to apply changes to this folder only or to this folder, subfolders, and files.

8 Click **OK**.

Did You Know?

You can compress files and folders with NTFS. Right-click the file or folder, click Properties, click the General tab, click Advanced, select the Compress contents to save disk space check box, and then click OK twice.

If your computer uses NTFS, you can use the advanced Encrypting File System (EFS) to protect sensitive data files on your computer. If someone tries to gain access to encrypted files or a folder on your computer, a unique file encryption key prevents that person from viewing it. When you encrypt a file, you also need to decide whether you want to encrypt the folder, too. When you encrypt a folder, you need to decide whether you want to encrypt all files and subfolders within it.

For Your Information

Managing and Backing Up Encryption Certificate

When you encrypt a file or folder, Windows uses information from your Encrypting File system certificate. A certificate is a digital document that verifies the identify of a person, which is issued by a trusted Certification Authority. If you lost the certificate or it becomes corrupted, you will not be able to recover an encrypted file or folder. To avoid this problem, you should back up your Encrypting File System (EFS) certificate. To manage and back up your EFS certificate, click the Start button, click Control Panel, double-click the User Accounts icon, click the Manage your file encryption certificates, and then follow the Encrypting File System wizard.

Encrypting Files Using BitLocker

If you have a two partition (also known as volumes) hard drive, you can use BitLocker (**New!**) to encrypt the entire system drive, including the Windows system files needed to startup and logon to Windows Vista. BitLocker helps protect your system and blocks hackers from accessing sensitive information behind the scenes. When you add files to your computer, BitLocker automatically encrypts them. When you copy files to another location, the files are decrypted. After you turn on BitLocker, it's critical that you create a recovery password, because BitLocker locks up the entire drive if it detects a problem during startup.

Turn On BitLocker to Encrypt the Entire System Disk

1. Click the **Start** button, then click **Control Panel**.

2. Double-click the **BitLocker Drive Encryption** icon in Classic view.

3. Click **Turn On BitLocker**.

4. Follow the BitLocker setup wizard.

5. Click the **Close** button.

Did You Know?

You can turn off or temporarily disable BitLocker. Click the Start button, then click Control Panel, double-click the BitLocker Drive Encryption icon in Classic view. To temporarily disable BitLocker, click Disable BitLocker Drive Encryption.

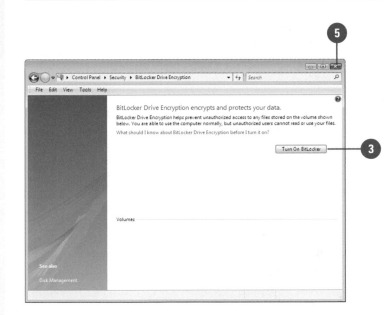

Avoiding Viruses and Other Harmful Attacks

Understanding Harmful Attacks

Using the Internet can expose your computer to a wide variety of harmful attacks, such as viruses, worms, and Trojan Horses. These attacks can come through e-mail, file transferring, and even possibly through Java and ActiveX, which are both programming languages used to enhance web pages.

A **virus** is an executable program whose functions range from just being annoying to causing havoc to your computer. A virus may display an innocuous warning on a particular day, such as Friday the 13th, or it may cause a more serious problem, such as wiping out your entire hard disk. Viruses are found in executable (.exe and .com) files, along with Microsoft Word and Microsoft Excel macro files. A **worm** is like a virus, but it can spread without human action across networks. For example, a worm might send e-mail copies of itself to everyone in your e-mail Address Book. A worm can consume memory causing your computer to stop responding or even take it over. A **Trojan Horse**, like it's mythological counterpart, is a program that appears to be useful and comes from a legitimate source, but actually causes problems.

Spreading Harmful Infections

Many viruses and other harmful attacks spread through file downloads and attachments in e-mail messages. Virus writers capitalize on people's curiosity and willingness to accept files from people they know or work with, in order to transmit malicious files disguised as or attached to benign files. When you start downloading files to your computer, you must be aware of the potential for catching a computer virus, worm, or Trojan Horse. Typically, you can't catch one from just reading a mail message or downloading a file, but you can catch one from opening or running an infected program, such as a file attached to an e-mail message, or one you download for free. And even though most viruses and other harmful attacks take the form of executable programs, data files that have macros or Visual Basic code attached to them, such as Word or Excel files, can also be infected with viruses.

Avoiding Harmful Attacks

There are a few things you can do to keep your system safe from the infiltration of viruses and other harmful attacks.

1) Make sure Windows Firewall is turned on. Windows Firewall helps block viruses and worms from reaching your computer, but it doesn't detect or disable them if they are already on your computer or come through e-mail. Windows Firewall doesn't block unsolicited e-mail or stop you from opening e-mail with harmful attachments. For more information on Windows Firewall, see "Connecting to the Internet" on page 135 and "Setting Up Windows Firewall" on page 137.

2) Make sure Automatic Updates is turned on. Windows Automatic Updates regularly checks the Windows Update web site for important updates that your computer needs, such as security updates, critical updates, and service packs. Each file that you download using Automatic Update has a digital signature from Microsoft to ensure it's authenticity and security. For more information, see "Updating Windows" on page 440.

3) Make sure you are using the most up-to-date antivirus software. New viruses and more virulent strains of existing viruses are discovered every day. Unless you update your virus checking software, new viruses can easily bypass outdated virus checking software. Companies such as McAfee and Symantec offer shareware virus checking programs available for download directly from their web sites. These programs monitor your system, checking each time a file is added to your computer to make sure it's not in some way trying to change or damage valuable system files.

4) Be very careful of the sites from which you download files. Major file repository sites, such as FileZ, Download.com, or TuCows, regularly check the files they receive for viruses before posting them to their web sites. Don't download files from web sites unless you are certain that the sites check their files for viruses. Internet Explorer monitors downloads and warns you about potentially harmful files and gives you the option to block them. For more information, see "Downloading Files from the Web" on page 160.

5) Be very careful of file attachments in e-mail you open. As you receive e-mail, don't open or run an attached file unless you know who sent it and what it contains. If you're not sure, you should delete it. The Attachment Manager provides security information to help you understand more about the file you're opening. To protect your computer from harmful attacks, see "Sending and Retrieving a File" on page 180, "Reading and Replying to E-mail" on page 178, and "Protecting Against E-mail Attacks" on page 345.

6) Make sure you activate macro virus checking protection in both Word and Excel. To do so, click the Tools menu, point to Macro on the expanded menu, click Security, and then make sure that the High Security Level option is selected. (In Office 2000, XP, or later, click the Tools menu, click Options, click the General tab, and then make sure the Macro Virus Protection option is selected.) And always elect not to run macros when opening a Word or Excel file that you received from someone who might not be using proper virus protection.

Avoiding Other Intruders

Spyware is software that collects personal information without your knowledge or permission. Typically, spyware is downloaded and installed on your computer along with free software, such as freeware, games, or music file-sharing programs. Spyware is often associated with **Adware** software that displays advertisements, such as a pop-up ad. Examples of spyware and unauthorized adware include programs that change your home page or search page without your permission. To avoid spyware and adware, read the fine print in license agreements when you install software, scan your computer for spyware and adware with detection and removal software (such as Ad-aware from Lavasoft), and turn on Pop-up Blocker. For details, see "Blocking Pop-Up Ads" on page 342.

Spam is unsolicited e-mail, which is often annoying and time-consuming to get rid of. Spammers harvest e-mail addresses from Web pages and unsolicited e-mail. To avoid spam, use multiple e-mail addresses (one for web forms and another for private e-mail), opt-out and remove yourself from e-mail lists, and turn on the Block Images And Other External Content In HTML E-mail option. For details, see "Protecting Against E-mail Attacks" on page 345.

Phishing is an e-mail scam that tries to steal your identity by sending deceptive e-mail asking you for bank and credit card information online. Don't be fooled by spoofed web site that look like the official site. Never respond to requests for personal information via e-mail; call the institution to investigate and report it.

Understanding Security on the Internet

No other web browser offers as many customizable features as Internet Explorer does, particularly advanced security features that are built into the program. To understand all the Internet Explorer security features, you first have to learn about security on the Internet in general.

When you send information from your computer to another computer, the two computers are not linked directly together. Your data may travel through multiple networks as it works its way across the Internet. Since your data is broadcast to the Internet, any computer on any of these networks could be listening in and capturing your data. (They typically aren't, but they could be.)

In addition, on the Internet it's possible to masquerade as someone else. E-mail addresses can be forged, domain names of sites can easily be misleading, and so on. You need some way to protect not only the data you send, but also yourself from sending data to the wrong place.

Furthermore, there is always the potential that someone (referred to as a "hacker") or something, such as a virus or worm, could infiltrate your computer systems. Once infiltrated, a hacker or virus can delete, rename, or even copy valuable information from your computer without your knowledge.

Security Zones

Through the use of **security zones**, you can easily tell Internet Explorer which sites you trust to not damage your computer and which sites you simply don't trust. In your company's intranet you would most likely trust all the information supplied on web pages through your company's network, but on the Internet you may want to be warned first of potential dangers a site could cause your sys-

tem. You can set up different levels of security based on different zones.

Certificates

When shopping on the Internet, you want to do business with only those companies that offer a certain level of security and promise to protect your buying information. In turn, those companies want to do business with legitimate customers only. A **certificate** or **digital ID** provides both the browser and the company with a kind of guarantee confirming that you are who you say you are and that the site is secure and genuine, not a fraud or scam. When you send an e-mail message, it also verifies your identity to your recipients.

A digital ID is made up of a public key, a private key, and a digital signature. When you digitally sign an e-mail, Windows Mail adds your public key and digital signature (the two together is the certificate) to the message. When your recipients receive the e-mail, your digital signature verifies your identity and your public key is stored in their Address Book so they can send you encrypted messages, which only you can open with your private key.

An independent company, called a **credentials agency**, issues three types of certificates: personal, authority, and publisher. A **personal certificate** identifies you so that you can access web sites that require positive identification, such as banks that allow online transactions. You can obtain a personal certificate from a credentials agency called VeriSign using the Security tab of the Options dialog box in Windows Mail. An **authority certificate** ensures that the web site you are visiting is not a fraud. Internet Explorer automatically checks site certificates to make sure that they're valid. A **publisher certificate** enables you to trust software that you download, such as ActiveX controls. Internet Explorer maintains a list of software companies whose certificates are valid and trustworthy. You can view your certificate settings on the Content tab of the Internet Options dialog box.

Content Advisor

Just about everyone can find objectionable material on the Internet. Parents might not want to subject their children to some of this material, such as strong language, violence, and other adult themes. However, most parents cannot spend every online minute with their children, censoring objectionable sites. In such cases, you can employ Internet Explorer's **Content Advisor** to screen out inappropriate sites, preventing youngsters from seeing things they shouldn't.

The Content Advisor works with different rating bureaus, such as the Recreational Software Advisory Council (RSAC), to rate sites within certain ranges. The RSAC's rating system is based on research that compiled a rating system to reflect different levels of violence, strong language, and so on. You decide exactly what kind of sites that your children can access, what ratings systems are used, which ranges are available to users within those sites, and whether users of your computer can see unrated sites.

You can also assign a supervisor password to allow a user to view such sites. As long as the user supplies the password you specified when you initially set up the content rating systems, the user can view sites where the material rates above the level chosen. You can turn off the Content Advisor at any time, opening up all sites on the Internet for viewing by any user without having to enter a password.

In order for the rating system to work, sites must subscribe to the system so that their ratings are passed to your computer when you access the sites. Most sites that want to offer quality information for children and those adult sites interested in making sure only individuals 18 years old or older are accessing their sites subscribe to rating systems like the RSAC. A site that voluntarily rates itself usually displays the RSAC logo on its home page. This logo is your indication that the site has properly rated itself and offers only materials that are appropriate to its rating.

Cookies

When you browse the Internet, you can access and gather information from web sites, but web sites can also gather information about you without your knowledge unless you set up Internet security on your computer. You can set Internet privacy options to protect your personal identity from unauthorized access. When you visit a web site, the site creates a **cookie** file, known as a **first-party cookie**, which stores information on your computer, such as your web site preferences or personal identifiable information, including your name and e-mail address. Not all cookies are harmful; many first-party-cookies save you time re-entering information on a return visit to a web site. However, there are also **third-party cookies**, such as advertising banners, which are created by web sites you are not currently viewing. Once a cookie is saved on your computer, only the web site that created it can read it. The privacy options allow you to block or permit cookies for web sites in the Internet zone; however, when you block cookies, you might not be able to access all the features of a web site. When a web site violates your cookie policy, a red icon appears on the status bar.

Creating Security Zones

Internet Explorer lets you create security zones based on where information comes from. For example, you might want to restrict access to web pages that can be viewed from the Internet, but not to those sites within your company's intranet. You can specify the level of security for each of the four available security zones: Local Intranet, Trusted Sites, Restricted Sites, and Internet. When you access a web page or download content from the site, Internet Explorer checks its security settings and determines the web site's zone. Internet Explorer displays a padlock icon in the status bar to indicate the web site is secure. All Internet web sites are assigned to the Internet zone until you assign individual web sites to other zones.

Select a Security Zone and Its Security Level

1. Click the **Start** button, click **Control Panel**, and then double-click the **Internet Options** icon in Classic view.

2. Click the **Security** tab.

3. Click the zone to which you want to assign security options.

4. If you want, click **Default Level** to reset the settings to Microsoft's suggested level.

5. Move the slider to the level of security you want to apply.

   TROUBLE? *If the slider is not available, click Default Level to change the security level to Medium and display the slider.*

6. If you want to specify individual security options, click **Custom Level**.

7. Scroll to a settings area, and then click the **Enable**, **Prompt**, or **Disable** option button.

8. Click **OK**.

9. Click **OK**.

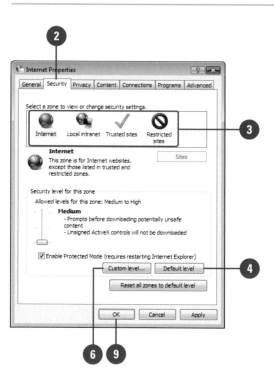

Add Sites to Your Restricted Sites Zone

① Click the **Start** button, click **Control Panel**, and then double-click the **Internet Options** icon in Classic view.

② Click the **Security** tab.

③ Click **Restricted Sites**.

④ Click **Sites**.

⑤ Type the full URL for the site.

⑥ Click **Add**.

⑦ Click **Close**, and then click **OK** again.

Did You Know?

You can reset default settings for security options. To return each option to its default settings for a specified security level, click the Reset Custom Settings list arrow, select a security level, and then click Reset.

You can remove a site from your Restricted Sites zone. Click the Tools menu, click Internet Options, click the Security tab, click Restricted Sites, and then click the Sites button. In the Web Sites box, click the site you want to remove, click Remove, and then click OK. Click OK to close the Internet Options dialog box.

You can enable Internet Explorer protection mode in Internet Properties. In the Internet Properties dialog box, click the Security tab, select the Enable Protected Mode (required restarting Internet Explorer check box, and then click OK.

⑤

Restricted sites

You can add and remove websites from this zone. All websites in this zone will use the zone's security settings.

Add this website to the zone:

www.shopping.com   [Add] ⑥

Websites:

[Remove]

[Close] ⑦

Security Zones

Zone	Description
Internet	Contains all web sites that are not assigned to any other zone; default is Medium
Local intranet	Contains all web sites that are on your organization's intranet and don't require a proxy server; default is Medium
Trusted sites	Contains web sites that you trust not to threaten the security of your computer; default is Low (allows all cookies)
Restricted sites	Contains web sites that you believe threaten the security of your computer; default is High (blocks all cookies)

For Your Information

Setting a Stronger Zone Defense

Internet Explorer also uses another zone called Local Machine, which provides security for your hard disk, but doesn't appear on the Security tab. In earlier versions of Internet Explorer, hackers were using low security levels to attack your computer. This is now stopped.

Setting Ratings Using the Content Advisor

If you have children who surf the Internet and you don't want to subject them to strong language, violence, or sexually explicit material, you can use the Content Advisor to restrict their access to inappropriate web sites. If a rated site matches your ratings specifications, the site can be viewed. If the site is rated above the level you've set, or if the site is not rated and you've restricted access to unrated sites, the site can be viewed only when the supervisor password is supplied.

Enable the Content Advisor Ratings

1. Click the **Start** button, click **Control Panel**, and then double-click the **Internet Options** icon in Classic view.

2. Click the **Content** tab.

3. Click **Enable**. This button toggles between Enable and Disable.

    The first time you use Content Advisor, set your initial settings.

4. Click **OK**, type a supervisor password twice, and then click **OK**.

Set the Content Advisor Ratings

1. Click the **Start** button, click **Control Panel**, and then double-click the **Internet Options** icon in Classic view.

2. Click the **Content** tab.

3. Click **Settings**. If necessary, type the supervisor password, and then click **OK**.

4. Click the category for which you want to set the rating.

5. Move the Rating slider to the rating level you want.

6. Click **OK**, and then click **OK** again.

Cleaning Up Internet Files and Information

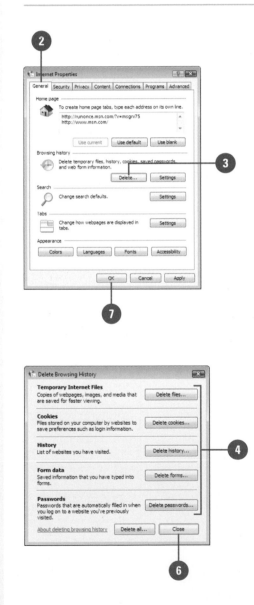

Microsoft
Certified
Application
Specialist

WINV-1.5.3

As you browse the Web, Internet Explorer stores information relating to what you have provided to Web sites when you log on (passwords) or fill out a form, the location of Web sites you have visited (history), and preference information used by Web sites (cookies). When you visit a Web site, Internet Explorer saves Web pages, images, and media (temporary Internet files) for faster viewing in the future, which can take up a lot of space on your hard disk. You can clean up the Internet files and information individually or all at once (**New!**), which will also improve your computer performance.

Delete Internet Files and Information

1. Click the **Start** button, click **Control Panel**, and then double-click the **Internet Options** icon in Classic view.

2. Click the **General** tab.

3. Click **Delete**.

4. Click the Delete buttons you want to clean up your computer:

    ◆ **Delete all.** Delete all information (listed below).

    ◆ **Delete temporary files.** Deletes files created while browsing.

    ◆ **Delete cookies.** Deletes information gathered by using Web sites.

    ◆ **Delete history.** Deletes list of Web sites you have visited.

    ◆ **Delete forms.** Deletes saved information you have enter into forms.

    ◆ **Delete passwords.** Deletes password used for automatic logon to Web sites.

5. Click **Yes** to confirm the deletion.

6. Click **Close**.

7. Click **OK**.

Protecting Internet Privacy

WINV-1.5.4

You can set Internet privacy options to protect your personal identity from unauthorized access (**New!**). The privacy options allow you to block or permit cookies for web sites in the Internet zone; however, when you block cookies, you might not be able to access all the features of a web site. When a web site violates your cookie policy, a red icon appears on the status bar. To find out if the web site you are viewing in Internet Explorer contains third-party cookies or whether any cookies have been restricted, you can get a privacy report. The privacy report lists all the web sites with content on the current Web page and shows how all the web sites handle cookies.

Control the Use of Cookies

1. Click the **Start** button, click **Control Panel**, and then double-click the **Internet Options** icon in Classic view.

2. Click the **Privacy** tab.

3. Drag the slider to select the level of privacy you want.

4. Click **OK**.

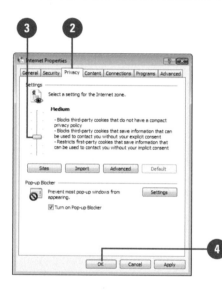

Delete All Cookies

1. Click the **Start** button, click **Control Panel**, and then double-click the **Internet Options** icon in Classic view.

2. Click the **General** tab.

3. Click **Delete**.

4. Click **Delete cookies**.

5. Click **Close**.

6. Click **OK**.

Protecting an Internet Identity

To further protect your privacy, you can use certificates to verify your identity and protect important information, such as your credit card number, on the Internet. A **certificate** is a statement verifying the identity of a person or the security of a web site. You can obtain your personal security certification from an independent Certification Authority (CA). A personal certificate verifies your identity to a secure web site that requires a certificate, while a web site certificate verifies its security to you before you send it information. When you visit a secure web site (one whose address may start with "https" instead of "http"), the site automatically sends you its certificate, and Internet Explorer displays a lock icon on the status bar. A certificate is also known as a Digital ID in other programs, such as Windows Mail, or the Windows Contacts.

Import a Certificate

1 Click the **Start** button, click **Control Panel**, and then double-click the **Internet Options** icon in Classic view.

2 Click the **Content** tab.

3 Click **Certificates**.

4 Click the tab with the type of certificate you want.

5 Click **Import**.

6 Follow the instructions in the Certificate Import Wizard to import a certificate.

7 Click **Close**.

8 Click **OK**.

> **Did You Know?**
>
> *You can let e-mail recipients know a message is from you with a certificate.* Click the Start button, click Windows Mail, click the Tools menu, click Options, click the Security tab, select the Digitally sign all outgoing messages check box, then click OK.

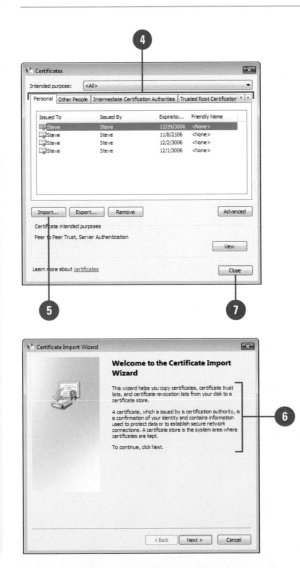

Protecting Against Phishing

Phishing is a technique people use to trick computer users into revealing personal for financial information. Typically, a phishing scam starts with an e-mail message that appears to come from a trusted source, such as a bank or credit card company, but actually directs recipients to provide information to a fraudulent Web site. Windows and Internet Explorer provide increase security to help protect you from phishing (**New!**) schemes. You can set phishing options in Internet Options in the Control Panel or on the Tools menu in Internet Explorer. You can check Web sites for phishing and report them to Microsoft if you think they are fraudulent.

Protect Against Phishing

1. Click the **Start** button, click **Control Panel**, and then double-click the **Internet Options** icon in Classic view.

2. Click the **Advanced** tab.

   TIMESAVER *In Internet Explorer, click the Tools button, point to Phishing Filter, and then click Phishing Filter Settings.*

3. Click the **Disable Phishing Filter**, **Turn off automatic website checking**, or **Turn on automatic website checking** option.

   TIMESAVER *In Internet Explorer, click the Tools button, point to Phishing Filter, and then click Turn Off Automatic Website Checking, select the turn on or off option, and then click OK.*

4. Click **OK**.

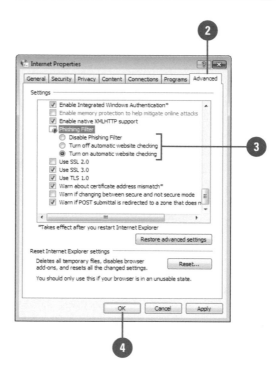

Check and Report a Web Site for Phishing

1. In Internet Explorer, click the **Tools** menu, and then point to **Phishing Filter**.

2. Click the command you want to perform:

   ◆ **Check This Website**. Click **Check This Website**, and then respond to the alerts as needed.

   ◆ **Report This Website**. Click **Report This Website**, specify the Website language, select the **I think this is a phishing website** check box, and then click **Submit**.

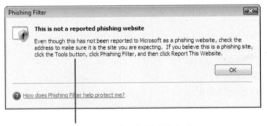

Results of check this Web site

Web site to submit a possible phishing site

Blocking Pop-Up Ads

Microsoft Certified Application Specialist WINV-1.5.5

The Pop-up Blocker prevents most unwanted pop-up windows from appearing. When Internet Explorer blocks an ad, a new window appears with an alert message in the Information Bar at the top. Blocked items are replaced in the window with a red "x". The Information Bar in Internet Explorer lets you temporarily or permanently open pop-ups, change Pop-up Blocker settings, and get Information Bar help. With the Pop-up Blocker Settings dialog box, you can allow or disallow pop-ups from specific sites, play a sound or show the Information Bar when a pop-up is blocked, and set a filter level to block pop-ups.

Set Options to Block Pop-Up Ads

1. Click the **Start** button, click **Control Panel**, and then double-click the **Internet Options** icon in Classic view.

2. Click the **Privacy** tab.

3. Select the **Turn on Pop-up Blocker** check box.

   TIMESAVER *In Internet Explorer, click the Tools button, point to Pop-up Blocker, and then click Turn Off Pop-up Blocker.*

4. Click **Settings**.

   TIMESAVER *In Internet Explorer, click the Tools button, point to Pop-up Blocker, and then click Pop-up Blocker Settings.*

5. To add a pop-up exception, enter a web site address, then click **Add**.

6. Select or clear check boxes to play sound or show on Information Bar when an ad is blocked.

7. Click the **Filter Level** list arrow, then click a pop-up filter: **High**, **Medium**, **Low**.

8. Click **Close**.

9. Click **OK**.

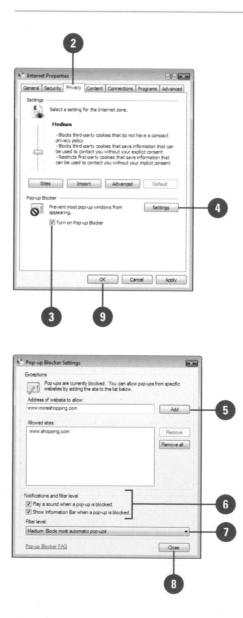

Using the Information Bar

Security Information Bar for Browsing

The Information Bar in Internet Explorer makes it easier for you to make informed decisions about potentially harmful content entering your computer. Internet Explorer displays the Information Bar below the address bar where you can view important security information about blocked pop-ups, downloads, security risks, and other harmful threats. When Internet Explorer blocks a pop-up ad or program from running on your computer, the Information Bar appears at the top of the window with information and options. If the default settings in Internet Explorer are turned on, the Information Bar appears when a web site tries to install an add-on, such as an ActiveX control, open a pop-up window, or download a file to your computer. A pop-up window typically display annoying ads. ActiveX controls provide added functionality to Internet Explorer, which makes using the Internet more enjoyable. However, it also opens the door for Spyware and Adware to invade your computer and privacy. When an outsider tries to enter your computer, the Information Bar appears, where you can click the message to take an action, such as block or unblock the content, or get more informa-

tion. See "Blocking Pop-Up Ads" on page 342 for information on turning on the Information Bar.

Security Information Bar for E-mail

Windows Mail adds a security option to stop pictures and other content from automatically downloading to your computer from contacts who are not in your address book. Spammers commonly use automatic picture download to confirm your e-mail address and send you more spam. Blocking the picture download provides a faster display, and reduces spam e-mail. When Windows Mail blocks images and other potential harm content in an e-mail message from downloading to your computer, the Information Bar appears at the top of the e-mail message with status information. Blocked items in e-mail are replaced with a red "x". You can follow the instructions on the Information Bar to view the blocked content. However, when you edit, print, forward, or reply to an e-mail message with blocked items, the blocked content is downloaded. See "Protecting Against E-mail Attacks" on page 345 for information on setting e-mail security options.

Information Bar alert

Information Bar for a pop-up window

Information Bar menu

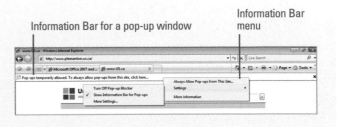

Managing Add-Ons

Add-on are programs that extend the functionality of Internet Explorer to perform a unique task, such as provide search toolbars or display Flash content. In most cases, add-ons are useful, but sometimes poorly built or old ones can slow down your computer, cause system crashes, or invade your privacy (such as Spyware or Adware that are sometimes deceptively installed). To help you work with add-ons, Internet Explorer includes the Add-on Manager, which provides a list of add-ons currently loaded or used by Internet Explorer. You can use the Add-on Manager to individually enable, disable, or update add-ons. The Add-on Manager can also detect add-ons related crashes in Internet Explorer and displays an option to disable it.

Manage Browser Add-Ons

① Click the **Start** button, click **Control Panel**, and then double-click the **Internet Options** icon in Classic view.

② Click the **Programs** tab.

③ Click **Manage add-ons**.

TIMESAVER *In Internet Explorer, click the Tools menu, and then click Manage Add-ons.*

④ Click **Show** list arrow, and then click the option with the type of add-ons you want to display.

⑤ Click the add-on you want to manage.

⑥ Click the **Enable or Disable** option.

⑦ Click **OK**.

⑧ Click **OK**.

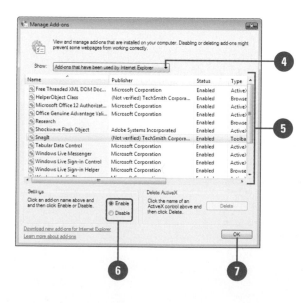

Protecting Against E-mail Attacks

In Windows Mail, security zones allow you to determine whether or not to run active content, such as ActiveX controls, from inside HTML e-mail messages, which potentially can carry viruses and other harmful threats. You can adjust the security zone levels using Internet Options in the Control Panel. To provide further protection, you can set options to let you know when an program tries to send mail with your e-mail address to contacts in your address book (which is a common way to propagate a virus), to not allow attachments to be saved or opened that might contain a virus, and to stop pictures and other content from automatically downloading to your computer (which is a common way spammers confirm your e-mail address to send more spam) from contacts who are not in your Address Book until you have a chance to read the message.

Protect Against E-mail Attacks in Windows Mail

1. Click the **Start** button, then click **Windows Mail**.

2. Click the **Tools** menu, then click **Options**.

3. Click the **Security** tab.

4. Click the security zone option you want: **Internet zone (Less secure)** or **Restricted sites zone (More secure)**.

5. Select the **Warn me when other applications try to send mail as me** check box.

6. Select the **Do not allow attachments to be saved or opened that could potentially be a virus** check box.

7. Select the **Block images and other external content in HTML e-mail** check box.

8. Click **OK**.

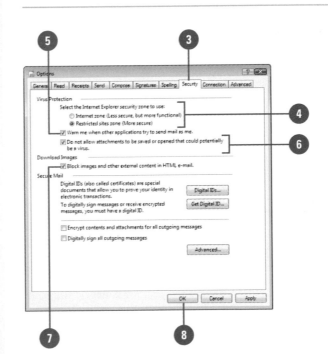

See Also

See "Avoiding Viruses and Other Harmful Attacks" on page 330 for information on security threats in e-mail.

Sending Secure E-mail

In Windows Mail, you can set security options to send e-mail messages with a digital ID or encryption. A digital ID verifies your identity to your recipients in the same way a picture ID verifies your identify when you write a check. Before you can send a digitally signed e-mail, you need to get a digital ID from an independent certification authority, which you can access from Windows Mail. Encryption prevents others on the Internet from intercepting and reading your e-mail. Before you can send an encrypted e-mail, your Windows Contacts needs to contain a digital ID for each recipient, which allows them to decrypt the message for reading.

Set Options to Send Secure E-mail in Windows Mail

1. Click the Start button, then click **Windows Mail**.

2. Click the **Tools** menu, then click **Options**.

3. Click the **Security** tab.

4. To get a digital ID, click **Get Digital ID**, and then follow the instructions.

5. To encrypt e-mail, select the **Encrypt contents and attachments for all outgoing messages** check box.

6. To digitally sign e-mail, select the **Digitally sign all outgoing messages** check box.

7. Click **Advanced**.

8. Select the check boxes to include my digital ID and add sender's certificates to my Windows Contacts.

9. To check for a revoked digital ID, click the **Only when online** option.

10. Click **OK**.

11. Click **OK** again.

Managing Files Using a Network

12

Introduction

Windows Vista comes with many tools for managing files and folders across multiple computers. One of the more powerful tools is the Network and Sharing Center. A **network** is a system of two or more computers connected together to share resources. It consists of at least one host and one client. Using the Network folder (accessible from the Start menu), you can view the entire network (hosts and clients), share files and folders with people from other parts of the network, and create and manage your network connections to these other computers. This chapter helps you set up you host and client computers so they can easily share files across your network.

In addition, Windows provides tools for sharing files and folders with computer that are not located in your home or in the same office (commonly referred to as remote computers). You can connect your computer to a network in a different location via modem, or via the internet using the Communications accessory provided. With wireless technology, such as laptop computers or Bluetooth-enabled devices (keyboards, cell phones and PDAs), you can seamlessly setup, discover and connect to wireless networks. You can also share and synchronize files between your laptop and your desktop computers using the Briefcase.

What You'll Do

Understand Network Services

View a Network

View the Network and Sharing Center

View Network Computer and Connection Properties

Join a Workgroup Network

Join a Domain Network

Connect to a Network Using a Modem

Connect to a Network over the Internet

Connect to a Wireless Network

Set Up a Wireless Network

Set Up a Wireless Computer Connection

Add a Wireless Device to a Network

Manage a Wireless Connection

Map and Disconnect a Network Drive

Create a Shortcut to a Network

Set Network Sharing Options

Control a Remote Computer

Share an Internet Connection

Change a Dial-Up Connection

Understanding Network Services

Windows is a secure, reliable network operating system that allows people using many different computers to share resources, such as programs, files, folders, printers, and an Internet connection. A single computer on the network, called a **server**, can be designated to store these resources. Other computers on the network, called **clients** or **workstations**, can access the resources on the server instead of having to store them. You can share resources using two or more client computers, or you can designate one computer to serve specifically as the server. If the workstation computers are close together in a single building or group of buildings, the network is called a **local area network (LAN)**. If the workstation computers are spread out in multiple buildings or throughout the entire country using dial-up or wireless connections, the network is called a **wide area network (WAN)**. To set up a network with multiple computers, you need to install a network adapter for each computer on your network and connect each computer to a network hub using network cable or wireless technology, known as Wi-Fi. Network adapters are usually hardware cards, called **network interface cards**, or **NICs**, inserted in a slot, or **USB (Universal Serial Bus)**, port in the back of your computer that connects it to the network. A **network hub** is a hardware device that connects multiple computers at a central location. When data arrives at one port of the network hub, it is copied to the other ports so that all connected network devices see the data. If you have two LANs or two sections of the same LAN on different floors of the same building with different network adapter types, you can connect them together with a hardware device called a **bridge**. If you have any number of LANs, you can connect them together with a hardware device called a **router**. If you want to share a printer or Internet connection with the computers on a network, you simply connect the printer or modem to the server, a computer on the network, or directly to a network hub, router, or bridge.

Share central resources through client/server networking

Windows offers a network configuration called **client/server networking**. Under this arrangement, a single computer is designated as a server, allowing access to resources for any qualified user. Client/server networking provides all users on a network a central location for accessing shared files. In a client/server network, individual computers are often grouped into domains. A **domain** is a collection of computers that the person managing the network creates in order to group together the computers to simplify the set up and maintenance of the network. The network administrator defines the domains that exist on the network and controls access to computers within those domains.

Domain

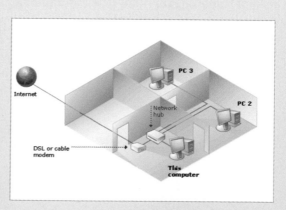

348

Share resources through peer-to-peer networking

Windows also offers a network configuration called **peer-to-peer networking**. Peer-to-peer networking enables two or more computers to link together without designating a central server. In a peer-to-peer network, individual computers are often organized into workgroups. A **workgroup** is a group of computers that perform common tasks or belong to users who share common duties and interests. In this configuration, any computer user can access resources stored on any other computer, as long as those resources are available for sharing. Peer-to-peer networking allows individual computer users to share files and other resources, such as a printer, with other users on the network without having to access a server. Workgroups are available on all Windows computers.

Share resources through network connections

Windows provides connectivity between your computer and a network, another computer, or the Internet using **Network Connections**. Whether you are physically connected using a direct cable or connected remotely using a dial-up or cable modem, you can connect securely to a network over the Internet using a **Virtual Private Network (VPN)** connection or set up your computer to let other computers connect to yours using an **incoming network connection**. VPN and incoming network connection are examples of WANs.

Share designated files and folders on your computer with other network users

Windows provides support for security, so even though your computer is connected to a network, you can designate which resources on your computer you want to share with others. Before network users can use any resources on your computer, they must be granted the required permission.

Workgroup

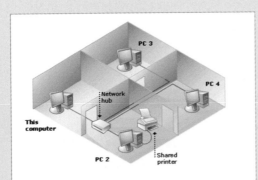

Wireless

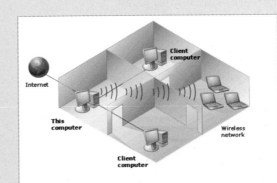

Viewing a Network

Microsoft
Certified
Application
Specialist

WINV-2.4.3,
WINV-2.4.4

The key to managing files and folders in a network environment is understanding the structure of your particular network. Most networks consist of multiple types of computers and operating systems. The Network folder lets you view the entire network or just your part of the network, to give you access to the servers, domains, and workgroups on the network. The Network folder also displays shared folders available on your immediate network. If you're working on a domain network, you can use Active Search Directory to help you find network resources, such as computer and printers.

View a Workgroup or Domain Network

1. Click the **Start** button, and then click **Network**.

2. Double-click a network computer icon to display the shared files, folders, and devices on the computer.

3. To open the Network and Sharing Center, click the **Network and Sharing Center** button on the toolbar.

4. When you're done, click the **Close** button.

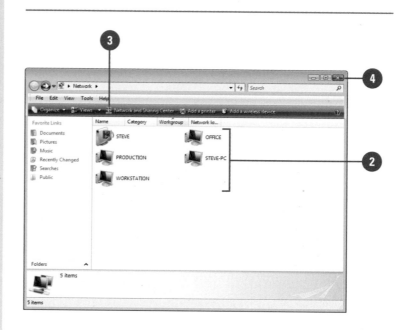

Did You Know?

A domain network and a workgroup are different. A domain network is a group of computers connected together to share and manage resources by an administrator from a central computer called a domain controller. A workgroup is a network of computers connected together to share resources, but each computer is maintained and shared separately.

Click to display network

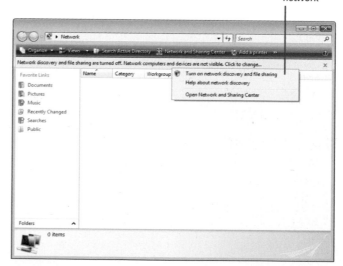

View a Shared Folder

1. Click the **Start** button, and then click **Network**.

2. Double-click a network computer icon.

3. Double-click a shared folder to display the shared files and folders in the folder.

4. When you're done, click the **Close** button.

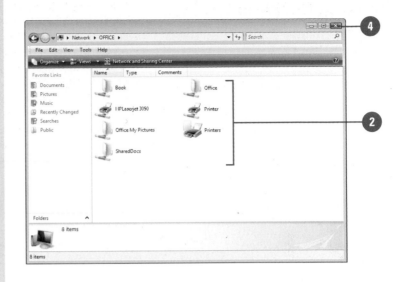

Search a Domain Network

1. Click the **Start** button, and then click **Network**.

2. Click the **Search Active Directory** button on the toolbar.

3. Click the **Find** list arrow, and then select the network resource you want to find.

4. Click the **In** list arrow, and then select where you want to search.

5. Specify the criteria for the search; tabs and information vary.

6. Click **Find Now**.

7. When you're done, click the **Close** button.

Viewing the Network and Sharing Center

The Network and Sharing Center (**New!**) provides a central location where you can view and modify network and sharing options for the computer connected to a network. From a network perspective, you can view a map of the network, view network connection status information, change the network location type (either Public or Private: Work or Home), and specify whether you want others on the network to see you, known as **network discovery**. When you connect to a network for the first time, Windows automatically detect it and asks you to choose a network location. When you change the network location, Windows automatically changes firewall settings for the type of network. In addition to viewing and setting network options, you can also turn sharing options on and off. The Network and Sharing Center visually display network maps and sharing on and off icons to make it easier to view status information.

View Network and Choose Network a Location

1 Click the **Start** button, and then click **Control Panel**.

2 Double-click the **Network and Sharing** icon in Classic view.

3 If necessary, click the down arrow (circle button) to the right of Network Discovery to display options.

4 Click the **Turn on network discovery** option.

5 Click **Apply**.

6 To specify a network location type, click **Customize**, click the **Public** or **Private** option, click **Next**, and then click **Close**.

7 When you're done, click the **Close** button.

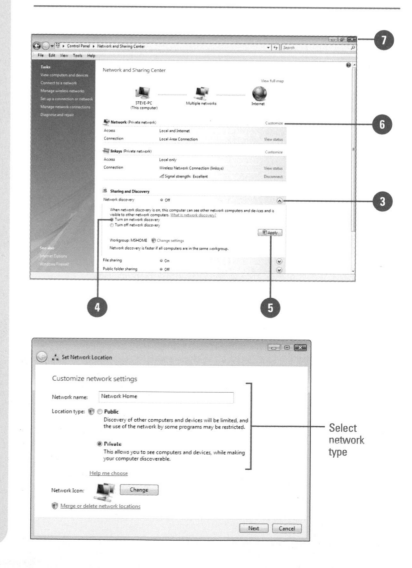

Select network type

View a Network Map

① Click the **Start** button, and then click **Control Panel**.

② Double-click the **Network and Sharing** icon in Classic view.

③ Click **View full map**.

④ Click the Network map of list arrow, and then select the network connection you want to view, which includes: **Local Area Connection - Network** and **Wireless Network Connection - Network**.

⑤ To open a networked device, double-click the icon.

⑥ When you're done, click the **Close** button.

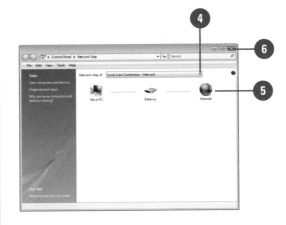

Did You Know?

You can use the Connection icon in the notification area to access commands. To see current networks, click the Connection icon on the taskbar in the notification area. You can also click links to connect to a network or open the Network and Sharing Center.

You can right-click the Connection icon to access more commands. Right-click the Connection icon on the taskbar in the notification area to turn on or off network activity animation or notification of new networks, connect to a network diagnose and repair a network problem, or open the Network and Sharing Center.

Security Alert

Networking with Windows Firewall

For security purposes, Windows Firewall is turned on (the default setting) to protect your computer against security threats, such as viruses, worms, and Trojan Horses, spread over the Internet or a network. Windows Vista automatically sets Windows Firewall settings to be compatible with your network. However, you might need to make adjustments for some programs, such as Internet games, to allow them to work properly. See "Setting Up Windows Firewall" on page 137 for more information.

Viewing Network Computer Properties

Names and locations are used to identify computers on a network. The computer's name refers to the individual machine, and the computer's location refers to how the machine is grouped together with other computers. Computers anywhere on the network can be located easily through the naming hierarchy and can be addressed individually by name. You can find the name and workgroup or domain of a computer on the network by examining the system properties. Workgroups and domains are available on all Windows computers.

View Network Computer Properties

① Click the **Start** button, and then click **Control Panel**.

② Double-click the **System** icon in Classic view.

③ Click **Change settings**.

④ Click the **Computer Name** tab.

⑤ To add a computer description, type a description.

⑥ To change a workgroup or domain, click **Change**, specify a new name, and then click **OK**.

⑦ Click **OK**.

See Also

See "Running DOS Commands" on page 46 for information on finding the IP configuration of a computer, and pinging another computer.

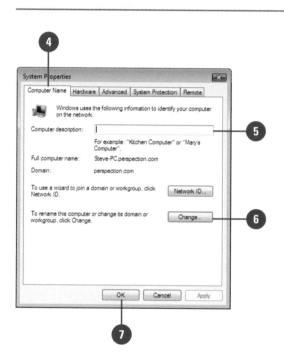

Viewing Network Connection Properties

WINV-7.4.1

A computer that uses a network must be configured so that other machines on the network recognize it. On a small network, you might be responsible for configuring your computer, or that responsibility might fall to the network administrator. You can view the status of the network connection and modify some of the network settings for your computer using the Network Connections window. A network connection consists of a network adapter and three types of components: client, service, and protocol. The **client** type allows you to access computers and files on the network. The **service** type allows you to share your computer resources, such as files and printers, with other networked computers. **Protocol** is the language that the computer uses to communicate with other computers on the network, such as TCP/IP. Knowing which components are installed on your computer helps you understand the capabilities and limitations of your computer on the network.

View Network Connection Properties

1 Click the **Start** button, and then click **Control Panel**.

2 Double-click the **Network and Sharing Center** icon in Classic view.

3 If the left pane, click **Manage network connections**.

4 Double-click the network connection you want to get status information.

> **TIMESAVER** *In the Network and Sharing Center, you can also click View status.*

5 If you have problems with your connection, click **Diagnose**.

6 To display network components installed and enabled, click **Properties**.

7 When you're done working with the components, click **OK**.

8 Click **Close**.

9 Click the **Close** button.

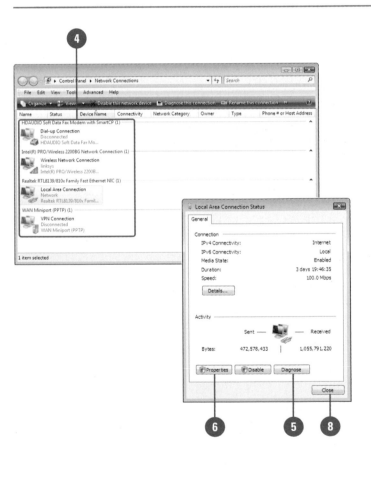

Joining a Workgroup Network

Before you can set up and configure a network at home or small office, you need to physically attach the hardware so the computers can communicate. This includes installing the network cards in all the computers, connecting the computers together using cables or wireless technology, installing a modem on the host computer, turning on all computers, printers, and external modems, and establishing a connection to the Internet. A home or small office network is typically a peer-to-peer network where individual computers are organized into workgroups with a host and several clients. The host is a computer on the network who shares an Internet connection with the other client computers on the network. The host computer must be turned on whenever a client computer needs to access the Internet. To join a workgroup, you can use a wizard in System properties. After you join, you can change the workgroup name to match the other ones in your network.

Join a Workgroup Network Using a Wizard

1. Click the **Start** button, and then click **Control Panel**.

2. Double-click the **System** icon in Classic view, and then click **Change settings**.

3. Click the **Computer Name** tab.

4. Click **Network ID**, and then click **Next** to continue.

5. Click the **This is a home computer; it's not part of a business network** option, and then click **Next** to continue.

6. Click **Finish**, and then restart your computer.

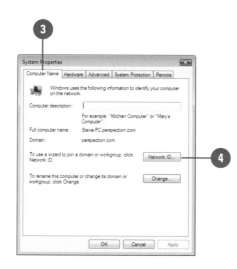

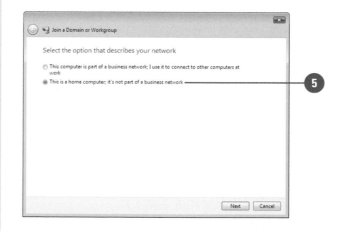

Change a Workgroup Network Name

1. Click the **Start** button, and then click **Control Panel**.

2. Double-click the **System** icon in Classic view, and then click **Change settings**.

3. Click the **Computer Name** tab.

4. Click **Change**.

5. Click the **Workgroup** option.

6. Type the workgroup name.

7. Click **OK**.

8. Click **OK**.

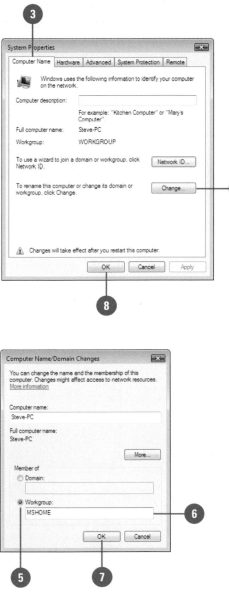

Joining a Domain Network

If you are not connected to a domain network, you can use the Network Identification Wizard to join a domain and create a local user account. If you already have a user account, you can use System Properties to join a domain. Before you join a domain, you need to connect your computer to a client/server network using a network adapter and network cable or wireless technology. After you connect a network adapter to your computer and start Windows Vista, your computer detects the network adapter and creates a local area connection. A local area connection is the only type of network connection that Windows automatically creates. Depending on your hardware setup, your Network Identification Wizard options might differ.

Join a Domain Network

1. Click the **Start** button, and then click **Control Panel**.

2. Double-click the **System** icon in Classic view, and then click **Change settings**.

3. Click the **Computer Name** tab.

4. Click **Change**.

5. Click the **Domain** option.

6. Type the domain name.

7. Click **OK**.

8. Click **OK**.

Join a Domain Network and Create a User Account

1. Click the **Start** button, and then click **Control Panel**.

2. Double-click the **System** icon in Classic view, and then click **Change settings**.

3. Click the **Computer Name** tab.

4. Click **Network ID**, and then click **Next** to continue.

5. Click the **This computer is part of a business network** option, and then click **Next** to continue.

6. Click the **My company uses a network with a domain** option, and then click **Next** to continue.

7. Read the page, and then click **Next** to continue.

8. Type a user name and password.

9. Type a domain name, and then click **Next** to continue.

10. Type a computer name and domain name, and then click **Next** to continue.

11. Click the **Add the following user** option, and then click **Next** to continue.

12. Click an access user level, and then click **Next** to continue.

13. Click **Finish**, and then restart your computer.

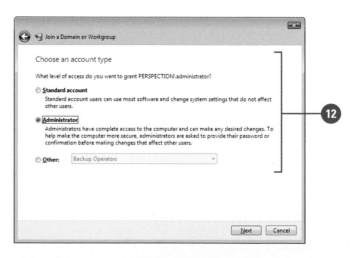

Connecting to a Network Using a Modem

If you have a modem installed on your computer, you can use a connection wizard to set up a dial-up connection to another computer or a network. Connecting to another computer or a network is useful when you need access to information stored on another computer or a network. You only need to set up a dial-up connection to a computer or a network once. After you set up the connection, you can use the Connect to a network dialog box to select the dial-up connection and establish a dial-up connection. When you are connected, Windows displays a connection icon in the notification area on the taskbar. You can point to the icon to display information about the connection or right-click the icon to perform tasks.

Create a Dial-Up Connection

1. Click the **Start** button, and then click **Connect To**.

2. Click **Set up a connection or network**.

3. In the left pane, click **Connect to a workplace**, and then click **Next** to continue.

4. Click **Dial Directly**, and then click **Next** to continue.

5. Type the phone number for calling the network.

6. To share this network connection, select the **Allow other people to use this connection** check box.

7. Click **Next** to continue.

8. Type user name, password and domain name.

9. Click **Connect**.

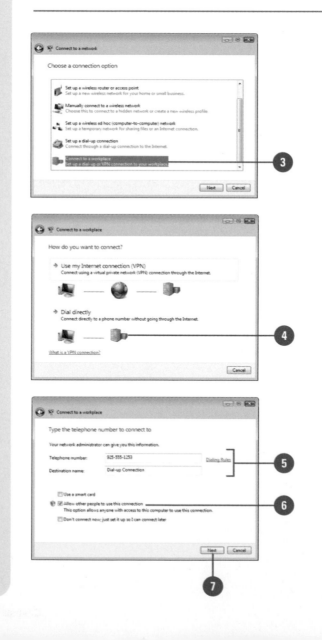

Establish a Dial-Up Connection

① Click the **Start** button, click **Connect To**, and then click the dial-up connection name.

② Select the dial up connection, and then click **Connect**.

③ Type your assigned user name and password.

④ To save your user name and password information, select the **Save this user name and password for the following users** check box, and then click an option to specify who can use the information.

⑤ Click **Dial**, and then wait for the connection.

⑥ When you're done, right-click the **Connection** icon in the notification area of the taskbar, and then click **Disconnect**.

Did You Know?

You can delete a connection. Right-click the Connection icon in the notification area, click Network and Share Center, click Manage network connections, right-click the connection you want to delete, and then click Delete.

See Also

See "Changing a Dial Up Connection" on page 380 for information on changing the settings for a dial-up connection.

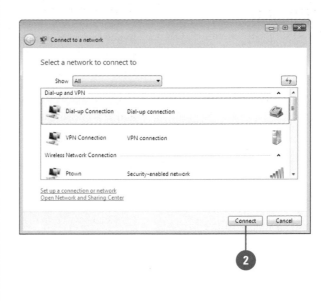

Connecting to a Network over the Internet

Microsoft
Certified
Application
Specialist

WINV-2.2.1,
WINV-2.2.4

You can create a VPN (Virtual Private Network) connection to connect to a network over the Internet. A VPN provides a secure connection between your computer and the network. The computer to which you want to connect must support a VPN and Internet connection. Before you create a connection, you need to have the name or IP (Internet Protocol) address of the VPN computer. You can use a connection wizard to set up a VPN connection. You only need to set up a VPN connection to a network once. When you are connected, Windows displays a connection icon in the notification area on the taskbar. You can point to the icon to display information about the connection or right-click the icon to perform tasks.

Create a VPN Connection

1. Click the **Start** button, and then click **Connect To**.

2. Click **Set up a connection or network.**

3. In the left pane, click **Connect to a workplace**, and then click **Next** to continue.

4. Click **Use my Internet connection (VPN)**, and then click **Next** to continue.

5. Type the host name or IP address to the computer to which you want to connect.

6. To share this network connection, select the **Allow other people to use this connection** check box.

7. Click **Next** to continue.

8. Type user name, password and domain name.

9. Click **Connect**.

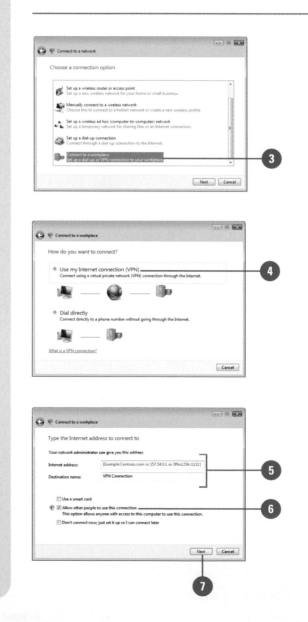

Establish a VPN Connection

1. Click the **Start** button, and then click **Connect To**, and then click the dial-up connection name.

2. Select the dial up connection, and then click **Connect**.

3. Type your assigned user name and password.

4. To save your user name and password information, select the **Save this user name and password for the following users** check box, and then click an option to specify who can use the information.

5. Click **Connect**, and then wait for the connection.

6. When you're done, right-click the **Connection** icon in the notification area of the taskbar, and then click **Disconnect**.

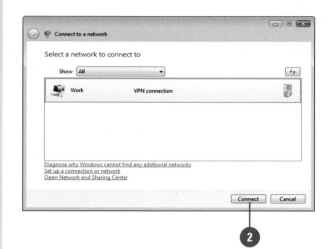

Connecting to a Wireless Network

Windows Vista provides updated wireless networking, enabling you to setup and manage wireless connections with a broad range of wireless hot spots that discover and connect to wireless networks (known as Wi-Fi). The Connection wizard makes it easy to setup a Wi-Fi network. You can quickly connect to an available wireless network with a security key or manually connect to one not recognized. As you walk through the manual process, you'll specify a network name, called the SSID (Service Set Identifier) and use a USB Flash drive (UFD)—recommended—to transfer and configure your network settings to your other wireless computers or devices. The SSID is broadcasted from your access point (AP)—typically a wireless router—to your other wireless devices. Windows Vista also provides updated support for Bluetooth-enabled hardware devices, allowing you to take advantage of the latest wireless devices, including wireless keyboards and mice, wireless printers, and connections with cell phones and PDAs.

Connect to an Available Wireless Network

1. Click the **Start** button, and then click **Connect To**.

2. Click **Set up a connection or network.**

3. Select the wireless network to which you want to connect.

4. Click **Connect**.

5. Type the security key or passphrase or if you have a USB flash drive with network settings for the wireless network, insert it now.

6. Click **Connect**.

7. To save this network, select the **Save this network** check box, and then select or clear the **Start this connection automatically** check box.

8. Click **Close**.

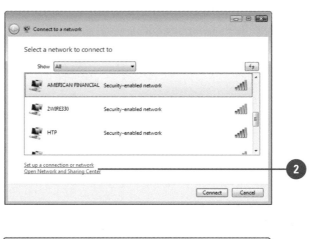

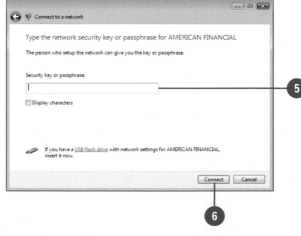

Manually Connect to a Wireless Network

1. Click the **Start** button, and then click **Connect To**.

2. Click **Set up a connection or network**.

3. Click **Manually connect to a wireless network**, and then click **Next** to continue.

4. Type the network name.

5. Specify a security type, and then specify an encryption type, if necessary.

6. Type a passphrase (point to the box and use the ScreenTip for help).

7. Click **Next** to continue.

8. Click **Connect to** or **Change connection settings**.

9. If necessary, click **Close**.

Did You Know?

You can perform a security check on your wireless network. After implementing lock down security measures, you can perform a security check. Install the free program NetStumbler available at *www.netstumber.com* onto a laptop or PDA.

Security Alert

Locking Down Your Wireless Network

Wireless networks (Wi-Fi) are a popular way to network home and small office computers. Unless you lock it down, hackers can take advantage of unsecured Wi-Fi networks. The following security techniques can keep you safe: (1) disable the SSID (Service Set Identifier) broadcast, so you no longer tell computers near by that you have a wireless network, (2) change the password on your access point, (3) use encryption, either WEP (Wired Equivalent Privacy), which is older and less secure (uses 64- or 128-bit non-changing encryption), or WPA (Wi-Fi Protected Access), which is much more secure (uses 256-bit constantly changes encryption), and (4) if necessary, enable Media Access Control (MAC) filtering, which tells your access point to grant access to only MAC addresses you enter. MAC is a unique address assigned to each wireless card.

Setting Up a Wireless Network

If you have a wireless router or access point, you can set up your own wireless network. A router directs communication traffic between two networks, such as a home or office network and the Internet. An access point provides wireless access to a wired Ethernet network. An access point plugs into a wired router and sends out a wireless signal, which other wireless computer and devices use to connect to a wired network. During the set up process, you need to specify a network name, choose file and printer sharing options, and a passphrase (a security key) to provide secure access. If you have a USB flash drive, you can save wireless network settings to the drive and use it to quickly add computers to your network.

Set Up a Wireless Network

1. Click the **Start** button, and then click **Connect To**.

2. Click **Set up a connection or network.**

3. In the left pane, click **Set up a wireless router or access point**, and then click **Next** to continue.

4. Read the screen, and then click **Next** to continue.

5. Type the network name (SSID), and then click **Next** to continue.

6. Type a passphrase or use the one generated, and then write it down so you can use it the first time that people connect to this network.

7. Click **Next** to continue.

8. Select the file and printer sharing option you want, and then click **Next** to continue.

9. If necessary, plug the USB flash drive into the USB port, select the drive from the list, and then click **Next** to continue.

10. Read the screen, and then click **Close.**

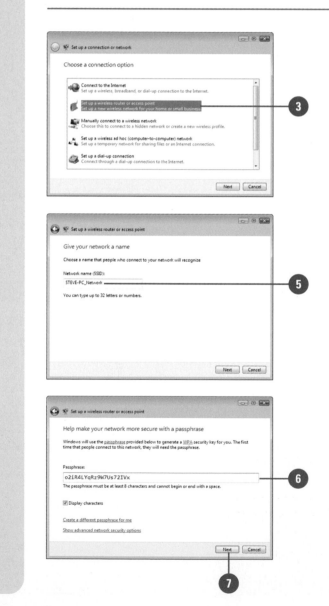

Setting Up a Wireless Computer Connection ▶

If you have two wireless computers, you can set up a connection between the two systems. During the set up process, you need to specify a network security type to keep the connection safe and a passphrase (a security key) to provide secure access. You can set the security type to Wired Equivalent Privacy (WEP), Wi-Fi Protected Access (WPA), or 802.1X authentication. WEP is a widely used network security type that uses an encrypted security key to provide a secure wireless environment. WPA improves on the security of WEP and checks to make sure the security key has not been modified. 802.1x is a sever authentication security type typically used for workplace networks. If you have a USB flash drive, you can save wireless network settings to the drive and use it to quickly add computers to your network.

Set Up a Wireless Connection to Another Computer

1 Click the **Start** button, and then click **Connect To**.

2 Click **Set up a connection or network.**

3 In the left pane, click **Set up a wireless ad hoc (computer-to-computer) network**, and then click **Next** to continue.

4 Read the screen, and then click **Next** to continue.

5 Type the network name, specify a security type.

6 Type a passphrase (point to the box and use the ScreenTip for help), and then write it down so you can use it the first time that people connect to this network.

7 Click **Next** to continue.

8 Select the file and printer sharing option you want, and then click **Next** to continue.

9 If necessary, plug in the USB flash drive, select the drive, and then click **Next** to continue.

10 Read the screen, and then click **Close**.

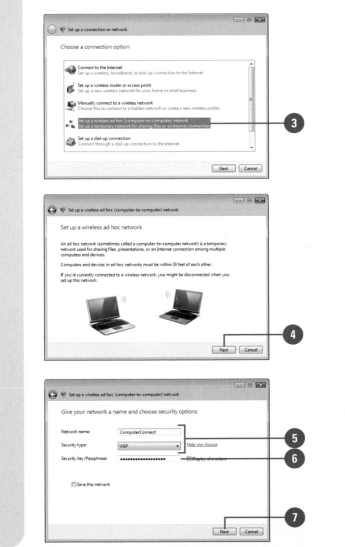

Adding a Wireless Device to a Network

If you have a USB flash drive, you can save wireless network settings to the drive and use it to quickly add computers to your network. You can use the Add a wireless device button in the Network folder to start a wizard which takes you step-by-step through the process. After you save your network settings on a USB flash drive, you can plug it into another computer and use the Wireless Network Setup Wizard in the AutoPlay dialog box to quickly set a network connection.

Save Network Settings on a USB Flash Drive

1. Click the **Start** button, and then click **Network**.

2. Click **Add a wireless device** button on the toolbar.

3. Select an available device, and the follow the online instructions.

4. If no devices are available, click **I want to add a wireless device or computer that is not on the list, using a USB flash drive**.

5. Click **Add the device or computer using a USB flash drive**.

6. Select the network to add devices to, and then click **Next** to continue.

7. Plug the USB flash drive into the USB port, select the drive from the list, and then click **Next** to continue.

8. Read the screen, and then click **Close**.

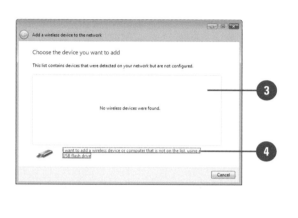

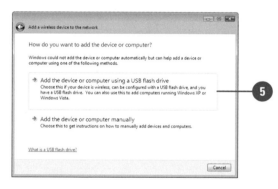

Set Up a Wireless Network Connection Using a USB Flash Drive

1 Insert the USB flash drive with the network setting into a USB port on the computer to which you want to set up a network connection.

2 In the AutoPlay dialog box, click **Wireless Network Setup Wizard**.

3 Click **OK** to continue.

4 Upon completion, click **OK**.

Did You Know?

What is Bluetooth wireless technology? Bluetooth technology uses radio waves to enable devices such as computers, printer, mice, or mobile phones, to communication wirelessly over a short distance. You can use Bluetooth to listen to music or use a mobile phone over wireless headphones, transfer files between laptop computers, or print to a wireless printer.

Managing a Wireless Connection

Microsoft
Certified
Application
Specialist

WINV-2.2.3

After you setup and connect to a wireless network, you can use the Manage Wireless Networks folder to view established wireless connections, add or remove wireless networks, or change the connection order. In the Manage Wireless Networks folder, each established wireless network appears, displaying security and connectivity information. You can use buttons on the toolbar to work with the wireless network connections. If you want to view or change connection and security properties for individual wireless connections, you can use the Wireless Network Properties dialog box. You can view the wireless network name, SSID, type, and availability, and enable automatic or preferred connect options or change the security type and key.

View Wireless Connections

1. Click the **Start** button, and then click **Control Panel**.

2. Double-click the **Network and Sharing Center** icon in Classic view.

3. If the left pane, click **Manage wireless networks**.

4. To add a wireless connection, click the **Add** button, and then follow the on-screen instructions.

5. Select the wireless network connection you want to modify.

6. To remove it, click the **Remove** button, and then click **OK**.

7. To change the connection order, click the **Move up** or **Move down** button.

8. When you're done, click the **Close** button.

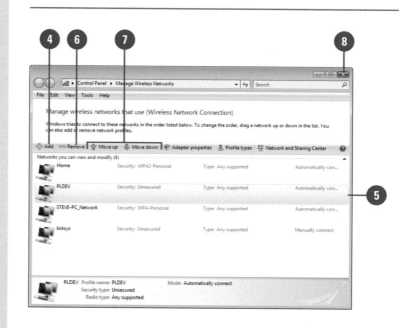

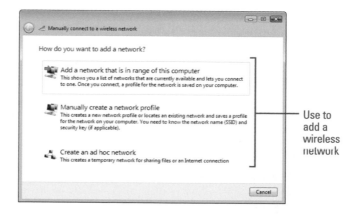

Use to add a wireless network

Display Wireless Connection and Security Properties

① Click the **Start** button, and then click **Control Panel**.

② Double-click the **Network and Sharing Center** icon in Classic view.

③ If the left pane, click **Manage wireless networks**.

④ Right-click the wireless connection you want to view, and then click **Properties**.

⑤ Click the **Connection** tab.

⑥ Select or clear the following connection check boxes:

   ◆ **Connect automatically when this network is in range.**

   ◆ **Connect to a more preferred network if available.**

   ◆ **Connect even if the networks is not broadcasting.**

⑦ Click the **Security** tab.

⑧ To change the security type, click the list arrow, and then select the type you want.

   When you change the security type, the other options change, which you can then modify.

⑨ Click **OK**, and then click the **Close** button.

⑤

Home Wireless Network properties

Connection | Security

Name: Home
SSID: Home
Network Type: Access point
Network Availability: All users

☑ Connect automatically when this network is in range
☑ Connect to a more preferred network if available
☐ Connect even if the network is not broadcasting

— ⑥

OK   Cancel

⑦

Home Wireless Network properties

Connection | Security

Security type: WPA2-Personal
Encryption type: AES
Network security key ••••••••
                      ☐ Show characters

— ⑧

OK   Cancel

⑨

Mapping and Disconnecting a Network Drive

Microsoft Certified Application Specialist WINV-2.4.2

Windows networking enables you to connect your computer to other computers on the network quite easily. If you connect to a network location frequently, you might want to designate a drive letter on your computer as a direct connection to a shared drive or folder on another computer. Instead of spending unnecessary time opening the Network folder and the shared drive or folder each time you want to access it, you can create a direct connection, called **mapping** a drive, to the network location for quick and easy access. If you no longer use a mapped drive, you can right-click the mapped drive in the Computer folder and then click Disconnect.

Map a Network Drive

1. Click the **Start** button, and then click **Network**.

2. Click the **Tools** menu, and then click **Map Network Drive**.

3. Click the **Drive** list arrow, and then select a drive letter.

4. Click **Browse**.

5. Select the folder you want to connect to.

6. Click **OK**.

7. To reconnect each time you log on to your computer, select the **Reconnect at logon** check box.

8. Click **Finish**.

9. To disconnect from a mapped drive, right-click the drive in the Computer folder, and then click **Disconnect**.

Did You Know?

You can also disconnect a mapped drive using the Tools menu. Click the Tools menu in the Network and Sharing Center, click Disconnect Network Drive, select the drive, and then click OK.

Map Network Drive

What network folder would you like to map?

Specify the drive letter for the connection and the folder that you want to connect to:

Drive: Z:

Folder: \\ALPHA\Books\Need Review   Browse...

Example: \\server\share

☑ Reconnect at logon

Connect using a different user name.

Connect to a Web site that you can use to store your documents and pictures.

Finish   Cancel

Creating a Shortcut to a Network

Instead of clicking numerous icons in the Network folder to access a network location, you can create a shortcut to the network location to provide easy access. A **shortcut** is a link that you can place in any location to gain instant access to a particular file, folder, or program on your hard disk or on a network just by double-clicking. The actual file, folder, or program remains stored in its original location, and you place an icon representing the shortcut in a convenient location, such as in a folder or on the desktop.

Create a Shortcut to a Network

1. Click the **Start** button, and then click **Network**.

2. Right-click a network computer icon or a folder on a network computer, and then click **Create Shortcut**.

   The shortcut appears on the desktop or in the folder.

3. Drag the shortcut icon to a convenient location.

Shortcut to a network

Setting Network Sharing Options

In the Network and Sharing Center you can set options to share files, printers, public folders, and media on the network. Sharing files, public folders, and printers provides a convenient way to share information and resources over a network. In addition, you can also share the media files in your Windows Media Player library over a network (**New!**). If you have a private network, you can play shared media files on another computer using Windows Media Player, or other networked digital media player (also called a digital media receiver), such as Xbox 360. When you open a shared media folder in the Network folder, the networked media player, such as Windows Media Player, opens, where you can play the shared media files as if the files were on your computer.

Set File or Public Folder Sharing Options

1. Click the **Start** button, and then click **Control Panel**.

2. Double-click the **Network and Sharing** icon in Classic view.

3. If necessary, click the down arrow (circle button) to the right of the File sharing to display options.

4. Click the **Turn on file sharing** or **Turn off file sharing** option.

5. If necessary, click the down arrow (circle button) to the right of the Public folder sharing to display options.

6. Select the sharing option you want.

7. Click **Apply**.

8. When you're done, click the **Close** button.

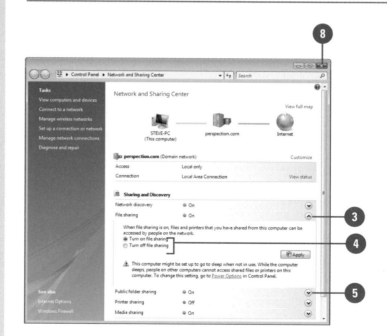

See Also

See "Sharing Folders or Files with Others" on page 92 for information on using the Shared Documents folder.

Set Media Sharing Options

1 Click the **Start** button, and then click **Control Panel**.

2 Double-click the **Network and Sharing** icon in Classic view.

3 If necessary, click the down arrow (circle button) to the right of the Media sharing to display options.

4 Click **Change**.

5 Select **Share my media** check box, and then click **OK**.

6 Select a share location, and then click **Allow**.

7 To change the media types, and star of parental ratings, click **Settings**, and then click **OK**.

8 Click **OK**.

9 When you're done, click the **Close** button.

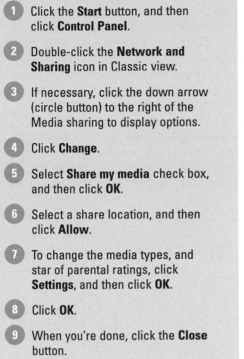

Change settings

Play Shared Media

1 Click the **Start** button, and then click **Network**.

2 Double-click a shared media icon.

Windows Media Player opens.

3 Use Windows Media Player to play the shared media files.

4 When you're done, click the **Close** button.

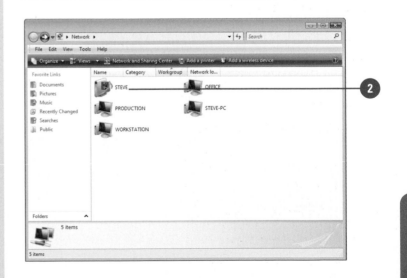

Controlling a Remote Computer

You can use Remote Desktop Connection to connect to a remote computer on your network or the Internet and use the remote computer as if you were working on it. Before you can connect to a remote computer, you need to turn on the Windows Vista computer and set the option to allow users to connect remotely to the computer. Doing this provides security for the remote computer. You can allow anyone to connect to the remote computer, or you can specify users with a password. You also need to have the name or IP (Internet Protocol) address of the remote computer and the user name and password you use to log on to the computer. You can also customize settings for the remote connection, which include the display size and color depth, when to use local or remote resources, and what programs to use and options to allow. Once you connect to the remote computer, the remote desktop appears on your screen. You can use the remote desktop as if you were working at the computer.

Set Up a Remote Computer

1. Click the **Start** button, and then click **Control Panel**.

2. Double-click the **System** icon in Classic view.

3. Click **Change settings**.

4. Click the **Remote** tab.

5. Select the **Allow Remote Assistance connections to this computer** check box.

6. Click **Advanced**.

7. Specify whether you want other to remotely control this computer, and how long a remote invitation is available, and then click **OK**.

8. Select the remote desktop connection option you want.

9. Click **Select Users**.

10. Click **Add**, type user names, and then click **OK**.

    TROUBLE? *Click Examples for help with user names.*

11. Click **OK**.

12. Click **OK**.

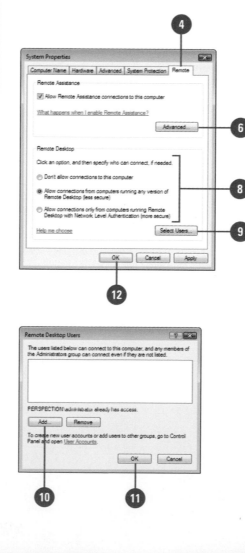

Connect to and Control a Remote Computer

① Establish a connection to your network.

② Click the **Start** button, point to **All Programs**, click **Accessories**, and then click **Remote Desktop Connection**.

③ Type the name or IP address of the remote computer.

④ Click **Options**.

⑤ If available, type a user name.

⑥ Click **Connect**.

⑦ If prompted, enter the needed connection credentials.

⑧ Use the remote desktop as if you were sitting in front of the remote computer.

⑨ Click the **Minimize** or **Restore Down** button to resize the remote desktop and to display the local desktop.

⑩ Use the local desktop.

⑪ When you're done, click the **Close** button, and then click **Yes** to disconnect.

Sharing an Internet Connection

If you have a home or small office network using Windows Vista, you can use Internet Connection Sharing (ICS) to connect all the computers on the network to the Internet with one connection, which saves you money on multiple connections. If you have a shared dial-up Internet connection no one is using, you can change settings to have the connection end automatically, or you can manually end the connection from your computer.

Share an Internet Connection

1. Click the **Start** button, and then click **Control Panel**.

2. Double-click the **Network and Sharing Center** icon in Classic view, and then click **Manage network connections** in the left pane.

3. Right-click the Internet Connection icon, and then click **Properties**.

4. Click the **Sharing** tab.

5. Select the **Allow other network users to connect through this computer's Internet connection** check box.

6. For a home network, select the adapter that connects you to the other networked computers.

7. If you want this connection to dial automatically, select the **Establish a dial-up connection whenever a computer on my network attempts to access the Internet** check box.

8. Select or clear the **Allow other network users to control or disable the shared Internet connection** check box.

9. To select specific services to share, click **Settings**, select the services you want, and then click **OK**.

10. Click **OK**.

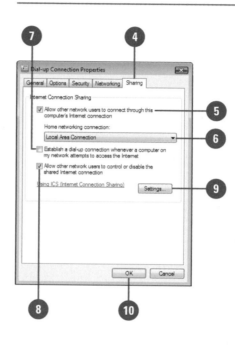

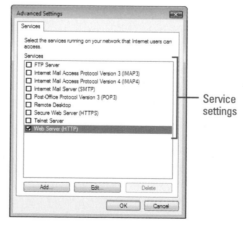

Service settings

End an Internet Connection

1. Click the **Start** button, and then click **Connect To**.

2. Select the connection you want to disconnect.

3. Click **Disconnect**.

   TIMESAVER *In the Network and Sharing Center, you can also click Disconnect.*

4. Click **Disconnect** to confirm.

5. If necessary, click **Close**.

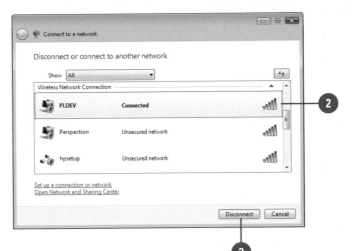

See Also

See "Creating an Internet Connection" on page 136 for information on creating a new shared Internet connection using the New Connection Wizard.

Did You Know?

Disable or enable a network connection. You can disable or enable a network connection by turning the network adapter for the connection off or on. To make this change, open the Network and Sharing Center, click Manage network connections in the left pane, right-click the connection you want to change, and then click Disable or Enable.

Changing a Dial-Up Connection

After you create a dial-up connection, you can change the settings to specify how the computer creates a dial-up connection to another computer. You can change the phone number, add dialing rules, and modify redial and hang up settings. You need to log on as an administrator to change some settings for a dial-up connection. When a computer is set up to share a dial-up connection to the Internet, these settings control the connection for the network users.

Change a Dial-Up Connection

1. Click the **Start** button, and then click **Control Panel**.

2. Double-click the **Network and Sharing Center** icon in Classic view, and then click **Manage network connections** in the left pane.

3. Right-click the **Dial-Up connection** icon, and then click **Properties**.

4. Click the **General** tab.

5. To change the number, double-click the text box, and then type a new number.

6. To use dialing rules, select the **Use dialog rules** check box, and then specify the area and country codes.

7. Click the **Options** tab.

8. Select the check boxes for the dialog options you want, and clear the others.

9. Set the idle time you want before the dial-up connection hangs up, and any redial options.

10. Click **OK**.

See Also

See "Connecting to a Network Using a Modem" on page 322 for information on creating a dial-up connection.

Going Mobile

13

Introduction

You no longer have to change mobile PC related options in different places. With the Windows Mobility Center, you can change or access mobile PC related options all in one place. In the Windows Mobility Center (**New!**), you can adjust volume level and power options, check your network connectivity, connect to an external display, enable presentation settings, and access the Sync Center, which helps you keep files up-to-date when you're working on different computers, such as a desktop computer and a laptop.

If you have a network projector at a remote location and you can connect to it, then you can operate the projector to give a presentation as if you were physically in the room. The Connect to the Network Project wizard makes it easy to establish a connection. Windows SideShow allows hardware manufacturers to build peripheral devices that you can use to view the information you need at a moments notice, such as e-mail or a meeting schedule.

Keeping track of the latest versions of all your files on your desktop computer and laptop can become a problem. With the Sync Center, you can keep files (including documents, music, photos, and in some case contacts) and other information up-to-date between your computer and mobile devices, network folders, and compatible programs. The Sync Center works with offline files and keeps them in sync.

If you have a Tablet PC or ink device, you can use the Pen and Input Devices and the Tablet PC Settings utilities in the Control Panel to customize and personalize the way you work. Windows Vista also comes standard with Tablet PC tools—Windows Journal, Tablet PC Input Panel, and Sticky Notes—that you can effectively use on a Tablet PC with a pen.

What You'll Do

View the Windows Mobility Center

Control Power Options

Keep Files in Sync

Work with Offline Files

Connect to a Network Projector

View Windows SideShow

Change Pen and Input Device Options

Work with Tablet PC Tools

Change Tablet PC Options

Viewing the Windows Mobility Center

Microsoft
Certified
Application
Specialist

WINV-5.2.1,
WINV-5.2.2

With the Windows Mobility Center (**New!**) , you can change or access mobile PC related options all in one place. You no longer have to change mobile PC related options in different places. In the Windows Mobility Center, you can adjust volume level and power options, check your network connectivity, connect to an external display, enable presentation settings, and access the Sync Center, which helps you keep files up-to-date when you're working on different computers, such as a desktop computer and a laptop. You can make an option change in Windows Mobility Center, or click the icon on a tile to open the utility in the Control Panel, where you can make additional changes.

View Windows Mobility Center

1 Click the **Start** button, and then click **Control Panel**.

2 Double-click the **Windows Mobility Center** icon in Classic view.

TIMESAVER *Click the battery meter icon in the notification area, and then click Windows Mobility Center, or press* ⊞*+X.*

3 Click a button or change an option for any of the following settings (options vary depending on your system):

   ◆ **Brightness** for the your display.

   ◆ **Volume** for the speakers.

   ◆ **Battery Status** for power usage.

   ◆ **Wireless Network** on and off.

   ◆ **Screen Rotation** for a Tablet PC.

   ◆ **External Display** add or remove.

   ◆ **Sync Center** to keep files up-to-date.

   ◆ **Presentation Settings** on and off for giving a presentation.

4 When you're done, click the **Close** button.

Change Presentation Settings

1. Click the **Start** button, and then click **Control Panel**.

2. Double-click the **Windows Mobility Center** icon in Classic view.

3. Click the Presentation Settings tile icon.

4. Select or clear the **Turn off the screen saver** check box.

5. Select or clear the **Set volume to** check box. If you select it, drag the slider to adjust it.

6. Select or clear the **Show this background** check box. If you select it, select a background and specify a position.

7. Click **OK**.

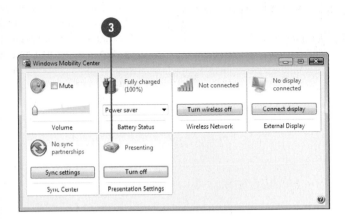

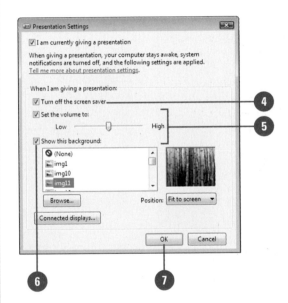

See Also

See "Controlling Power Options" on page 350 for information on using battery power and usage.

See "Keeping Files in Sync" on page 352 for information on keeping files up-to-date on different computers.

See "Using Multiple Monitors" on page 106 for information on using more than one monitor.

See "Controlling the Volume" on page 260 for information on using the volume control.

Controlling Power Options

Microsoft Certified Application Specialist

WINV-2.1,
WINV-7.1.3

You can change power options properties (**New!**) for a portable or laptop computer to reduce power consumption and maximize battery life. For example, if you often leave your computer for a short time while working, you can set your computer to go into **standby**, a state in which your monitor and hard disks turn off after being idle for a set time. If you are often away from your computer for an extended time, you can set it to go into **hibernation**, a state in which your computer first saves everything in memory on your hard disk and then shuts down. To help you set power options, you can choose one of the power plans included with Windows or modify one to suit your needs. A **power plan** is a predefined collection of power usage settings. The power options you see vary depending on your computer's hardware configuration. Windows detects what is available on your computer and shows you only the options that you can control.

Select and Modify a Power Plan

1. Click the **Start** button, and then click **Control Panel**.

2. Double-click the **Power Options** icon in Classic view.

3. Click the power plan option you want: **Balanced**, **Power saver**, **High performance**, or custom.

4. Click **Change plan settings** below the selected option.

5. Specify the amount of time before Windows turns off the display or puts the computer to sleep.

6. Click **Save Changes**.

Did You Know?

You can create a custom power plan. In Power Options, click Create a power plan in the Navigation pane, select a power plan close to the one you want, type a name, click Next, modify the power options, and then click Create. To delete a custom plan, click Change plan settings, click Delete this plan, and then click Yes.

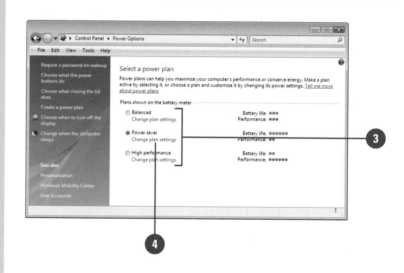

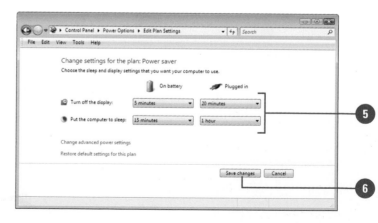

Define Power Button and Set Password Protection

1 Click the **Start** button, and then click **Control Panel.**

2 Double-click the **Power Options** icon in Classic view.

3 In the Navigation pane, click **Choose what the power buttons do.**

4 Specify the options you want when you press the power or sleep button, or when you close the lid.

5 Select the **Require a password (recommended)** or **Don't require a password** option.

6 Click **Save Changes.**

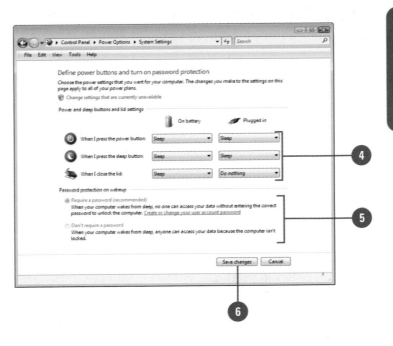

Set Advanced Options

1 Click the **Start** button, and then click **Control Panel.**

2 Double-click the **Power Options** icon in Classic view.

3 Click **Change plan settings** below the selected power plan option.

4 Click **Change advanced power settings**.

5 Click the plus sign (-) and minus sign (-) icons to display the option you want to change.

6 Click the option list arrow, and then select a setting.

7 When you're done, click **OK**.

8 Click **Save Changes.**

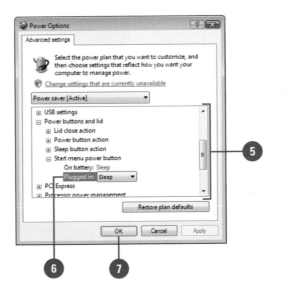

Keeping Files in Sync

Microsoft
Certified
Application
Specialist

WINV-2.5.4, WINV-2.5.5,
WINV-2.5.6

Keeping track of the latest versions of all your files on your desktop computer and laptop can become a problem. With the Sync Center (**New!**), you can keep files (including documents, music, photos, and in some case contacts) and other information up-to-date between your computer and mobile devices, network folders, and compatible programs. You can keep files in sync (short for *synchronization*) in one direction (changes on one computer get changed on the other) or in both directions (changes on both computers get changed on both). The Sync Center compares files between the two computers and then copies the latest version in the appropriate place. If the same files gets changed on both computers, the Sync Center asks you to resolve it. The Sync Center also works with offline files and keeps them in sync.

Sync with a Device

① Establish a connection between your computer and the mobile device, network folder, or program.

② Click the **Start** button, and then click **Control Panel.**

③ Double-click the **Sync Center** icon in Classic view.

> **TIMESAVER** *Click the Start button, point to All Programs, click Accessories, and then click Sync Center.*

④ In the left pane, click **Set up new sync partnerships**.

⑤ Click the name of the device in the list of partnerships.

⑥ Click the **Set Up** button on the toolbar.

⑦ Follow the wizard instructions to select the settings and sync schedule you want. When you're done, click **Finish**.

⑧ To start syncing now, click the **Sync** button on the toolbar.

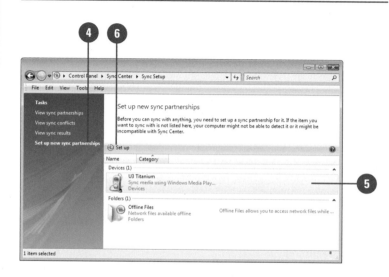

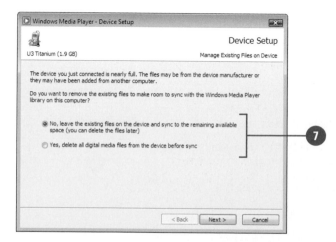

Sync All Offline Files

1. Click the **Start** button, and then click **Control Panel**.

2. Double-click the **Sync Center** icon in Classic view.

3. Click the **Offline Files** sync partnership.

4. If you want to sync the contents of a folder, open it up.

5. Click the **Sync All** button on the toolbar.

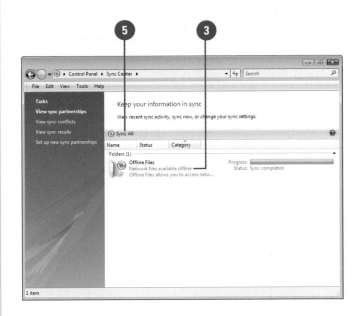

Sync Individual Offline Files

1. Click the **Start** button, and then click **Control Panel**.

2. Double-click the **Sync Center** icon in Classic view.

3. Double-click the **Offline Files** sync partnership.

4. Select the folder you want to sync.

5. To open the folder to view its contents, click the **Browse** button on the toolbar. When you're done, click the **Close** button.

6. Click the **Sync** button on the toolbar.

7. To schedule the time you want to sync this folder, click the **Schedule** button on the toolbar, and then follow the wizard instructions.

Working with Offline Files

The Sync Center works with offline files and keeps them in sync. An offline file is a copy of a network file that is stored on your local computer for use when the network connection is not available. Before you can make a network file available offline, you need to enable offline files in the Offline Files utility in the Control Panel, where you can also set disk usage, security, and network options. When you make a network file available offline, the Windows automatically creates a copy on your local computer. Whenever the network versions are not available, the Sync Center opens the offline copy and then syncs it back with the network version when the connection becomes available again.

Change Offline Files Settings

1. Click the **Start** button, and then click **Control Panel.**

2. Double-click the **Offline Files** icon in Classic view.

3. Click the **General** tab.

4. To disable or enable offline files, click the **Disable Offline Files** or **Enable Offline Files.**

5. Click the **Disk Usage** tab.

6. To change disk space allocation for offline files, click **Change Limits,** drag the slider to adjust space usage, and then click **OK.**

7. Click the **Encryption** tab.

8. Click **Encrypt** or **Unencrypt** to add or remove file security.

9. Click the **Network** tab.

10. Select the check box and specify time, if you want to automatically work offline on a slow network.

11. Click **OK.**

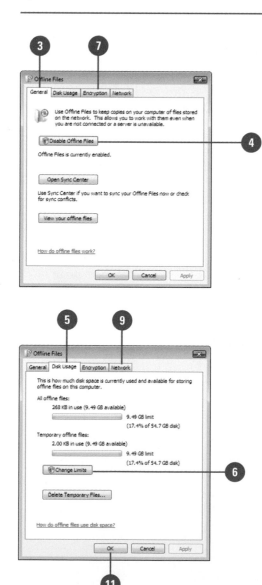

Make Files Available Offline

① Open the network file or folder you want to make available offline.

② Right-click the file or folder, and then click **Always Available Offline**.

TIMESAVER *Select the file or folder, and then click the Work Offline button on the toolbar.*

③ To check if you're working offline or not, open the network folder with the offline files, and check the Details pane for offline status information.

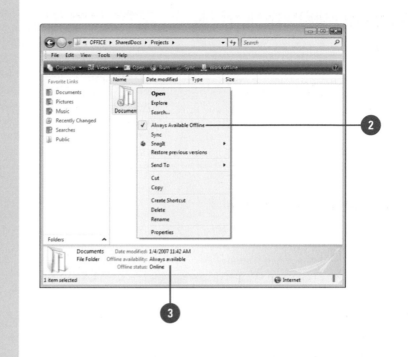

View Offline Files

① Click the **Start** button, and then click **Control Panel.**

② Double-click the **Offline Files** icon in Classic view.

③ Click the **General** tab.

④ Click the **View your offline files** button.

⑤ When you're done, click the **Close** button on the window with the offline files.

⑥ Click **OK** to close the Offline Files dialog box.

Connecting to a Network Projector

Microsoft
Certified
Application
Specialist

WINV-5.2.3

A network projector (**New!**) is a video projector that is connected to a wireless or local area network. If you have a network projector at a remote location and you can connect to it, then you can operate the projector to give a presentation as if you were physically in the room. The audience for the presentation needs to be in the same room as the network projector and the presentation can't be viewed over a network. To connect to a network projector, you can search for one on your network or you can enter a network or Web address provided from your network administrator or the person in charge of the network projector. If the projector icon you select contains a lock, it's security-enabled and requires a password.

Connect to a Network Projector

① Click the **Start** button, point to **All Programs**, click **Accessories**, and then click **Connect to a Network Projector**.

② Click one of the following commands:

◆ **Search for a projector**. Select a projector from the list, and then click Next to continue.

◆ **Enter the projector address**. Type a network address. The address can be a Web address (http://server.com/...) or a network path (\\server\...)

③ If the projector is security-enabled, type a projector password.

④ Click **Connect**.

The Network Presentation dialog box opens and then minimizes on the taskbar.

⑤ Use the dialog box to pause and resume the presentation, or disconnect to exit the presentation.

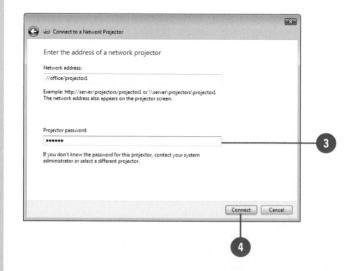

Viewing Windows SideShow

Windows SideShow (**New!**) allows hardware manufacturers to build peripheral devices—such as LCD displays, remote controls, Personal Digital Assistances (PDA), cell phones, or TVs—that can be used to view the information you need at a moments notice. Some devices are integrated into your computer, while other are separate from your computer. You can use Windows SideShow devices to check e-mail messages, view meeting schedules, or find addresses and phones numbers without having to start up your computer. To find a Windows SideShow device, check the Microsoft Web site for details and look for the Windows SideShow logo on the hardware device. This innovative technology is just getting started, so new hardware will continue to expand as Windows Vista continues to grow. You install gadgets, or add-in programs to determine what information you want to gather and display using a Windows SideShow device. After you install a gadget, you can use Windows SideShow in the Control Panel to turn it on.

View Windows SideShow

1. Click the **Start** button, and then click **Control Panel**.

2. Double-click the **Windows SideShow** icon in Classic view.

3. To check more gadgets, click **Get more gadgets online**.

   Your Web browser opens, displaying the gadgets you want install. Follow the online instructions.

4. Click the **Close** button to exit your Web browser.

5. Click the **Close** button.

Changing Pen and Input Device Options

If you have a Tablet PC or ink device, you can use the Pen and Input Devices utility (**New!**) in the Control Panel to set the options you want. You can adjust how quickly you tap the screen when you double-tap or the distance the pointer can move between tapping when you double-tap, and then test your settings to make sure they are what you want. If you want more visual feedback when you perform a specific pointer action, you can displays the ones you want. A flick is a quick stroke of the pen to navigate and perform shortcuts using your tablet pen. On the Flicks tab, you can select options to use flicks to perform common commands and adjust the sensitivity slider to set the right recognition level for your flicks.

Change Pen Options

1 Click the **Start** button, and then click **Control Panel**.

2 Double-click the **Pen and Input Devices** icon in Classic view.

3 Click the **Pen Options** tab.

4 Select the pen action you want to change.

5 Click **Settings**.

6 Drag the sliders to adjust the speed and spatial tolerance you want, and then double-tap the graphic to test the adjustments.

7 Click **OK**.

8 Select or clear the Pen buttons check boxes.

9 Click **OK**.

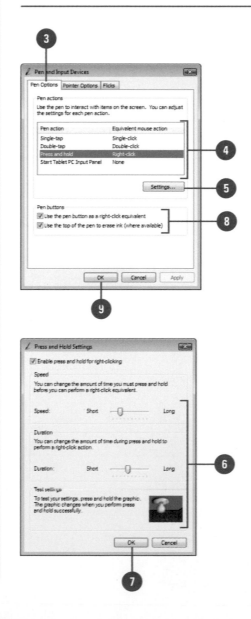

Change Pointer Options and Flicks

1 Click the **Start** button, and then click **Control Panel.**

2 Double-click the **Pen and Input Devices** icon in Classic view.

3 Click the **Pointer Options** tab.

4 Select the visual feedback check boxes you want:

- ◆ **Single-tap**
- ◆ **Double-tap**
- ◆ **Press the pen button**
- ◆ **Press the pen button and tap**

5 Select or clear the **Show pen cursors instead of mouse cursors when I use my pen** check box.

6 Click the **Flicks** tab.

7 Select the **Use flicks to perform command actions quickly and easily** check box.

8 Click the **Navigation flicks** or **Navigation flicks and editing flicks** option.

9 Drag the **Relaxed** slider to adjust sensitivity.

10 Select or clear the **Display flicks icon in the notification area** check box.

11 Click **OK**.

Did You Know?

You can take flick training. Click the Flicks tab in the Pend and Input Devices dialog box, click Practice using flicks, and then follow the wizard instructions.

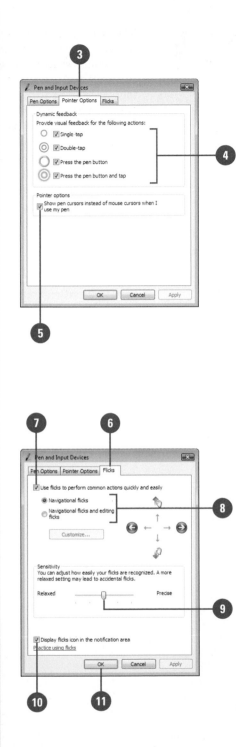

Working with Tablet PC Tools

Windows Vista comes standard with Tablet PC tools that you can effectively use on a Tablet PC with a pen. The tools are also available on a standard PC and you can them with a mouse, but not as effectively. Windows Vista comes with three tools: Windows Journal, Tablet PC Input Panel, and Sticky Notes. Windows Journal allows you to handwrite notes and draw pictures that mimic a notebook pad.Tablet PC Input Panel allows you to enter text without using a standard keyboard. You use the writing pad or the character pad to convert your handwriting into typed text. You can also use the on-screen keyboard to enter characters. Sticky Notes allows you to create notes that mimic the paper version and add writing to a 30 second voice note.

Handwrite Journal Entries

1 Click the **Start** button, point to **All Programs**, click **Accessories**, click **Tablet PC**, and then click **Windows Journal**.

2 Click the **Pen** button arrow on the toolbar, and then select a pen style.

3 Handwrite notes or make a drawing.

4 To make corrections, click the **Erase** button arrow, select an eraser size, and then drag to erase on the page.

5 Use many of the common tools on the toolbar and menus to create a handwritten document.

6 When you're done, click the **Save** button on the toolbar, type a name, specify a location, and then click **Save**.

7 Click the **File** menu, and then click **Exit**.

Use the Tablet PC Input Panel

1. Open a document to insert handwriting.

2. Click the **Start** button, point to **All Programs**, click **Accessories**, click **Tablet PC**, and then click **Tablet PC Input Panel**.

3. To write continuously, click the **Writing Pad** button, handwrite a message, and then click the **Insert** button.

4. To convert handwriting to text, click the **Character Pad** button, handwrite characters, and then click the **Insert** button.

5. To use an on-screen keyboard, click the **On-Screen Keyboard** button, and then click the keys.

6. When you're done, click the **Tools** menu, and then click **Exit**.

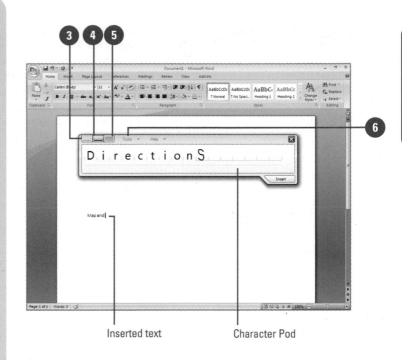

Inserted text   Character Pod

Create Sticky Notes

1. Click the **Start** button, point to **All Programs**, click **Accessories**, click **Tablet PC**, and then click **Sticky Notes**.

2. Write a note in the note pad area.

3. To create a new note, click **New Note**.

4. To create a 30 second voice note, click the **Record** button, speak, and then click the **Stop** button.

5. To move between notes, click the **Previous Note** or **Next Note** button.

6. To delete a note, click the **Delete This Note** button.

7. When you're done, click the **Tools** menu, and then click **Exit**.

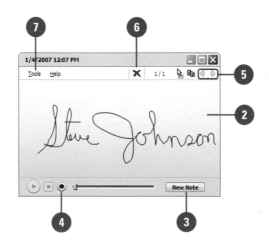

Changing Tablet PC Options

If you have a Tablet PC, you can use the Tablet PC utility (**New!**) in the Control Panel to set the options you want. You can specify whether you are right-handed or left handed and calibrate your tablet pen to improve accuracy on the screen. You can also change the screen orientation and preview the results. The Tablet PC utility also connects you to display brightness settings in Windows Mobility Center, and pen and input device settings in the Pen and Input Device utility in the Control Panel.

Change Tablet PC Options

1. Click the **Start** button, and then click **Control Panel.**

2. Double-click the **Tablet PC** icon in Classic view.

3. Click the **General** tab.

4. Click the **Right-handed** or **Left-handed** option.

5. To calibrate your tablet pen for more accuracy, click **Calibrate**.

6. Click the **Display** tab.

7. Select the orientation, preview, and rotation sequence you want, and use the link to change display brightness using Windows Mobility Center.

8. Click the **Handwriting Recognition** tab.

9. Select the **Use the personalized recognizer (recommended)** check box

10. Click **OK**.

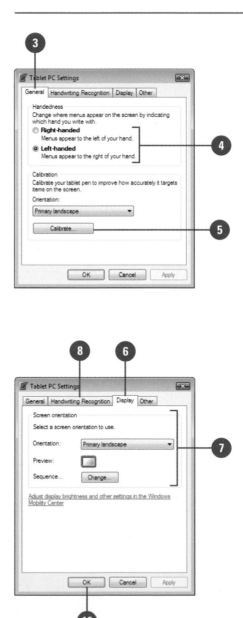

Did You Know?

You can access pen and input device settings from Tablet PC Settings. In the Tablet PC utility, click the Other tab, and then click the Go to Pen and Input Devices link.

Printing and Faxing

14

Introduction

After you create a document or picture, or open a web page or an e-mail, you can use Windows printing options to create a hard copy. You can print files from a folder window or within a program. The Add a Printer Wizard makes it easy to install a printer directly attached to your computer or connected to a network. After you send a print job to the printer, you can check the status, pause and resume the print job, or cancel it. If a printer is not working the way you want, you can change printer properties, such as a printer's computer connection or network location, sharing options, related software drivers, color management options, graphics settings, installed fonts, and other advanced settings. To customize your print jobs, you can also change printer preferences, such as orientation, page order, pages per sheet, paper size, paper tray selection, copy count, print quality, and color.

Windows also provides you with complete fax facilities from your computer. After the fax is set up, you can configure fax settings, send and receive faxes, track and monitor fax activity, and view faxes. Using Windows Fax and Scan, you can send and receive faxes, fax or e-mail scanned documents, and forward faxes as e-mail attachments from your computer. You can also change the send and receive properties for the fax to work with your phone line.

Understanding Printers

Although there are many different kinds of printers, there are two main categories: ink-jet and laser. An **ink-jet printer** works by spraying ionized ink on a sheet of paper. Ink-jet printers are less expensive and considerably slower than laser printers, but they still produce a good quality output. A **laser printer** utilizes a laser beam to produce an image on a drum, which is rolled through a reservoir of toner and transferred to the paper through a combination of heat and pressure. Laser printers are faster and produce a higher quality output than ink-jets, but they are also more expensive. Ink-jet and laser printers are combined with other hardware devices, such as a copier and scanner, into a multi-function device. A **multi-function device** provides common device functionality at a lower cost than purchasing each device separately. Printers are classified by two main characteristics: resolution and speed. Printer resolution refers to the sharpness and clarity of a printed page. For printers, the resolution indicates the number of dots per inch (dpi). For example, a 300-dpi printer is one that is capable of printing 300 distinct dots in a line one-inch long, or 90,000 dots per square inch. The higher the dpi, the sharper the print quality. Printer speed is measured in pages per minute (ppm). The speed of printers varies widely. In general, ink-jet printers range from about 4 to 10 ppm, while laser printers range from about 10 to 30 ppm. The speed depends on the amount of printer memory (the more the better) and the page's contents: if there is just text or the page has only one color, the ppm is in the high range, but when a page contains graphics and/or has multiple colors, the ppm rate falls to the low range.

Ink-jet printer

Laser printer

Multi-function device

Viewing Printers

Microsoft Certified Application Specialist   WINV-7.6.1

After you install a printer, the printer appears in the Printers and Faxes window and in a program's Print dialog box, where you can view and change printer properties and personal preferences. Every installed printer on your computer is represented by an icon in the Printers and Faxes window. When you select a printer icon, status information for that printer appears in the Details section of the task pane, such as number of documents to be printed, and whether the printer is ready to print. A printer icon appears in the window without a cable indicates a **local printer**, while a printer icon with a cable indicates a **network printer**. A local printer is a printer connected directly to your computer, and a network printer is one connected to a network to which you have access. A printer icon that appears with a hand indicates that other network users share the printer directly connected to your computer, known as a **shared printer**.

View Printer Properties

1. Click the **Start** button, and then click the **Control Panel**.

2. Double-click the **Printers** icon in Classic view.

3. Click a printer icon.

4. Click the **Close** button.

Did You Know?

You can access additional buttons on the toolbar in the Printers window. In the Printers window, the toolbar display several commands, such as Add a printer, See what's printing, Set as default. However, there are more commands available on the toolbar. Click the double arrow (>>) to display a menu with additional commands, such as Rename this printer, Pause printing, and Share.

You can display printer status by displaying views in the Printers window. In the Printers window, click the Views button on the toolbar, and then click Tiles or Details. Printer status appears along with the printer name.

Printer status   Local printer

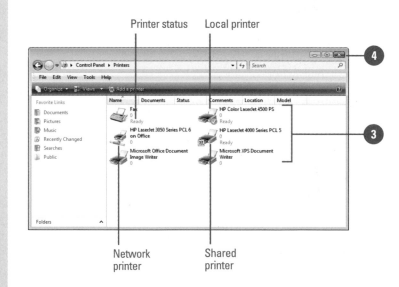

Network printer   Shared printer

Installing a Printer

Microsoft Certified Application Specialist WINV-3.6.1, WINV-3.6.3

To install a printer, you do not need to shut down your computer. Simply attach the printer cable to the appropriate connector on your computer, according to the manufacturer's instructions, and plug in the power cord. If you connect your printer to your computer through a USB port, Windows detects the new hardware device and installs the printer, and you are ready to print. Otherwise, you can use the Add Printer Wizard in conjunction with the Found New Hardware Wizard to detect and install the printer. The Add Printer Wizard asks you a series of questions to help you install either a local or network printer, establish a connection, and print a test page.

Set Up a Local Printer Using the Add Printer Wizard

1. Click the **Start** button, and then click the **Control Panel**.

2. Double-click the **Printers** icon in Classic view.

3. Click the **Add a printer** button on the toolbar.

4. Click **Add a local printer**.

5. Select the **Use an existing port** or **Create a new port** option, and then click **Next** to continue.

6. Select the printer manufacturer and model, and then click **Next** to continue.

7. Type a printer name.

8. Select or clear the **Set as the default printer** check box, and then click **Next** to continue.

9. To test the printer, click **Print a test page**.

10. Click **Finish**.

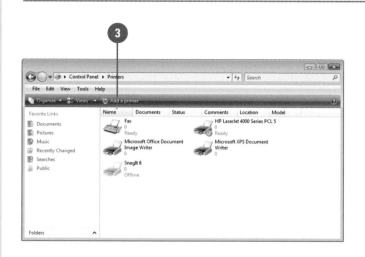

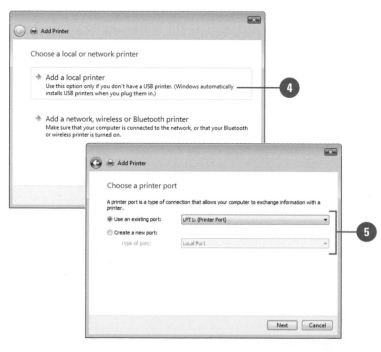

Set Up a Network Printer Using the Add Printer Wizard

1. Click the **Start** button, and then click the **Control Panel**.

2. Double-click the **Printers** icon in Classic view.

3. Click the **Add a printer** button on the toolbar.

4. Click **Add a network, wireless or Bluetooth printer**.

5. Select the printer you want to install, and then click **Next** to continue.

6. If necessary, click **Install driver** to install the printer driver.

7. If available, type a name for the printer.

8. Select or clear the **Set as the default printer** check box, and then click **Next** to continue.

9. To test the printer, click **Print a test page**.

10. Click **Finish**.

Did You Know?

You can display printer and communication ports. Click the Start button, click Control Panel, double-click the Printers icon in Classic view, click the File menu, click Server Properties, and then click the Ports tab. The available ports don't have a printer name associated with it.

For Your Information

Understanding USB Ports

A **port** is the location on the back of your computer where you connect the printer cable. You can connect the cable to either a printer port, which is labeled LPT1 or LPT2, to a communications port, which is labeled COM1 or COM2, or to a Universal Serial Bus port, which is labeled USB. A printer port is called a **parallel port**, which sends more than one byte simultaneously. A communications port is called a **serial port**, which sends information one byte at a time. The USB port is a new technology that is expected to replace parallel and serial ports. A **USB (Universal Serial Bus) port** is an external hardware interface on the computer that allows you to connect a USB device. A single USB port can be used to connect up to 127 peripheral devices, such as mice, modems, and keyboards, and supports data transfer rates of 480 Mbs (480 million bits per second). USB also supports plug and play installation and **hot plugging**, which is the ability to add and remove devices to a computer while the computer is running and have the operating system automatically recognize the change.

Specifying a Default Printer

If your computer is connected to more than one printer, you can choose the default printer you want Windows to use to print your files unless you specify another one. The default printer is typically the printer that you use most often. When you start a print job without specifying a particular printer, the job is sent to the default printer. You can select a default printer in the Printers and Faxes window or when you set up a new printer. The default printer displays a black dot with a check mark in the printer icon.

Select a Default Printer

1. Click the **Start** button, and then click the **Control Panel**.

2. Double-click the **Printers** icon in Classic view.

3. Right-click the printer icon you want to set as the default, and then click **Set as Default Printer**.

   TIMESAVER *Select the printer, and then click the Set as default button.*

4. Click the **Close** button.

Current default printer

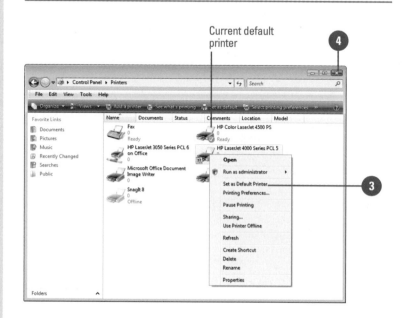

Renaming or Deleting a Printer

If you have trouble identifying a printer, or if you just want to change the name, you can rename it. You rename the same way you rename a file or folder. When you rename a printer, the new name appears in the Print dialog box for all your programs. If you no longer use a printer, you can delete it. When you delete the default printer, Windows displays a warning and changes the default printer to another available printer.

Rename a Printer

1. Click the **Start** button, and then click the **Control Panel**.

2. Double-click the **Printers** icon in Classic view.

3. Right-click the printer icon you want to rename, and then click **Rename**.

   TIMESAVER *Select the printer, and then click the Rename this printer button.*

4. Type a new name for the printer, and then press Enter.

5. Click the **Close** button.

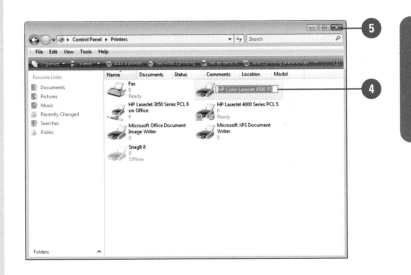

Delete a Printer

1. Click the **Start** button, and then click the **Control Panel**.

2. Double-click the **Printers** icon in Classic view.

3. Right-click the printer icon you want to delete, and then click **Delete**.

   TIMESAVER *You can also press the Delete key.*

4. Click **OK** to confirm the deletion.

5. If the printer is the default, click **OK**.

6. Click the **Close** button.

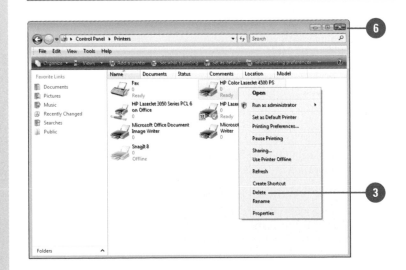

Sharing a Printer

If you have a printer connected to your computer and your computer is connected to a network, you can share your printer with other network users. Before you can share a printer, you need to turn on printer sharing using the Network Setup Wizard, which you can accomplish by using the Sharing tab in the Printer Properties dialog box. After you share a printer, the printer icon appears with a hand in the Printers and Faxes window. For security purposes, if Windows Firewall is enabled (the default setting) on the computer with the shared computer, then you need to select File and Printer Sharing on the Exceptions tab in Windows Firewall for others to use the shared printer.

Share a Printer

1. Click the **Start** button, and then click the **Control Panel**.

2. Double-click the **Printers** icon in Classic view.

3. Right-click the printer you want to share, and then click **Sharing**.

   TROUBLE? *If sharing options are not available, click the Change sharing options button, and then follow the instructions to turn on print sharing.*

4. Select the **Share this printer** check box.

5. Type a name for the printer (eight characters recommended), or use the suggested one.

6. If other computers on the network are using different versions of Windows, click **Additional Drivers** to install other drivers for the other computers, select the check boxes for the operating systems you want, and then click **OK**.

7. If prompted, insert the Windows Vista DVD into your drive or provide a driver location, and then click **OK**.

8. Click **OK**.

9. Click the **Close** button.

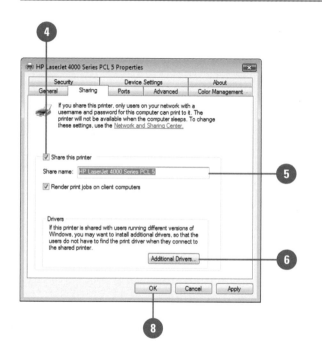

Printing Documents

If you have a group of documents that you want to print, you can print them all directly from a folder window without having to open each one in its program. The program needs to be installed on your computer to complete the job.

Print Documents Using the Default Printer

1. Open the folder that contains the documents you want to print.

2. Select the documents.

3. Click the **Print** button on the toolbar.

4. Select the options you want, and then click **Print**.

Print Documents Using a Specific Printer

1. Click the **Start** button, and then click the **Control Panel**.

2. Double-click the **Printers** icon in Classic view.

3. Open the folder (in a separate window) that contains the documents you want to print.

4. Select the documents.

5. Drag the selected documents onto the printer you want to use, and then click **Yes**.

> **TROUBLE?** *If a program requires the use of the default printer, you need to change the printer to the default.*

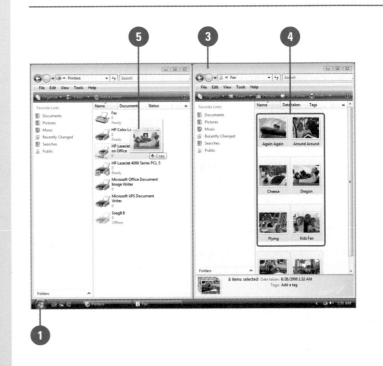

Managing Printers and Print Jobs

Microsoft Certified Application Specialist

WINV-7.6.2

After you send a print job to the printer from the Print dialog box in a program, or drag files to the Printer icon in the Printers and Faxes window, you can check the status. To check the status of a printer or manage multiple print jobs, you can double-click the appropriate printer icon in the Printers and Faxes window or on the taskbar in the notification area. A window opens showing the **print queue**, which is the list of files to be printed. You can use this window to cancel print jobs, temporarily pause print jobs, view printer properties, and so on. If you are having problems with a printer or print job, you can **defer**, or halt, the printing process to avoid getting error messages. With deferred printing, you can send a job to be printed even if your computer is not connected to a printer. To do this, you pause printing, and the file waits in the print queue until you turn off pause printing.

Pause Printing

1. Click the **Start** button, and then click the **Control Panel**.

2. Double-click the **Printers** icon in Classic view.

3. Right-click the printer icon you want to pause, and then click **Pause Printing**.

   TIMESAVER *Select the printer, and then click the Pause printing button, or click the File menu, and then click Pause Printing.*

4. To resume printing, right-click the printer icon you want to pause, and then click **Resume Printing**.

5. Click the **Close** button.

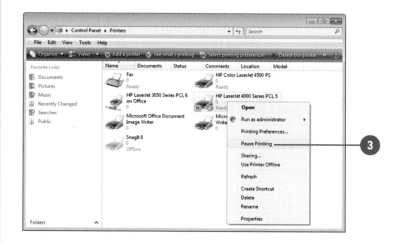

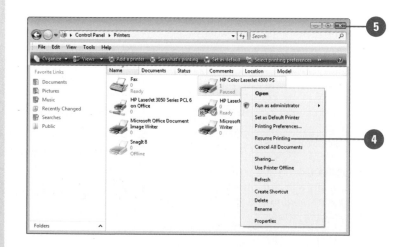

Pause a Print Job

1. Click the **Start** button, and then click the **Control Panel**.

2. Double-click the **Printers** icon in Classic view.

3. Double-click the printer icon.

4. Right-click the document you want to pause, and then click **Pause**.

5. To resume the document printing, right-click the document you want to resume, and then click **Restart**.

6. Click the **Close** button.

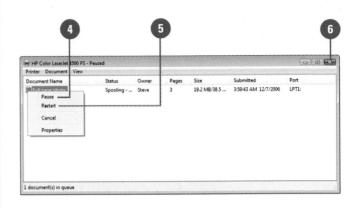

Cancel a Print Job

1. Click the **Start** button, and then click the **Control Panel**.

2. Double-click the **Printers** icon in Classic view.

3. Double-click the printer icon.

4. Right-click the document you want to stop, and then click **Cancel**.

5. To cancel all documents, click the **Printer** menu, click **Cancel All Documents**, and then click Yes to confirm the cancelation.

6. Click the **Close** button.

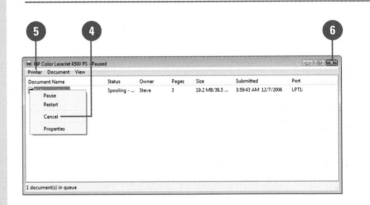

Security Alert

Displaying Printer Notification

For security purposes, if Windows Firewall is turned on (the default setting), printer notification information, such as "Ready" or "Paused," in the Printers and Faxes folder is slightly delayed and your computer no longer receives other printer notifications, such as "Print job completed" or "Printer out of paper".

Changing Printer Properties

Viewing printer properties gives you information about a printer's computer connection or network location, sharing options, related software drivers, color management options, graphics settings, installed fonts, and other advanced settings, such as **spooling**. Spooling, also known as **background printing**, is the process of storing a temporary copy of a file on the hard disk and then sending the file to the print device. Spooling allows you to continue working with the file as soon as it is stored on the disk instead of having to wait until the file is finished printing.

Change General and Device Properties

1. Click the **Start** button, and then click the **Control Panel**.

2. Double-click the **Printers** icon in Classic view.

3. Right-click the printer icon you want to change, and then click **Properties**.

   TIMESAVER *Select the printer, and then click the Set printer properties button.*

4. Click the **General** tab.

5. If you want, change the printer name or location, and then type a comment.

6. Click the **Device Settings** tab.

7. Click the plus sign (+) to expand the options you want to change.

8. Click an option link.

9. Click an option list arrow, and then select a setting.

10. Click **OK**.

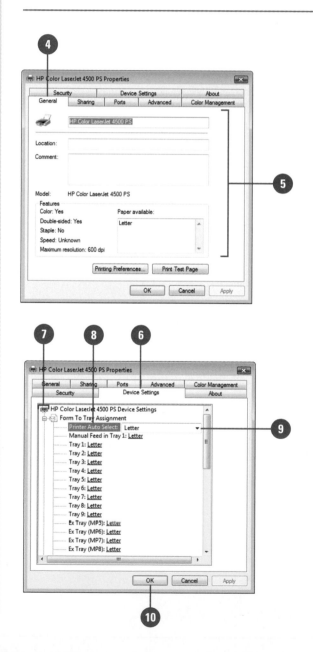

Change Spooling Settings

1. Click the **Start** button, and then click the **Control Panel**.

2. Double-click the **Printers** icon in Classic view.

3. Right-click the the printer icon you want to change, and then click **Properties**.

4. Click the **Advanced** tab.

5. Click the **Spool print documents so program finishes printing faster** option.

6. Click a spooling option to specify when you want the printer to start printing your documents.

7. To keep documents in the spooler after they are printed, select the **Keep printed documents** check box.

8. To print documents that have completed spooling before other documents, select **Print spooled documents first** check box.

9. Click **OK**.

Changing Printer Preferences

In addition to printer properties, you can also view and change personal printer preferences, such as orientation, page order, pages per sheet, paper size, paper tray selection, copy count, and print quality and color. When you change personal printing preferences from the Printers and Faxes folder, the default settings are changed for all documents you print to that printer. When you change personal preferences from the Print or Page Setup dialog boxes within a program, the settings are changed for individual documents. The available printing preferences depend on the printer.

Change Printer Preferences

1 Click the **Start** button, and then click the **Control Panel**.

2 Double-click the **Printers** icon in Classic view.

3 Select the printer icon you want to change.

4 Click the **Select Printing Preferences** button on the toolbar.

5 Click the tab with the option you want to change; tabs and options vary depending on the printer.

6 Change the printer preferences you want to modify.

7 Click **OK**.

8 Click the **Close** button.

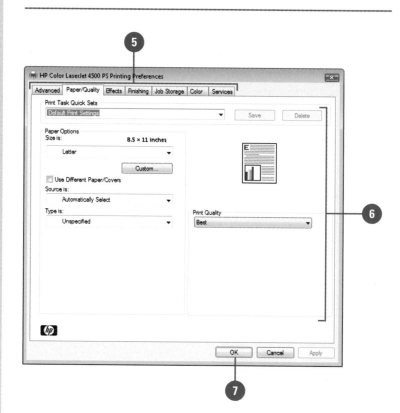

Understanding Faxes

Windows Fax and Scan is a program that allows you to send and receive faxes, fax or e-mail scanned documents, and forward faxes as e-mail attachments from your computer. From Windows Fax and Scan, you can monitor the progress of incoming and outgoing fax activity.

Before you can use Windows Fax and Scan, you need a fax device for sending and receiving faxes. The fax device can be directly attached to your computer, known as a **local fax**, or located on a network, known as a **fax server**. Window Fax and Scan makes it easy to setup a fax device with the Fax Setup Wizard. You can only connect to one local fax, however you can connect to multiple fax servers or devices on a network. To start the Fax Setup Wizard and set up a fax, start Windows Fax and Scan, click Fax in the left pane, click the Tools menu, click Fax Accounts, click Add to start the Fax Setup Wizard. In the wizard, click Connect to a fax server on my network, and then follow the on-screen instructions.

Once your fax is installed, you can use Windows Fax and Scan to send and receive faxes, manage incoming and outgoing faxes, and change fax device properties. You can also send faxes from a folder window or the Print dialog box in a program. When you print using a fax printer, Windows Fax and Scan starts and opens the New Fax window, where you can send a fax just like you send an e-mail message.

With the Fax Cover Page Editor, you can create and edit cover pages to use when you send a fax. The Fax Cover Page Editor is a full page editor that makes it easy to insert common fax page items, such as recipient, subject, number of pages, and message, and to format the page to create a professional look. You can also customize a few samples that come with the program.

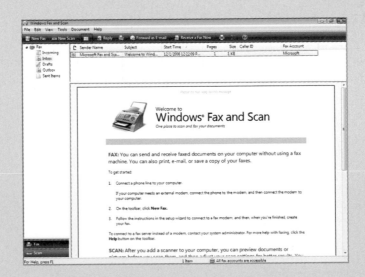

Setting Up a Fax

If your computer has a fax modem installed, you can send and receive faxes through your computer. If you are not sure, you can use the Phone and Modem Options utility in the Control Panel to check if you have one installed. Using Windows Fax and Scan (**New!**), you can send and receive faxes, fax or e-mail scanned documents, and forward faxes as e-mail attachments from your computer. The Fax Setup Wizard helps you set up the Fax Service using a modem or a fax server. Afterwards, you can enter some personal information for the fax cover page, a phone number, and some option for the way you want to send and receive faxes.

Install a Modem

1. If necessary, attach an analog phone line to your computer, and then turn the fax on. You can't use a digital phone line to send or receive faxes.

   If your computer has a built-in modem, Windows automatically detects and sets it up.

2. Click the **Start** button, and then click **Control Panel**.

3. Double-click the **Phone And Modem Options** icon in Classic view.

4. On first use, enter information about your current location, and then click **OK**.

5. Click the **Modems** tab.

   If you have a modem installed, it appears in the modem list.

6. Click **Add**.

7. Follow the Add Hardware Wizard instructions to complete the installation.

8. Click **OK**.

5

Phone and Modem Options

Dialing Rules | Modems | Advanced

The following modems are installed:

Modem	Attached To
HDAUDIO Soft Data Fax Modem with Sma...	COM3

Add... | Remove | Properties

OK | Cancel | Apply

6 **8**

Set Up for Faxing

1. Click the **Start** button, point to the **All Programs**, and then click **Windows Fax and Scan**.

   ◆ You can also double-click the Fax icon in the Printers window to open Windows Fax and Scan.

2. In the left pane, click **Fax**.

   If you're connecting to a fax device for the first time, the New Fax button starts the Fax Setup Wizard.

3. Click the **New Fax** button on the toolbar.

   If the wizard doesn't start, click the Tools menu, click Fax Accounts, and then click Add.

4. Click **Connect to a fax modem** or **Connect to a fax server on my network**.

5. Follow the wizard instructions to complete the set up; options vary depending on the fax modem you set up.

   Upon completion, the New Fax window opens.

6. Click the **Close** button on the New Fax window.

7. Click the **Tools** menu, and then click **Sender Information**.

8. Enter the information you want cover pages to display.

9. Click **OK**.

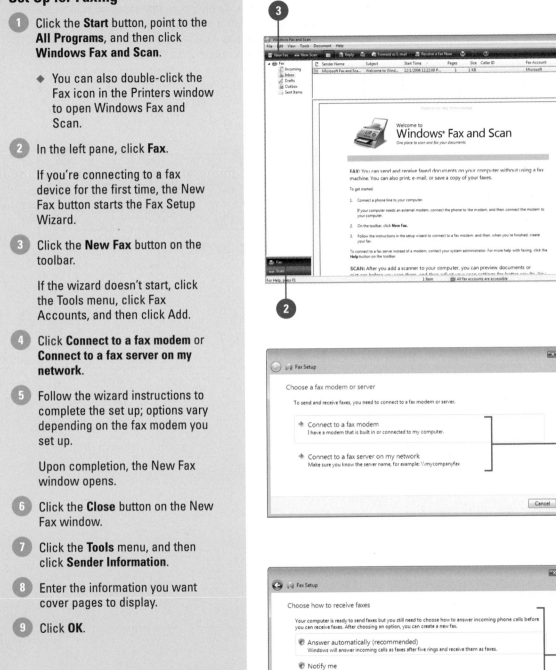

Creating a Fax Cover Page

A cover page is typically a one page cover memo sent along with a fax containing the fax sender, a recipient, number of pages, a short message, and the transmission date and time. You can use the Fax Cover Page Editor to create your own cover pages or to customize cover page templates, known as common cover pages, that come with the program. You can copy and modify common cover pages without affecting the original templates. You can also edit existing cover pages and rename or delete personal cover pages as needed.

Create a Cover Page from Scratch

1. Click the **Start** button, point to the **All Programs**, **Windows Fax and Scan**, and then click the **Fax** tab.

2. Click the **Tools**, click **Cover Pages**, and then click **New**.

3. Click the **View** menu, and then click **Grid Lines**.

4. Click the **Insert** menu, point to **Recipient**, **Sender**, or **Message**, and then click an item.

5. Press and hold Ctrl, and then click the items you want to select.

6. Drag the items to a new location, or use the alignment buttons on the toolbar.

7. Use the formatting buttons on the toolbar to format the text.

8. Use the drawing tools on the toolbar to add shapes and lines.

9. Click the **File** menu, and then click **Save As**.

10. Type a name for the cover page.

11. Click **Save**.

12. Click the **Close** button on the Fax Cover Page Editor.

13. Click **Close**.

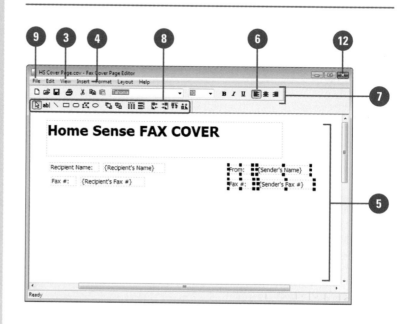

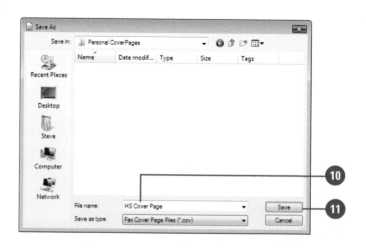

Copy a Cover Page Template

1. Click the **Start** button, point to the **All Programs, Windows Fax and Scan**, and then click the **Fax** tab.

2. Click the **Tools**, and then click **Cover Pages**.

3. Click **Copy**.

4. Select a common fax cover page.

5. Click **Open**.

6. Click **Close**.

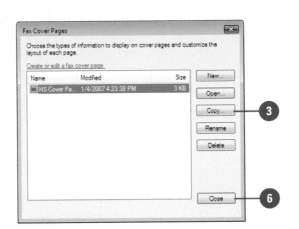

Rename or Delete a Cover Page

1. Click the **Start** button, point to the **All Programs, Windows Fax and Scan**, and then click the **Fax** tab.

2. Click the **Tools**, and then click **Cover Pages**.

3. Click a cover page.

4. To rename the cover page, click **Rename**, type a new name (include the extension .cov), and then press Enter.

5. To delete the cover page, click **Delete**, and then click Yes to confirm it.

6. Click **Close**.

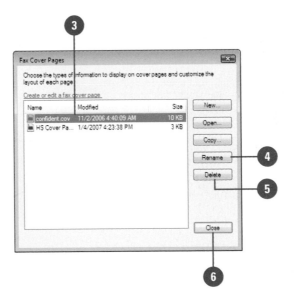

Sending a Fax

After you install and configure your fax, you can send a fax using the New Fax window. You can send a cover page fax from the Printer window or from within Windows Fax and Scan, or a document fax from a program. When you send a fax, the New Fax window opens to help you create and send a fax. When you send a document fax, the program in which you open or create the document prints it to the fax device. When you print to a fax device, Windows Fax and Scan starts and opens the New Fax window where you can send the fax.

Send a Fax

1. Click the **Start** button, point to the **All Programs**, **Windows Fax and Scan**, and then click the **Fax** tab.

2. Click the **New Fax** button.

3. Click the **Cover Page** list arrow, and then select a cover page.

4. Click the **To** button, select a recipients you want, click the **To** button, and then click **OK**.

5. Type a subject.

6. Click the **Dialing rule** list arrow, and then select a rule.

7. Type the message you want.

8. Click the **Send** button on the toolbar.

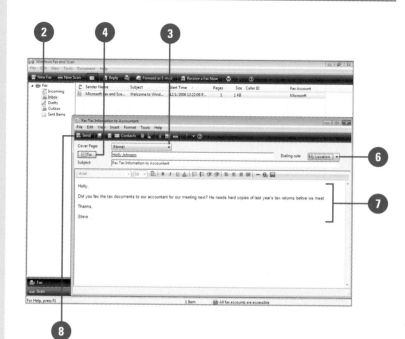

Send a Fax from a Document

1. Start the program and open or create the document you want to send as a fax.

2. Click the **File** menu, and then click **Print**.

   ◆ For a Microsoft Office 2007 program, click the Office button, point to Print, and then click Print.

3. Click the Fax printer as your printer.

4. Click **Print** or **OK**.

   Windows Fax and Scan opens and starts a new fax.

5. Click the **Cover Page** list arrow, and then select a cover page.

6. Click the **To** button, select a recipients you want, click the **To** button, and then click **OK**.

7. Type a subject, and any cover page notes you want.

8. Click the **Dialing rule** list arrow, and then select a rule.

9. Type the message you want.

10. Click the **Send** button on the toolbar.

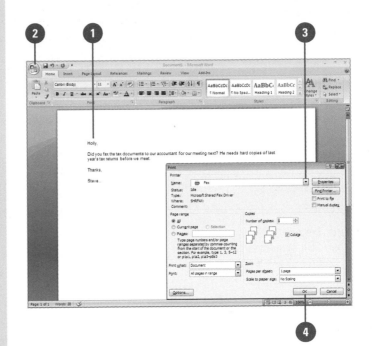

Did You Know?

You can scan and fax a document. Scan the document using a scanner, open the scanned document in a program, and then print it to the fax directly from the program.

Managing Outgoing Faxes

After you send a fax, its sent to the Outbox folder of the Fax Console. The Outbox is a storage area for all faxes waiting to be sent, or in the process of being sent. From the Outbox, you can pause and resume faxes, restart failed faxes, and remove individual faxes as necessary. If a fax is being sent to multiple recipients, the fax for each recipient appears separately, so you can pause or delete a fax to one of the multiple recipients without affecting the others. When you change the status of a fax in the Outbox, the Status column changes to indicate the new state of the fax. Once a fax is sent successfully, it is moved to the Sent Items folder.

Cancel or Restart an Outgoing Fax

1 Click the **Start** button, point to the **All Programs**, **Windows Fax and Scan**, and then click the **Fax** tab.

2 Click the **Outbox** icon.

3 To cancel a fax, click the fax, and then click the **Delete** button.

4 To restart a failed fax, click the fax, click the **Document** menu, and then click **Restart**.

5 When you're done, click the **Close** button.

Did You Know?

You can't remove a fax from a remote fax printer without deleting the fax printer. Click the remote fax printer from the Printer window, and then click the Delete this printer button on the toolbar.

Pause or Resume an Outgoing Fax

1. Click the **Start** button, point to the **All Programs**, **Windows Fax and Scan**, and then click the **Fax** tab.

2. Click the Outbox icon.

3. To pause a fax, click the fax, and then click the click the **Document** menu, and then click **Pause**.

4. To resume a fax, click the paused fax, click the **Document** menu, and then click **Resume**.

5. When you're done, click the **Close** button.

View a Sent Fax

1. Click the **Start** button, point to the **All Programs**, **Windows Fax and Scan**, and then click the **Fax** tab.

2. Click the Sent Items icon.

3. Review the fax information.

4. When you're done, click the **Close** button.

Receiving a Fax

If you have a phone line attached to your computer, you can set up Windows Fax and Scan to receive faxes automatically or manually. If the phone line is a dedicated fax line and set to receive faxes automatically, Windows Fax and Scan automatically stores the fax in your Inbox, just like an e-mail in your e-mail program. If the phone line is used for voice and fax calls, Windows Fax and Scan waits for you to answer the call before it receives the fax.

Receive a Fax Manually

1. When you receive a call for a fax, click to receive the call to open the Fax Status Monitor dialog box.

2. Click **Answer call**, if necessary.

3. Click **View Details** to see details about the call.

4. If there are problems with the fax or if you don't want to receive it, click **Disconnect**.

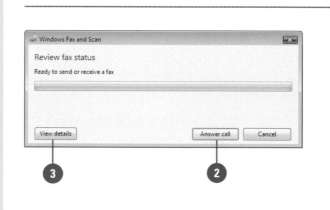

Change Receive Answer Mode

1. Click the **Start** button, point to the **All Programs**, **Windows Fax and Scan**, and then click the **Fax** tab.

2. Click the **Tools** menu, and then click **Fax Settings**.

3. Click the **General** tab.

4. Select the **Allow the device to receive fax calls** check box.

5. Click the **Manually answer** or **Automatically answer after X rings** option.

6. Click the **Tracking** tab, and then select the **Received** check box.

7. Click **OK**.

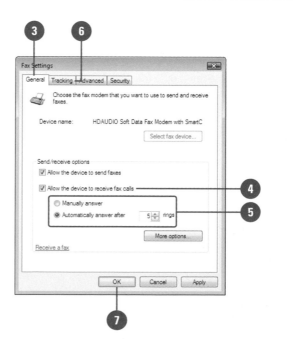

Reviewing a Fax

After you receive a fax, you can use Fax Console to view, print, save, or e-mail the fax. Windows Fax and Scan informs you when a fax arrived, who sent it, how many pages were received, and the status of the job.

Review a Received Fax

1. Click the **Start** button, point to the **All Programs**, **Windows Fax and Scan**, and then click the **Fax** tab.

2. To review the status of a fax being received, click the **Incoming** icon.

3. Click the **Inbox** icon.

4. Click the fax you want to view.

5. Use the buttons on the toolbar to do the following:

   ◆ Reply to the fax as another fax.

   ◆ Forward the fax as another fax.

   ◆ E-mail the fax as an attachment to a message.

   ◆ Print the fax to your printer.

   ◆ Delete the fax.

6. To save the fax as a TIF file, click the **File** menu, click **Save As**, specify a name and location, and then click **Save**.

7. When you're done, click the **Close** button.

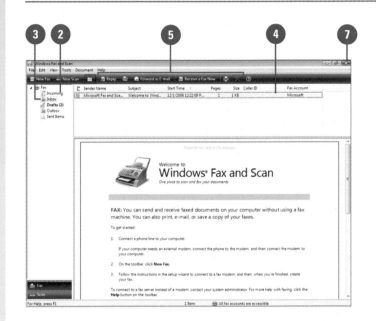

Did You Know?

You can sort faxes by a variety of different categories. In Windows Fax and Scan, click the View menu, point to Arrange By, and then select the way you want to sort. You can arrange by Fax Account, Caller ID, Subject, and Number of Pages to name a few.

Changing Fax Properties

You can change the send and receive properties for a fax device to effectively work with your phone line. You can change the number of times the the fax device tries to resend a fax. You can also change where to store a fax when you receive it. If you need to specify the use of a Transmitting Station Identifier (TSID), which is an identification sent along with a fax to identify the source, and a Called Subscriber Identifier (CSID), which is an identification sent back to the sending fax device to confirm the identity of the source, you can specify those settings as well.

Change Send Properties

1. Click the **Start** button, point to the **All Programs**, **Windows Fax and Scan**, and then click the **Fax** tab.

2. Click the **Tools** menu, and then click **Fax Settings**.

3. Click the **General** tab.

4. Select the **Allow the device to send faxes** check box.

5. To change TSID or CSID, click **More options**, type the information, and then click **OK**.

6. Click the **Advanced** tab.

7. Type the number of redialing attempts.

8. Type the number of minutes to dial again for a redial.

9. To send faxes at a specific time when discount phone charges apply, specify a start and end time.

10. Click **OK**.

Change Receive Properties

1. Click the **Start** button, point to the **All Programs**, **Windows Fax and Scan**, and then click the **Fax** tab.

2. Click the **Tools** menu, and then click **Fax Settings**.

3. Click the **General** tab.

4. Select the **Allow the device to receive fax calls** check box.

5. Click the **Manually answer** or **Automatically answer after X rings** option.

6. Click **More options**.

7. If you want, select the **Print a copy to** check box, and then select a printer.

8. If you want, select the **Save a Copy to** check box, and then select a folder.

9. Click **OK**.

10. Click **OK**.

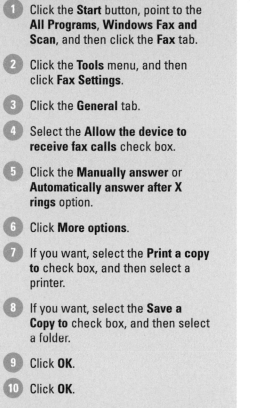

Changing Fax Options

As you send and receive faxes, you can have fax track and notify you when events take place. For example, you can show a progress indicator when faxes are incoming or outgoing and display notifications when faxes arrive. You can also set fax options to automatically open the Fax Monitor when a fax is being sent or received and archive faxes for backup purposes.

Change Tracking Options

1. Click the **Start** button, point to the **All Programs**, **Windows Fax and Scan**, and then click the **Fax** tab.

2. Click the **Tools** menu, and then click **Fax Settings**.

3. Click the **Tracking** tab.

4. Select the check boxes in the Notifications you want.

5. Select the check boxes for the Fax Monitor you want.

6. Click **OK**.

Change Archive Options

1. Click the **Start** button, point to the **All Programs**, **Windows Fax and Scan**, and then click the **Fax** tab.

2. Click the **Tools** menu, and then click **Fax Settings**.

3. Click the **Advanced** tab.

4. Click **Move Folder**, select a folder, and then click **OK**.

5. Click **OK**.

Maintaining Your Computer

Introduction

Windows Vista offers a number of useful tools for managing such routine tasks as installing and removing programs, and formatting, copying, and repairing disks. Windows also provides tools to find and fix disk problems, speed up disk access, and clean up disk space. By periodically finding and repairing disk errors, you can keep your files in good working condition and prevent disk problems that might cause you to lose your work. You can also schedule these tasks to run on a regular basis. If you find Windows performing sluggishly even after performing routine maintenance, you can adjust system processing and memory settings to improve performance.

Keeping your computer up-to-date is another way to keep your computer in good working condition and protect it against new and ongoing attacks over the Internet. Windows Update scans your computer for any software components or fixes (including security and high priority updates) that need to be installed and automatically or manually downloads them from the Internet. Each file that you download using Windows Update has a digital signature from Microsoft to ensure it's authenticity and security. If problems do occur, you can undo harmful changes to your computer and restore its settings, or you can use one of several startup options to help you start Windows in a safe environment with basic files and drivers where you can restore settings and fix the problems.

Understanding Disk File Systems

A disk must be formatted with a **file system** that allows it to work with the operating system to store, manage, and access data. Two of the most common file systems are FAT (or FAT32, which is an improvement on FAT technology) and NTFS. Disks on DOS, Windows 3.1, or Windows 98/Me computers use the FAT file system, while disks on computers running Windows NT 4.0, Windows 2000, Windows XP and later can use either the NTFS or FAT system. NTFS is a newer file system that improves on some of the shortcomings of FAT disks that make them less desirable on a network. NTFS is the preferred file system for Windows Vista.

There are important differences between FAT and NTFS file systems:

FAT

When you format a disk with the FAT file system, a formatting program divides the disk into storage compartments. First it creates a series of rings, called **tracks**, around the circumference of the disk. Then it divides the tracks into equal parts, like pieces of a pie, to form sectors. The number of sectors and tracks depends on the size of the disk.

Although the physical surface of a disk is made of tracks and sectors, a file is stored in clusters. A cluster, also called an **allocation unit**, is one or more sectors of storage space. It represents the minimum amount of space that an operating system reserves when saving the contents of a file to a disk. Thus, a file might be stored in more than one cluster.

Each cluster is identified by a unique number. The first two clusters are reserved by the operating system. The operating system maintains a file allocation table (or FAT) on each disk that lists the clusters on the disk and records the status of each cluster, whether it is occupied (and by which file), available, or defective. Each cluster in a file "remembers" its order in the chain of clusters—and each cluster points to the next one until the last cluster, which marks the end of the file. The FAT and FAT32 formats provide compatibility with other operating systems on your computer, which means you can configure your computer for a dual-boot or multi-boot setup and you can backup a previous operating system.

NTFS

NTFS features a built-in security system that does not allow users to access the disk unless they have a user account and password with the necessary rights and permissions. NTFS protects disks from damage by automatically redirecting data from a bad sector to a good sector without requiring you to run a disk-checking utility. Given the reliability and the built-in repair mechanisms of NTFS disks, only rarely do they require maintenance. This is an example of **fault tolerance**, the ability of a disk to resist damage, which is a critical issue with disks on a network computer.

Selecting a file system

NTFS does not support floppy disks, so all floppies are formatted with FAT. If you are running Windows on a stand-alone computer, you can choose either FAT or NTFS, but in most cases, the file system has already been determined either by the person who originally set up the computer or by the manufacturer from whom you purchased the computer. If your computer is a client on a Windows network, it is likely that your hard

disk uses NTFS. Because NTFS is more suited to network demands, such as a high level of security and resistance to system failure, network administrators format network disks with NTFS whenever possible. Sometimes, however, users on a network want or need to use a non-Windows operating system. Also, a user might need a computer that is capable of running Windows XP. The disks on that computer would then be formatted with FAT.

NTFS disk drive

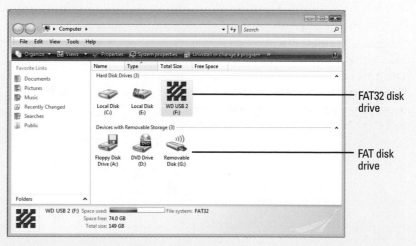

FAT32 disk drive

FAT disk drive

Formatting a Disk

Formatting a disk—including hard disks, USB flash drives and flash memory cards—prepares it so that you can store information on it. Formatting removes all information from the disk, so you should never format a disk that has files you want to keep. When you format a disk, you need to specify the certain settings; Windows has default settings recommended. Capacity is how much data the disk or partition can hold, such as the physical size, storage size, and sector size. A file system is the overall structure in which files are named, stored, and organized. NTFS and FAT32 are types of file systems. Disk allocation unit size, or cluster size, is a group of sectors on a disk. The operating system assigns a unique number to each cluster, and then keeps track of files according to which clusters they use. If your hard disk uses the FAT or FAT32 file system, you can convert it to the NTFS format.

Format a Disk

1. With a disk in the drive, click the **Start** button, and then click **Computer**.

2. Right-click the drive, and then click **Format**.

3. Specify the capacity, file system, and allocation unit size.

4. Select the **Quick Format** check box to perform a quick format, or clear the **Quick Format** check box to perform a full format and disk scan for bad sectors.

5. To use a disk to start up your computer and run MS-DOS, select the **Create an MS-DOS startup disk** check box.

6. Click **Start**, click **OK** to format the disk, and then click **OK** when it's done.

7. Click **Close**.

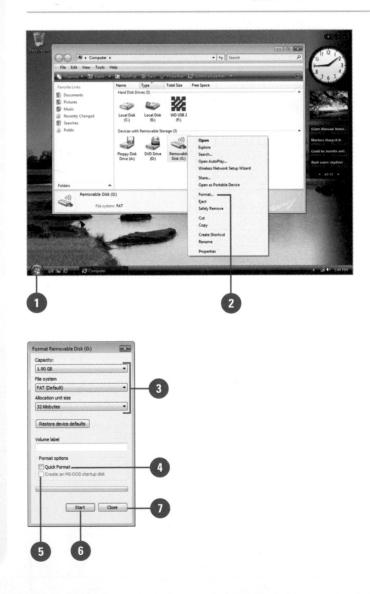

Convert a Disk

1. Click the **Start** button, point to **All Programs**, click **Accessories**, and then click **Command Prompt**.

2. Type **convert** *drive* **: /fs:ntfs /v**, and then press Enter.

   Where *drive* is the drive letter of the drive you wanted converted to NTFS.

3. If you upgraded your computer, type **Y**, and then press Enter to delete the backup, or type **N**, and then press Enter to cancel the procedure.

4. If you're asked to force a dismount, type **N**, and then press Enter.

5. If you need to restart the system to complete the conversion, type **Y**, and then press Enter.

6. Click the **Close** button.

7. Click the **Start** button, point to the Arrow, and then click **Shut Down**, and then wait for the computer to restart and convert the drive.

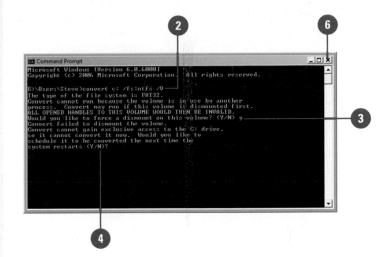

Did You Know?

You can check the format of a disk.
Click the Start button, click Computer, click the disk you want to check, and then check the Details pane.

See Also

See "Detecting and Repairing Disk Errors" on page 433 for information on bad sectors.

Displaying Disk and Folder Information

As you work with files, folders, and programs, you should know the size of the disk and how much space remains available. A disk can store only a limited amount of data. Hard disks can store large amounts of data (in gigabytes), while removable disks, such as a USB flash drive or flash memory card, store smaller amounts. You can use the Properties command on a disk to display the disk size or the amount of used and free space, and to change a disk label, which is a name you can assign to a hard or removable disk. Besides checking hard disk drive or floppy disk information, you can also use the Properties command on a folder to find out the size of its contents. This can be helpful when you want to copy or move a folder to a removable disk or CD/DVD.

Determine Free Space on a Disk

1. With a disk in the drive, click the **Start** button, and then click **Computer**.

2. Click the drive, and then click the **Properties** button on the toolbar.

3. Right-click the drive, and then click **Properties**.

4. On the **General** tab, identify the amount of free space on the disk.

5. Click **OK**.

Used and free disk space

Did You Know?

You can display basic system information. Click the Start button, click Control Panel, double-click the System icon in Classic view. The basic information about your computer includes system rating, processor, memory (RAM), system type, network information, and Windows activation.

You can access and display system information from the Welcome Center. Click the Start button, point to All Programs, click Accessories, click Welcome Center, and then click View computer details. You can click Show more details to access System properties in the Control Panel.

For Your Information

Understanding File Sizes

When you create a file, it takes up space on a disk. Files with text are smaller than files with graphics. The size of a file is measured in bytes. A byte is a unit of storage capable of holding a single character or pixel. It's the base measurement for all other incremental units, which are kilobyte, megabyte, and gigabyte. A kilobyte (KB) is 1,024 bytes of information while a megabyte (MB) is 1,048,576 bytes, which is equal to 1,024 kilobytes. A gigabyte (GB) is equal to 1,024 megabytes.

Transferring Files Using a Disk

You can copy files from your computer to a disk if you need to either transfer files from one stand-alone computer to another. You can also save a copy of important files to prevent losing them in the event of a power failure or a computer problem.

Copy Files to a Disk

1. With the disk in the drive, click the **Start** button, and then click **Computer**.

2. Open the folder, and then select the files you want to copy.

3. Right-click the selected files, and then point to **Send To**.

4. Click a disk from the submenu.

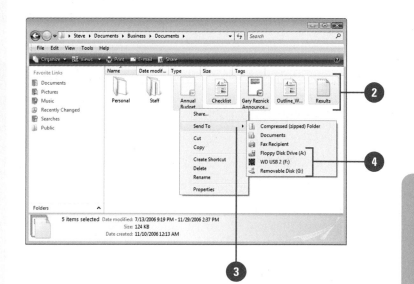

Copy Files from a Disk

1. With the disk in the drive, click the **Start** button, and then click **Computer**.

2. Open the disk window, and then select the files you want to copy.

3. Drag the selected files to copy the selected items.

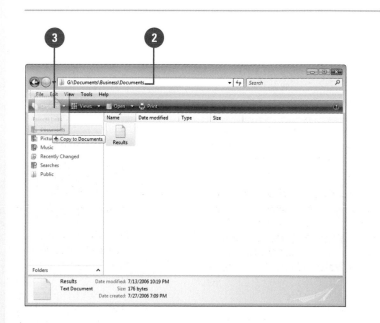

Setting Disk Quotas for Users

If you are using a computer with multiple users, you can set up disk quotas, so a single user cannot fill the entire disk. Disk quotas (**New!**) are not enabled by default, so you need to turn this feature on before you can use it. You can enable and set different disk quotas for individual users. If a user exceeds the quota, you can specify whether to allow or deny disk space. If you're not sure what to set, you can create quota logs to monitor disk usage and then decide what you want to do.

Set Disk Quotas

1. Click the **Start** button, and then click **Computer**.

2. Right-click a hard disk drive, and then click **Properties**.

3. Click the **Quota** tab.

4. Click **Show Quota Settings**.

5. Select the **Enable quota management** check box.

6. Select the **Deny disk space to users exceeding quota limit** check box.

7. Click the **Do not limit disk usage** option or click the **Limit disk space to** option and specify the disk space limit.

8. Select either of the log event check boxes to create a record of disk usage.

9. To set specific limits for individual users, click **Quota Entries**.

   ◆ In the Quota Entries window, click the **Quota** menu, click **New Quota Entry**, and then select a user and fill in property information.

10. Click **OK**.

11. Click **OK**.

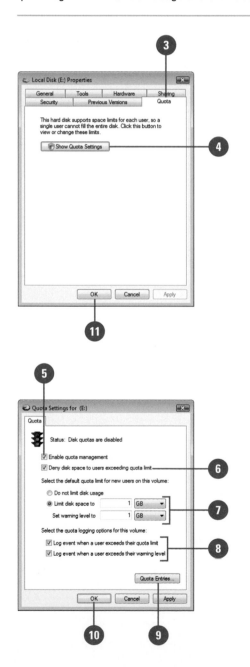

Detecting and Repairing Disk Errors

Microsoft
Certified
Application
Specialist   WINV-3.2.3

Sometimes an unexpected power loss or program error can create inaccessible file segments that take up space on a disk. The Check Disk program that comes with Windows helps you find and repair damaged sections of a disk. Check Disk can also be used to find physical disk errors or **bad sectors**. The program doesn't physically repair your media, but it moves data away from any bad sectors it finds. To keep your hard disk drive working properly, you should run Check Disk from time to time. When you run Check Disk, all files must be closed for the process to run. While the Check Disk process is running, your hard disk will not be available to perform any other task.

Check a Disk for Errors

1 Click the **Start** button, and then click **Computer**.

2 Right-click the disk you want to check, and then click **Properties**.

3 Click the **Tools** tab.

4 Click **Check Now**.

5 Select the **Automatically fix file system errors** check box, and then select the **Scan for and attempt recovery of bad sectors** check box.

6 Click **Start**.

7 When it's done, click **OK**.

8 Click **OK**.

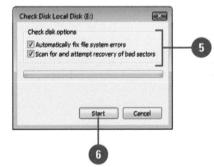

> **Did You Know?**
>
> **You should run Check Disk before the Disk Defragmenter.** For best results, run Check Disk to check for errors on your disk before you start the disk defragmentation process.

Optimizing a Disk

Microsoft Certified Application Specialist   WINV-7.1.2

When you delete files from a disk, you create empty spaces that might be fragmented over different areas of the disk. When you create a new file on a fragmented disk, parts of the file are stored in these empty spaces, resulting in a single file that is broken into many parts, which takes longer to retrieve or store when you open or save the file. A file broken up in this way is called a **fragmented file**, which is undetectable to the user. You can use Disk Defragmenter to place all of the parts of a file in one **contiguous**, or adjacent, location. This procedure, which efficiently arranges all of the files and unused space, is called **optimization**. Optimization makes your programs run faster and your files open more quickly. You can also set of schedule (**New!**) to run Disk Defragmenter on a regular basis. While the Disk Defragmenter works, you can use your computer to carry out other tasks; however, your computer will operate more slowly, so it's best to wait.

Defragment a Disk

1. Click the **Start** button, point to **All Programs**, click **Accessories**, click **System Tools**, and then click **Disk Defragmenter**.

2. Click **Defragment now**.

3. To stop the process, click **Cancel Defragment**.

4. Click **OK**.

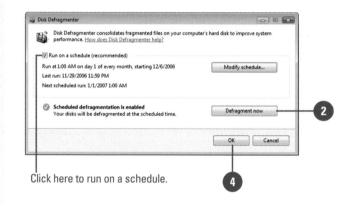

Click here to run on a schedule.

Schedule a Disk Defragment

1. Click the **Start** button, point to **All Programs**, click **Accessories**, click **System Tools**, and then click **Disk Defragmenter**.

2. Select the **Run on a schedule (recommended)** check box.

3. Click **Modify schedule**.

4. Click the list arrows, and then specify how often, what day, and what time.

5. Click **OK**.

6. Click **OK**.

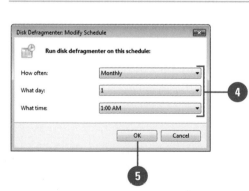

Cleaning Up a Disk

Cleaning up a disk involves removing unneeded files to make room for other files on your computer, which can be difficult if you don't know the significance of each file. You can use a Windows program called Disk Cleanup to clean up your hard disk drive safely and effectively. Disk Cleanup searches your drive, then lists temporary files, Internet cache files, the Recycle Bin, and unnecessary program files that you can safely delete. Disk Cleanup also gives you the option to remove Windows components and installed programs that you no longer use. You can select the types of files you want Disk Cleanup to delete. Before you select and delete files, make sure you will not need them in the future. If you have multiple users on your computer, you can specify whether to clean up only your files or all the files on the computer (**New!**).

Clean Up a Disk

1. Click the **Start** button, point to **All Programs**, click **Accessories**, click **System Tools**, and then click **Disk Cleanup**.

2. Click **My files only** or **Files from all users on this computer**.

3. If necessary, click the **Drives** list arrow, select a disk, and then click **OK**.

    Wait while Disk Cleanup calculates how much space it can free up.

4. Select the check boxes for the folders and files you want to delete.

5. To view the contents of a folder, click **View Files**, and then click the Close button.

6. Click **OK**, and then click **Yes**.

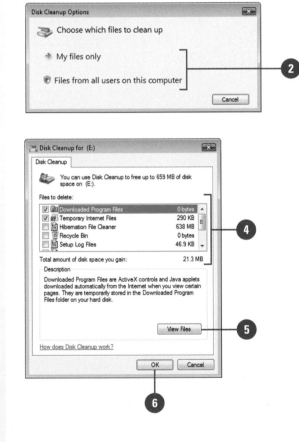

Scheduling Tasks

Task Scheduler is a program that enables you to schedule tasks, to run regularly, such as Disk Cleanup, at a time convenient for you. Task Scheduler starts each time you start Windows. With Task Scheduler, you can schedule a task to run daily, weekly, monthly, or at certain times (such as when the computer starts or idles), change the schedule for or turn off an existing task, or customize how a task runs at its scheduled time. You can create a basic task using the Create Basic Task wizard or a more complex task using the Create Task dialog box (**New!**). Before you schedule a task, be sure that the system date and time on your computer are accurate, as Task Scheduler relies on this information to run.

Scheduled a Basic Task

1. Click the **Start** button, point to **All Programs**, click **Accessories**, click **System Tools**, and then click **Task Scheduler**.

2. In the Actions pane, click **Create Basic Task**.

3. Type a name and description for the scheduled task, and then click **Next** to continue.

4. Click a scheduled task time interval option, and then click **Next** to continue.

5. Specify a start time and a recurring interval, and then click **Next** to continue.

6. Select an action option, and then click **Next** to continue.

7. Specify the information or options related with the selected action, and then click **Next** to continue.

8. Click **Finish**.

9. To run, end, disable, or delete a task, click the **Task Scheduler Library**, select the task in the console window, and then click the command you want at the bottom of the Actions pane. To edit a task, select it, and then make changes at the bottom of the console window.

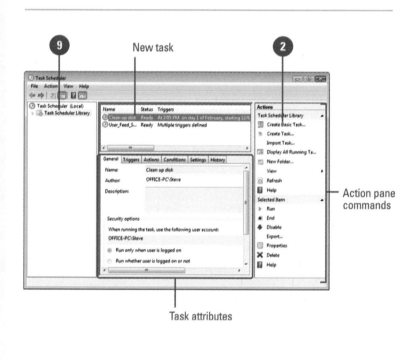

New task

Action pane commands

Task attributes

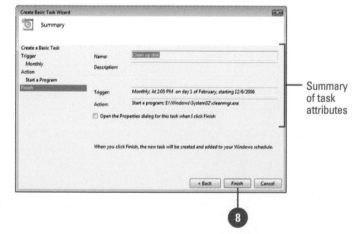

Summary of task attributes

Adding or Removing Windows Components

Windows Vista comes with a collection of components, such as Internet Explorer, Windows Mail, Windows Media Player, or Windows Messenger, you can use to get work done and have fun on your computer. When you install Windows Vista, not all the components on the installation disc are installed on your computer. You can use the the Programs and Features utility (**New!**) in the Control Panel to install additional components. When you install a new program on your computer, the Start menu highlights the menus you need to click to start the program. If you are no longer using a Windows component, you can remove it to save disk space.

Add or Remove a Windows Component

1. Click the **Start** button, and then click **Control Panel**.

2. Double-click the **Programs and Features** icon in Classic view.

3. In the left pane, click **Turn Windows features on or off**.

4. Click the plus sign (+) to expand a category or click the minus sign (-) to collapse a category.

   A blue check box indicates that only some of the items in a component group are installed.

5. Select a check box to add the item, or clear a check box to remove an item.

6. When you're done, click **OK**.

7. If prompted, insert the Windows Vista DVD into the drive.

8. Click OK if prompted to restart your computer.

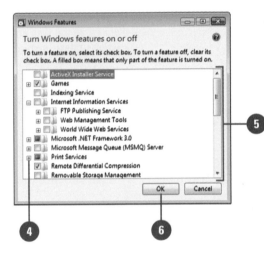

Installing or Uninstalling a Program

WINV-3.1.2, WINV-3.1.3,
WINV-7.5.2

Windows comes with a collection of accessory programs with simple functionality. If you need more functionality, software programs are available for purchase. Before you can use a software program, you need to install it using a separate installer program. Most software programs come with their own installation program, which copies the program files to different places on your computer, some in a program folder and others in the Windows folder. When you install a new program on your computer, the Start menu highlights the menus you need to click to start the program. If you no longer use a program or a Windows update, you can remove it from your computer, which saves hard disk space. The Programs and Features utility (**New!**) in the Control Panel provides a faster display and shows you all the programs and/or software updates installed on your computer. Windows keeps track of all the files you install, so you should uninstall a program or system update, instead of deleting folders and files to remove it.

Install a Software Program

1. Close all running programs, and then insert the program installation disc into the drive.

   If the disc starts, the AutoPlay dialog box opens. Start the setup and follow the instructions provided to install the software.

   IMPORTANT *Only users with administrator privileges can add or remove programs.*

2. If the disc doesn't start or you're installing from a network or different drive, click the **Start** button, and then click **Computer**.

3. Double-click the CD or DVD icon with the installation set up.

4. Double-click the set up file, and then follow the installation instructions.

Start of installation

Uninstall, Change, or Repair a Software Program

1 Click the **Start** button, and then click **Control Panel.**

2 Double-click the **Programs and Features** icon in Classic view.

3 In the left pane, click **View installed updates** or **Uninstall a program** to display the software you want.

4 Click the program you want to uninstall or change.

5 Click the **Uninstall, Change,** or **Repair** button on the toolbar; availability varies depending on the program.

6 If prompted, click **Yes** to confirm the removal. If an uninstall program starts, follow the instructions.

7 When it's done, click **OK,** and then click the **Close** button.

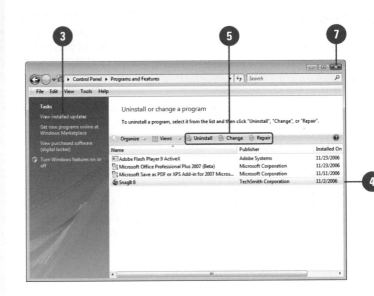

Did You Know?

You can turn the Start menu highlight off. Right-click the Start button, click Properties, click Customize, clear the Highlight newly installed programs check box, and then click OK twice.

See Also

If you encounter a problem after removing a Windows update or component, see "Restoring Computer Settings" on page 444 for information on restoring Windows to a previous state using the System Restore Wizard.

Updating Windows

Microsoft
Certified
Application
Specialist

WINV-1.3.2, WINV-1.3.3,
WINV-3.1.4, WINV-3.3.2

Microsoft continues to improve Windows Vista with new features or security fixes, known as updates. Windows Update allows you to keep your computer up-to-date with the latest system software and security updates over the Internet. You can choose to have Windows regularly check for critical updates and download them in the background (which doesn't interfere with other downloads), or you can manually select the ones you want to install using the Windows Update Web site. Automatic updates occur at scheduled times or by notification acceptance. If you're busy, you can ignore/hide the update to install it later. The Windows Update Web site displays express (only high priority) and custom (high priority, software, and hardware) installation update options. High priority updates are critical for your system to run properly, while software and hardware updates are optional. Windows Update confidentially scans your computer for updates that need to be installed.

Update Windows Automatically

1. Click the **Start** button, point to **All Programs**, and then click **Windows Update**.

2. In the left pane, click **Change settings**.

   IMPORTANT *If you're part of a network, options are grayed out.*

3. Click the automatic update option you want to use:

   ◆ Install updates automatically (recommended), then specify a time.

   ◆ Download updates, but let me choose whether to install them.

   ◆ Check for updates but let me choose whether to download and install them.

   ◆ Never check for updates (not recommended).

4. Click **OK**, and then click **Close** button.

5. If a Windows Update icon appears in the notification area, click the alert or icon, and then follow any instructions as needed.

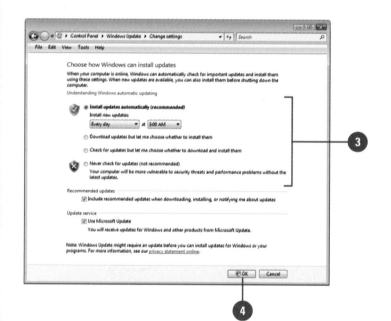

Update Windows Manually

1. Click the **Start** button, point to **All Programs**, and then click **Windows Update**.

2. Click **Check for updates**.

3. If necessary, click the **Install** button.

4. Wait for the updates to be downloaded from the Web and installed on your computer.

5. If prompted, click **OK** to restart your computer.

6. Click the **Close** button.

Can click here too.

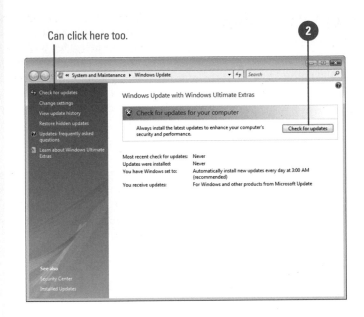

Did You Know?

You can View update history. Click the Start button, point to All Programs, click Windows Update, and then click View update history in the left pane to view the installed updates. When you're done, click OK, and then click the Close button.

You can install updates when not available or resume after an interruption. If your computer is turned off or in hibernate or standby mode during a scheduled update, updates are installed the next time you start your computer. If you lose an Internet connection during a download, Windows Update resumes where it left off.

Improving Computer Performance

Microsoft Certified Application Specialist WINV-7.3.5

The Performance Information and Tools utility (**New!**) in the Control Panel provides a central location for you to determine the performance of your computer, print out a report, and access tools to increase performance. The utility analyzes your computer and provides a rating score for the critical components on your computer, which include processor, memory (RAM), graphics, gaming graphics, and primary hard disk. To help you improve performance, you can access performance related tools in the Navigation pane.

Optimize Computer Performance

1. Click the **Start** button, and then click **Control Panel**.

2. Double-click the **Performance Information and Tools** icon in Classic view.

3. Click **Update my score** to the latest information.

4. To view and print details, click **View and print details**, click **Print this page**, click **Print**, and then click the **Close** button.

5. In the left pane, click links to performance improvement tools:

   ◆ **Manage startup programs.** Remove or disable unnecessary startup programs.

   ◆ **Adjust visual effects.** Set to Adjust for best performance option.

   ◆ **Adjust indexing options.** Reduce the number of folder to index.

   ◆ **Adjust power settings.** Set to use Balanced power plan.

   ◆ **Open Disk Cleanup.** Delete unnecessary or temporary files.

   ◆ **Advanced tools.** Displays additional tools, including Disk Defragmenter and ReadyBoost.

6. When you're done, click the **Close** button.

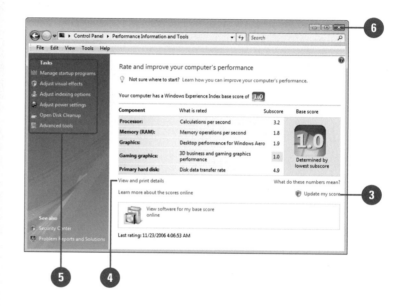

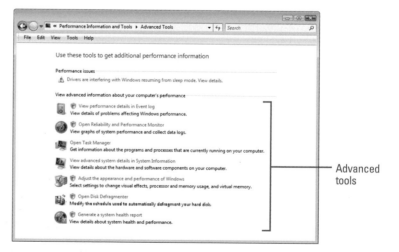

Advanced tools

Boosting Speed with Removable Media

WINV-7.1.1,
WINV-7.3.2

You can use Windows ReadyBoost (**New!**) to speed up your computer by using disk space on certain removable media devices, such as USB flash drives. When you insert a compatible removable media device (one that uses fast flash memory), the AutoPlay dialog box opens and provides the option to use Windows ReadyBoost. Before you can use it, you need to turn it on and specify the amount of space you want to allocate. Windows provides a recommended space amount. In general, ReadyBoost recommends one to three times the amount of random access memory (RAM) installed on your computer for the best performance results.

Use Windows ReadyBoost

1. With removable media in the drive, click the **Start** button, and then click **Computer**.

2. Click the drive, and then click the **Properties** button on the toolbar.

3. Click the **ReadyBoost** tab.

4. Click the **Use this device** option.

5. If you want, drag the slider to specify the space to reserve for system speed.

6. Click **OK**.

7. To use ReadyBoost, remove the device, re-insert it, and then use the AutoPlay dialog box to start it.

For Your Information

Changing the Size of Virtual Memory

If you are running out of virtual memory (using hard disk space as RAM), you can increase the minimum size of the paging file (**a virtual memory**). The Initial size is set to installed RAM plus 300 MB and the Maximum size is set to 3 times installed RAM. To increase the size, double-click the System icon in the Control Panel, click Advanced system settings in the left pane, click the Advanced tab, click Settings (under Performance), clear the Automatically manage paging file size for all drives check box, click the drive you want, click Custom size, type a new size in the Initial or Maximum size, click Set, and then click OK.

Restoring Computer Settings

Windows Vista is a reliable operating system, but any time you make changes to your computer, such as adding or removing software and hardware, you run the risk of causing problems with your operating system. To alleviate potential problems, you can use System Restore, a program installed with Windows Vista, to undo harmful changes to your computer and restore its settings. System Restore returns your computer system, but not your personal files, to an earlier time, before the changes were made to your computer, called a **restore point**. As you work with your computer, System Restore monitors your changes and creates restore points on a daily basis or at important system events, but you can also create your own restore point at any time. If you have recently performed a system restoration, you can use System Restore to undo your most recent restoration. System Restore is turned on by default when you install Windows Vista, but you can turn it off or change System Restore options. However, you need at least 300 MB of free space on each hard disk.

Set System Protection

1. Click the **Start** button, and click the **Control Panel**.

2. Double-click the **System** icon in Classic view.

3. In the left pane, click the **System Protection**.

4. Select the check box next to the disk you want to protect and restore.

5. Click **OK**.

6. Click the **Close** button.

Did You Know?

You can start System Restore from a command prompt. At the command prompt, type **rstrui.exe**, and then press Enter.

Restore the System

1. Close all programs and make sure no one else is logged on to the computer.

2. Click the **Start** button, point to **All Programs**, click **Accessories**, click **System Tools**, and then click **System Restore**.

3. Click the **Recommended restore** or **Choose a different restore point** option.

4. Click **Next** to continue.

5. If you are choosing a restore point, select it, and then click **Next** to continue.

6. Review the restore point information, and then click **Finish**.

7. Wait for the system to be restored, and log on when prompted.

8. When it's done, click **OK**, and then click the **Close** button.

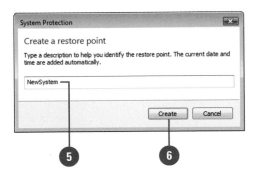

Create a Restore Point

1. Click the **Start** button, and click the **Control Panel**.

2. Double-click the **System** icon in Classic view.

3. In the left pane, click the **System Protection**.

4. Click **Create**.

5. Type a restore point name.

6. Click **Create**.

7. When it's done, click **OK**, and then click the **Close** button.

Using Previous Versions

Previous versions (**New!**) are shadow copies of files and folders that you back up using the Back Up Files wizard or Windows automatically saves as part of a restore point. You can use previous versions of files to restore files that become damaged or you accidentally modify or delete. If System Protection is turned on, Windows automatically creates shadow copies of files—except Windows system files—that have been modified since the last restore point was made. You can restore individual files or complete folders. When you restore a file or folder, the current file or folder is replace by the restored one. It's important to realize that you cannot undo a restore.

Restore a File or Folder Using Previous Versions

① Open the folder with the file or folder you want restore.

② Right-click it, and then click **Restore previous version**.

③ Click an item in the list.

IMPORTANT *You cannot undo a file or folder previous version restore.*

④ Click **Restore**.

If the Restore button is not available, you cannot restore a previous version of the file or folder.

⑤ Click **OK**.

See Also

See "Restoring Computer Settings" on page 444 for information on turning on System Protection.

Starting Windows When Problems Occur

If you have a problem starting Windows, you can use one of several startup options to help you start Windows in a safe environment where you can restore settings and fix the problem. Safe Mode is a good place to start. If a problem does not occur when you start in Safe Mode, you can eliminate basic Windows files and drivers as possible causes of the problem. If you added a device or changed driver, you can use Safe Mode to remove the device or restore the changed driver. You can also use Choosing Last Known Good Configuration to restore settings saved when your computer was last shut down properly.

Start Windows When Problems Occur

1. Restart your computer.

2. As your computer boots, press and hold F8.

3. Use the arrow keys to select a startup option, and then press Enter.

4. If you have a dual-boot system, select the operating system you want, and then press Enter.

5. Restore any recent system changes, or remove any newly installed software that might be causing the problem.

6. Shutdown your computer.

7. Start your computer to see if it works properly.

8. If problems persist, try a different startup option, or seek assistance from a support technician.

Did You Know?

You can use Startup Repair to fix Windows Vista problems. Restart your computer with the Windows installation disc in the drive, click Repair your computer, select your operating system, click Next, click Startup Repair, and then follow the on-screen instructions.

Computer Startup Options	
Option	**Description**
Safe Mode	Starts with basic files and drivers and without a network connection
Safe Mode With Networking	Starts with basic files and drivers and a network connection
Safe Mode With Command Prompt	Starts with basic files and drivers and without a network connection to the command prompt
Enable Boot Logging	Starts and logs startup information in the *ntbtlog.txt* file
Enable VGA Mode	Starts using the basic VGA driver
Last Known Good Configuration	Starts using Registry settings saved at the last properly done shutdown
Directory Services Restore Mode	Restores active directory services
Debugging Mode	Starts and sends debugging information to another computer using a serial cable
Start Windows Normally	Starts the computer normally
Reboot	Restarts the computer
Return To OS Choices Menu	Displays operating system selection screen

Setting Startup and Recovery Options

If you installed more than one operating system on your computer (known as a **dual-boot**), such as Windows XP and Windows Vista, you can select the default operating system you want to use when you start up your computer. You can also specify how much time to display the list of operating systems for a dual boot before the default starts. If you have problems starting Windows, you can set options to instruct Windows what to do. You can set options to automatically restart and create a system log of events to track where the problem occurs.

Set Windows Startup and Recovery Options

1. Click the **Start** button, and then click **Control Panel**.

2. Double-click the **System** icon in Classic view.

3. In the left pane, click **Advanced system settings**.

4. Click **Settings** (under Startup And Recovery).

5. Click the **Default operating system** list arrow, and then select the operating system you want to start as default.

6. Select the system startup check boxes you want to use and specify the time you want to wait to select the operating system or recovery options.

7. Select the system failure check boxes you want to use.

8. Click **OK**.

9. Click **OK**.

10. Click the **Close** button.

Managing Hardware

Introduction

A **hardware device** is any physical device that you plug into and is controlled by your computer. This device can be a network or modem card that you install inside your computer. It can be a printer or a scanner that you plug into the outside of the computer. When you plug or insert a hardware device into the appropriate port or expansion slot, Windows attempts to recognize the device and configure it for you using plug-and-play technology. Plug-and-play automatically tells the device drivers (software that operates the hardware and comes with Windows Vista) where to find the hardware device. After a hardware device is installed, you can change settings and options to customize the way the device works. Plug-and-play technology will recognize most any kind of hardware device, such as a mouse, modem, keyboard, game controller, laptop battery, or secondary monitor just to name a few.

All hardware devices can be managed or removed from the Control Panel. Most hardware devices are managed under the Device Manager, but some have their own program for managing them (for example, Game Controller is located in the Control Panel).

Understanding Plug and Play Hardware

Windows includes **plug and play** support for hardware, making it easy to install and uninstall devices quickly. With plug and play support, you simply plug the device in, and Windows sets the device to work with your existing hardware and resolves any system conflicts. When you install a hardware device, Windows installs related software, known as a **driver**, that allows the hardware to communicate with Windows and other software applications. Plug and play tells the device drivers where to find the hardware devices. Plug and play matches up physical hardware devices with the software device drivers that operate them and establish channels of communication between each physical device and its driver. With plug and play, you can be confident that any new device will work properly with your computer and that your computer will restart correctly after you install or uninstall hardware. Microsoft recommends that you use only device drivers with the Designed for Microsoft Windows Vista logo, which have a digital signature from Microsoft, indicating that the product was tested for compatibility with Windows Vista. You might need to be logged on as an administrator or a member of the Administrators group in order to install a hardware device. In order to install a plug and play device, you need to do the following:

1) Gather your original Windows Vista installation disc, the hardware device that you want to install, and the discs that come with the device, if available.

2) Turn off your computer before you physically install a hardware device, such as a network card or a sound card, inside your computer. To install a hardware device that plugs into the outside of your computer, such as a scanner, printer or other USB (universal serial bus) device, you can plug it in without turning off your computer. If your USB device uses a power cord, you need to connect the device to the power cord and turn it on before you connect the USB device to your computer.

3) Follow the manufacturer's instructions to plug the new device into your computer.

4) Turn on your computer, or start the Add Hardware utility program in the Control Panel. Windows tries to detect the new device and install the device drivers. If Windows doesn't recognize the new hardware device, the device might not be plug and play compatible or installed correctly. Turn off your computer, check the device documentation and installation carefully, and then turn on your computer again. If the device driver is not available on your computer, Windows asks you to insert into the appropriate drive the Windows Vista installation disc or the disc that comes with the device from the manufacturer. After the driver software is installed, you can disconnect and reconnect the device without taking any further action.

5) Follow the instructions on the screen until a message indicates that you are finished. Windows notifies all other devices of the new device so there are no conflicts and manages the power requirements of your hardware and peripherals by shutting them down or conserving power when you are not using them. If you are working in another program when you install or uninstall a device, plug and play lets you know that it is about to change your computer configuration and warns you to save your work.

6) Use the Safely Remove Hardware Icon in the notification area to safely unplug or eject plug and play hardware. The Safely Remove Hardware dialog box helps you stop the device, so it's safe to remove.

Plug and play finds new hardware

Found New Hardware

Windows needs to install driver software for your Unknown Device

The Found New Hardware Wizard installs the new hardware

Locate and install driver software (recommended)
Windows will guide you through the process of installing driver software for your device.

Ask me again later
Windows will ask again the next time you plug in your device or log on.

Don't show this message again for this device
Your device will not function until you install driver software.

Cancel

Safely removes hardware

Safely Remove Hardware icon

Installing Hardware Devices

Before you install a new hardware device, be sure to carefully read the product installation guide provided by the manufacturer. If the hardware device comes with an installation disc, it is recommended that you use the manufacturer's disc and related instructions to install the hardware. If the product documentation instructs you to perform a typical plug and play installation, turn off your computer, physically connect your hardware to your computer, and then turn on your computer again. In most cases, Windows detects your new hardware device and installs it or starts the Add Hardware Wizard. The Add Hardware Wizard installs hardware devices by asking you a series of questions to set up the necessary software for the new hardware device. If Windows doesn't detect the new hardware, you can start the Add Hardware Wizard in the Control Panel and select the new hardware device to install it. You might need to be logged on as an administrator in order to install a hardware device.

Install a Hardware Device Using the Add Hardware Wizard

1. Click the **Start** button, and then click **Control Panel**.

2. Double-click the **Add Hardware** icon in Classic view, and then click **Next** to continue.

3. Click the **Search for and install the hardware automatically (Recommended)** or **Install the hardware that I manually select from a list (advanced)** option, and then click **Next** to continue.

4. If necessary, select a hardware category or **Show All Devices**, and the click **Next** to continue.

5. Click the manufacturer and model, or click **Have Disk** to locate files, and then click **Next** to continue.

6. Type or use the name provided, and then click **Next** to continue.

7. Click **Finish**.

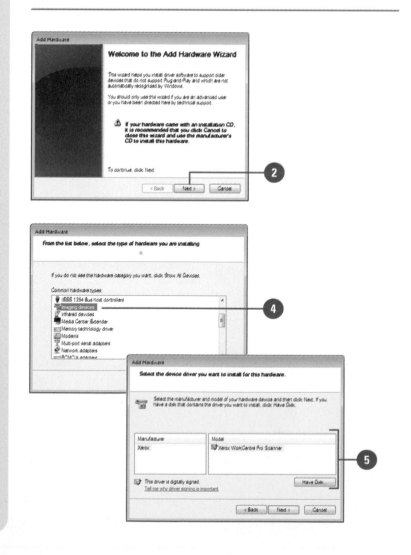

Viewing System Hardware

Microsoft
Certified
Application
Specialist

WINV-3.3.1, WINV-3.3.2,
WINV-3.3.3

When you install a new operating system, such as Windows Vista, it is important to make sure that you are using the latest software drivers with your system hardware. If you are not using the latest software drivers, your hardware devices might not work to full capacity. You can view your system hardware using a Windows utility called the Device Manager. Device Manager provides you with a list of the hardware types, also known as **hardware classes**, which are attached to your computer. With the Device Manager, you can determine the software driver versions being used with your system hardware, update the software driver with a newer version, roll back to a previous driver version if the device fails with the new one, or uninstall a driver. After viewing your software driver version numbers, you can contact the manufacturer or visit their web site to determine the latest versions. Most manufacturers allow you to download drivers from their web sites for free.

Use the Device Manager

1. Click the **Start** button, and then click **Control Panel**.

2. Double-click the **Device Manager** icon in Classic view.

3. Click the plus sign (+) next to the hardware category you want to expand.

4. Click the device you want to view.

5. Click the **Properties** button on the toolbar.

6. To work with drivers, click the Driver tab. You can any of the following buttons:

   ◆ **Driver Details**. View driver details.

   ◆ **Update Driver**. Update the driver.

   ◆ **Roll Back Driver**. Roll back to a previously installed driver.

   ◆ **Disable**. Disable the driver and the device.

   ◆ **Uninstall**. Remove the driver.

7. Click **OK**.

8. Click the **Close** button.

Viewing Hardware Settings

One reason you might want to view hardware settings is if you plan to install any legacy hardware. **Legacy hardware** is any device not designed for Windows Vista plug and play support. If you have a hardware device that is not designed for Windows Vista plug and play, it is important to find out current hardware resource settings to avoid conflicts during installation, such as having two devices with the same resource settings. Before you actually place a legacy hardware device in your computer, you should browse through the devices currently attached to your computer system and ensure that your computer has the available resources to install the hardware device. With the Device Manager, you can view the device resources that are being used with your system hardware and determine whether your computer has the available resources to install a legacy or plug and play hardware device. Generally, you cannot install non plug and play hardware without performing some manual setup with the Device Manager. Check with the hardware manufacturer for installation specifics.

View Hardware Settings

1. Click the **Start** button, and then click **Control Panel**.

2. Double-click the **Device Manager** icon in Classic view.

3. Click the plus sign (+) next to the resource category you want to expand.

4. Click the device you want to view.

5. Click the **Properties** button on the toolbar.

6. Use the tabs to view or modify device settings and resources.

7. Click **OK**.

8. Click the **Close** button.

No conflicts

Changing Windows Update Driver Settings

When you connect a new device to your computer, you can specify how you want Windows Update (**New!**) to find a software driver for the device. The default setting is to automatically check for a driver on your computer or online from the Microsoft Windows Update Web site. However, if you want more control over the process, you can change it to have Windows ask you each time you connect a new device before to check for drivers or never check for drivers. You can use System Properties to specify the option you want.

Change Windows Update Driver Settings

1. Click the **Start** button, and then click **Control Panel**.

2. Double-click the **System** icon in Classic view.

3. In the left pane, click **Advanced system settings**.

4. Click the **Hardware** tab.

5. Click **Windows Update Driver Settings**.

6. Select the option you want to use.

7. Click **OK**.

8. Click **OK**.

9. Click the **Close** button.

Changing Mouse Settings

A mouse does not require adjustments after you plug it in and start Windows. However, you can use Mouse properties in the Control Panel to change the way your mouse works and the way the pointer looks and behaves. For the mouse, you can switch the role of the buttons, or you can change the double-clicking speed. For the mouse pointer, you can modify its appearance using a pointer scheme, increase or decrease its speed, improve its visibility with a pointer trail, or set it to be hidden when you are typing. If your button has a wheel, roll the wheel with your forefinger to move up or down in a document or on a web page.

Change Button Settings

1. Click the **Start** button, and then click **Control Panel**.

2. Double-click the **Mouse** icon in Classic view.

3. Click the **Buttons** tab.

4. To reverse the mouse buttons, select the **Switch primary and secondary buttons** check box.

5. To adjust the double-click speed, drag the slider.

6. Click **OK**.

Did You Know?

You can change the mouse wheel speed. In the Control Panel, double-click the Mouse icon, click the Wheel tab, click the following number of lines at a time option, type a number or click the One screen at a time option, and then click OK.

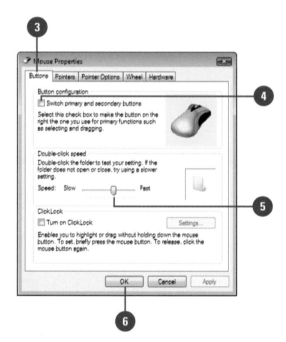

Change Pointer Appearance

① Click the **Start** button, and then click **Control Panel**.

② Double-click the **Mouse** icon in Classic view.

③ Click the **Pointers** tab.

④ Click the **Scheme** list arrow, and then select a pointer scheme.

⑤ Click **OK**.

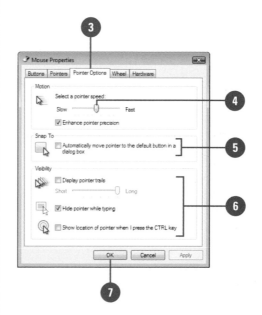

Change Pointer Options

① Click the **Start** button, and then click **Control Panel**.

② Double-click the **Mouse** icon in Classic view.

③ Click the **Pointer Options** tab.

④ To adjust the pointer speed, drag the **Motion** slider.

⑤ To snap the pointer to a button, select the **Automatically move pointer to the default button in a dialog box** check box.

⑥ To display a trail after the pointer, hide the pointer while you type, or show the pointer location, select the visibility check box you want.

⑦ Click **OK**.

Changing Keyboard Settings

While your keyboard should just work when you start up your computer, you can use Keyboard properties in the Control Panel to adjust the rate at which a character is repeated when you hold down a key, and the time delay before it starts repeating. You can also adjust the blink rate of the insertion point.

Change Keyboard Settings

1 Click the **Start** button, and then click **Control Panel**.

2 Double-click the **Keyboard** icon in Classic view.

3 Click the **Speed** tab.

4 To adjust the character repeat delay, drag the slider.

5 To adjust the character repeat rate, drag the slider.

6 Click **OK**.

See Also

See "Changing Language Options" on page 112 for information on changing languages and keyboard layouts.

3

Keyboard Properties

Speed | Hardware

Character repeat

Repeat delay:
Long ———————————— Short

Repeat rate:
Slow .... Fast

Click here and hold down a key to test repeat rate:

Cursor blink rate

None .... Fast

OK | Cancel | Apply

4

5

6

Changing Phone Dialing Options

When phone numbers or dialing settings to an Internet Service Provider or a network change, you need to update the phone dialing options your modem uses to make a dial-up connection. You can use Phone and Modem properties in the Control Panel to add, edit, and customize phone dialing options on your computer for one or more locations. For example, you can change country, region or area codes, disable call waiting, and set up a credit card number to pay for calls. You can also set access rules for dialing local, long distance, and international calls. If you no longer use a dialing location, you can remove it.

Change Phone Dialing Options

1 Click the **Start** button, and then click **Control Panel.**

2 Double-click the **Phone and Modem Options** icon in Classic view.

3 Click the **Dialing Rules** tab, and then click a dialing location.

4 Click **Edit**, and then click the **General** tab.

5 Change the country/region or area code.

6 Specify the dialing rules you want.

7 If you want, select the **To disable call waiting** check box.

8 To apply area code dialing rules, click the **Area Code Rules** tab, and then click **New** to create one.

9 To use a calling card, click the **Calling Card** tab, select a calling card option, or click **New** to create your own.

10 Click **OK.**

11 Click **OK.**

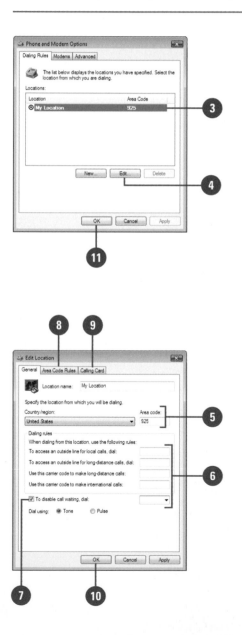

Changing Modem Options

A **modem** is a hardware device that allows two computers to transmit information over a phone line. A modem translates the binary information from the computer to an analog signal (known as modulation) that can pass over the phone line. At the receiving end, another modem translates the analog signal back to binary information (known as demodulation) that can be used by the computer. If you are having problems with your modem, you can test it. With the results of the test you can consult the modem documentation or a support technician to help you fix the problem. If requested, you can change data transmission settings, such as data bits, parity, stop bits, or modulation.

Change Modem Hardware Settings

1. Click the **Start** button, and then click **Control Panel.**

2. Double-click the **Phone and Modem Options** icon in Classic view.

3. Click the **Modems** tab.

4. Click the modem you want to change, and then click **Properties**.

5. Click the **Modem** tab.

6. Change the maximum port speed and speaker volume.

7. Click the **Advanced** tab, and then click **Change Default Preferences**.

8. Click the **Advanced** tab.

9. Change the setting for data bits, parity, stop bits, or modulation.

10. Click **OK**.

11. Click **OK**, and then click **OK** again.

Did You Know?

You can test a modem. In Phone and Modem Options, click the Modems tab, select a modem, click Properties, click the Diagnostics tab, and then click Query Modem, wait for and view the results, and then click OK twice.

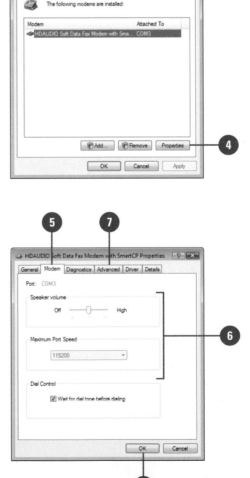

Managing Color

Color management is a system that makes sure the color you see on your display or printer is the color you want. Not all hardware displays color in the same way; each hardware device uses different characteristics, or methods, when rendering and processing color on a specific device. Even programs don't all render and process color the same way. Color Management controls the relationship between the device characteristics and the display conditions to produce the most accurate results. A color profile describes the color characteristics of a specific device. With the Color Management (**New!**) properties in the Control Panel, you can add or remove a color profile, associate a different color profile with a device, change the default profile, and change the color options, such as rendering intent and color space. Color profiles are typically added when you install a hardware device or software program that requires it. Windows Vista supports the standard ICC color standard and can add to it with Windows Color System.

View Color Profiles

1. Click the **Start** button, and then click **Control Panel.**

2. Double-click the **Color Management** icon in Classic view.

3. Click the **Devices** tab.

4. Click the **Device** list arrow, and then click the device you want to view.

   If a device uses a color profile, it appears in the list.

5. If you want to change the color profile, select the **Use my settings for this device** check box.

6. Use the **Add**, **Remove**, and **Profiles** buttons to modify profile associations.

7. To view all profiles on your computer or add a profile, click the **All Profiles** tab.

8. To change specific attributes and characteristics of a profile, click the **Advanced** tab.

9. Click **Close**.

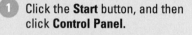

Adding a Secondary Monitor

Microsoft Certified Application Specialist

WINV-3.5.1, WINV-3.5.2, WINV-3.5.3

If you need more space on your desktop to work, you can add a secondary monitor to your computer. This allows you to view and work with more than one full size window on the screen at the same time. One monitor serves as the primary display while the other serves as the secondary display. You can set different screen resolutions and different color quality settings for each monitor. You can connect multiple monitors to individual video cards or to a single card that supports multiple video ports. If you have a docked or undocked portable computer or desktop computer with two video ports on one video card, you use DualView to add a secondary monitor and expand the size of your desktop. DualView is similar to the multiple monitor feature, but you cannot select the primary display, which is always the LCD display screen on a portable computer and the monitor attached to the first video out port on a desktop computer. You don't need to purchase and install another video adapter on your computer.

Set Secondary Monitor Options

1. Click the **Start** button, and then click **Control Panel**.

2. Double-click the **Personalize** icon in Classic view, and then click **Display settings**.

3. Click the secondary monitor.

4. To change the screen resolution, drag the **Resolution** slider.

   Changes to the screen resolution appear in the preview.

5. Select the **Extend the desktop onto this monitor** check box.

6. Click **OK**.

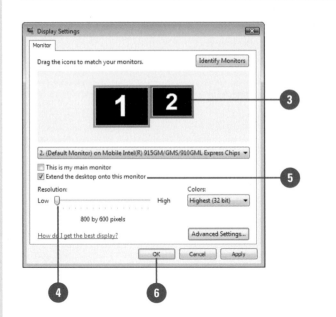

Did You Know?

You can change resolution and color quality on either monitor. On the Settings tab, click the monitor icon for the monitor you want to change, adjust the resolution or color quality, and then click OK.

Change the Movement Between Monitors

1. Click the **Start** button, and then click **Control Panel**.

2. Double-click the **Personalize** icon in Classic view, and then click **Display settings**.

3. Click **Identify Monitors**.

4. Click the monitor icons and drag them to positions that represent how you want to move items from one monitor to another.

5. Click **OK**.

   You can drag items across the primary monitor until it appears on the secondary monitor.

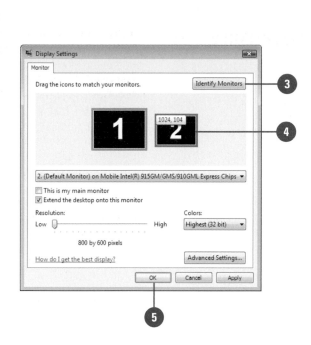

Change the Primary Monitor

1. Click the **Start** button, and then click **Control Panel**.

2. Double-click the **Personalize** icon in Classic view, and then click **Display settings**.

3. Click the monitor icon that represents the monitor you want as the primary one.

4. Select the **This is my main monitor** check box.

   TROUBLE? *This check box is unavailable if you select the current primary monitor.*

5. Click **OK**.

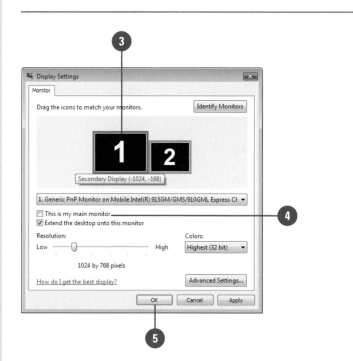

Changing Game Controller Settings

A **game controller** is a hardware device, such as a joystick or game pad, that controls a program, typically a game. You can use Game Controllers properties in the Control Panel to add, configure, and customize game controllers on your computer. For example, you can add older gaming devices so you can play those games on your computer. You can also test, calibrate, and troubleshoot your game controllers. If you no longer use a game controller, you can remove it from your computer.

Test a Game Controller

1. Click the **Start** button, and then click **Control Panel**.

2. Double-click the **Game Controllers** icon in Classic view.

3. Click the controller you want to test.

4. Click **Properties**.

5. Click the **Test** tab.

6. Test the controller by moving or pressing each control, and then view the results.

7. Click **OK**.

8. Click **OK**.

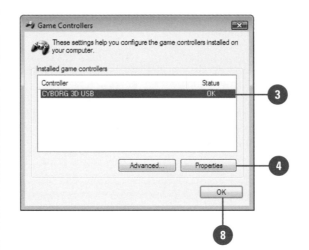

Did You Know?

You can reset a game controller. In the Control Panel, double-click the Game Controller icon, click a controller, click Properties, click the Settings tab, click Reset To Default, and then click OK twice.

You can calibrate a game controller. In the Control Panel, double-click the Game Controller icon, click a controller, click Properties, click the Settings tab, click Calibrate, follow the wizard instructions, and then click OK twice.

Removing Hardware Devices

If you no longer use a hardware device, or if you have an older hardware device that you want to upgrade, you need to remove the hardware device drivers and related software before you remove the physical hardware device from your computer. With the Device Manager, you can quickly and easily remove hardware devices and any related device drivers. Before you remove a legacy device, printing the device settings is a good idea in case you need to reinstall the device later.

Remove a Hardware Device

1. Click the **Start** button, and then click **Control Panel**.

2. Double-click the **Device Manager** icon in Classic view.

3. Click the plus sign (+) next to the hardware category you want to expand.

4. Click the device you want to remove.

5. Click the **Uninstall** button.

6. Click **OK**.

7. Click the **Close** button.

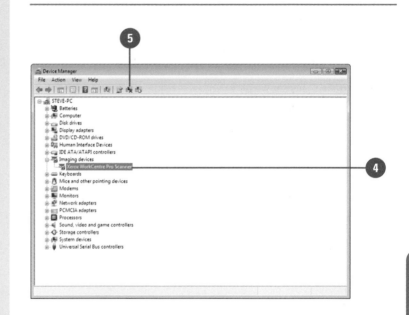

Did You Know?

You can quickly delete a printer. Click the Start button, click Control Panel, double-click the Printers icon, right-click the printer you want to delete, click Delete, and then click Yes.

You can safely unplug or eject plug and play hardware from the notification area. If the Safely Remove Hardware icon appears in the notification area on the taskbar, double-click it, select a device, click Stop, click Close, and then unplug or eject the device. You can also right-click the Safely Remove Hardware icon, and then select a drive or device.

Backing Up Your Computer

17

Introduction

It is vital that you make backup copies of the files on your computer on a regular basis so you don't lose valuable data if your computer encounters problems. The term **back up** (or **backup**, when referring to the noun or adjective) refers to the process of using a special software program designed to read your data quickly, compress it into a small, efficient space, then store it on an external medium, such as a set of disks, a network drive, or a tape cartridge.

Windows Vista includes the Back up and Restore Center (**New!**). Using the Back up and Restore Center has several advantages over simply copying files to a removable disk. Your files are compressed as they are copied so that you can fit more onto a removable disk, and it splits a large file across two or more disks (saving disk space), something you cannot do with the Copy command. Also, in an emergency, Backup offers several data-recovery aids to help you locate and restore important files quickly.

If your computer system crashes and Windows cannot start, you can use the Windows Vista installation disc, which contains the files necessary to start Windows. You can use the Startup Repair and other tools on the System Recovery Options menu to repair the problem or restore data from a backup.

Developing a Backup Strategy

With Backup, you can back up files from a local or network hard drive to a removable disk, a CD or DVD, a network drive, or a tape drive that is attached to your computer. Before you back up files, it is a good idea to develop a backup strategy. A **backup strategy** is a method for regularly backing up your work that balances tradeoffs between safety, time, and media space. For example, if safety were your only concern, you could back up your entire hard drive every hour. But you would not have any time to work, and you would spend a fortune on backup mediums. If spending minimal time and money on backups were your only concern, you might back up only a few crucial files once a month. The best choice is a balance between the two extremes. The **backup medium** that you use to store backed up files from a hard drive is usually a set of removable disks, writeable CDs or DVDs, or a tape cartridge designed to store computer data.

Because backups take time each time you perform them, you should back up only the files that change on a regular basis; back up all of the files on your computer at less frequent intervals. For example, because software program files don't change, you can easily reinstall them from their original program CDs or DVDs, so you do not need to back them up as often as your personal document files, which might change on a daily or weekly basis. Ask yourself how much work you can afford to lose. If you cannot afford to lose the work accomplished in one day, then you should back up once a day. If your work does not change much during the week, back up once a week.

Depending on the number and size of your files and the backup device you are using, the backup can take a few minutes to a few hours to complete. If you are planning to back up large amounts of information, such as your entire hard drive, it is best to start the backup at the end of the day and use a large capacity tape or removable disk, if possible, so you do not have to swap multiple disks. When a file does not fit on a tape or disk, Backup splits the file, fitting what it can on the current disk and then prompting you to insert the next tape or disk. When you perform a backup, Backup creates a **backup set**, also known as a **backup job**, which contains the compressed copies of the files you backed up. The backup job is stored in the backup file with the .bkf extension. You can store more than one backup job in a specified backup file. An incremental backup copies only the files that have changed since your most recent normal or incremental backup. It also clears the archive attribute for each file that is backed up. Therefore, the first incremental backup after a normal backup copies all files that have changed since the normal backup, and the second incremental backup copies only those files that have changed since the first incremental backup, and so on.

Lastly, keeping your computer's clock set to an accurate time is crucial to the success of your backups and other file maintenance. When setting a backup schedule, Windows will be looking at your system's clock to commence backups. Make sure your computer's time is accurately set throughout the year to ensure proper time stamping for your backups, as well as, other file properties.

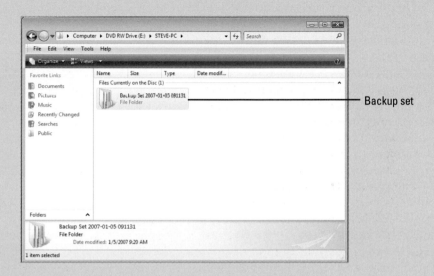

Backup set

Backup

Restore

Understanding Backup Permissions

Backup Permissions

You must have certain permissions to back up files and folders. If you are an administrator or a backup operator in a local group using Windows Vista, you can back up any file and folder on the computer to which the local group applies. However, if you are not an administrator or a backup operator and you want to back up files, then you must be the owner of the files and folders you want to back up, or you must have one or more of the following permissions for the files and folders you want to back up: Read, Read and Execute, Modify, or Full Control. You can also restrict access to a backup file by selecting the *Allow only the owner and the administrator access to the backup data* check box in the Backup Job Information dialog box. If you select this option, only an administrator or the person who created the backup file will be able to restore the files and folders.

    To add a user to the Backup Operators group, double-click the Administrative Tools icon in the Control Panel, and then double-click the Computer Management icon in the Administrative Tools window. This opens the Computer Management Window. Next, click the arrow next to Local Users and Groups in the console tree, click Groups in the console tree, and then double-click Backup Operators in the Details pane. Next, click Add in the Backup Operators Properties dialog box, type the domain and user name of the person you want to make a backup operator in the form \\Domain\user name, and then click OK. For more information about using Computer Management, see Chapter 18, "Administering Your Computer."

Backup permissions

File Systems

You can back up and restore data on either FAT or NTFS volumes. However, if you have backed up data from an NTFS volume used in Windows Vista, it is recommended that you restore the data to an NTFS volume used in Windows Vista instead of Windows 2000, or you could lose data as well as some file and folder features. For more information about FAT and NTFS disk file systems, see Chapter 15, "Maintaining Your Computer."

Exploring the Backup and Restore Center

Using the Backup Wizard in the Backup and Restore Center (**New!**), you can pick the day, time, and how often you want to back up your files, folders, and settings. You can also specify the type of data to back up, such as documents, photos, or music. Windows Vista takes care of the rest. And you won't be interrupted while you work, because automatic data backup occurs in the background, regardless of when you've scheduled your backup. You can continue to use your computer, even when it's backing up. Easily backing up your data is only part of the story—you also need a way to get your files back where they belong if something happens to them. Using the Restore Wizard, you can choose only what you want to restore—whether it's an individual file, a group of photos, or even your entire system and its related settings. Windows Vista takes care of putting the files back where they were before they were lost.

Start Backup and Restore Center

1 Click the **Start** button, and then click the Control Panel.

2 Double-click the **Backup and Restore Center** icon in Classic view.

3 Click any of the following buttons to perform the task you want:

◆ **Back up files**. Back up selected files and folders.

◆ **Back up computer**. Back up the entire system.

◆ **Restore files**. Restore selected files and folders.

◆ **Restore computer**. Restore the entire system.

4 Click the **Close** button.

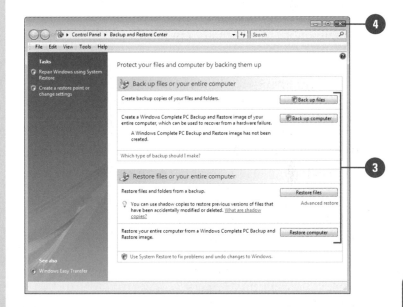

Performing a Backup Using a Wizard

Microsoft
Certified
Application
Specialist

WINV-4.7.1

The Backup Wizard walks you through the process of backing up files on your computer. You can back up every file on your computer, or selected files and folders. Backing up your entire computer is a good idea in case you have a problem with Windows and it doesn't start properly. Typically, you back up your entire computer after you make major changes to your system and you back up changes to individual files, folders, and settings on a regular schedule. During the wizard process, you select the back up location, choose the day, time, and how often you want to back up your files, folders, and settings. You can also specify the type of data to back up, such as documents, photos, or music. While the back up takes place you can continue to use your computer, yet it may be a little slower.

Back up Every File Using a Wizard

1 Click the **Start** button, and then click the Control Panel.

2 Double-click the **Backup and Restore Center** icon in Classic view.

3 Click **Back up computer**.

4 Select the option where you want to back up your computer, and then select the specific location.

5 Click **Next** to continue.

6 Confirm your backup settings, and then click **Start backup**.

7 If prompted to insert a disc, insert a CD or DVD, and then click **OK**.

8 If prompted to format the disc, click **Format**.

The progress dialog box opens, displaying back up status.

9 When it's done, click **Close**.

Back up Selected Files Using a Wizard

1. Click the **Start** button, and then click the **Control Panel**.

2. Double-click the **Backup and Restore Center** icon in Classic view.

3. Click **Back up files**.

4. Select the option where you want to back up your files, and then select the specific location.

5. Click **Next** to continue.

6. To find out what files are included in the back up of a category or file type, point to the one you want, and then read about the details.

7. Select the check boxes with the data you want to back up and clear the ones you don't want to include.

8. Click **Next** to continue.

9. Select how often you want to create a backup. Specify how often, what day, and what time.

10. Click **Save settings and start backup**.

11. If prompted to insert a disc, insert a DVD, and then click **OK**.

12. If prompted to format the disc, click **Format**.

    The progress dialog box opens, displaying back up status.

13. When it's done, click **Close**.

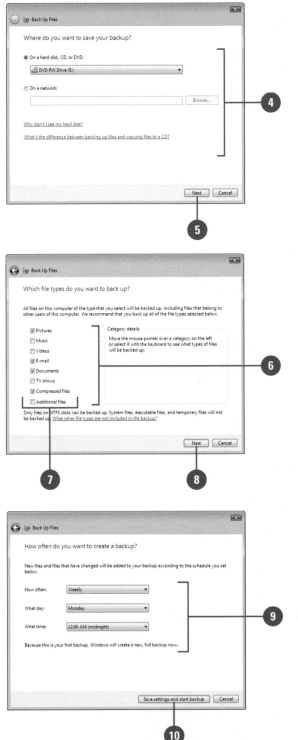

Changing Backup Settings

After you complete a back up, you can make modifications to the backup settings. You can change the backup schedule or the types of files backed up. Instead of selecting individual files and folders, the Backup Wizard provides file types and categories for you to select. For example, you can select Pictures, Music, Videos, E-mail, Documents, TV shows, Compressed files, or Additional system and temporary files. If you need to perform a manual back up, you can choose Back up now in the Backup Status and Configuration dialog box.

Change Backup Settings

1. Click the **Start** button, and then click the **Control Panel**.

2. Double-click the **Backup and Restore Center** icon in Classic view.

3. Click **Change settings** under the Back up files button.

4. Click **Change backup settings**.

5. Select the option where you want to back up your files, and then select the specific location.

6. Click **Next** to continue.

7. Select the check boxes with the data you want to back up and clear the ones you don't want to include.

8. Click **Next** to continue.

9. Select how often you want to create a backup. Specify how often, what day, and what time.

10. Select or clear the **Clear a new, full backup now in addition to saving settings** check box.

11. Click **Save settings and start backup** or **Save settings**.

12. Upon completion, click the **Close** button.

13. Click the **Close** button.

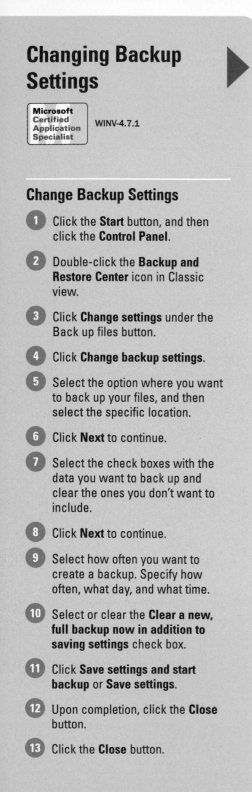

Perform a Manual Backup Using Current Settings

1 Click the **Start** button, and then click the **Control Panel**.

2 Double-click the **Backup and Restore Center** icon in Classic view.

3 Click **Change settings** under the Back up files button.

4 Click **Back up now.**

The backup starts.

5 To stop the backup, click the stop this backup link.

6 Upon completion, click the **Close** button.

7 Click the **Close** button.

Scheduling a Backup

Microsoft
Certified
Application
Specialist

WINV-4.7.2

Scheduling backups according to a backup strategy can help you perform backups on a regular basis and protect your data. Typically, late at night or on the weekends, when nobody is around, is a good time to perform backups. Backup makes it easy to schedule backups any time you want to perform them. You can schedule a backup to run once, every day, every week, or every month. If you have a back up scheduled for a certain time and you need to cancel it, you can turn off automatic back ups and then turn it back on later. And if your computer is turned off at the time the backup is scheduled to occur, the backup process will begin when you next turn on your computer.

Schedule a Backup

1. Click the **Start** button, and then click the **Control Panel**.

2. Double-click the **Backup and Restore Center** icon in Classic view.

3. Click **Change settings** under the Back up files button.

    The Backup Status and Configuration dialog box opens.

4. Click **Change backup settings**.

5. Click **Next** to continue.

6. Click **Next** to continue.

7. Click the **How often** list arrow, and then select an interval.

8. Click the **What day** list arrow, and then select a day of the week.

9. Click the **What time** list arrow, and then select a time.

10. Click **Save settings and exit**.

11. Click the **Close** button to close the Backup Status and Configuration dialog box.

12. Click the **Close** button.

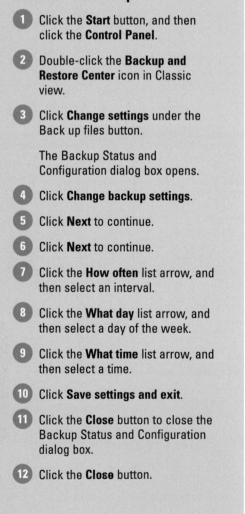

Turn Off Automatic Backup

① Click the **Start** button, and then click the **Control Panel**.

② Double-click the **Backup and Restore Center** icon in Classic view.

③ Click **Change settings** under the Back up files button.

④ Click **Turn off**.

⑤ Click the **Close** button to close the Backup Status and Configuration dialog box.

⑥ Click the **Close** button.

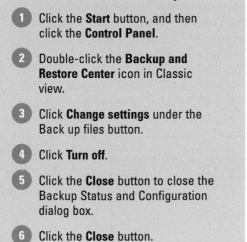

Backup Status and Configuration

Automatic file backup is turned on

Windows will scan your computer for new and updated files and add them to your backup based on the schedule you set.

What file types are not included in the backup?

Backup status

ⓘ The last file backup was successful.

Backup location: DVD RW Drive (E:)

Last successful backup: 1/5/2007 5:19 AM
Next backup: 1/8/2007 12:00 AM

🔘 Back up now
Scan for new or updated files and add them to your backup.

🔘 Change backup settings
Adjust your current backup settings or start a new, full backup.

Automatic backup is currently on   [🔘 Turn off]

⑤   ④

Backup Status and Configuration

Automatic file backup is configured but turned off

Windows is not scanning your computer for new and updated files.

What file types are not included in the backup?

Backup status

ⓘ The last file backup was successful.

Backup location:

Last successful backup: 1/5/2007 9:25 AM
Next backup: Disabled

🔘 Back up now
Scan for new or updated files and add them to your backup.

🔘 Change backup settings
Adjust your current backup settings or start a new, full backup.

Automatic backup is currently off   [🔘 Turn on]

Automatic Backup disabled

Restoring Files Using a Wizard

WINV-4.7.3

The real value in backing up your files becomes apparent if you lose or damage some files, or need information from a document that has changed a great deal over time. You can restore a single file, several files, or an entire hard drive. Using the Restore Wizard, you can specify which files you want to restore and where you want them to be placed. When you create a backup set, a **catalog**, or index of the backed up files, is built and stored on the backup medium. When you store the catalog on the backup medium, it speeds up the process when you want to restore the files.

Restore a Backup

1. Click the **Start** button, and then click the **Control Panel**.

2. Double-click the **Backup and Restore Center** icon in Classic view.

3. Click **Restore files**.

4. Click the **Files from the lastest backup** or **Files from an older backup** option.

5. To view the Recycle Bin, click the **See recently deleted files (Recycle Bin)** link, and then click the **Close** button when you're done.

6. Click **Next** to continue.

7. If necessary, select an older backup, and then click **Next** to continue.

8 Click **Add files** or **Add folders**, select the file or folder you want to restore, and then click **Open**.

9 If you can't find a file or folder, click **Search**.

10 Type the characters you want to find in the title of the file or folder, and then press Enter.

11 Select the check boxes with the files or folder you want to add to the restore list.

12 Click **Add**.

13 Click **Next** to continue.

14 Click the **In the original location** or **In the following location** option.

15 If you are changing the locations, select the **Restore the files to their original subfolders** check box. If you select this option, then select or clear the **Create a subfolder for the drive letter** check box.

16 Click **Start restore**.

The progress dialog box opens, displaying the restore status.

17 When it's done, click **Finish**.

18 Click the **Close** button.

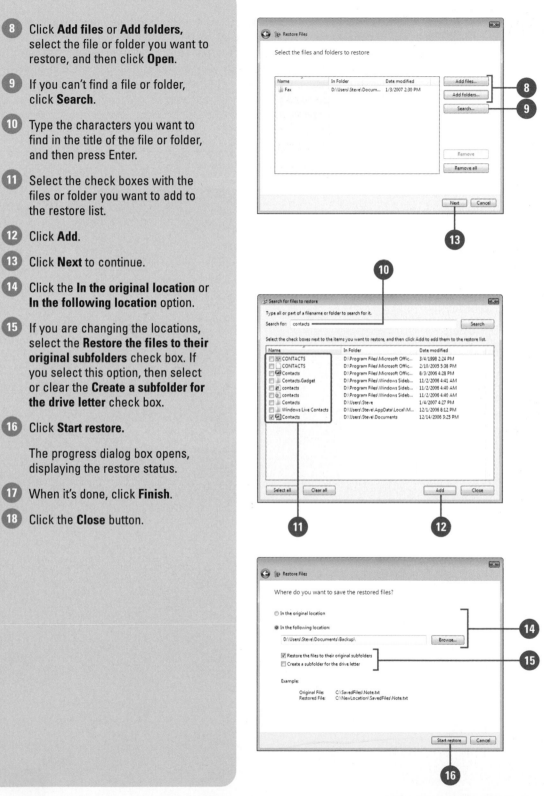

Restoring Files Using Advanced Settings

Restore a Backup Using Advanced Settings

1 Click the **Start** button, and then click the **Control Panel**.

2 Double-click the **Backup and Restore Center** icon in Classic view.

3 Click **Advanced restore** under the Restore files button.

4 Click **Advanced restore**.

5 Click the option to specify what you want to restore:

- ◆ **Files from the latest backup made on this computer.**

- ◆ **Files from an older backup made on this computer.**

- ◆ **Files from a backup made on a different computer.**

6 Click **Next** to continue.

7 If necessary, select an older backup, or the location of a back up in another location, and then click **Next** to continue.

If you need to restore files from an older backup made on this computer or files from a back up made on a different computer, you can select additional options using the Advanced restore button. The advanced options allow you to select an older backup set or one stored in a different location. You can also decide where to put the restored files. You can put them back in their original place, or select a new location. The Restore Wizard walks you through the process, so you can restore the files and folder you want.

8 Click **Add files** or **Add folders,** select the file or folder you want to restore, and then click **Open**.

9 If you can't find a file or folder, click **Search**.

10 Type the characters you want to find in the title of the file or folder, and then press Enter.

11 Select the check boxes with the files or folder you want to add to the restore list.

12 Click **Add**.

13 Click **Next** to continue.

14 Click the **In the original location** or **In the following location** option.

15 If you are changing the locations, select the **Restore the files to their original subfolders** check box. If you select this option, then select or clear the **Create a subfolder for the drive letter** check box.

16 Click **Start restore**.

The progress dialog box opens, displaying the restore status.

17 When it's done, click **Finish**.

18 Click the **Close** button.

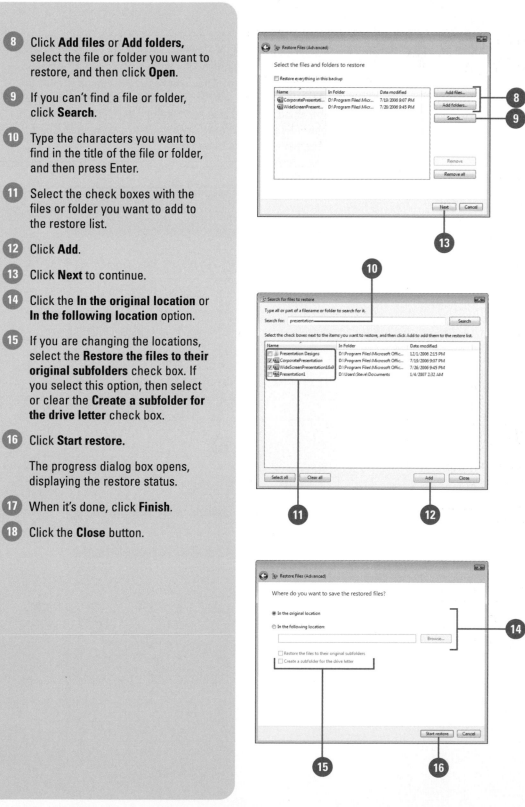

Copying Files From the Backup

If you need a few backed up files or folders and know exactly where they are located on the back up media, you can open up the backed up media drive and navigate directly to the files and folder like any other external drive. You can use the Copy and Paste commands to copy the files and folder you need to another place on your computer. If you prefer, another method, you can also use the Copy To Folder command on the Edit menu. This method is useful when you are copying files and folder to disks, networks, and other drives.

Copy Files from the Backup

1. Click the **Start** button, and then click **Computer**.

2. Locate the drive with your backup files.

3. Double-click the drive and any folders to locate the files or folders you want to copy.

4. Select the files or folders you want to copy.

5. Right-click the selected files or folders, and then click **Copy**.

6. Display the folder where you want to copy the backed up files or folders.

7. Right-click a blank area of the folder, and then click **Paste**.

Did You Know?

You can extract all files from a backup. Open the Backup Set folder with the files or folders you want to extract, select a folder, click the Extract all files button on the toolbar, click Browse, select a destination folder, click OK, and then click Extract.

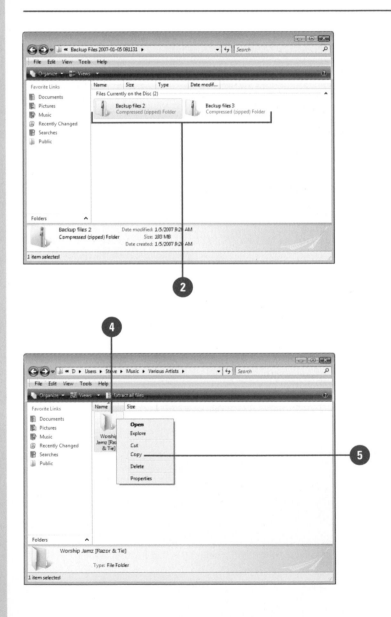

Restoring Your Computer

To restore your computer, you need to exit the Backup and Restore Center and run Windows Complete PC Restore from the System Recovery Options menu. You can access the Recovery Options menu from a recovery partitions using the F8 key at startup or from a Windows installation disc. Windows Complete PC Restore reformats your hard disk and erases all your data and programs, and then restores it. Before you start the complete restore process, be sure to have the removable media (your back up material) available.

Restore Your Computer

1. Click the **Start** button, and then click the **Control Panel**.

2. Double-click the **Backup and Restore Center** icon in Classic view.

3. Click **Restore computer**.

   An alert appears, explaining the process to restore your computer.

4. Click **Close**.

5. Click the **Close** button.

6. Insert your Windows installation disc into your drive, and then restart your computer.

7. At startup, press F8.

8. Select **Repair your computer** on the Advanced Boots Options menu, and then press Enter.

9. Follow the on-screen instructions to complete the process.

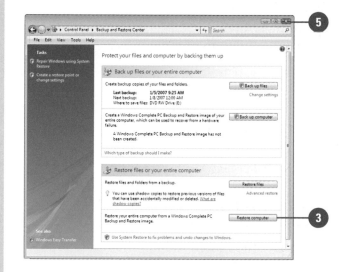

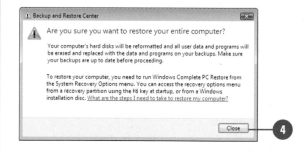

Deleting a
Backup Set

Each time you perform a backup, Backup creates a backup set containing the backed up files. You can store more than one backup set in a backup file. After backing up files for a while, you might find a number of unneeded backup sets accumulating in a backup file. You can delete these sets quickly and easily from the backup file within Backup. When you delete a backup set, only the backup set is deleted, but the backup file, such as Backup.bkf, remains in the backup location. If you want to delete the backup file, drag the file icon into the Recycle Bin as you would any other Windows file.

Delete a Backup Set

1. Click the **Start** button, and then click **Computer**.

2. Locate the drive with your backup files.

3. Double-click the drive and any folders to locate the Backup Set.

4. Select the **Backup Set** folder.

5. Press the Delete key.

6. Click **Yes** to conform the deletion.

7. To permanently delete the Backup Set, right-click the **Recycle Bin**, and then click **Empty Recycle Bin**.

Administering Your Computer

18

Introduction

If you have purchased a computer and set it up in your home, you are that computer's administrator. Computers on a network in a company or an institution, such as at a university, are called clients. The clients are managed by one or more system or network administrators, who have the task of ensuring that the network and its services are reliable, fast, and secure. Although most network administration takes place on the server (host, as described in earlier chapters), clients must also be administered. Windows Vista includes administrative tools that make it easy to ensure that client computers are operating as they should.

You can use the administrative tools to track and view the activity on your computer. You can set up criteria for gathering event information, and then Windows automatically gathers that information for you. In the event of a problem, you can view that data to help you find and fix the problem.

When you open an administrative tool, Windows uses a two-pane view that is similar to Windows Explorer. The hierarchy of tools in the left pane of the window is called a **console tree**, and each main category of tools is called a **node**. The nodes in the console tree allow you to manage and monitor system events and performance, and make adjustments as necessary.

Exploring Windows Administrative Tools

Windows Vista offers a set of tools that helps you administer your computer and ensure it operates smoothly. The Administrative Tools window, opened from the Control Panel, provides tools that allow you to configure administrative settings for local and remote computers. If you are working on a shared or network computer, you might need to be logged on as a computer administrator or as a member of the Administrators group in order to view or modify some properties or perform some tasks with the administrative tools. You can open User Accounts in the Control Panel to check which account is currently in use or to check with your system administrator to determine whether you have the necessary access privileges. Many Windows users won't ever have to open the Administrative Tools window, but computers on a network will probably require administrative support.

View Administrative Tools

1 Click the **Start** button, and then click **Control Panel.**

2 Double-click the **Administrative Tools** icon in Classic view.

3 When you're done, click the **Close** button.

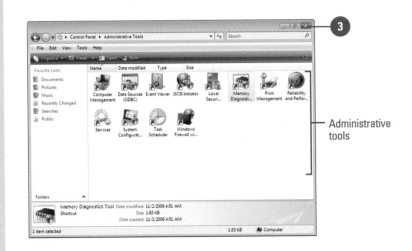

Administrative tools

Did You Know?

You can add Administrative Tools to the Start menu. Right-click the Start button, click Properties, click the Start Menu tab, click Customize, scroll down the list, click the Display on the All Programs menu and the Start menu option under System Administrative Tools, and then click OK twice.

Monitoring Activity with Event Viewer

Every time you start Windows, an event-logging service notes any unusual event that occurs, such as a failed logon, the installation of a new driver for a hardware device, the failure of a device or service to start, or a network interruption. For some critical events, such as when your disk is full, a warning message appears on your screen. Most events, however, don't require immediate attention, so Windows logs them in an event log file that you can view using the Event Viewer tool. Event Viewer maintains several logs in two categories: Windows Logs and Applications and Services Logs. Windows Logs maintains three logs: System, for events logged by Windows operating system components; Security, for security and audit events (such as who logged on); and Application, for Windows program events. Applications and Services Logs maintains individual program and service logs. When you are troubleshooting problems on your computer, you can use the Event Viewer logs to monitor what activity took place.

Monitor Activities

1. Click the **Start** button, and then click **Control Panel**.

2. Double-click the **Administrative Tools** icon in Classic view.

3. Double-click the **Event Viewer** icon.

4. Click arrow next to the log category to expand it, and then click the log in which you want to monitor events.

5. Double-click an event.

6. Click the **Up Arrow** button or the **Down Arrow** button to display other events.

7. Click **Close**.

8. When you're done, click the **Close** button.

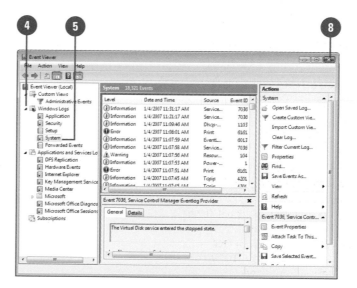

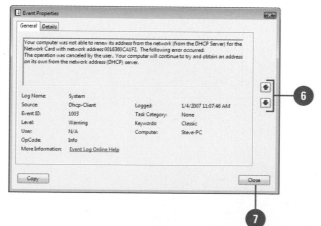

Managing an Event Log

Event logs grow in size as you work on your computer, but Event Viewer provides tools that help you view just the information you need and store the information you want to save for later. For example, you can apply a **filter** that allows you to view only events matching specified criteria, such as all events associated with a certain user. You can also search for a specific event using similar criteria. You probably don't want your active log to include events that happened long ago. With Event Viewer, you can **archive**, or save, your log periodically and then clear the archived events. Most administrators archive event logs on a regular schedule.

Sort and Filter an Event Log

1. Click the **Start** button, and then click **Control Panel**.

2. Double-click the **Administrative Tools** icon in Classic view.

3. Double-click the **Event Viewer** icon, and then select the event log you want to sort or filter events.

4. Click the **View** menu, point to **Sort By**, and then click the sort method you want.

5. In the Action pane, click **Filter Current Log**.

6. Select the event type check boxes in which you want to filter.

7. Specify filter information by specific value.

8. Click **OK**.

9. When you're done, click the **Close** button.

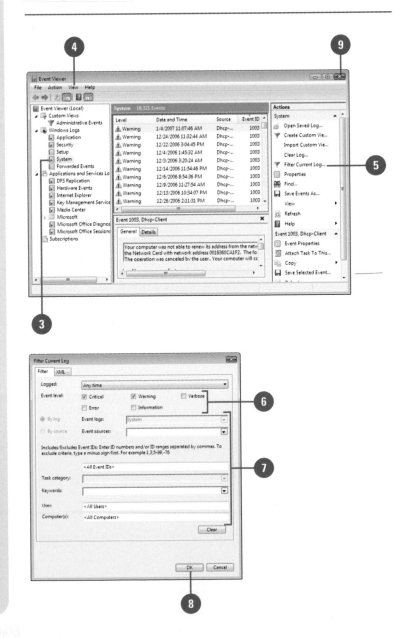

Save an Event Log

① Click the **Start** button, and then click **Control Panel**.

② Double-click the **Administrative Tools** icon in Classic view.

③ Double-click the **Event Viewer** icon, and then select the event log you want to save.

④ In the Action pane, click **Save Log File As** or **Save Events As**.

⑤ Select a location for the log file.

⑥ Type a name for the log file.

⑦ Click **Save**.

⑧ When you're done, click the **Close** button.

Did You Know?

You can open the log file from the Event Viewer. In the Event Viewer, click Open Saved Log in the Action pane, select the log file, and then click Open.

You can find information in the Event Viewer. In the Event Viewer, click Find in the Action pane, type what you want to find, and then click Find Next. When you're done, click Close.

Changing Log Settings

You can control how any log in the Event Viewer collects data by defining a maximum log size (the default is 512K) and instructing Event Viewer how to handle an event log that has reached its maximum size. Only users with administrative rights can change log settings. In addition to specifying a maximum log size, you can also choose from three log options when the log is full: new events can automatically overwrite the oldest events, new events can overwrite only events older than a specified number of days, or Event Viewer will not overwrite events, in which case you must manually clear a full log before it can resume logging events.

Change Log Settings

1. Click the **Start** button, and then click **Control Panel**.

2. Double-click the **Administrative Tools** icon in Classic view.

3. Double-click the **Event Viewer** icon.

4. Select the log in which you want to change settings.

5. In the Action pane, click the **Properties**.

6. Click the **General** tab.

7. Specify the maximum log size.

8. Select an option when the maximum size is reached.

9. Click **OK**.

10. When you're done, click the **Close** button.

6

Log Properties - Application (Type: Administrative)

General | Subscriptions

Full Name:	Application
Log path:	%SystemRoot%\System32\Winevt\Logs\Application.evtx
Log size:	1.07 MB(1,118,208 bytes)
Created:	Thursday, November 30, 2006 4:21:59 PM
Modified:	Tuesday, January 02, 2007 6:33:09 PM
Accessed:	Thursday, November 30, 2006 4:21:59 PM

☑ Enable logging

Maximum log size (KB): 20480

When maximum event log size is reached:

● Overwrite events as needed (oldest events first)
○ Archive the log when full, do not overwrite events
○ Do not overwrite events (Clear logs manually)

7

8

Clear Log

OK | Cancel | Apply

9

Checking Memory for Problems

If a problem arises related to the memory on your computer, Windows automatically tries to detected it and displays an alert message, which allows you to run the Memory Diagnostic Tool. If you also suspect a memory problem, you can run the Memory Diagnostic Tool from Administrator Tools. When the memory tool starts, you can have the program restart your computer and run the memory tool immediately or run it later. While the memory tool runs, a progress bar indicates the status of the test. When the test is done, Windows restarts again. If the results indicate a problem, you should contact your computer or memory manufacturer for information about fixing the problem.

Check for Memory Problems

1. Click the **Start** button, and then click **Control Panel**.

2. Double-click the **Administrative Tools** icon in Classic view.

3. Double-click the **Memory Diagnostics Tool** icon.

4. Click **Restart now and check for problems** or **Check for problems the next time I start my computer** option.

5. Follow the on-screen instructions to complete the test.

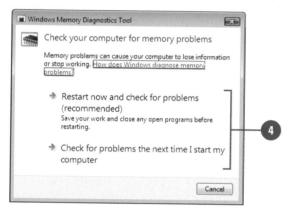

Viewing and Creating Performance Charts

**Microsoft
Certified
Application
Specialist**

WINV-7.3.1

On a daily basis, your system generates a variety of performance data, such as your computer's memory or processor use, or the amount of congestion on a device. As the system administrator, you can use the Reliability and Performance tool to create charts from the data that enable you to observe how a computer's processor behaves over time. The types of performance data you monitor and record are called **performance objects**. Each performance object has a set of counters associated with it that provides numeric information. The Reliability and Performance tool charts the numeric data gathered from the counters and provides graphical tools to make it easier to analyze and track the performance of your computer. Performance charts include statistics about each counter you select, but unless you know how your system should perform, these statistics might not be very meaningful. For this reason, administrators create baseline charts—charts made when the computer or network is running at a normal level. When there are problems, the administrator can create another performance chart that can be compared to the baseline chart.

View Resource Performance Chart

1. Click the **Start** button, and then click **Control Panel**.

   TIMESAVER *You can display performance usage graphs in the Task Manager on the Performance tab. Press Ctl+Alt+Del, click Task Manager, and then click Resource Monitor.*

2. Double-click the **Administrative Tools** icon in Classic view.

3. Double-click the **Reliability and Performance Monitor** icon.

4. In the left pane, click **Reliability and Performance**.

5. Click a bar (**CPU**, **Disk**, **Network**, or **Memory**) to display program specific information.

6. Click the bar again to hide the specific programs.

7. When you're done, click the **Close** button.

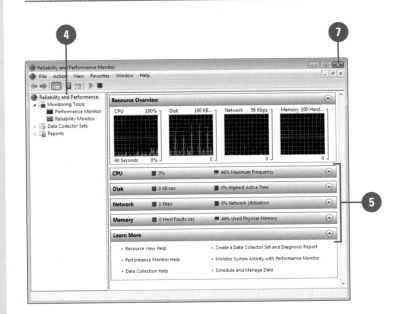

View a Reliability Chart

1. Click the **Start** button, and then click **Control Panel**.

2. Double-click the **Administrative Tools** icon in Classic view.

3. Double-click the **Reliability and Performance Monitor** icon.

4. In the left pane, click the arrow next to **Monitoring Tools**, and then click **Reliability Monitor**.

5. Click the plus (+) sign or minus (-) sign to display program specific information.

6. Click the **Close** button.

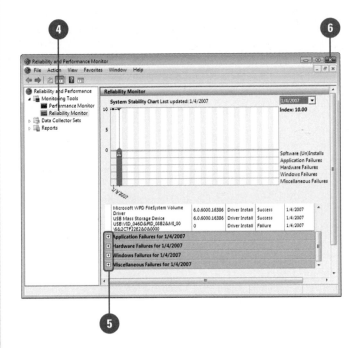

View or Create a Performance Chart

1. Click the **Start** button, and then click **Control Panel**.

2. Double-click the **Administrative Tools** icon in Classic view.

3. Double-click the **Reliability and Performance Monitor** icon.

4. In the left pane, click the arrow next to **Monitoring Tools**, and then click **Performance Monitor**.

5. To add counts and create a chart, click the **Add** button on the System Monitor toolbar.

6. Click the counter you want, and then click **Add**. You can continue to add other counters.

7. When you're done, click **OK**.

8. Click the **Close** button.

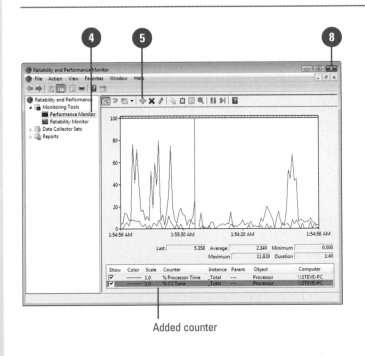

Added counter

Monitoring Local Security Settings

Using Windows Vista, you can view and monitor local security settings with the Local Security Settings tool to ensure that computer users are adhering to the organization's security policies. For example, you can set user account and password options to require computer users to create complex passwords of a specific length and change them on a regular basis. A **complex password** contains characters from at least three of the four following categories: uppercase (A through Z), lowercase (a through z), numbers (0 through 9), and nonalphanumeric (!, $, *, etc.). In addition to setting security options, you can also **monitor**, or **audit**, the success or failure of security related events, such as account logon and logoff activities, user account changes, and program launches. When an event that you have chosen to audit is triggered, it appears in the Event Viewer in the Security node.

Change Password Policies

1 Click the **Start** button, and then click **Control Panel**.

2 Double-click the **Administrative Tools** icon in Classic view.

3 Double-click the **Local Security Policy** icon.

4 Click the arrow next to Account Policies.

5 Click the **Password Policy** folder.

6 Double-click the policy you want to change.

7 Change the policy setting.

8 Click **OK**.

You can continue to change other password policies.

9 When you're done, click the **Close** button.

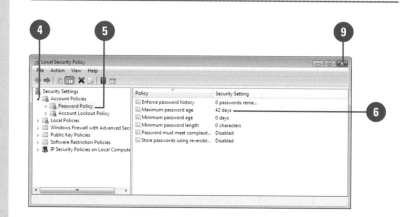

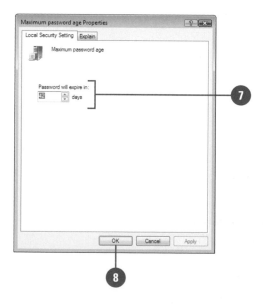

Audit Policies

1. Click the **Start** button, and then click **Control Panel**.

2. Double-click the **Administrative Tools** icon in Classic view.

3. Double-click the **Local Security Policy** icon.

4. Click the arrow next to Local Policies.

5. Click the **Audit Policy** folder.

6. Double-click the audit policy you want to change.

7. Select the **Success** and/or **Failure** check box.

8. Click **OK**.

   You can continue to change other audit policies.

9. When you're done, click the **Close** button.

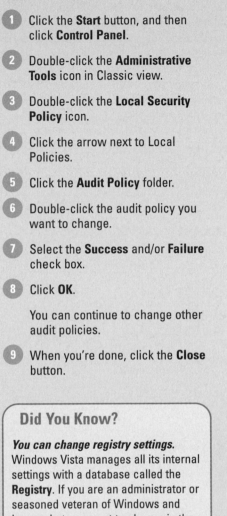

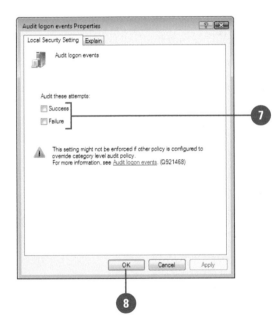

Did You Know?

You can change registry settings.
Windows Vista manages all its internal settings with a database called the **Registry**. If you are an administrator or seasoned veteran of Windows and know what you want to change in the Registry, you can fix a problem with your system or a program, or you can enhance the functionality of Windows. Click the Start button, point to Programs, click Accessories, click Run, type ***regedt32***, click OK, open the folder and double-click the item you want to change, and then click OK. When you're done, click the Close button.

Viewing Computer Management Tools

Computer Management consolidates administrative tools, such as Event Viewer and Performance, into a single window that you can use to manage a local or remote computer. The three nodes in the Computer Management window (System Tools, Storage, and Services and Applications) allow you to manage and monitor system events and performance and to perform disk-related tasks. Each node contains **snap-in tools**, which come in two types: stand-alone or extension. Stand-alone snap-ins are independent tools, while extension snap-ins are add-ons to current snap-ins. The selected tool appears in the right pane, and you can use the toolbars and menus that appear to take appropriate action with the tool.

View Management Tools

1. Click the **Start** button, and then click **Control Panel**.

2. Double-click the **Administrative Tools** icon in Classic view.

3. Double-click the **Computer Management** icon.

   TIMESAVER *To open Computer Management, right-click Computer on the Start menu, and then click Manage.*

4. Click the arrow next to the category you want to view.

5. Click the item you want to view.

6. Double-click the item you want to change, adjust the setting, and then click **OK**.

   You can continue to change other items.

7. When you're done, click the **Close** button.

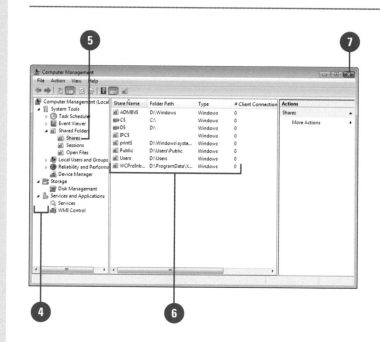

Managing Disks

Microsoft Certified Application Specialist

WINV3.2.2

The Storage node in the Computer Management window provides you with tools, such as Disk Defragmenter and Disk Management, to help you manage your disks. The Disk Management tool is a graphical tool for managing disks that allows you to partition unallocated portions of your disks into volumes. A **volume** is a fixed amount of storage on a disk. A single disk can contain more than one volume, or a volume can span part of one or more disks. Each volume on a disk is assigned its own drive letter, which is why the term volume is often synonymous with the term drive. Thus, the same physical disk might contain two volumes. Each volume can use a different file system, so you might have a single disk partitioned into two volumes, each with its own file system. You might partition a single hard disk in two different ways: first, with a single NTFS volume, and second, with one NTFS volume and one FAT volume, which can be helpful if you have a computer with two operating systems, Windows 98/Me on the FAT volume and Windows Vista on the NTFS volume.

View Disk Settings

1 Click the **Start** button, and then click **Control Panel**.

2 Double-click the **Administrative Tools** icon in Classic view.

3 Double-click the **Computer Management** icon.

TIMESAVER *To open Computer Management, right-click Computer on the Start menu, and then click Manage.*

4 Click the arrow next to **Storage**.

5 Click **Disk Management**.

The volumes on your computer display in the right pane.

6 Click the drive you want to modify.

7 Click the **Action** menu, point to **All Tasks**, and then click a command, such as **Format**, **Change Drive Letter and Paths**, **Mark Partition as Active**, or **Delete Volume**.

8 When you're done, click the **Close** button.

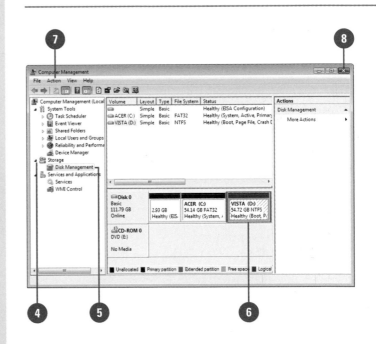

Managing Local Users and Groups

Microsoft Certified Application Specialist

WINV-1.6

In Windows Vista, you can manage the access privileges and permissions of local user and group accounts. A local user account is an individual account with a unique set of permissions, while a group account is a collection of individual accounts with the same set of permissions. You can change local user and group accounts in the Computer Management window using the Local Users And Groups tool. This security feature limits individual users and groups from accessing and deleting files, using programs such as Backup, or making accidental or intentional system-wide changes. You can create or modify a user account, disable or activate a user account, identify members of groups, and add or delete members to and from groups.

Manage Local Users and Groups

1. Click the **Start** button, and then click Control Panel.

2. Double-click the **Administrative Tools** icon in Classic view.

3. Double-click the **Computer Management** icon.

4. Click the arrow next to **System Tools**.

5. Click the arrow next to **Local Users and Groups**.

6. Click the **Users** or **Groups** folder.

7. Double-click the account you want to change.

8. Change the settings you want; add members if requested.

9. Click **OK**.

   You can continue to change other settings.

10. When you're done, click the **Close** button.

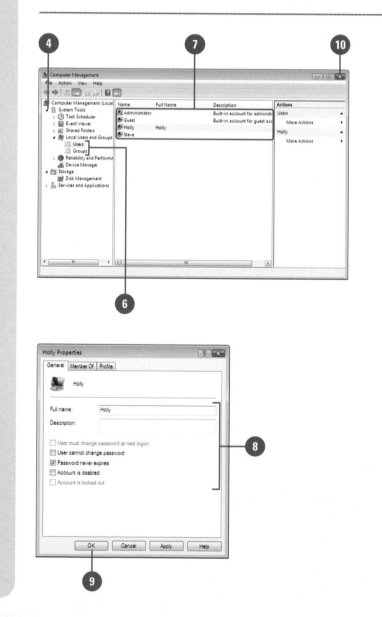

Viewing and Saving System Information

WINV-7.3.4

If you are having problems with Windows Vista or a program installed on your computer and can't figure out what to do, you can use System Information to locate valuable information for a support technician. For most people, the information in System Information is difficult to understand. However, if a support technician asks you for information about your system, you know where to find it. After you find the information, you can save and send it to the support technician.

View and Save System Information

1. Click the **Start** button, point to **All Programs**, click **Accessories**, click **System Tools**, and then click **System Information**.

2. Click **System Summary** to view the main information about your system.

3. Click a plus sign (+) to view a system area.

4. Click the item you want to view.

5. Click the **File** menu, and then click **Save**.

6. Select a folder.

7. Type a name for the file.

8. Click **Save**.

9. When you're done, click the **Close** button.

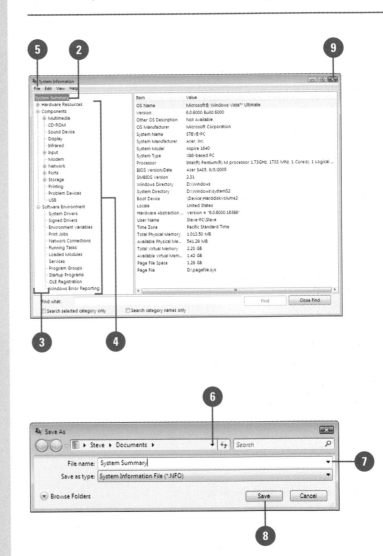

Did You Know?

You can display basic system information. Click the Start button, click Control Panel, double-click the System icon in Classic view. The basic information about your computer includes system rating, processor, memory (RAM), system type, network information, and Windows activation.

Setting System Configuration Options

If you're experiencing problems with your system, you can use the System Configuration tool from Administrator Tools to help you troubleshoot and configure your computer. To help you troubleshoot your system, you can select an option to start Windows Vista with a minimal set of resources, which can help you successfully boot and narrow down the problem. After you reboot successfully, you can start to select services and startup items to add them into the equation and determine what works and what doesn't. If you need to launch an administrator tool during the process, you can do it from the Tools tab.

Change System Configuration Options

1. Click the **Start** button, and then click **Control Panel**.

2. Double-click the **Administrative Tools** icon in Classic view.

3. Double-click the **System Configuration** icon.

4. Click the **General** tab.

5. To change the way Windows starts up, click the option you want: Normal, Diagnostic, or Selective.

6. Click the tab with the options you want to change:

   ◆ **Boot.** Select options to perform a safe boot.

   ◆ **Services.** Select what services (code segments) start up.

   ◆ **Startup.** Select what programs start when Windows starts.

   ◆ **Tools.** Launch an administrator related tool.

7. When you're done, click the **OK** button.

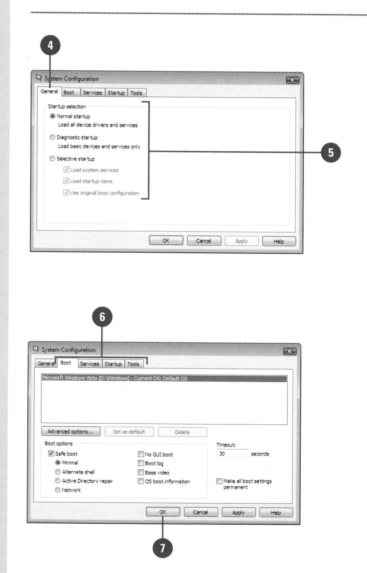

Appendix

Introduction

If you're upgrading to Windows Vista from a previous version of Windows, this appendix describes how to prepare and install Windows Vista. The temptation is to insert the Windows Vista disc and start the installation, but you can avoid problems by making sure your computer is ready for Windows Vista. Before you install Windows Vista, you need to check your computer hardware and software and make several setup decisions that relate to your computer. The Windows Vista Setup Wizard walks you through the installation process.

Microsoft is continually updating and enhancing Windows Vista. Instead of releasing multiple updates individually, periodically Microsoft releases an update, known as a Service Pack (SP), which provides all-in-one access to the most up-to-date drivers, tools, enhancements, and other critical updates (which were formally referred to as hotfixes). Service packs, as well as, individual updates are available free for download and installation over the Internet using the Windows Update Web site.

If you purchased a new computer that came with Windows Vista already installed on it, you can use the Transfer Files And Setting Wizard to transfer the files and customized settings from your old computer to your new one.

What You'll Do

Prepare to Install Windows Vista

Install Windows Vista

Update to a Windows Vista Service Pack

Transfer Files and Settings from Another Computer

Get Windows Vista Extras

Learn About Windows Live

Preparing to Install Windows Vista

The Windows Vista Setup Wizard guides you through many of the choices you need to make, but there are some decisions and actions you need to make before you start the wizard. To ensure a successful installation, do the following:

Make sure your hardware components meet the minimum requirements. Your computer hardware needs to meet the following minimum hardware requirements to be **Windows Vista PC Capability Ready**: A modern processor (at least 800MHz1), 512 MB of system memory, and a graphics processor that is DirectX 9 capable.

To get an even better Windows Vista experience, including the Windows Aero user experience, your computer hardware needs to meet the following hardware requirements to be **Windows Vista PC Premium Ready**: 1 GHz 32-bit (x86) or 64-bit (x64) processor1; 1 GB of system memory; support for DirectX 9 graphics with a WDDM driver, 128 MB of graphics memory (minimum), Pixel Shader 2.0 and 32 bits per pixel; 40 GB of hard drive capacity with 15 GB free space; DVD-ROM Drive3, audio output capability; and Internet access capability.

Features available in specific premium editions of Windows Vista, such as the ability to watch and record live TV, may require additional hardware. Beyond the basic requirements, some software and hardware services, such as networking, voice and video conferencing, and sound playback, call for you to meet additional requirements; see Windows Vista documentation for specific details.

Make sure your hardware and software are compatible using the Windows Vista Upgrade Advisor. If you are running a Windows XP-based computer, you can run the Windows

Vista Upgrade Advisor, which scans your computer and creates an easy-to-understand report of all known system, device, and program compatibility issues, and recommends ways to resolve them. Upgrade Advisor can also help you choose the edition of Windows Vista that best fits the way you want to use your computer. The Upgrade Advisor software is available on the Install window and the Microsoft Web site at *www.microsoft.com/windowsvista/getready/upgradeadvisor*.

Make sure you have the required product key information. On the back of the Windows Vista DVD packaging is a unique 25-character product key, such as KFEPC-12345-MHORY-12345-IROFE, that you need to enter during the Windows Vista Setup Wizard installation to complete the process. Keep the product key in a safe place, and do not share it with others. The unique product key allows you to activate and use Windows. Product activation and product registration are not the same. Product activation is required and ensures that each Windows product is not installed on more than the limited number of computers allowed in the software's end user license agreement. Activation is completely anonymous and requires no personal identification information to complete. To complete the activation process, you enter a unique 25-character product key during the Windows Vista Setup Wizard installation process or when using the Activate Windows program located on the Start menu. You have a 30-day grace period in which to activate your Windows product installation. If the grace period expires and you have not completed activation, all features will stop working except the product activation feature. During the activation process, you can also register your copy of Windows Vista. Product registration is not required, but completing the process ensures that you receive product update and support information from Microsoft.

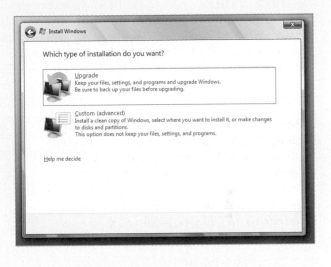

Determine whether you want to perform an in-place upgrade or install a new copy of Windows Vista.

After you start the Windows Vista Setup Wizard, you need to decide whether to upgrade your current operating system or to perform an entirely new installation, known as a clean install. A clean install includes completely erasing your hard drive and reformatting it with a new file system, which eliminates incompatibilities and makes your system run better. See Chapter 15, "Maintaining Your Computer," for more information about file systems. Before you perform a clean install, you need to backup your files and settings on a CD, removable, or network drive before you begin. After a clean install you still need to re-install all of your programs. To perform a clean install, you also need the Full Edition of Windows Vista, which is more expensive than the Upgrade version. You can upgrade from Windows 2000 or XP to Windows Vista. Earlier Windows operating systems are not supported for upgrading, so

those users will need to perform a clean install.

Back up your files in case you need to restore your current operating system. If you're upgrading from an earlier version of Windows or performing a clean install, you should back up your current files so you can correct any problems that might arise during the installation. You can back up files to a removable disk, a DVD-R or DVD-RW drive, a tape drive, or another computer on your network. See Chapter 17, "Backing Up Your Computer," for more information.

Make sure you have the required network information. If you are connecting to a network, you need the following information from your network administrator: name of your computer, name of the workgroup or domain, and a TCP/IP address if your network doesn't use a DHCP (Dynamic Host Configuration Protocol) server. If you are not sure whether you are connecting to a workgroup or a domain, select the workgroup option. You can always connect to a domain after you install Windows Vista Business.

Installing Windows Vista

The Windows Vista Setup Wizard guides you step-by-step through the process of installing Windows Vista. When the installation is finished, you are ready to log on to Windows Vista. Be aware that your computer restarts several times during the installation process. Depending on the type of installation you need to perform, either upgrade or clean, you start the Windows Vista Setup Wizard in different ways. If you perform an upgrade or clean install on a Windows version, you simply start your computer and insert the Windows Vista installation CD to start the Windows Vista Setup Wizard. However, if you perform a clean install on a nonsupported operating system or a blank hard disk, you need to start your computer by inserting the Windows Vista installation DVD into the DVD drive, which starts the Windows Vista Setup Wizard. A clean install requires you to select additional options as you step through the wizard, but the steps are basically the same.

Install Windows Vista

1 Insert the Windows Vista DVD into your DVD drive, and then start your computer.

2 Click **Install Windows Vista**.

3 Click an option whether to get important updates for installation.

4 Type the 25-character product key.

TROUBLE? *If you don't have a product key, you can use Windows Vista for a 30-day trial period. Leave the product key blank, and then continue.*

5 Click **Next**, and then if necessary, click **No** to continue the installation as a trial.

> **Did You Know?**
>
> *You can clean up your old installation to save space.* Click the Start button, point to All Programs, click Accessories, click System Tools, click Disk Cleanup, click Files From All Users On This Computer, if requested select a drive and click OK, select the check box next to your old Windows version, and then click OK.

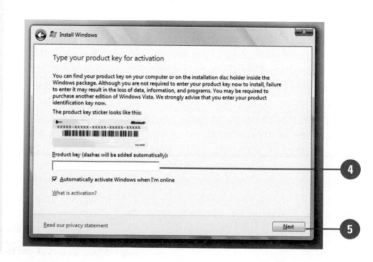

6. Select the edition you want to install, and then click **Next** to continue.

7. Click the type of installation you want: **Upgrade** or **Custom (advanced)**.

8. Click the **I accept the license terms** check box, and then click **Next** to continue.

9. Wait while Setup copies and installs Windows Vista on your computer. Your computer might reboot several times during this process.

10. As prompted, select the initial options you want. Options vary depending on the installation type.

   ◆ **Windows protection.** Select **Use recommended settings**, **Install important updates only**, or **Ask me later**.

   ◆ **User accounts.** Enter user account names and passwords to share the computer, and then click **Next**.

   ◆ **Time zone, date, and time.** Select a time zone, date, and time, and then click **Next**.

11. Click **Start** and then wait while Setup configures Windows Vista and prepares your desktop.

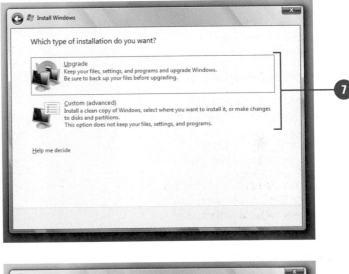

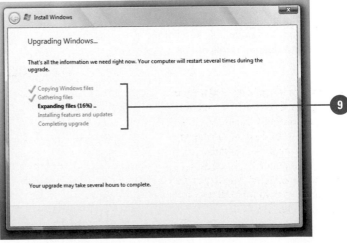

Updating to a Windows Vista Service Pack

Microsoft is continually updating and enhancing Windows Vista. Instead of releasing multiple updates individually, periodically Microsoft releases an update, known as a Service Pack (SP), which provides all-in-one access to the most up-to-date drivers, tools, enhancements, and other critical updates (which were formally referred to as hotfixes). Service packs as well as individual updates are available free for download and installation over the Internet using the Windows Update web site. With the enhanced Windows Update web site, Microsoft makes it easy to securely download and install this important update over the Internet. After you complete the installation, turn on Automatic Updates to help you keep your computer up-to-date and secure. If you're experiencing problems with the service pack and need to reinstall it again, you can uninstall (or remove) it from your computer using Programs and Features in the Control Panel.

Download and Install a Service Pack or Other Updates

1. Click the **Start** button, point to **All Programs**, and then click **Windows Update**.

   Windows connects to the Internet.

2. If prompted to install Windows Update software, click **Yes**.

3. If necessary, click **Check for updates**, and then wait for the update scan to complete.

4. If available, select a service pack or any other updates you want to install.

5. Click **Install Updates**.

6. Review the End User License Agreement, and then click **I accept the license terms** option.

7 Click **Finish**.

Windows Update downloads the updates, and then starts the installation.

8 If prompted, follow any additional installation instructions.

While updating your computer, Windows checks your system for compatibility and archives files in case of removal later.

9 Wait for the updates to be installed on your computer.

10 If prompted, click **OK** to restart your computer, and then turn on Automatic Updates.

11 Click the **Close** button in your browser as needed.

Uninstall a Windows Vista Service Pack

1 Click the **Start** button, click **Control Panel**, and then double-click the **Programs and Features** icon in Classic view.

2 In the Navigation pane, click **View installed updates**.

> **TIMESAVER** *You can also click Installed Updates in Navigation pane of Windows Update.*

3 Select the service pack you want to uninstall.

4 Click **Uninstall**.

5 Click **Yes** to confirm the removal, and then follow the instructions.

6 When it's done, click **OK**.

7 Click the **Close** button.

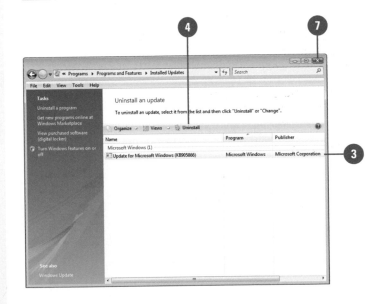

Transferring Files and Settings from Another Computer

Instead of trying to re-create Windows settings manually from an old computer on a new Windows Vista computer, you can use Windows Easy Transfer. If you have a removable hard drive, a CD or DVD burner drive, a direct connect cable, such as an Easy Transfer Cable (a special USB cable designed for Windows Easy Transfer), or you are connected to a computer over a network, you can use Windows Easy Transfer to transfer settings for Windows, such as user accounts, folder and taskbar options, desktop and display properties, and Internet Explorer browser and Outlook Express mail setup options, and files or entire folders, such as My Documents and Favorites. However, it's not meant for transferring your computer programs.

Prepare the Old Computer

1. Click the Start button, point to **All Programs**, click **Accessories**, and then click **Welcome Center**.

   The Welcome Center window opens.

2. Double-click the **Transfer files and settings** icon.

3. Read the welcome screen, and then click **Next** to continue.

4. Click **Start a new transfer**.

5. Click **My old computer**.

6. Click the option for the way you want to transfer the files and settings, select or specify the related options you want for the transfer method, and then click **Next** to continue.

7. Click an option to specify the way you want to transfer your data, and then click **Next** to continue.

8. Click **Transfer**.

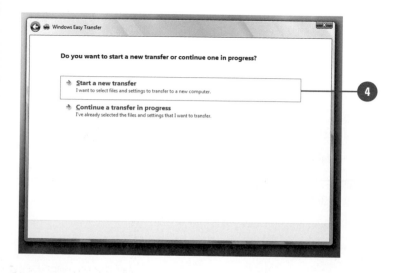

508

Transfer Files and Settings to the New Computer

1. Click the **Start** button, point to **All Programs**, click **Accessories**, and then click **Welcome Center**.

2. Double-click the **Transfer files and settings** icon.

3. Read the welcome screen, and then click **Next** to continue.

4. Click **Continue a transfer in progress**.

5. Click **My new computer**.

6. Click the option for the way you want to transfer the files and settings, select or specify the related options you want for the transfer method, and then click **Next** to continue.

7. Click an option to specify the location of the files and settings, and then click **Next** to continue.

8. Click **Transfer**.

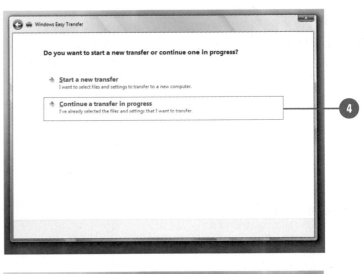

Getting Windows Vista Extras

Microsoft Windows Vista Ultimate provides additional programs, services, and premium content you can download from the Web. You can find out more about the available resources provided by Windows Ultimate Extras and download the extras you want using Windows Update. A section of the Windows Update window provides a list of currently available extras you can download and install on your computer.

Get Windows Vista Ultimate Extras

① Click the **Start** button, point to **All Programs**, click **Accessories**, and then click **Welcome Center**.

② Double-click the **Windows Ultimate Extras** icon.

The Windows Update window opens.

③ If prompted to install Windows Update software, click **Yes**.

④ To find out more about Windows Ultimate Extras, click **Learn about Windows Ultimate Extras** to access the Microsoft Web site.

⑤ If necessary, click **Check for updates**, and then wait for the update scan to complete.

⑥ If available, select the Windows Extras you want to install.

⑦ Click **Install Updates**.

⑧ Review the End User License Agreement, and then click **I accept the license terms** option, and then click **Finish**.

⑨ If prompted, follow any additional installation instructions.

⑩ If prompted, click **OK** to restart your computer, and then turn on Automatic Updates.

⑪ Click the **Close** button.

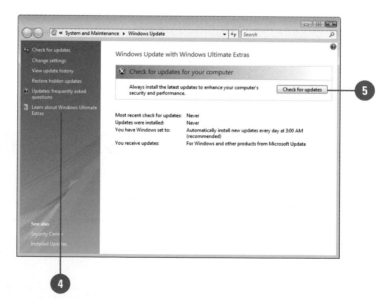

Learning About Windows Live

Microsoft Windows Live (**New!**) is a set of online services that allows you to stay informed, connected, and protected using specialized Web tools for Windows Vista. Windows Live provides information tools, such as Live Search, Live.com, and Windows Live Toolbar to help you find the information you need, and provide a personalized search portal and easy access toolbar. In addition, Windows Live provides communication tools, such as Windows Live Mail, Windows Live Messenger, and Windows Live Spaces to help you send and receive messages and create your own blogs. If you need help making sure your computer is secure, you can subscribe to Windows Live OneCare and let Microsoft do the job for you.

Learn About Windows Live

1. Click the **Start** button, point to **All Programs**, click **Accessories**, and then click **Welcome Center**.

   The Welcome Center window opens.

2. Double-click the **Go online to learn about Windows Live** icon.

   Your Web browser opens, display the Windows Live Web site.

3. Read about Windows Live.

4. Click links (**Informed**, **Connected**, or **Protected**) at the top of the page to find out more about Windows Live.

5. When you're done, click the **Close** button.

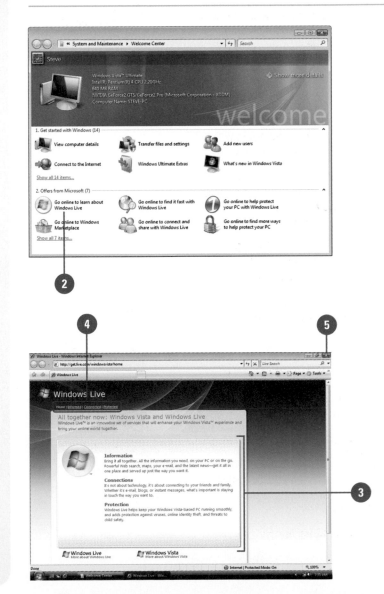

New! Features

Microsoft Windows Vista

Microsoft Windows Vista comes with new features that make your computer significantly easier and faster to use than earlier versions of Windows. Windows Vista makes it easier to use the Start menu, open files and programs, find information, and accomplish other common tasks, such as send and receive secure e-mail, browse the Internet securely, scan and view pictures, play music and videos, and change settings. Windows Vista delivers the Windows Areo user experience, Instant Searches, Explorers, Sidebars and Gadgets, improved Internet Explorer, Windows Media Center, and advanced security and protection.

Only New Features

If you're already familiar with Microsoft Windows XP, you can access and download all the tasks in this book with Microsoft Windows Vista New Features to help make your transition to the new version simple and smooth. The Microsoft Windows Vista New Features, as well as other XP to Vista transition helpers, are available on the Web at *www.perspection.com*.

What's New

If you're searching for what's new in Windows Vista, just look for the icon: New!. The new icon appears in the table of contents and throughout this book so you can quickly and easily identify a new or improved feature in Windows Vista. The following is a brief description of each new feature, and it's location in this book.

Windows Vista

◆ **Windows Aero (p. 2)** An new dynamic user interface in Windows Vista.

◆ **Explorer windows (p. 2)** Explorer windows give you more information and control while simplifying how you work with your files.

◆ **Search folders (p. 2)** A Search Folder is simply a search that you save. Opening a Search Folder instantly runs that saved search, displaying up-to-date results immediately.

◆ **Welcome Center (p. 4)** The Welcome Center displays options to view basic computer details, transfer files and settings, add new users, connect to the

Internet, install Windows Ultimate Extras, view new feature in Windows Vista, and view Microsoft offers available on the Web.

- **Live taskbar thumbnails (p. 6, 55)** Windows Aero displays a Live thumbnail of the window, showing the content of that window.

- **Windows flip and windows flip 3D (p. 6)** Flip allows you to flip through open windows (by using Alt+Tab), providing a Live thumbnail of each window

- **Instant search (p. 10, 70)** The Instant Search box helps you quickly find and start any program or file on your computer. After you add or edit file properties or data associated with a file, you can use the Instant Search box to quickly find a file by the file property.

- **Gadgets (p. 12)** Gadgets are mini-applications that can connect to Web services, such as an RSS feed.

- **Windows sidebar (p. 12)** Windows Sidebar is a pane on the side of the Windows Vista desktop that gives you quick access to gadgets such as news headlines and updates.

- **Help and Support (p. 20-21)** Microsoft Help and Support is a resource of information, training, and support to help you learn and use Windows Vista.

- **Contacts (p. 29)** Stores names, addresses, and other contact information.

- **Windows Calendar (p. 29)** Manages appointments and tasks using personal calendars.

- **Windows Defender (p. 29)** Helps protect your computer from spyware and other harmful intruders.

- **Windows Live Messenger (p. 29, 208-232)** Sends and receives instant messages to online contacts; you need to download the program.

- **Windows DVD Maker (p. 29, 306-308)** Burns pictures and videos to DVDs.

- **Windows Mail (p. 29, 165-200)** Sends and receives faxes or scanned pictures and documents.

- **Windows Fax and Scan (p. 29)** Sends and receives faxes or scanned pictures and documents.

- **Windows Meeting Space (p. 29)** Provides an online place to share files, programs, or your desktop.

- **Windows Media Center (p. 29)** Provides entertainment options for digital and on-demand media.

- **Windows Photo Gallery (p. 29, 240-242, 254)** Provides an online place to share files, programs, or your desktop.

- **Window Views PCs (p. 55)** The available views include Extra Large, Large, Medium and Small Icons, List, Details, and Tiles.

- **Personal folder (p. 58)** The personal folder only contains files and folders associated with a user account and are unique for each user on the computer.

- ◆ **Recently Changed folder (p. 60)** The Recently Changed folder in the Navigation pane of an Explorer window makes it easy to locate recently changed documents.

- ◆ **Address bar (p. 62)** The Address bar appears at the top of every Explorer window and displays the current location on your computer or network.

- ◆ **Explorer layout (p. 64)** The layout for each Explorer window includes a Menu Bar, Details pane, Preview pane, and Navigation pane.

- ◆ **Navigation pane (p. 63)** The Navigation pane provides links to commonly used folders and saved searches to reduce the number of clicks it takes to locate a file or folder.

- ◆ **Filtering (p. 64)** Filtering displays only files with the properties you select by heading type.

- ◆ **Stacking (p. 64)** Stacking displays all of the files in the view into piles by heading type.

- ◆ **Grouping (p. 64)** Grouping displays a sequential list of all of the files by heading type.

- ◆ **Natural language search (p. 75)** If using properties and boolean filters seems a little too much for you to handle, you can find files using natural language search.

- ◆ **Indexing (p. 78-79)** Windows keeps track of files in indexed locations and stores information about them in the background using an index, like the one found in the back of this book, to make locating files faster and easier.

- ◆ **Live System format (p. 94)** The Live File System format allows you to copy files to a disc at any time, like a USB drive, while the Mastered format needs to copy them all at once.

- ◆ **Public folder (p. 90)** The Public folder contains subfolders to help you organize the files you are sharing, and include Documents, Downloads, Music, Pictures and Videos.

- ◆ **Speech recognition (p. 130)** Speech recognition is the ability to convert a spoken voice into electronic text.

- ◆ **Change Screen Text Size (p. 107)** Windows Vista allows you to increase the Dots Per Inch (DPI) scale, which is the number of dots that a device can display or print per linear inch.

- ◆ **Ease of Access Center (p. 126-127)** The Ease of Access Center allows you to check the status of and start or stop the Magnifier, Narrator, and On-Screen Keyboard accessibility programs.

- ◆ **Tabbed Browsing (p. 142)** Internet Explorer creates separate tabs for each one, so you can view multiple Web sites in a single window.

- ◆ **Feed (p. 150)** A feed delivers frequently updated Web content to your browser on a continuous basis. A feed, also known as RSS (Really Simple Syndication) feed, XML feed, syndicated content, or Web feed, is usually offered on a subscription basis and typically free of charge.

- ◆ **Junk mail filter (p. 186-187)** Junk e-mail can seem like a never ending battle as it keeps piling up. Windows Mail provides the Junk E-mail Options dialog box to help you reduce the amount of junk e-mail you receive.

- ◆ **Shared calendars (p. 199-200)** You can use Windows Mail to share and publish calendars over the Internet.

- ◆ **MTV URGE music service (p. 262)** Windows Media Player provides special integration with URGE, an online music service provided by MTV networks.

- ◆ **Better protection from spyware (p. 324-325)** Windows Defender helps you protect your computer from spyware and other potentially harmful software that attempts to install itself or run on your computer.

- ◆ **Phishing filter (p. 340)** Phishing is a technique people use to trick computer users into revealing personal for financial information. Windows and Internet Explorer provide increase security to help protect you from phishing schemes.

- ◆ **Network center (p. 352-353)** The Network and Sharing Center provides a central location where you can view and modify network and sharing options for the computer connected to a network.

- ◆ **Windows SideShow (p. 391)** Windows SideShow allows hardware manufacturers to build peripheral devices—such as LCD displays, remote controls, Personal Digital Assistances (PDA), cell phones, or TVs—that can be used to view the information you need at a moments notice.

- ◆ **Network map (p. 352-353)** Network and Sharing Center displays a network map of your networking configuration.

- ◆ **Create your own DVDs (p. 307-308)** With Windows DVD Maker, you can insert video, pictures and audio, and combine it with titles and predefined menus to create a DVD video disc that you can play on a TV using a DVD player.

- ◆ **Encrypting file system (p. 328)** If your computer uses NTFS, you can use the advanced Encrypting File System (EFS) to protect sensitive data files on your computer.

- ◆ **Windows BitLocker drive encryption (p. 329)** If you have a two partition (also known as volumes) hard drive, you can use BitLocker to encrypt the entire system drive.

- ◆ **Windows mobility center (p. 382)** With the Windows Mobility Center, you can change or access mobile PC related options all in one place.

- ◆ **Presentation settings (p. 383)** As a presenter you can change all the settings you use regularly.

- ◆ **Power management (p. 384-385)** You can change power options properties for a portable or laptop computer to reduce power consumption and maximize battery life.

- ♦ **Sync center (p. 386-387)** With the Sync Center, you can keep files (including documents, music, photos, and in some case contacts) and other information up-to-date between your computer and mobile devices, network folders, and compatible programs.

- ♦ **Network projection (p. 390)** A network projector is a video projector that is connected to a wireless or local area network.

- ♦ **Tablet PC (p. 392-395)** If you have a Tablet PC or ink device, you can use the Pen and Input Devices utility in the Control Panel to set the options you want. Windows Vista comes with three Tablet PC tools: Windows Journal, Tablet PC Input Panel, and Sticky Notes.

- ♦ **Windows update (p. 440-441)** Windows Update allows you to keep your computer up-to-date with the latest system software and security updates over the Internet.

- ♦ **Windows ReadyBoost (p. 443)** You can use Windows ReadyBoost to speed up your computer by using disk space on certain removable media devices, such as USB flash drives.

- ♦ **System restore (p. 445)** System Restore returns your computer system, but not your personal files, to an earlier time, before the changes were made to your computer, called a restore point.

- ♦ **Windows backup (p. 467-482)** Using the Backup Wizard in the Backup and Restore Center, you can pick the day, time, and how often you want to back up your files, folders, and settings.

- ♦ **Previous versions (p. 446)** Previous versions are shadow copies of files and folders that you back up using the Back Up Files Wizard or Windows automatically saves as part of a restore point.

- ♦ **Windows easy transfer (p. 508-509)** Instead of trying to re-create Windows settings manually from an old computer on a new Windows Vista computer, you can use Windows Easy Transfer.

What Happened To . . .

- ♦ **My Documents** The folder has a new name. It's now called Documents.

- ♦ **Messenger in Windows Media Center** Messenger is not available in this version.

- ♦ **NetBEUI protocol** NetBIOS Extended User Interface (NetBEUI) is a network protocol usually used in small LANs. NetBEUI is not supported by Windows Vista and has mostly been replaced by TCP/IP.

- ♦ **Task pane** The Task pane has been replaced by the new toolbar at the top of the folder. Many of the tasks that used to appear in the Task pane now appear on the toolbar.

- ♦ **Utility Manager** This option has been replaced by the Ease of Access Center.

- ◆ **Accessibility Wizard** The wizard has been replaced by an optional questionnaire in the Ease of Access Center.

- ◆ **Windows Address Book** The Address Book has been replaced by Windows Contacts.

- ◆ **Search Assistant** This feature has been replaced by the Instant Search box.

- ◆ **Windows Messenger** This program has been replaced by Windows Live Messenger.

- ◆ **Fax Console** This program has been replaced by Windows Fax and Scan.

- ◆ **Windows Picture and Fax Viewer** This has been replaced by Windows Fax and Scan.

- ◆ **Internet games** Internal games no longer come standard on Windows. However, you can access them at *www.msn.microsoft.com*.

Microsoft Certified Applications Specialist

About the MCAS Program

The Microsoft Certified Applications Specialist (MCAS) certification is the globally recognized standard for validating expertise with the Microsoft Office suite of business productivity programs. Earning an MCAS certificate acknowledges you have the expertise to work with Microsoft Office programs. To earn the MCAS certification, you must pass a certification exam for Microsoft Windows Vista. Additional exams are available for the Microsoft Office desktop applications of Microsoft Office Word, Microsoft Office Excel, Microsoft Office PowerPoint, Microsoft Office Outlook, or Microsoft Office Access. (The availability of Microsoft Certified Applications Specialist certification exams varies by program, program version, and language. Visit *www.microsoft.com* and search on *Microsoft Certified Applications Specialist* for exam availability and more information about the program.) The Microsoft Certified Applications Specialist program is the only Microsoft-approved program in the world for certifying proficiency with Microsoft Office programs.

What Does This Logo Mean?

It means this book has been approved by the Microsoft Certified Applications Specialist program to be certified courseware for learning Microsoft Windows Vista and preparing for the certification exam. This book will prepare you for the Microsoft Certified Applications Specialist exam for Microsoft Windows Vista. Each certification level has a set of objectives, which are organized into broader skill sets. Throughout this book, content that pertains to a Microsoft Certified Applications Specialist objective is identified with the following MCAS certification logo and objective number below the title of the topic:

Microsoft Certified Application Specialist

WINV-1.1.1
WINV-2.2.1

Windows Vista Objectives

C

Windows Vista Objectives *(continued)*

C

C

C

Preparing for a MCAS Exam

Every Microsoft Certified Applications Specialist certification exam is developed from a list of objectives based on how Microsoft Office programs are actually used in the workplace. The list of objectives determine the scope of each exam, so they provide you with the information you need to prepare for MCAS certification. Microsoft Certified Applications Specialist Approved Courseware, including the On Demand series, is reviewed and approved on the basis of its coverage of the objectives. To prepare for the certification exam, you should review and perform each task identified with a MCAS objective to confirm that you can meet the requirements for the exam.

Taking a MCAS Exam

The Microsoft Certified Applications Specialist certification exams are not written exams. Instead, the exams are performance-based examinations that allow you to interact with a "live" Office program as you complete a series of objective-based tasks. All the standard ribbons, tabs, toolbars, and keyboard shortcuts are available during the exam. Microsoft Certified Applications Specialist exams for Office 2007 programs consist of 25 to 35 questions, each of which requires you to complete one or more tasks using the Office program for which you are seeking certification. A typical exam takes from 45 to 60 minutes. Passing percentages range from 70 to 80 percent correct.

The Exam Experience

After you fill out a series of information screens, the testing software starts the exam and the Office program. The test questions appear in the exam dialog box in the lower right corner of the screen.

◆ The timer starts when the first question appears and displays the remaining exam time at the top of the exam dialog box. If the timer and the counter are distracting, you can click the timer to remove the display.

◆ The counter at the top of the exam dialog box tracks how many questions you have completed and how many remain.

◆ If you think you have made a mistake, you can click the Reset button to restart the question. The Reset button does not restart the entire exam or extend the exam time limit.

◆ When you complete a question, click the Next button to move to the next question. It is not possible to move back to a previous question on the exam.

◆ If the exam dialog box gets in your way, you can click the Minimize button in the upper right corner of the exam dialog box to hide it, or you can drag the title bar to another part of the screen to move it.

Tips for Taking an Exam

◆ Carefully read and follow all instructions provided in each question.

◆ Make sure all steps in a task are completed before proceeding to the next exam question.

◆ Enter requested information as it appears in the instructions without formatting unless you are explicitly requested otherwise.

◆ Close all dialog boxes before proceeding to the next exam question unless you are specifically instructed otherwise.

◆ Do not leave tables, boxes, or cells "active" unless instructed otherwise.

◆ Do not cut and paste information from the exam interface into the program.

◆ When you print a document from an Office program during the exam, nothing actually gets printed.

◆ Errant keystrokes or mouse clicks do not count against your score as long as you achieve the correct end result. You are scored based on the end result, not the method you use to achieve it. However, if a specific method is explicitly requested, you need to use it to get credit for the results.

◆ The overall exam is timed, so taking too long on individual questions may leave you without enough time to complete the entire exam.

◆ If you experience computer problems during the exam, immediately notify a testing center administrator to restart your exam where you were interrupted.

Exam Results

At the end of the exam, a score report appears indicating whether you passed or failed the exam. An official certificate is mailed to successful candidates in approximately two to three weeks.

Getting More Information

To learn more about the Microsoft Certified Applications Specialist program, read a list of frequently asked questions, and locate the nearest testing center, visit:

www.microsoft.com

Index